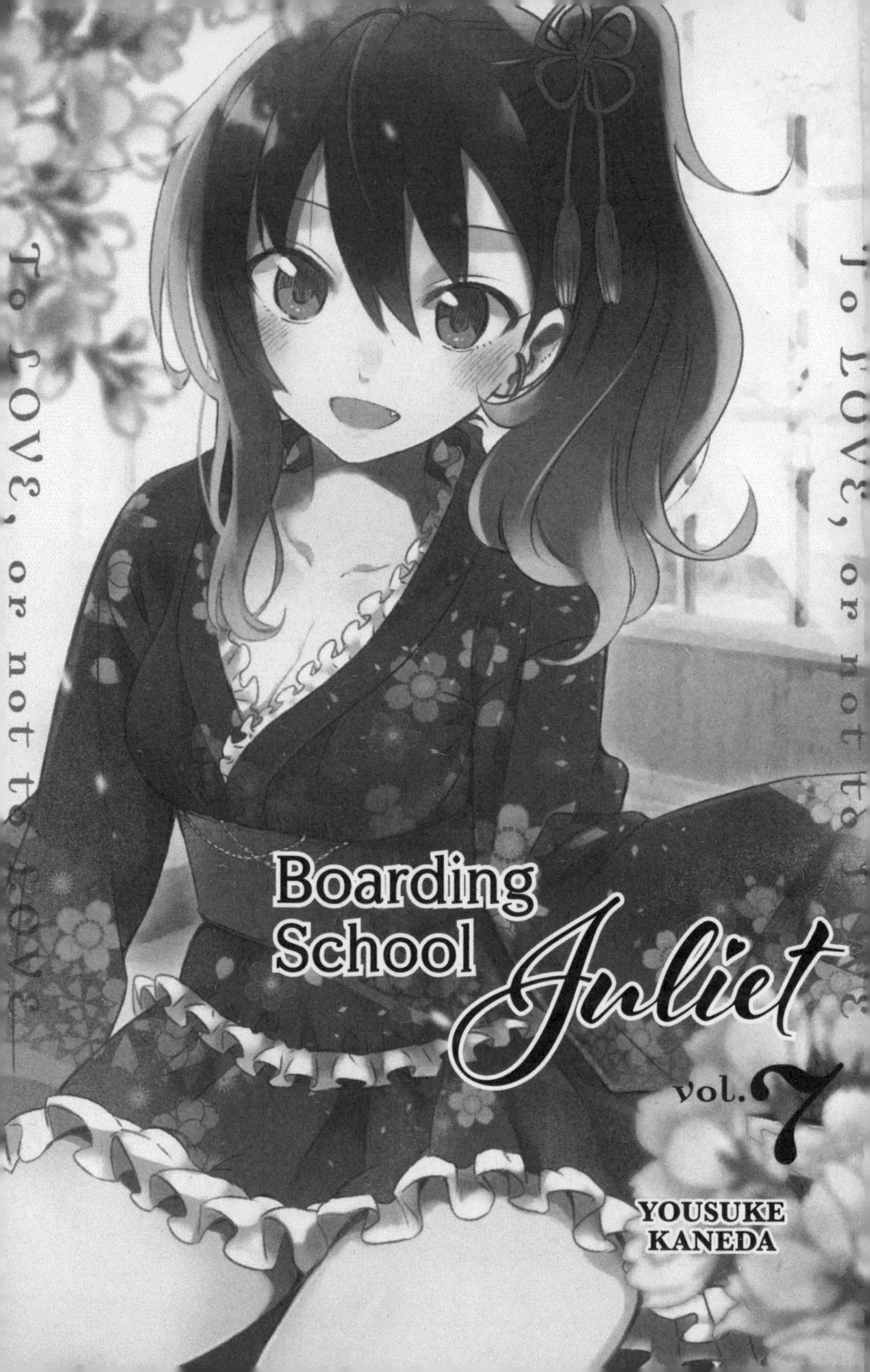
To LOVE, or not to LOVE
To LOVE, or not to LOVE
Boarding School
Juliet
vol.7
YOUSUKE KANEDA

THE PLAYERS

character

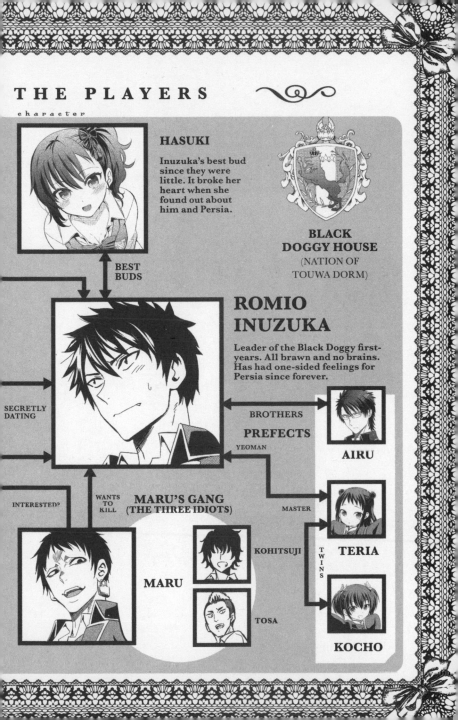

HASUKI

Inuzuka's best bud since they were little. It broke her heart when she found out about him and Persia.

BLACK DOGGY HOUSE
(NATION OF TOUWA DORM)

BEST BUDS

ROMIO INUZUKA

Leader of the Black Doggy first-years. All brawn and no brains. Has had one-sided feelings for Persia since forever.

SECRETLY DATING

BROTHERS

PREFECTS

YEOMAN

AIRU

INTERESTED?

WANTS TO KILL

MARU'S GANG
(THE THREE IDIOTS)

MASTER

MARU

KOHITSUJI

TERIA

TWINS

TOSA

KOCHO

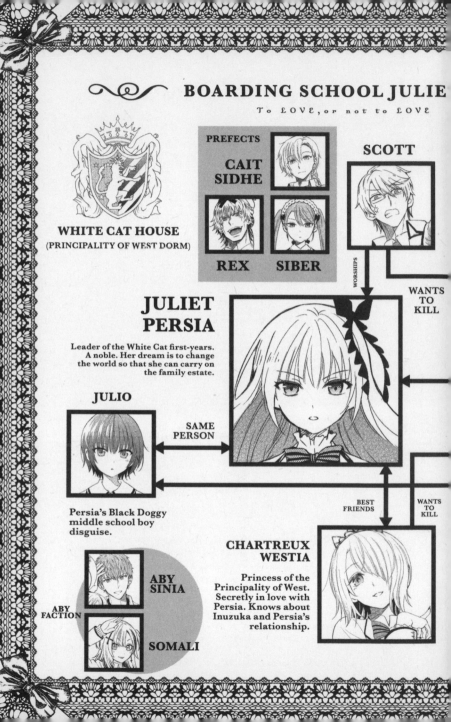

BOARDING SCHOOL JULIE

To LOVE, or not to LOVE

WHITE CAT HOUSE
(PRINCIPALITY OF WEST DORM)

PREFECTS

CAIT SIDHE

REX   **SIBER**

SCOTT

WORSHIPS

WANTS TO KILL

JULIET PERSIA

Leader of the White Cat first-years. A noble. Her dream is to change the world so that she can carry on the family estate.

JULIO

SAME PERSON

Persia's Black Doggy middle school boy disguise.

ABY SINIA

ABY FACTION

SOMALI

BEST FRIENDS

WANTS TO KILL

CHARTREUX WESTIA

Princess of the Principality of West. Secretly in love with Persia. Knows about Inuzuka and Persia's relationship.

contents

story

At boarding school Dahlia Academy, attended by students from two
feuding countries, one first-year longs for a forbidden love. His name:
Romio Inuzuka, leader of the Black Doggy House first-years. The apple
of his eye: Juliet Persia, leader of the White Cat House first-years. It all
begins when Inuzuka confesses his feelings to her. This is Inuzuka and
Persia's star-crossed, secret love story...

On the two-night, three-day school camping trip, Inuzuka tries his
darnedest to set up some secret alone time with Persia. When Persia reacts
with an apparently cold attitude, it's the last straw for Hasuki. At long last,
Hasuki and Persia collide head-on!

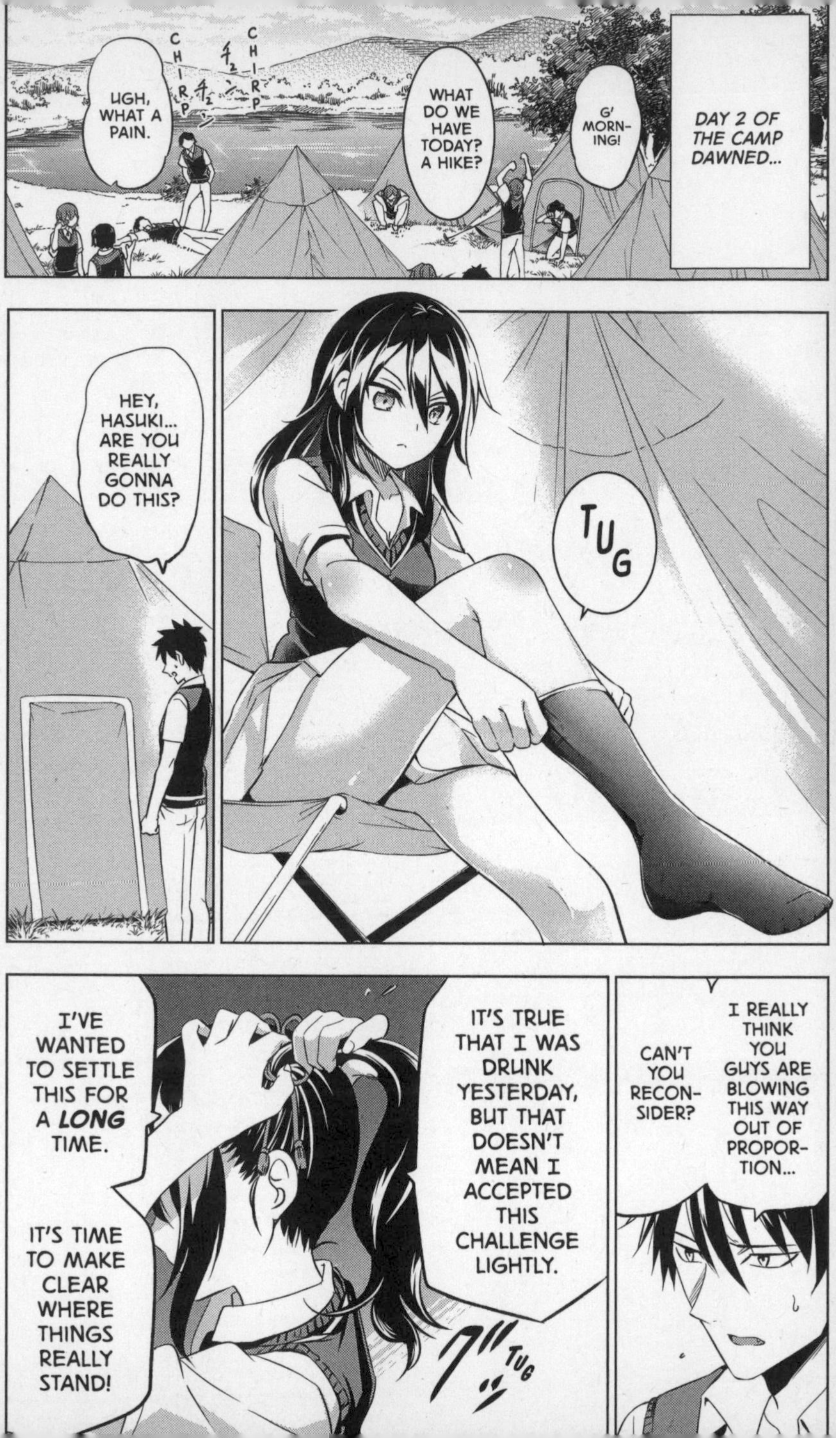
DAY 2 OF THE CAMP DAWNED...
G' MORNING!
WHAT DO WE HAVE TODAY? A HIKE?
CHIRP
CHIRP
UGH, WHAT A PAIN.
TUG
HEY, HASUKI... ARE YOU REALLY GONNA DO THIS?
I REALLY THINK YOU GUYS ARE BLOWING THIS WAY OUT OF PROPORTION...
CAN'T YOU RECONSIDER?
IT'S TRUE THAT I WAS DRUNK YESTERDAY, BUT THAT DOESN'T MEAN I ACCEPTED THIS CHALLENGE LIGHTLY.
I'VE WANTED TO SETTLE THIS FOR A LONG TIME.
IT'S TIME TO MAKE CLEAR WHERE THINGS REALLY STAND!
TUG

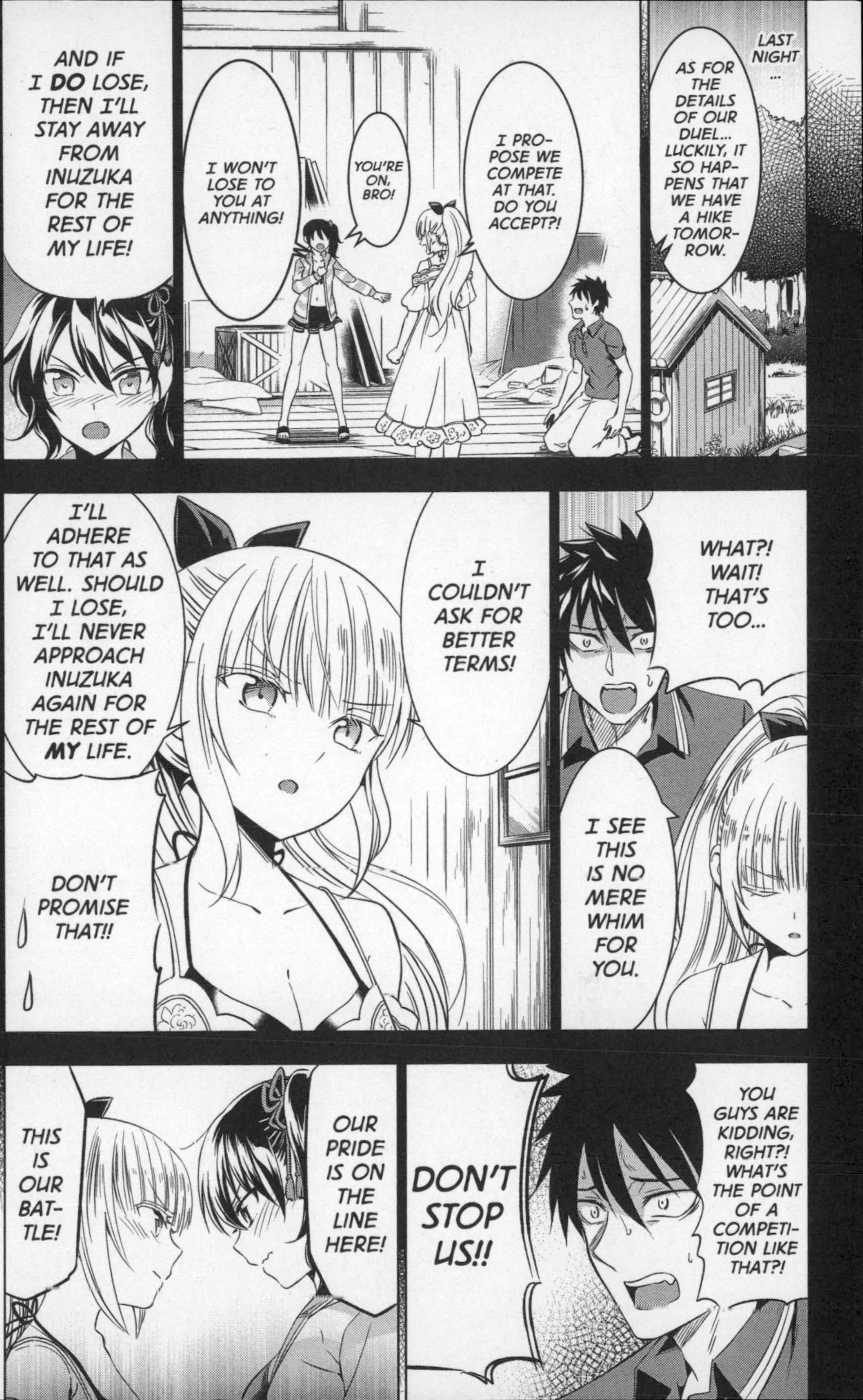
LAST NIGHT...
AS FOR THE DETAILS OF OUR DUEL... LUCKILY, IT SO HAPPENS THAT WE HAVE A HIKE TOMORROW.
I PROPOSE WE COMPETE AT THAT. DO YOU ACCEPT?!
YOU'RE ON, BRO!
I WON'T LOSE TO YOU AT ANYTHING!
AND IF I **DO** LOSE, THEN I'LL STAY AWAY FROM INUZUKA FOR THE REST OF MY LIFE!
WHAT?! WAIT! THAT'S TOO...
I SEE THIS IS NO MERE WHIM FOR YOU.
I COULDN'T ASK FOR BETTER TERMS!
I'LL ADHERE TO THAT AS WELL. SHOULD I LOSE, I'LL NEVER APPROACH INUZUKA AGAIN FOR THE REST OF **MY** LIFE.
DON'T PROMISE THAT!!
YOU GUYS ARE KIDDING, RIGHT?! WHAT'S THE POINT OF A COMPETITION LIKE THAT?!
DON'T STOP US!!
OUR PRIDE IS ON THE LINE HERE!
THIS IS OUR BATTLE!

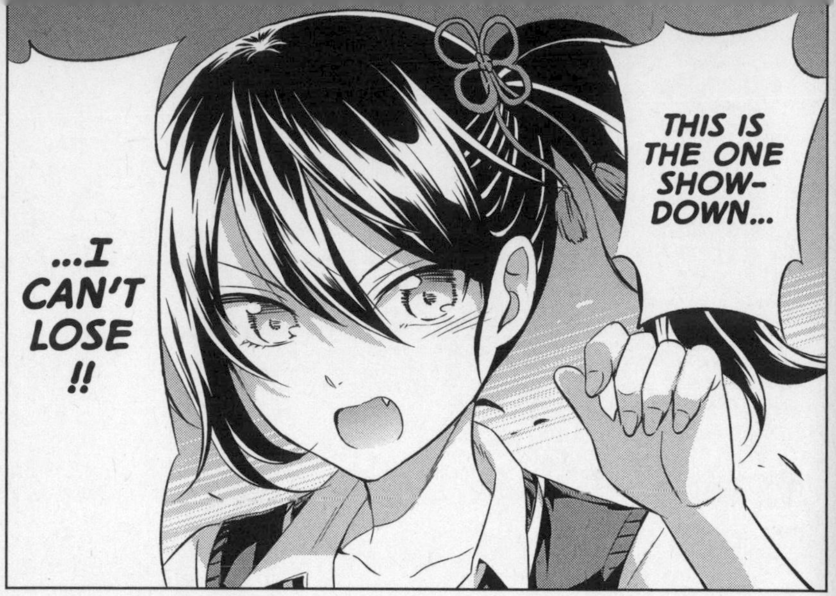
THIS IS THE ONE SHOW-DOWN...
...I CAN'T LOSE !!

ACT 32:

ROMIO & JULIET & HASUKI II

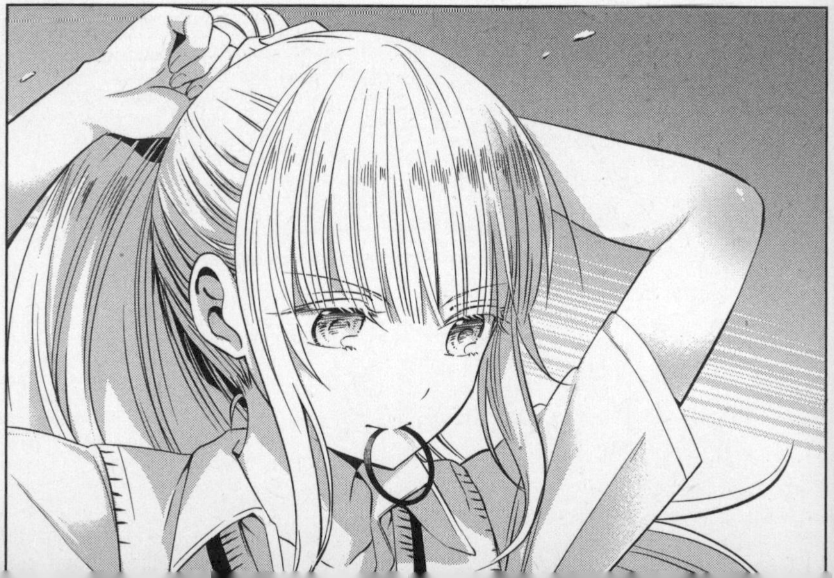

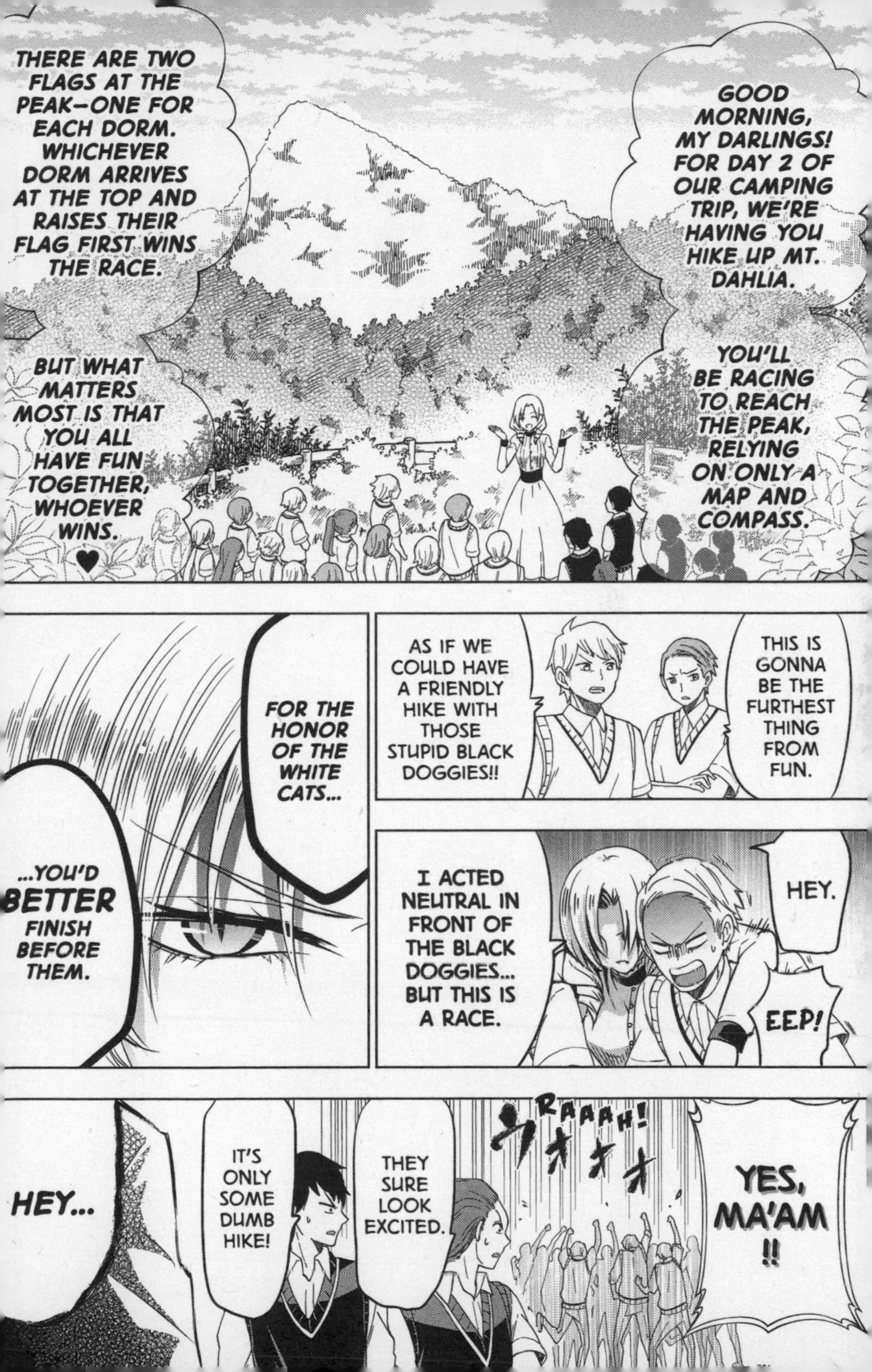
GOOD MORNING, MY DARLINGS! FOR DAY 2 OF OUR CAMPING TRIP, WE'RE HAVING YOU HIKE UP MT. DAHLIA.
YOU'LL BE RACING TO REACH THE PEAK, RELYING ON ONLY A MAP AND COMPASS.
THERE ARE TWO FLAGS AT THE PEAK—ONE FOR EACH DORM. WHICHEVER DORM ARRIVES AT THE TOP AND RAISES THEIR FLAG FIRST WINS THE RACE.
BUT WHAT MATTERS MOST IS THAT YOU ALL HAVE FUN TOGETHER, WHOEVER WINS. ♥
THIS IS GONNA BE THE FURTHEST THING FROM FUN.
AS IF WE COULD HAVE A FRIENDLY HIKE WITH THOSE STUPID BLACK DOGGIES!!
HEY.
EEP!
I ACTED NEUTRAL IN FRONT OF THE BLACK DOGGIES... BUT THIS IS A RACE.
FOR THE HONOR OF THE WHITE CATS...
...YOU'D BETTER FINISH BEFORE THEM.
YES, MA'AM!!
RAAAH!
THEY SURE LOOK EXCITED.
IT'S ONLY SOME DUMB HIKE!
HEY...

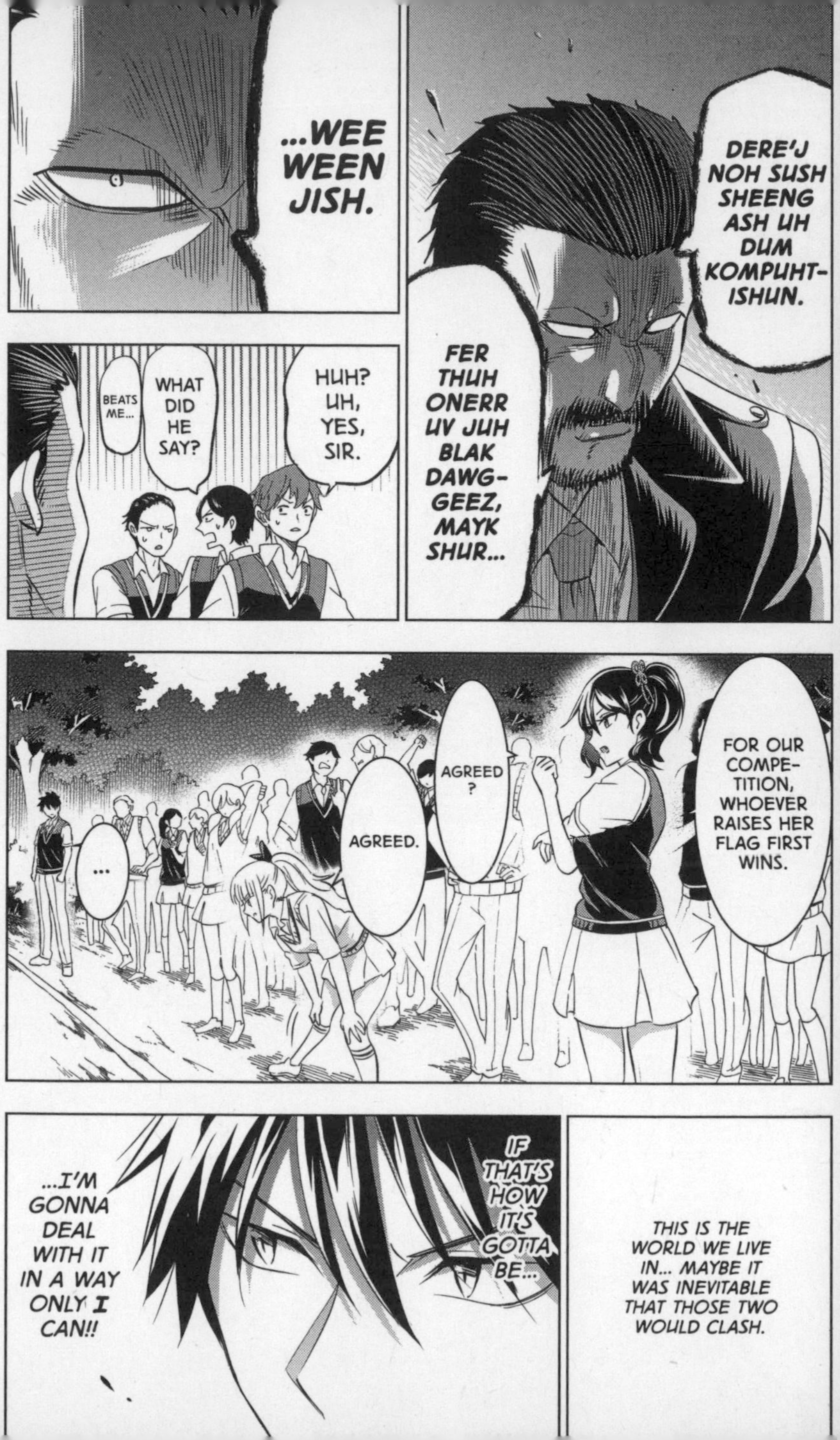
DERE'J NOH SUSH SHEENG ASH UH DUM KOMPUHT-ISHUN.
FER THUH ONERR UV JUH BLAK DAWG-GEEZ, MAYK SHUR...
...WEE WEEN JISH.
HUH? UH, YES, SIR.
WHAT DID HE SAY?
BEATS ME...
FOR OUR COMPE-TITION, WHOEVER RAISES HER FLAG FIRST WINS.
AGREED?
AGREED.
...
THIS IS THE WORLD WE LIVE IN... MAYBE IT WAS INEVITABLE THAT THOSE TWO WOULD CLASH.
IF THAT'S HOW IT'S GOTTA BE...
...I'M GONNA DEAL WITH IT IN A WAY ONLY I CAN!!

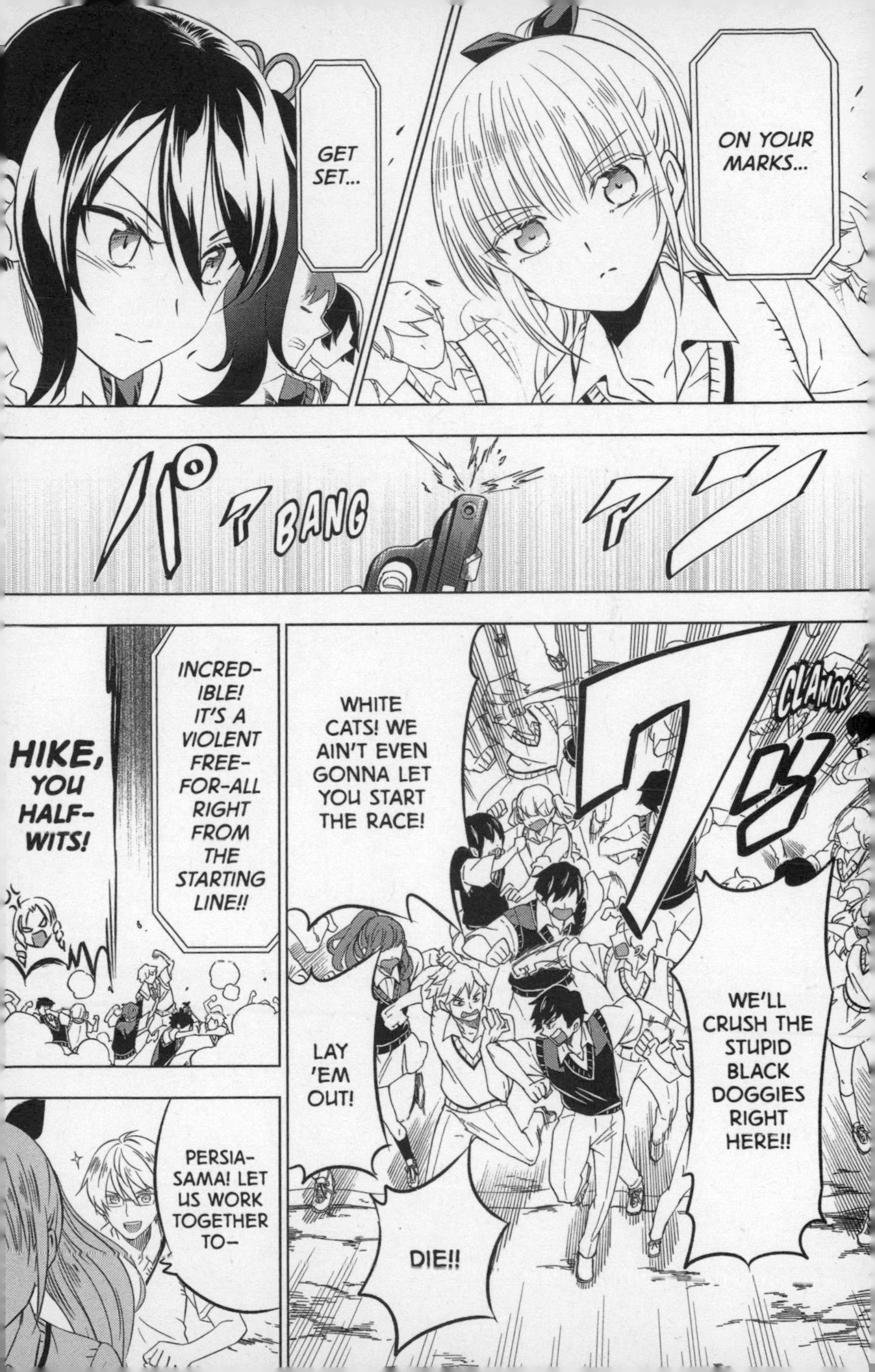
ON YOUR MARKS...
GET SET...
パァ
BANG
ァン
CLAMOR
ワッ
WE'LL CRUSH THE STUPID BLACK DOGGIES RIGHT HERE!!
WHITE CATS! WE AIN'T EVEN GONNA LET YOU START THE RACE!
LAY 'EM OUT!
DIE!!
INCREDIBLE! IT'S A VIOLENT FREE-FOR-ALL RIGHT FROM THE STARTING LINE!!
HIKE, YOU HALF-WITS!
PERSIA-SAMA! LET US WORK TOGETHER TO–

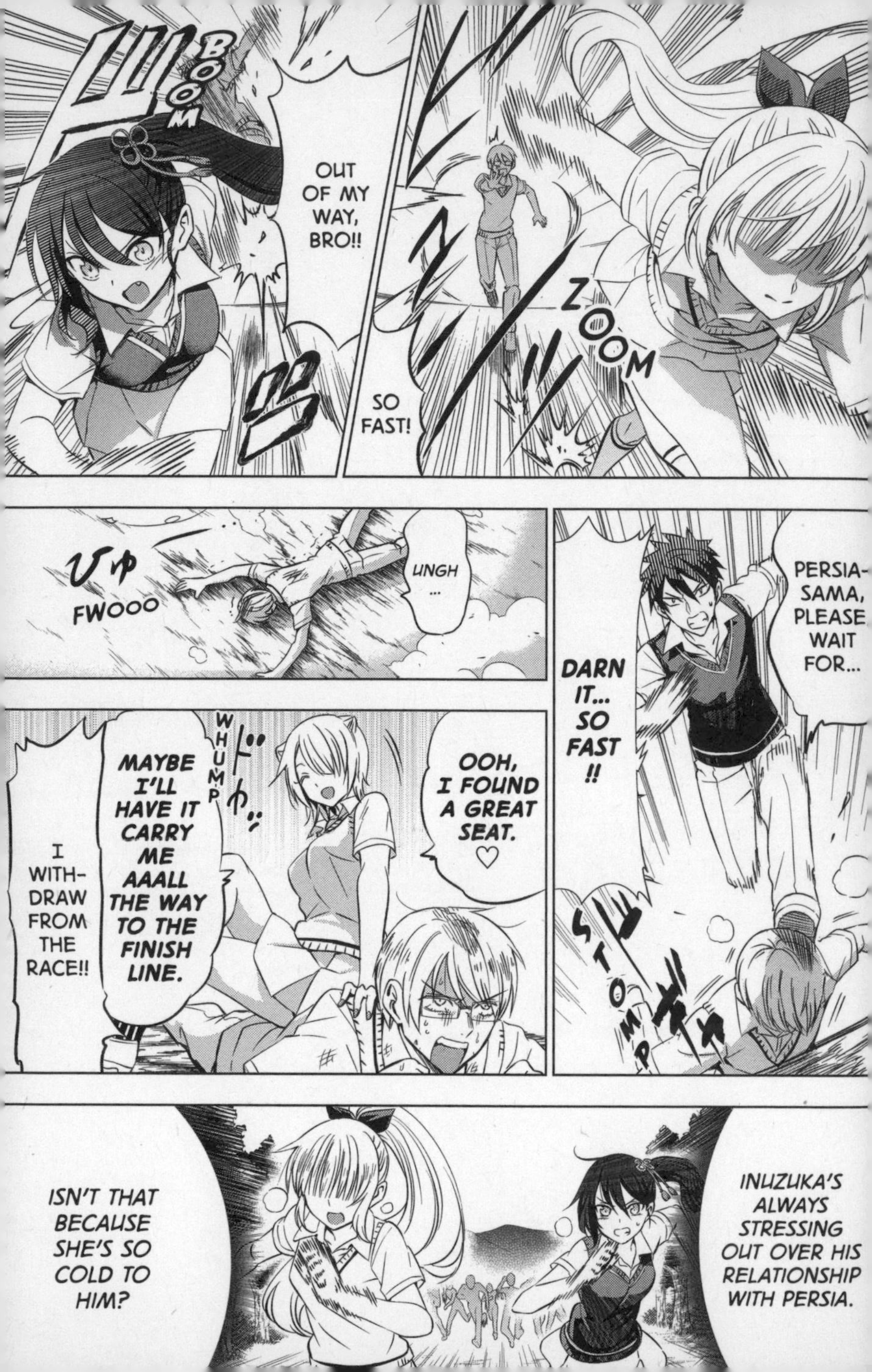
ZOOM
SO FAST!
BOOM
OUT OF MY WAY, BRO!!
PERSIA-SAMA, PLEASE WAIT FOR...
DARN IT... SO FAST!!
STOMP
UNGH...
FWOOO
OOH, I FOUND A GREAT SEAT. ♡
WHUMP
MAYBE I'LL HAVE IT CARRY ME AAALL THE WAY TO THE FINISH LINE.
I WITH-DRAW FROM THE RACE!!
INUZUKA'S ALWAYS STRESSING OUT OVER HIS RELATIONSHIP WITH PERSIA.
ISN'T THAT BECAUSE SHE'S SO COLD TO HIM?

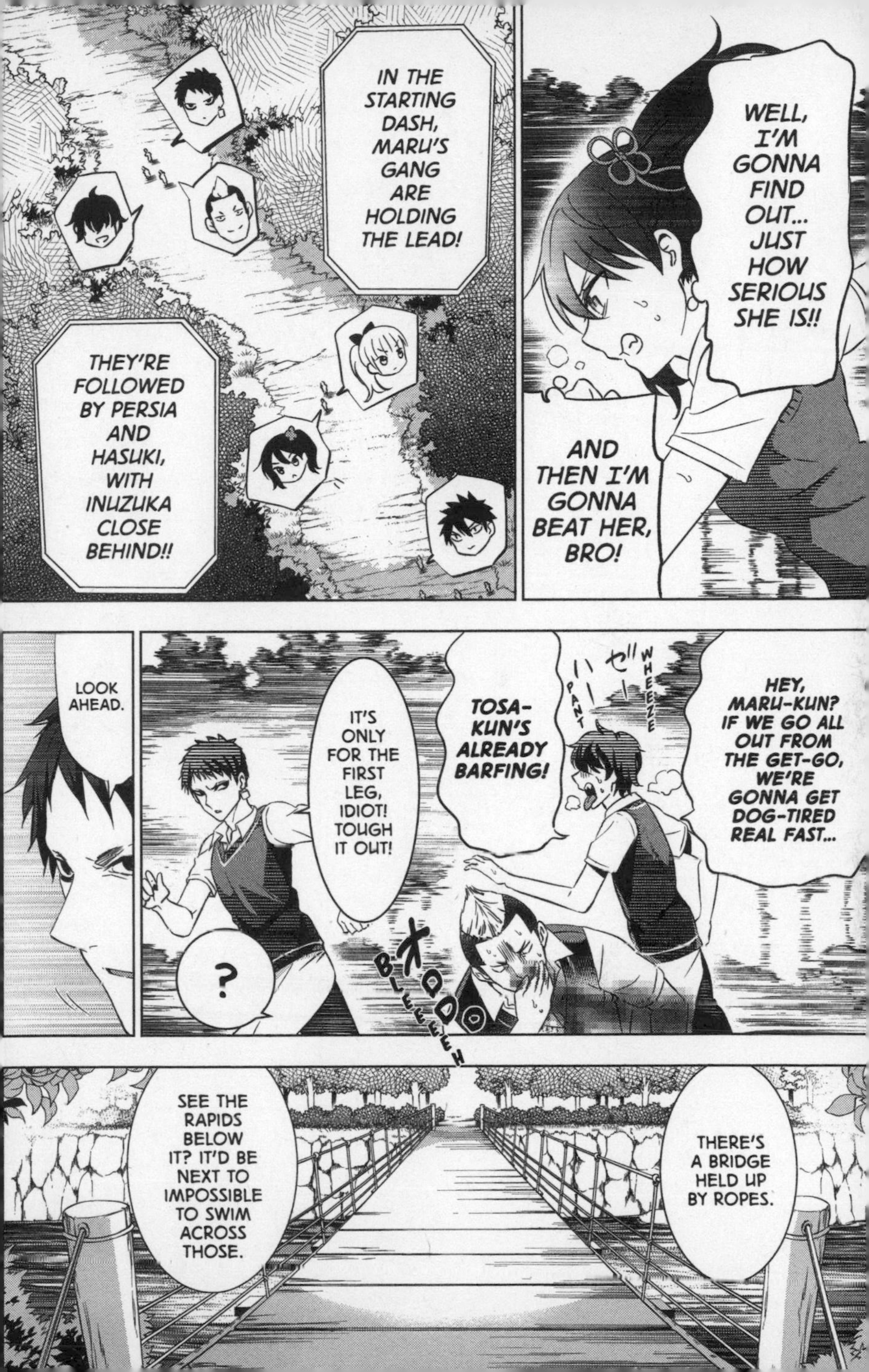
WELL, I'M GONNA FIND OUT... JUST HOW SERIOUS SHE IS!!
AND THEN I'M GONNA BEAT HER, BRO!
IN THE STARTING DASH, MARU'S GANG ARE HOLDING THE LEAD!
THEY'RE FOLLOWED BY PERSIA AND HASUKI, WITH INUZUKA CLOSE BEHIND!!
HEY, MARU-KUN? IF WE GO ALL OUT FROM THE GET-GO, WE'RE GONNA GET DOG-TIRED REAL FAST...
WHEEZE
PANT
TOSA-KUN'S ALREADY BARFING!
IT'S ONLY FOR THE FIRST LEG, IDIOT! TOUGH IT OUT!
?
BLEEEEEEH
LOOK AHEAD.
THERE'S A BRIDGE HELD UP BY ROPES.
SEE THE RAPIDS BELOW IT? IT'D BE NEXT TO IMPOSSIBLE TO SWIM ACROSS THOSE.

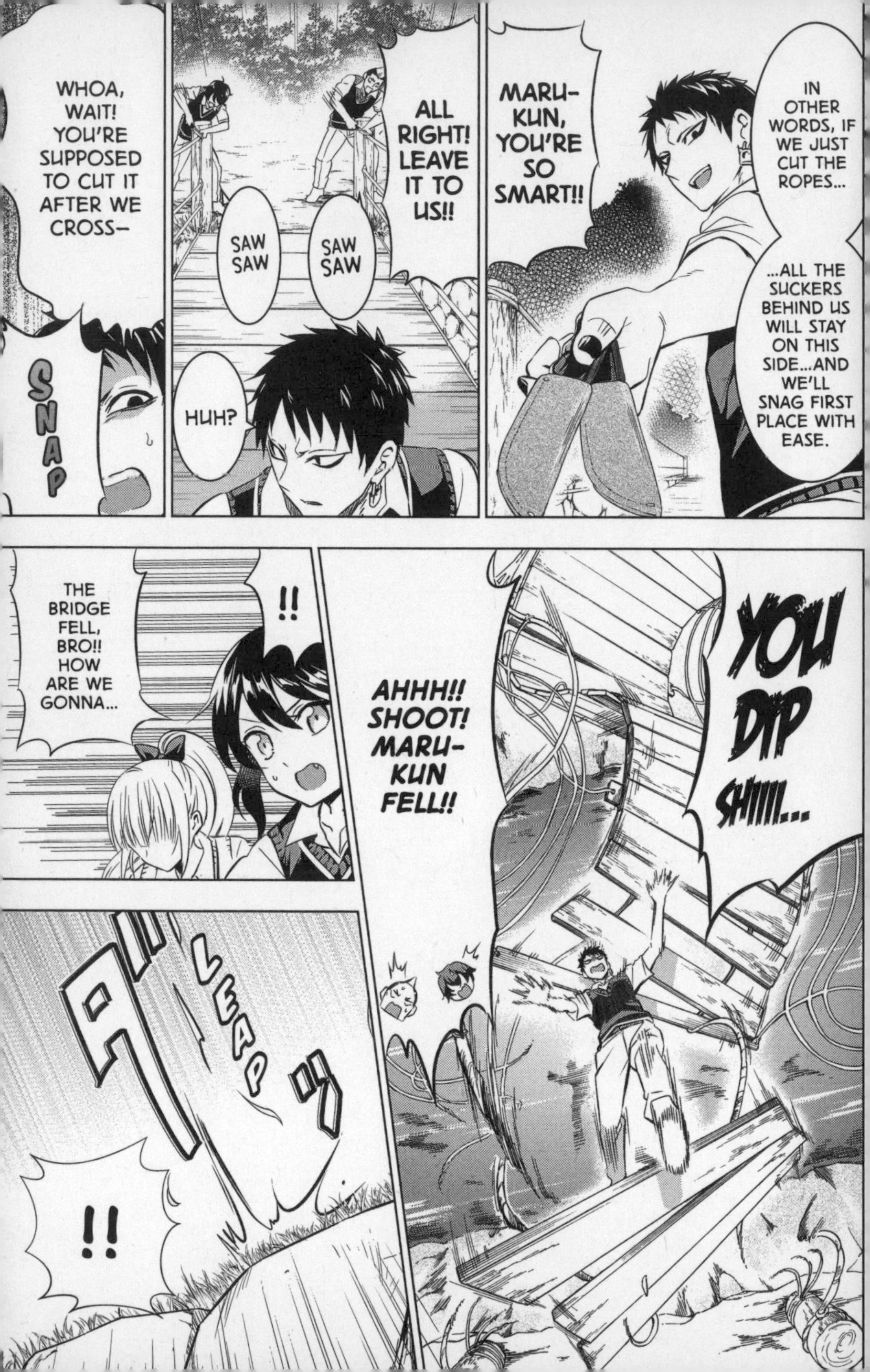
IN OTHER WORDS, IF WE JUST CUT THE ROPES...
...ALL THE SUCKERS BEHIND US WILL STAY ON THIS SIDE...AND WE'LL SNAG FIRST PLACE WITH EASE.
MARU-KUN, YOU'RE SO SMART!!
ALL RIGHT! LEAVE IT TO US!!
SAW SAW
SAW SAW
HUH?
WHOA, WAIT! YOU'RE SUPPOSED TO CUT IT AFTER WE CROSS—
SNAP
YOU DIP SHIIII...
AHHH!! SHOOT! MARU-KUN FELL!!
!!
THE BRIDGE FELL, BRO!! HOW ARE WE GONNA...
LEAP
!!

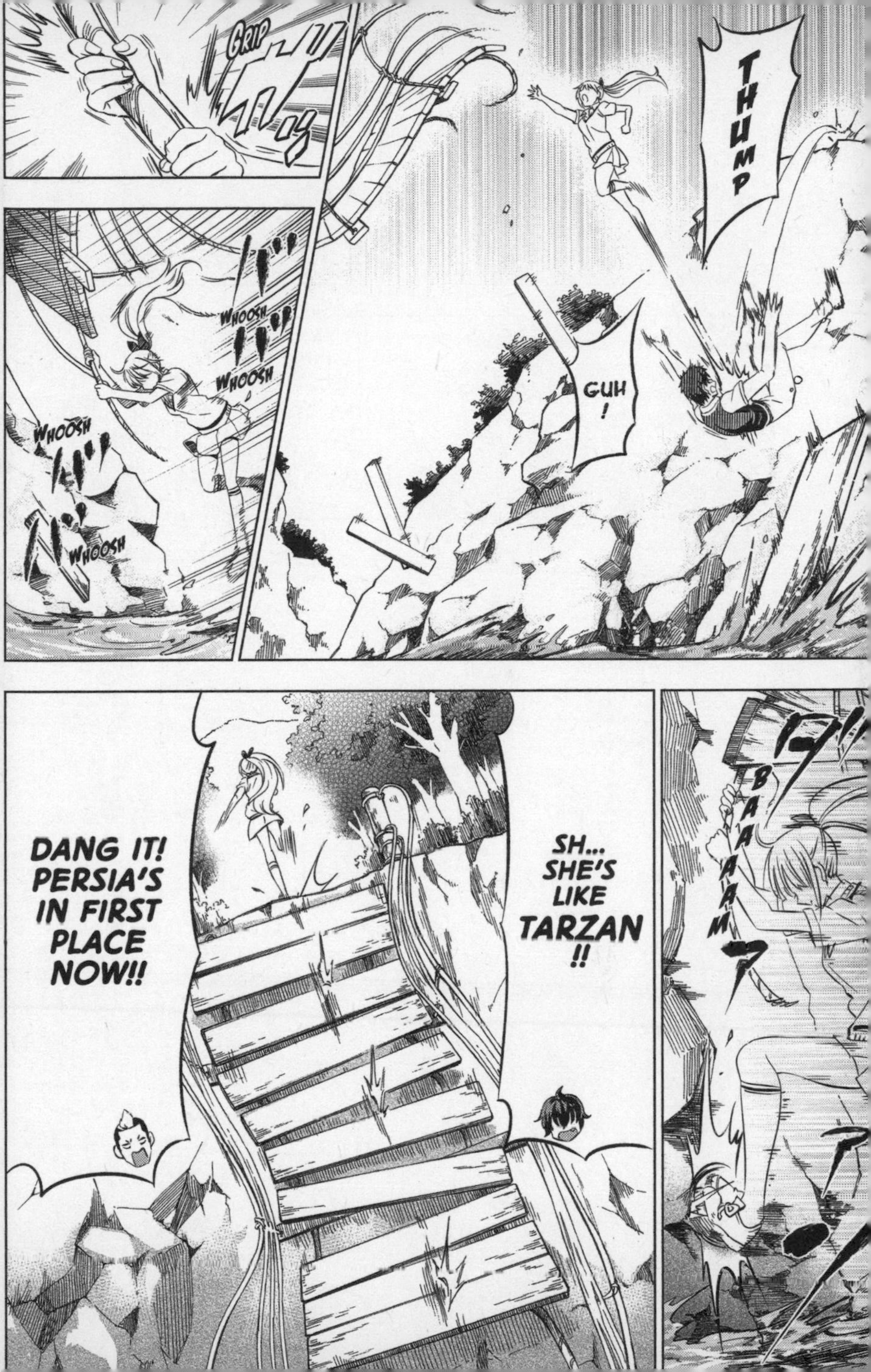
THUMP
GUH!
GRIP
WHOOSH
WHOOSH
WHOOSH
WHOOSH
BAAAAAM
SH... SHE'S LIKE TARZAN!!
DANG IT! PERSIA'S IN FIRST PLACE NOW!!

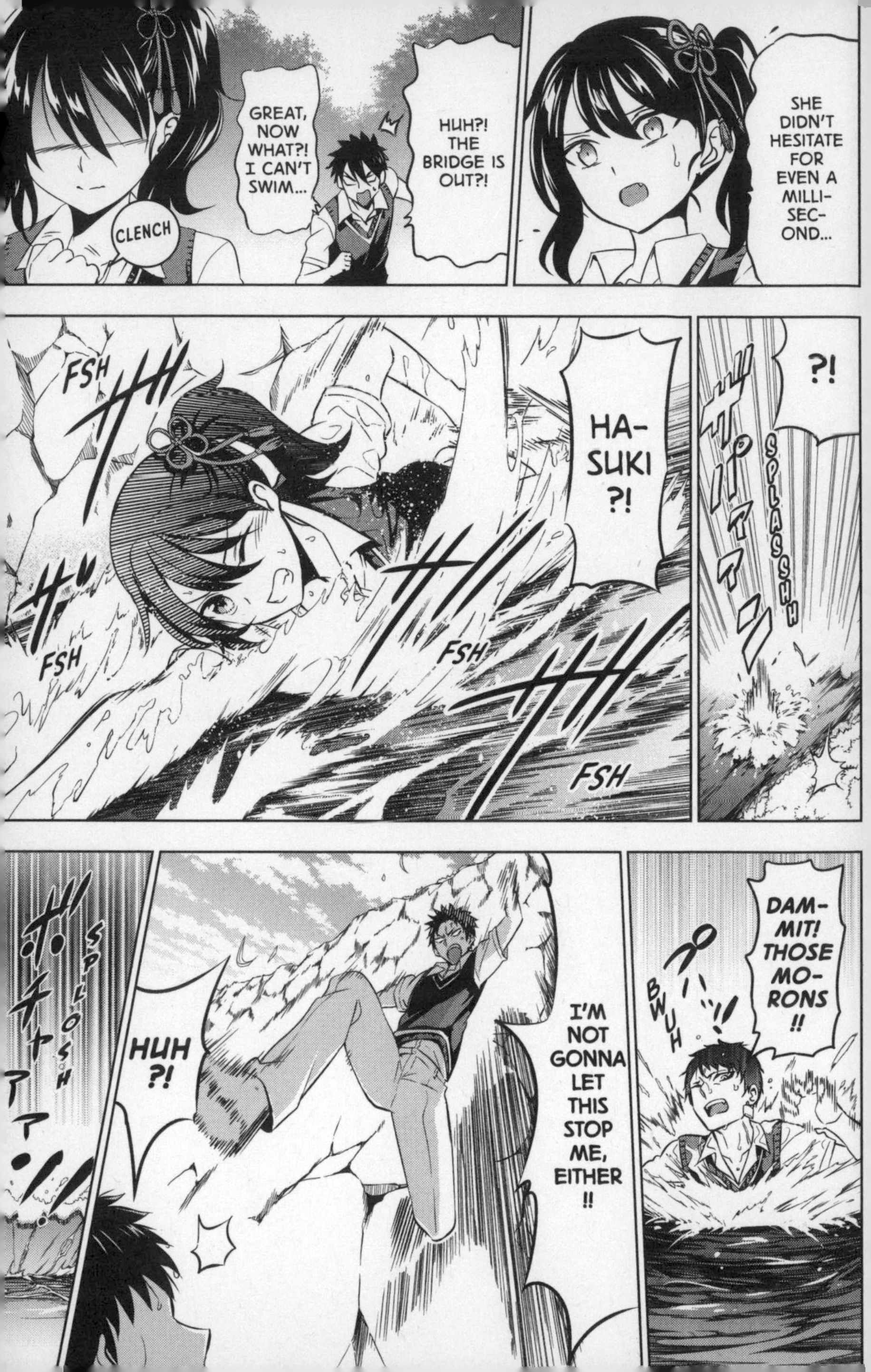
SHE DIDN'T HESITATE FOR EVEN A MILLI-SEC-OND...
HUH?! THE BRIDGE IS OUT?!
GREAT, NOW WHAT?! I CAN'T SWIM...
CLENCH
?!
SPLASSHH
HA-SUKI ?!
FSH
FSH
FSH
FSH
DAM-MIT! THOSE MO-RONS !!
BWUH
I'M NOT GONNA LET THIS STOP ME, EITHER !!
HUH ?!
SPLOOSH

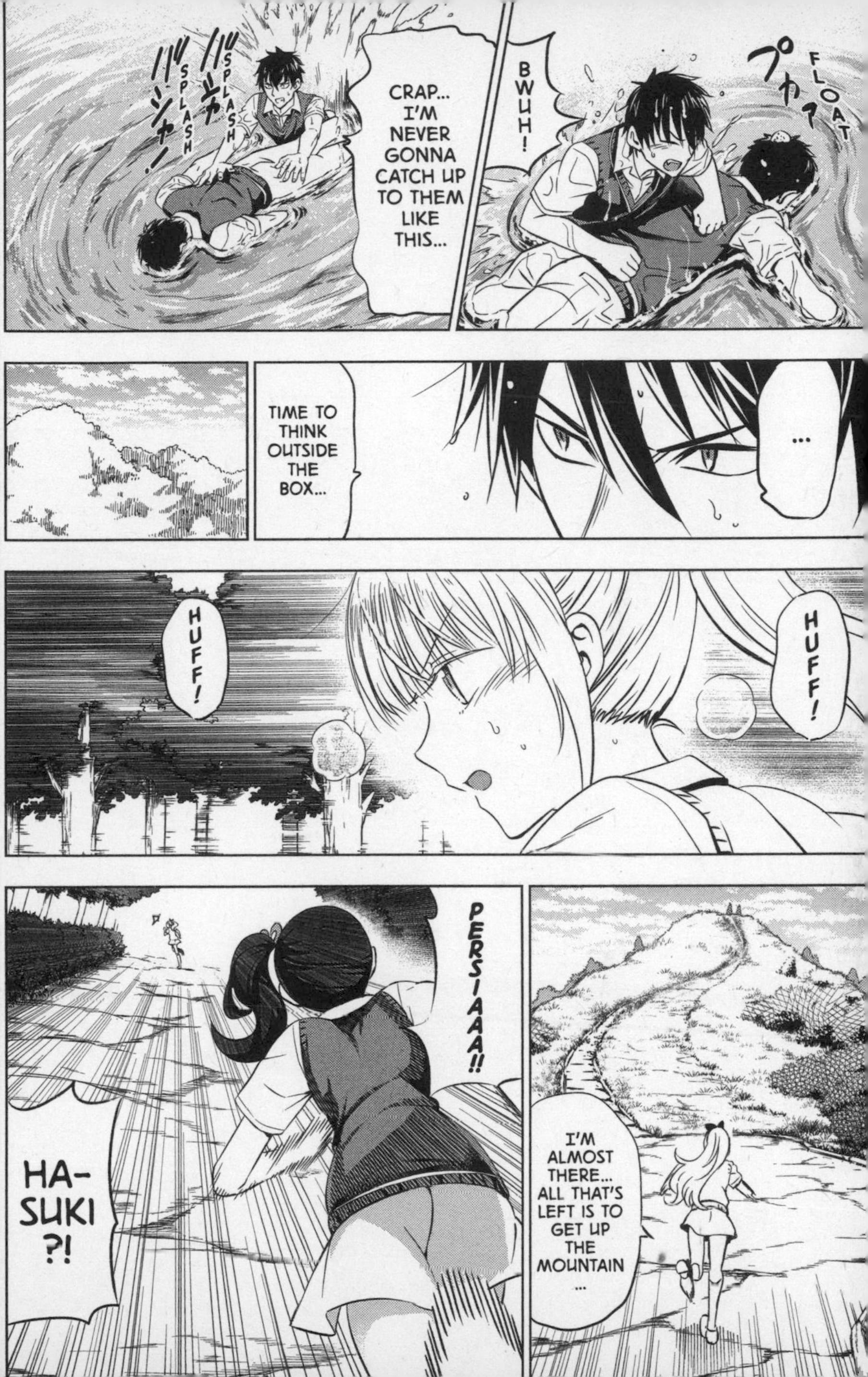
FLOAT
BWUH!
CRAP... I'M NEVER GONNA CATCH UP TO THEM LIKE THIS...
SPLASH
SPLASH
...
TIME TO THINK OUTSIDE THE BOX...
HUFF!
HUFF!
I'M ALMOST THERE... ALL THAT'S LEFT IS TO GET UP THE MOUNTAIN...
PERSIAAA!!
HA-SUKI?!

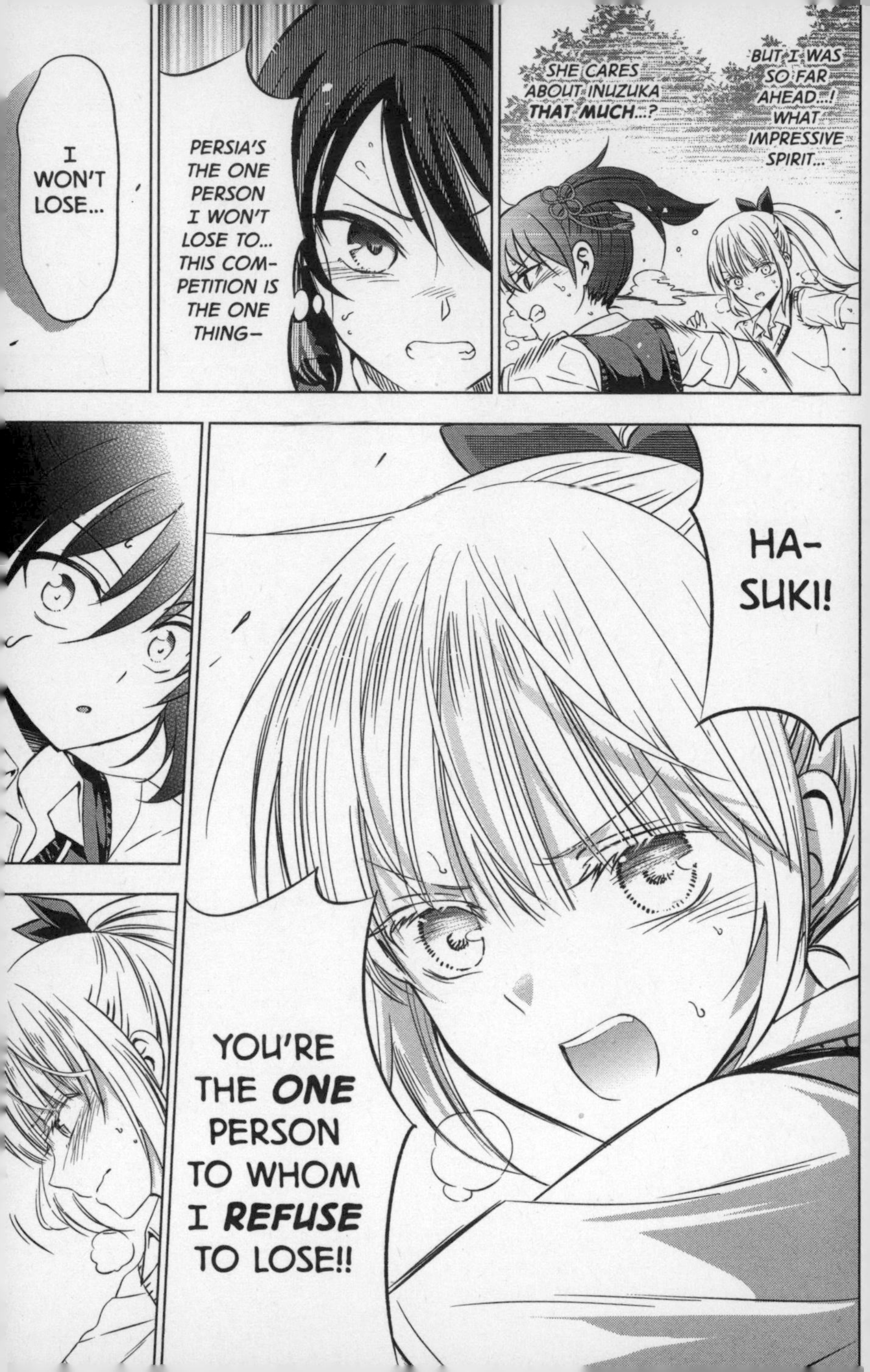
BUT I WAS SO FAR AHEAD...! WHAT IMPRESSIVE SPIRIT...
SHE CARES ABOUT INUZUKA **THAT MUCH**...?
PERSIA'S THE ONE PERSON I WON'T LOSE TO... THIS COMPETITION IS THE ONE THING—
I WON'T LOSE...
HA-SUKI!
YOU'RE THE ***ONE*** PERSON TO WHOM I ***REFUSE*** TO LOSE!!

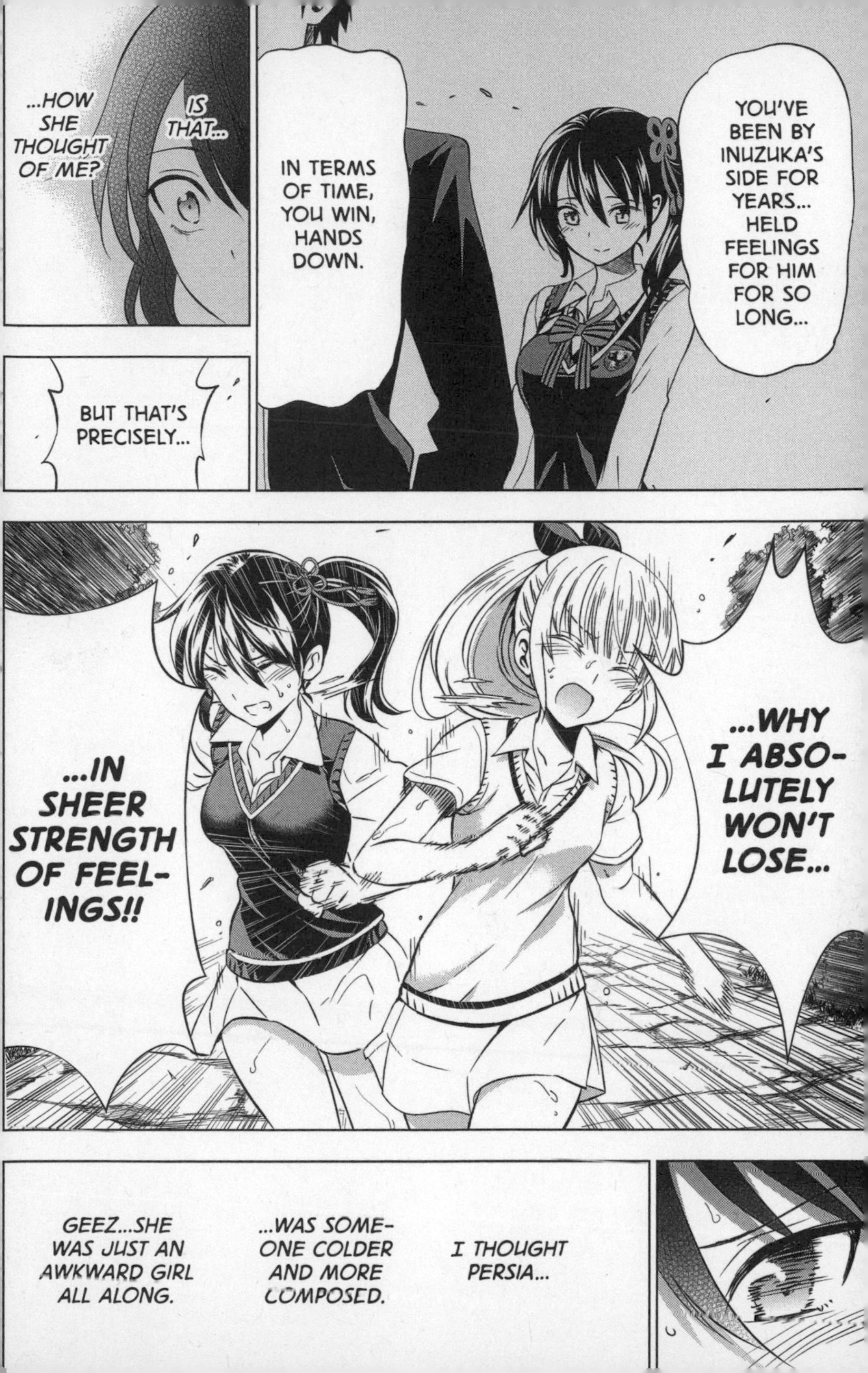
YOU'VE BEEN BY INUZUKA'S SIDE FOR YEARS... HELD FEELINGS FOR HIM FOR SO LONG...
IN TERMS OF TIME, YOU WIN, HANDS DOWN.
IS THAT...
...HOW SHE THOUGHT OF ME?
BUT THAT'S PRECISELY...
...WHY I ABSO-LUTELY WON'T LOSE...
...IN SHEER STRENGTH OF FEEL-INGS!!
I THOUGHT PERSIA...
...WAS SOME-ONE COLDER AND MORE COMPOSED.
GEEZ...SHE WAS JUST AN AWKWARD GIRL ALL ALONG.

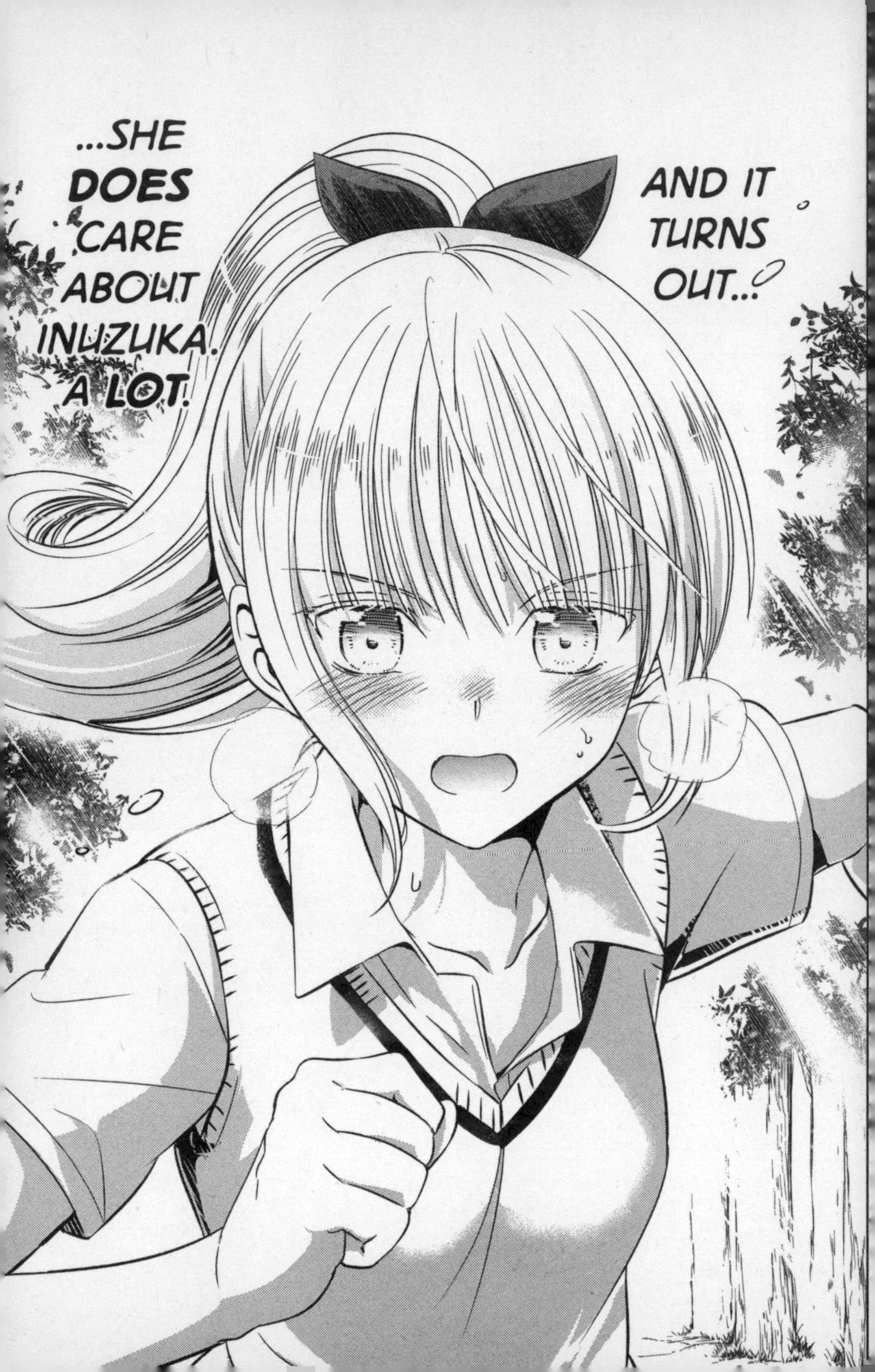
AND IT TURNS OUT...
...SHE DOES CARE ABOUT INUZUKA. A LOT.

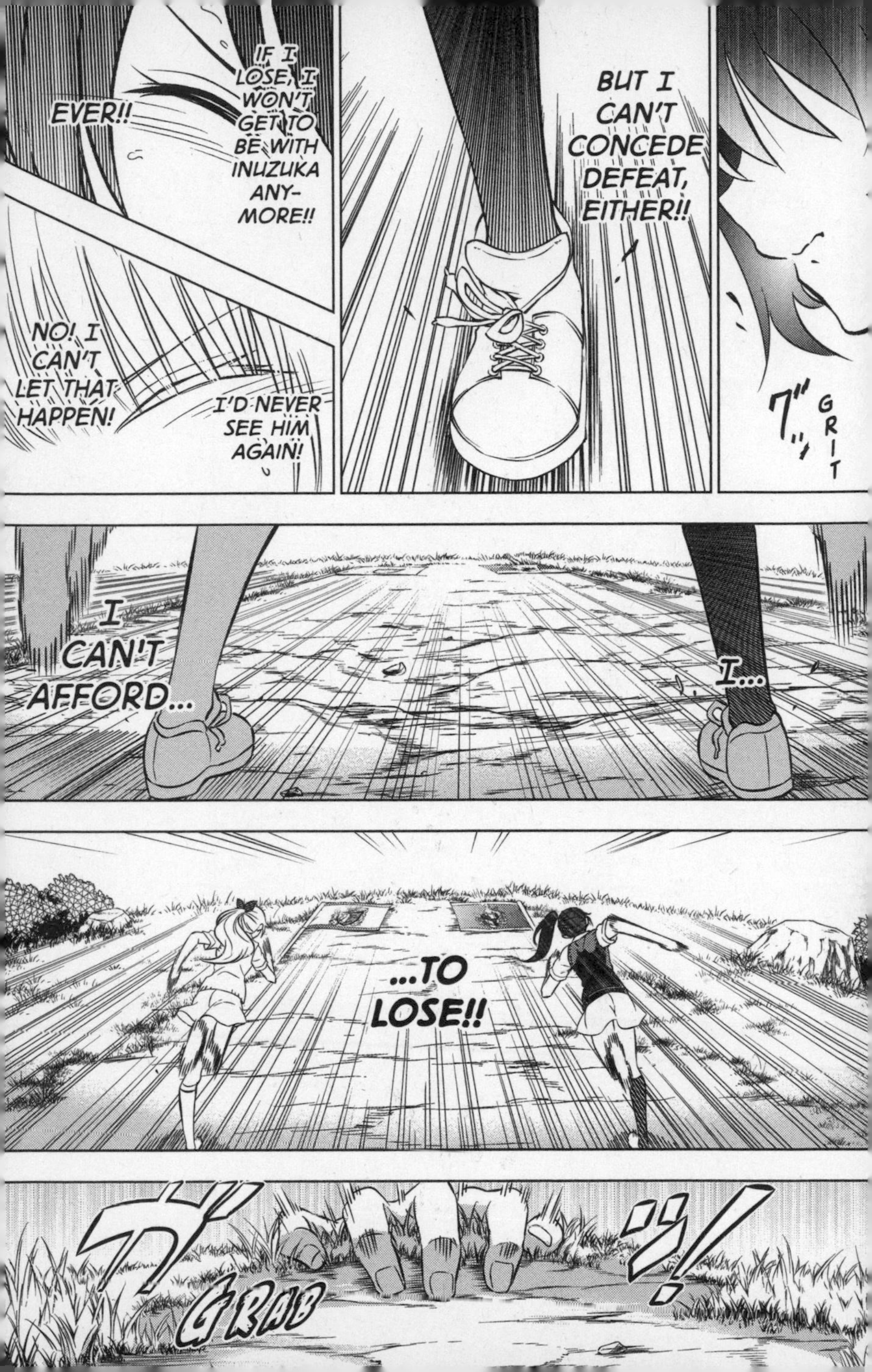
GRIT
BUT I CAN'T CONCEDE DEFEAT, EITHER!!
IF I LOSE, I WON'T GET TO BE WITH INUZUKA ANYMORE!!
EVER!!
I'D NEVER SEE HIM AGAIN!
NO! I CAN'T LET THAT HAPPEN!
I...
I CAN'T AFFORD...
...TO LOSE!!
GRAB

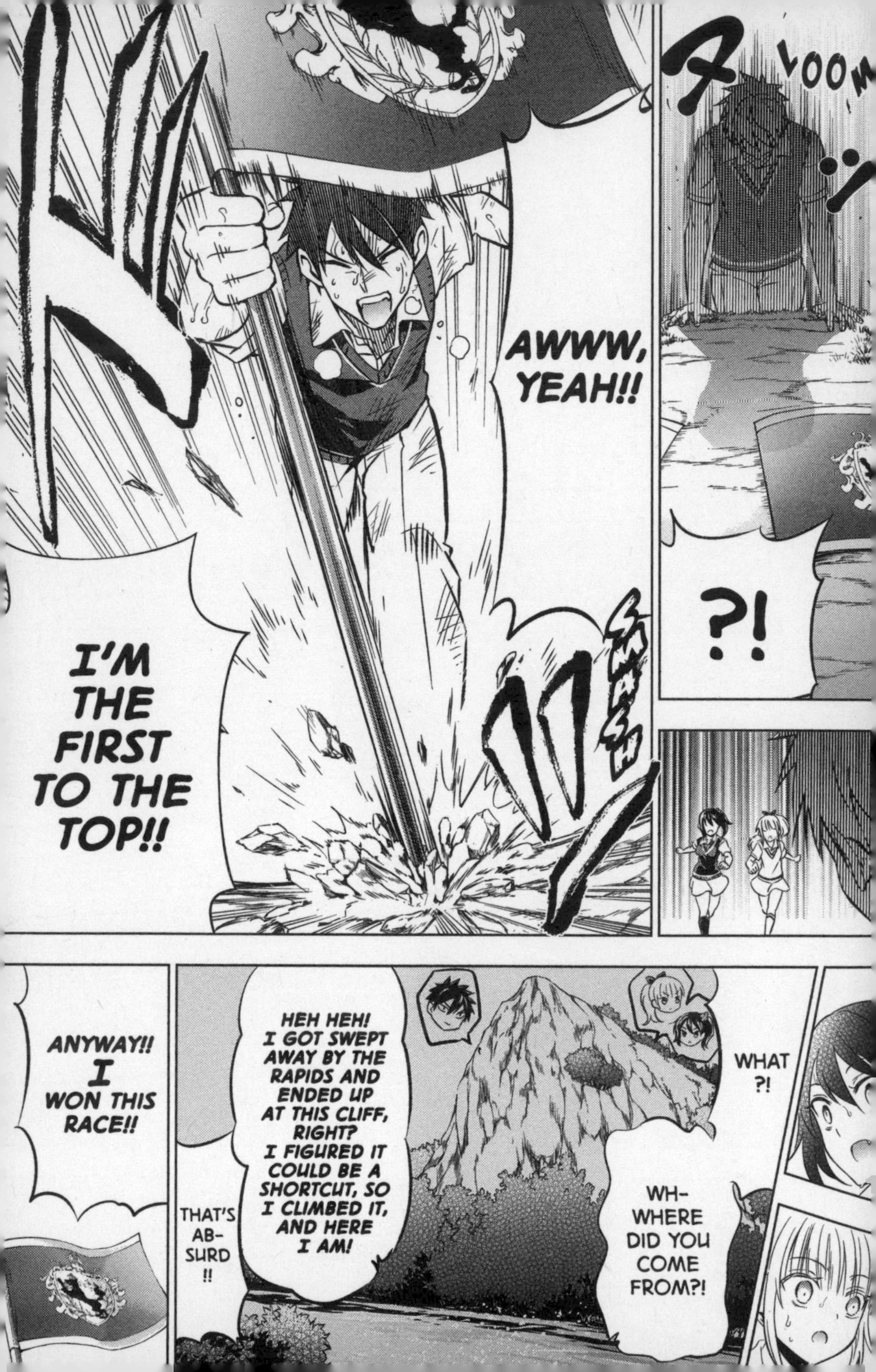
VOOM
?!
AWWW, YEAH!!
I'M THE FIRST TO THE TOP!!
WHAT?!
WH-WHERE DID YOU COME FROM?!
HEH HEH! I GOT SWEPT AWAY BY THE RAPIDS AND ENDED UP AT THIS CLIFF, RIGHT? I FIGURED IT COULD BE A SHORTCUT, SO I CLIMBED IT, AND HERE I AM!
THAT'S AB-SURD!!
ANYWAY!! I WON THIS RACE!!

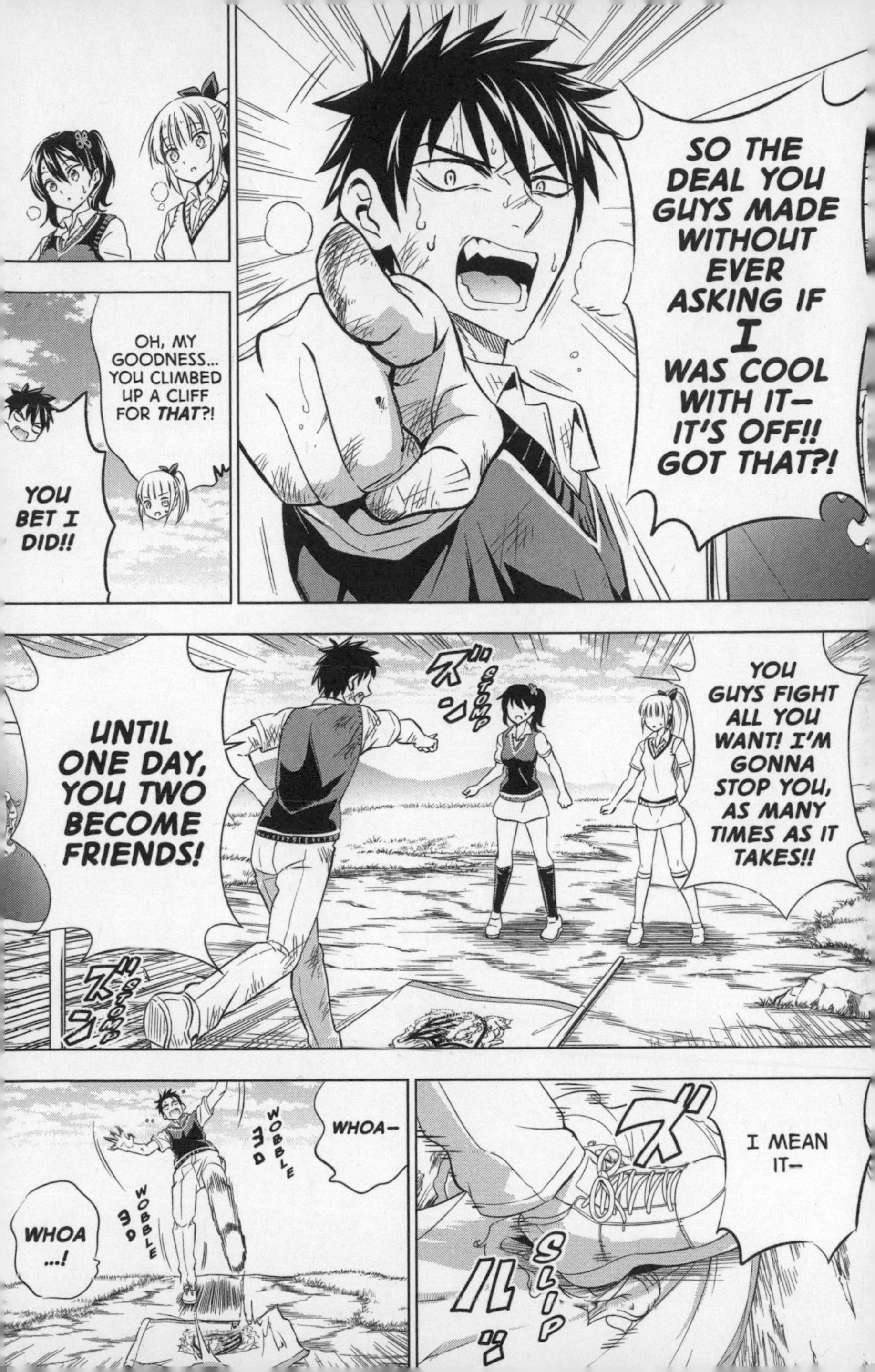
SO THE DEAL YOU GUYS MADE WITHOUT EVER ASKING IF I WAS COOL WITH IT— IT'S OFF!! GOT THAT?!
OH, MY GOODNESS... YOU CLIMBED UP A CLIFF FOR THAT?!
YOU BET I DID!!
YOU GUYS FIGHT ALL YOU WANT! I'M GONNA STOP YOU, AS MANY TIMES AS IT TAKES!!
STOMP
UNTIL ONE DAY, YOU TWO BECOME FRIENDS!
STOMP
I MEAN IT—
SLIP
WHOA—
WOBBLE
WOBBLE
WHOA ...!

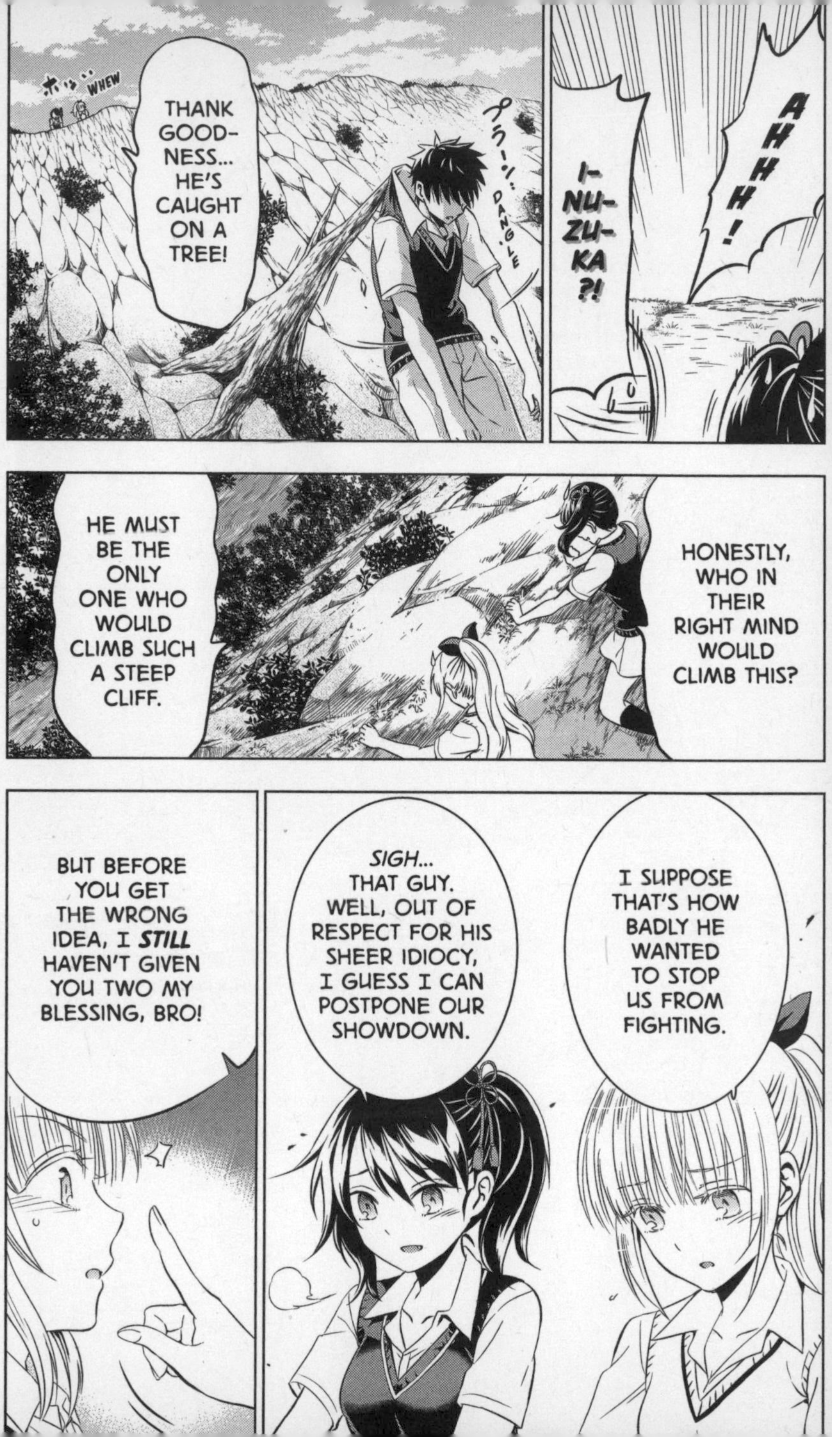
AHHH!
I-NUZUKA?!
WHEW
THANK GOODNESS... HE'S CAUGHT ON A TREE!
DANGLE
HONESTLY, WHO IN THEIR RIGHT MIND WOULD CLIMB THIS?
HE MUST BE THE ONLY ONE WHO WOULD CLIMB SUCH A STEEP CLIFF.
I SUPPOSE THAT'S HOW BADLY HE WANTED TO STOP US FROM FIGHTING.
SIGH... THAT GUY. WELL, OUT OF RESPECT FOR HIS SHEER IDIOCY, I GUESS I CAN POSTPONE OUR SHOWDOWN.
BUT BEFORE YOU GET THE WRONG IDEA, I ***STILL*** HAVEN'T GIVEN YOU TWO MY BLESSING, BRO!

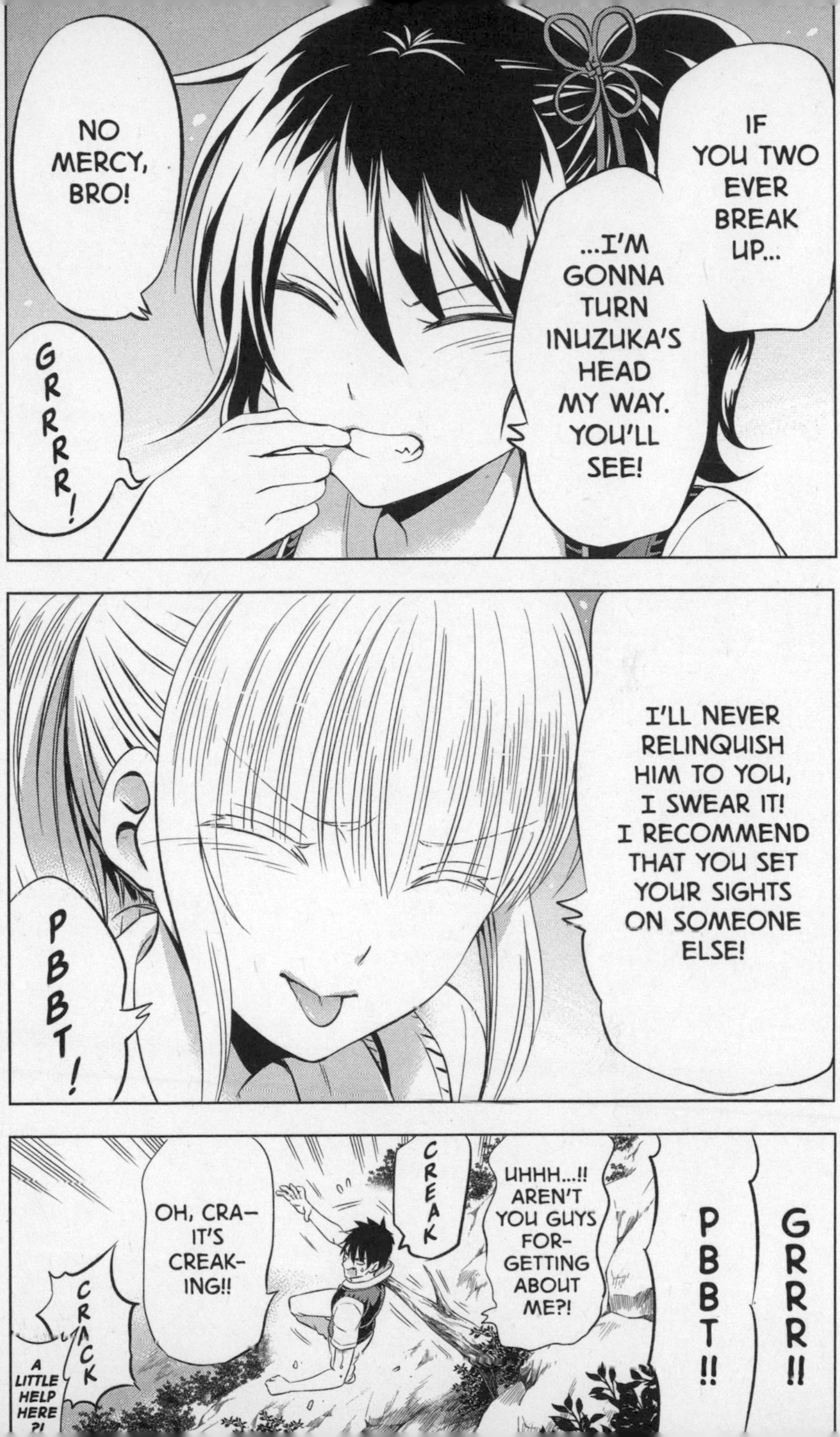
IF YOU TWO EVER BREAK UP...
...I'M GONNA TURN INUZUKA'S HEAD MY WAY. YOU'LL SEE!
NO MERCY, BRO!
GRRRR!
I'LL NEVER RELINQUISH HIM TO YOU, I SWEAR IT! I RECOMMEND THAT YOU SET YOUR SIGHTS ON SOMEONE ELSE!
PBBT!
GRRR!!
PBBT!!
UHHH...!! AREN'T YOU GUYS FOR-GETTING ABOUT ME?!
CREAK
OH, CRA— IT'S CREAK-ING!!
CRACK
A LITTLE HELP HERE?!

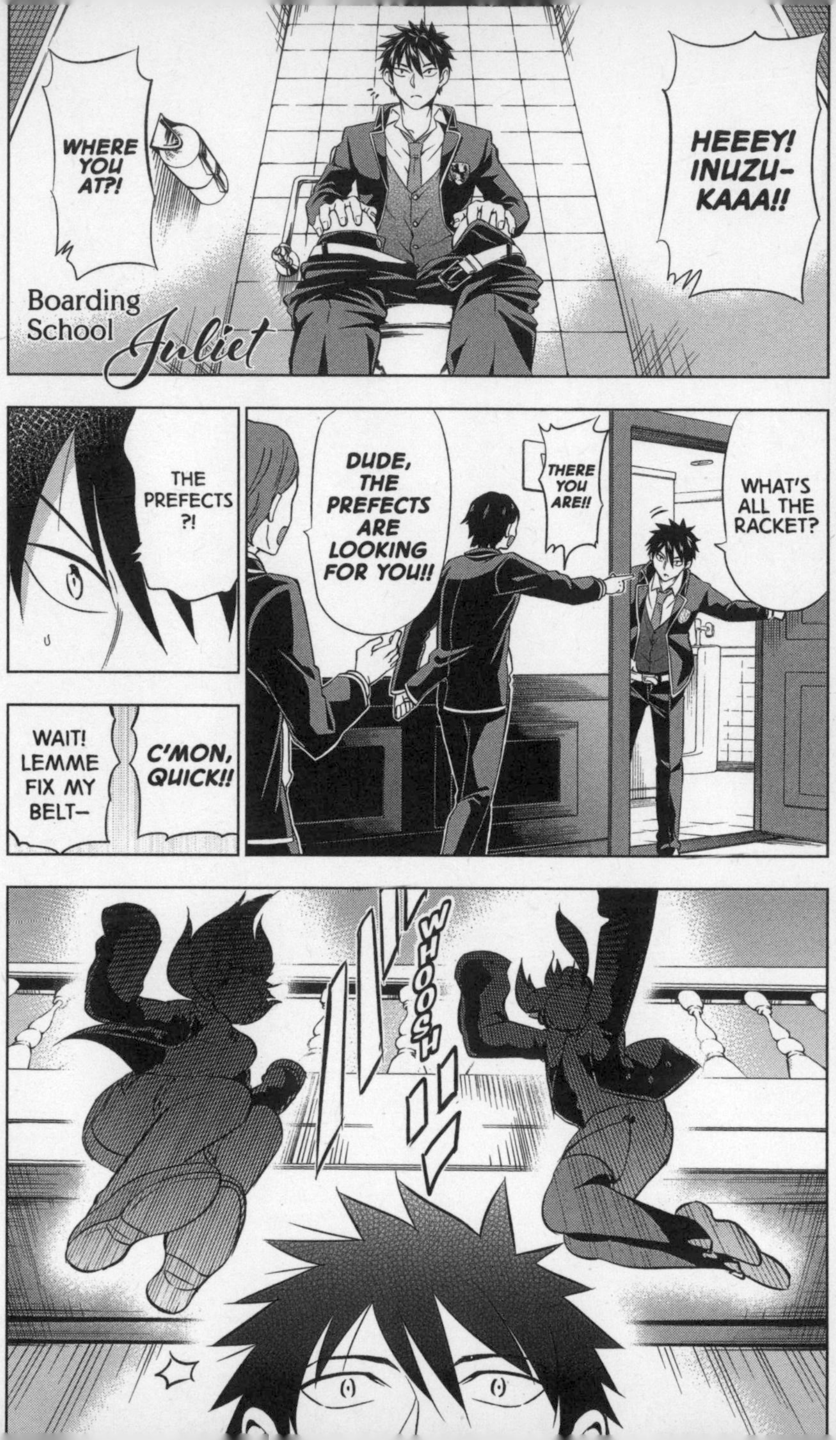
HEEEY! INUZU-KAAA!!
WHERE YOU AT?!
Boarding School Juliet
WHAT'S ALL THE RACKET?
THERE YOU ARE!!
DUDE, THE PREFECTS ARE LOOKING FOR YOU!!
THE PREFECTS?!
C'MON, QUICK!!
WAIT! LEMME FIX MY BELT—
WHOOSH

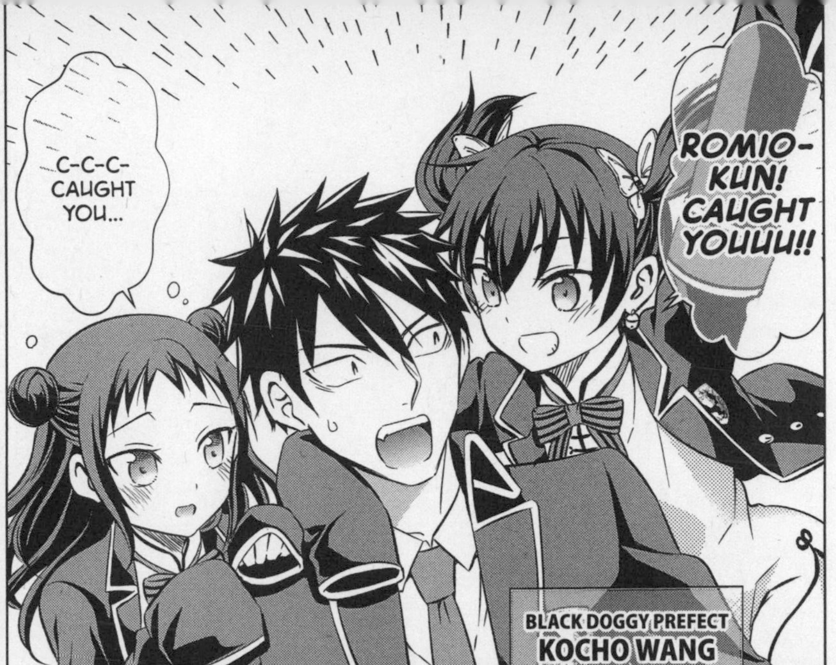
ROMIO-KUN! CAUGHT YOUUU!!
C-C-C-CAUGHT YOU...
BLACK DOGGY PREFECT KOCHO WANG SECOND-YEAR
BLACK DOGGY PREFECT TERIA WANG SECOND-YEAR
ACT 33:
ROMIO & THE TWINS I

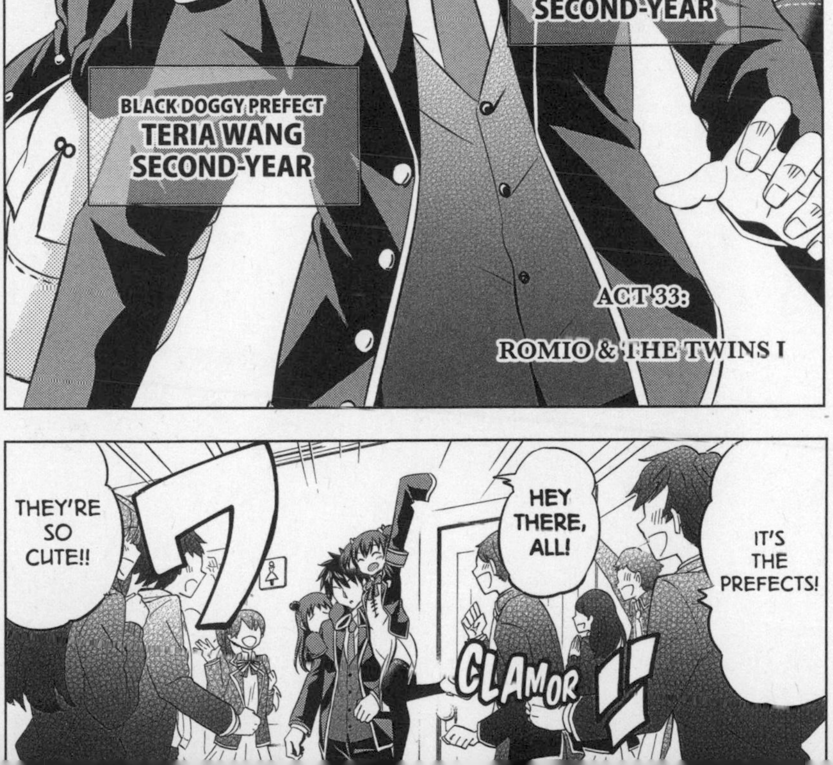
IT'S THE PREFECTS!
HEY THERE, ALL!
CLAMOR
THEY'RE SO CUTE!!

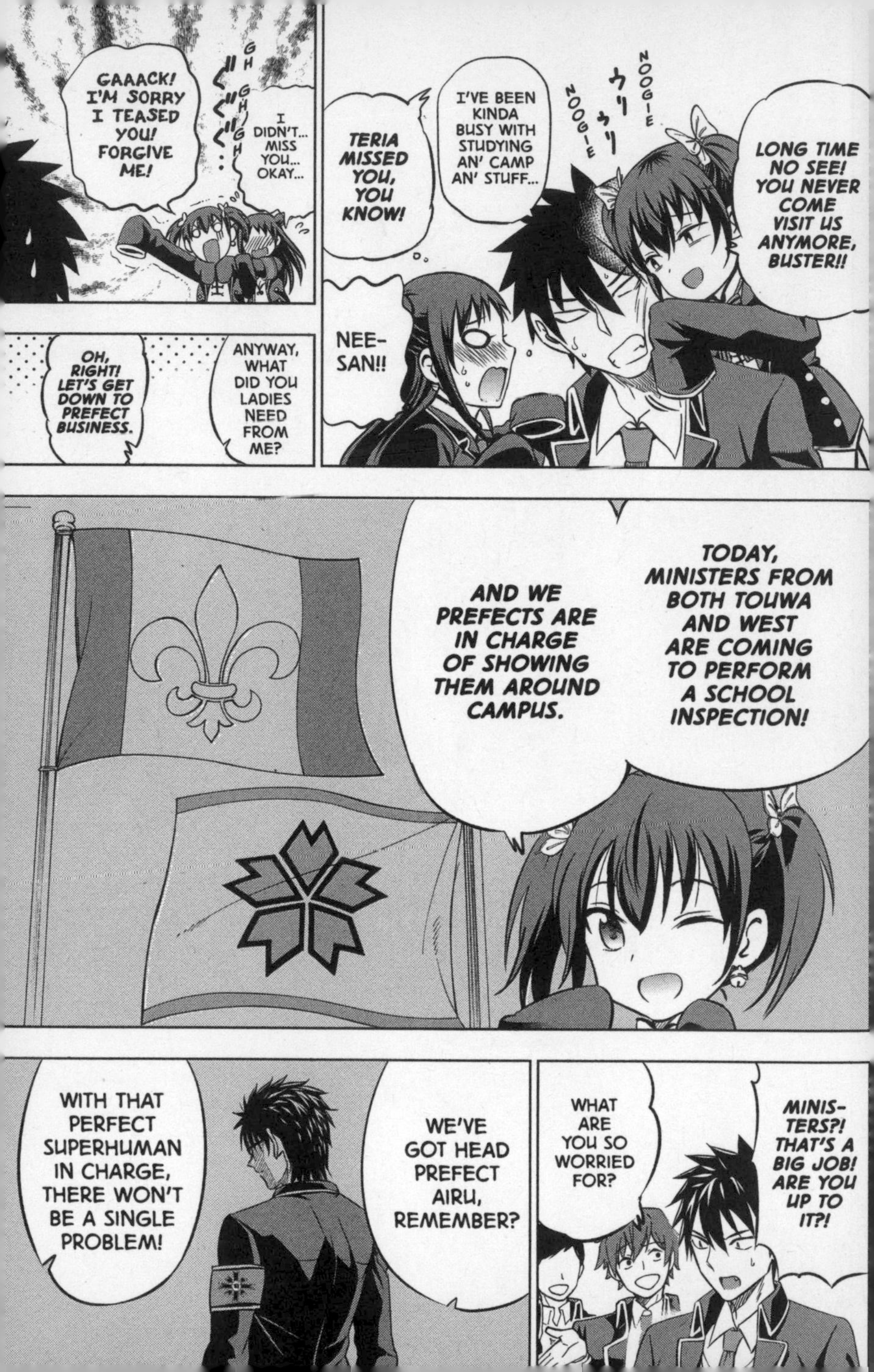
LONG TIME NO SEE! YOU NEVER COME VISIT US ANYMORE, BUSTER!!
NOOGIE NOOGIE
I'VE BEEN KINDA BUSY WITH STUDYING AN' CAMP AN' STUFF...
TERIA MISSED YOU, YOU KNOW!
NEE-SAN!!
GH GH GH
I DIDN'T... MISS YOU... OKAY...
GAAACK! I'M SORRY I TEASED YOU! FORGIVE ME!
ANYWAY, WHAT DID YOU LADIES NEED FROM ME?
OH, RIGHT! LET'S GET DOWN TO PREFECT BUSINESS.
TODAY, MINISTERS FROM BOTH TOUWA AND WEST ARE COMING TO PERFORM A SCHOOL INSPECTION!
AND WE PREFECTS ARE IN CHARGE OF SHOWING THEM AROUND CAMPUS.
MINIS-TERS?! THAT'S A BIG JOB! ARE YOU UP TO IT?!
WHAT ARE YOU SO WORRIED FOR?
WE'VE GOT HEAD PREFECT AIRU, REMEMBER?
WITH THAT PERFECT SUPERHUMAN IN CHARGE, THERE WON'T BE A SINGLE PROBLEM!

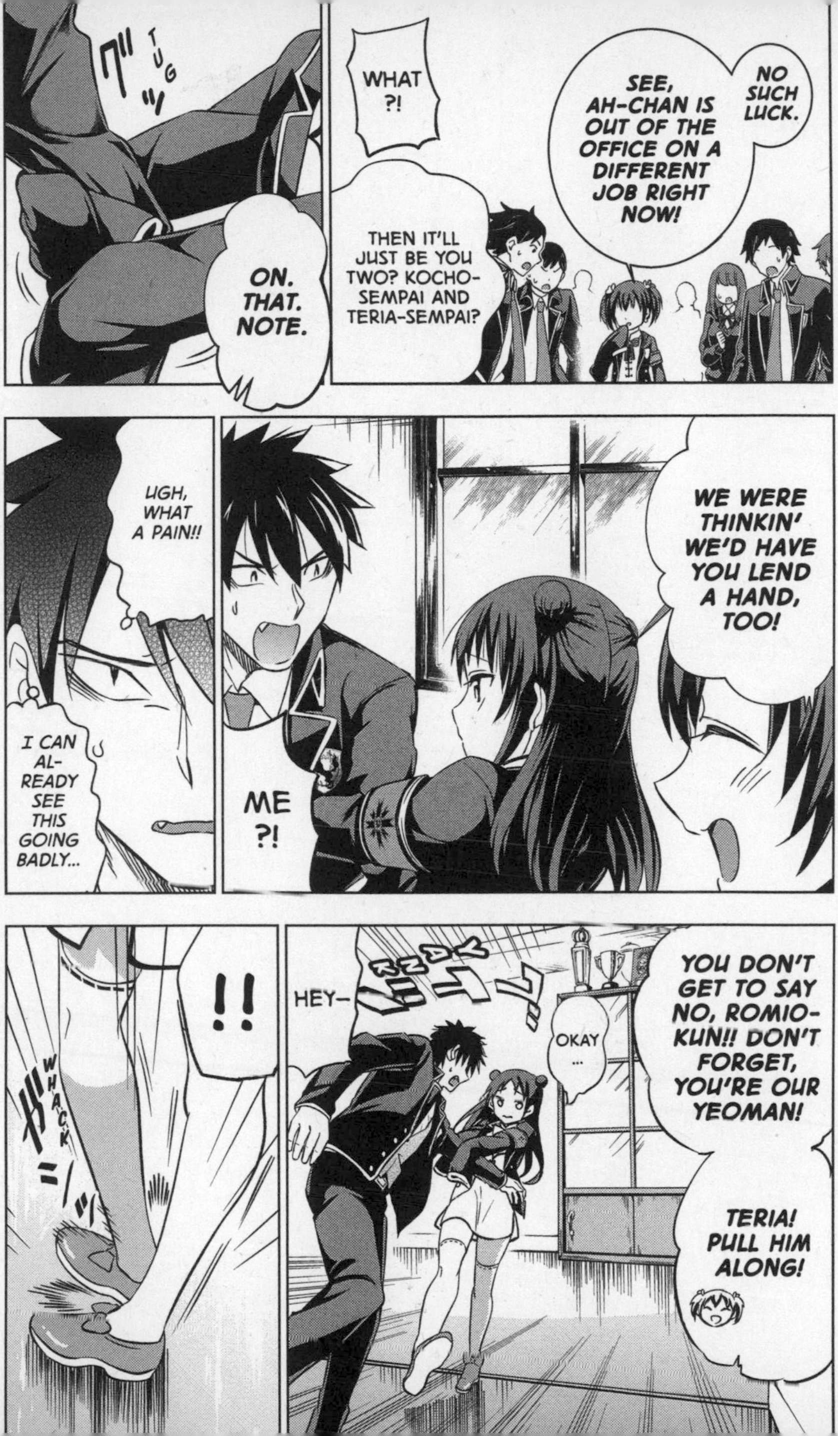
NO SUCH LUCK.
SEE, AH-CHAN IS OUT OF THE OFFICE ON A DIFFERENT JOB RIGHT NOW!
WHAT?!
THEN IT'LL JUST BE YOU TWO? KOCHO-SEMPAI AND TERIA-SEMPAI?
ON. THAT. NOTE.
TUG
WE WERE THINKIN' WE'D HAVE YOU LEND A HAND, TOO!
ME?!
UGH, WHAT A PAIN!!
I CAN AL-READY SEE THIS GOING BADLY...
YOU DON'T GET TO SAY NO, ROMIO-KUN!! DON'T FORGET, YOU'RE OUR YEOMAN!
TERIA! PULL HIM ALONG!
OKAY...
YANK
HEY–
!!
WHACK

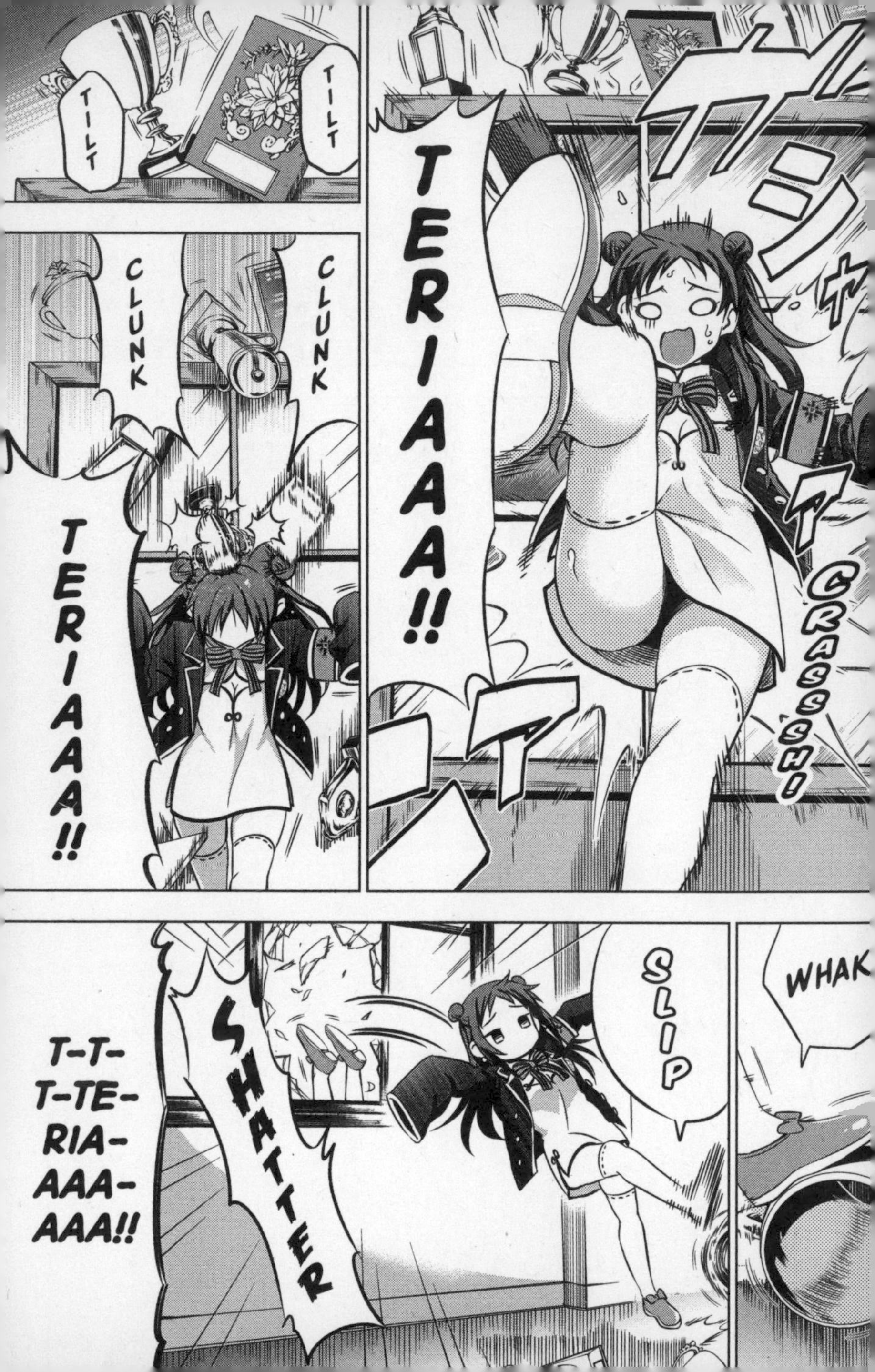
TERIAAAA!!
CRASSSH!
TILT
TILT
CLUNK
CLUNK
TERIAAAAA!!
WHAK
SLIP
SHATTER
T-T-T-TE-RIA-AAA-AAA!!

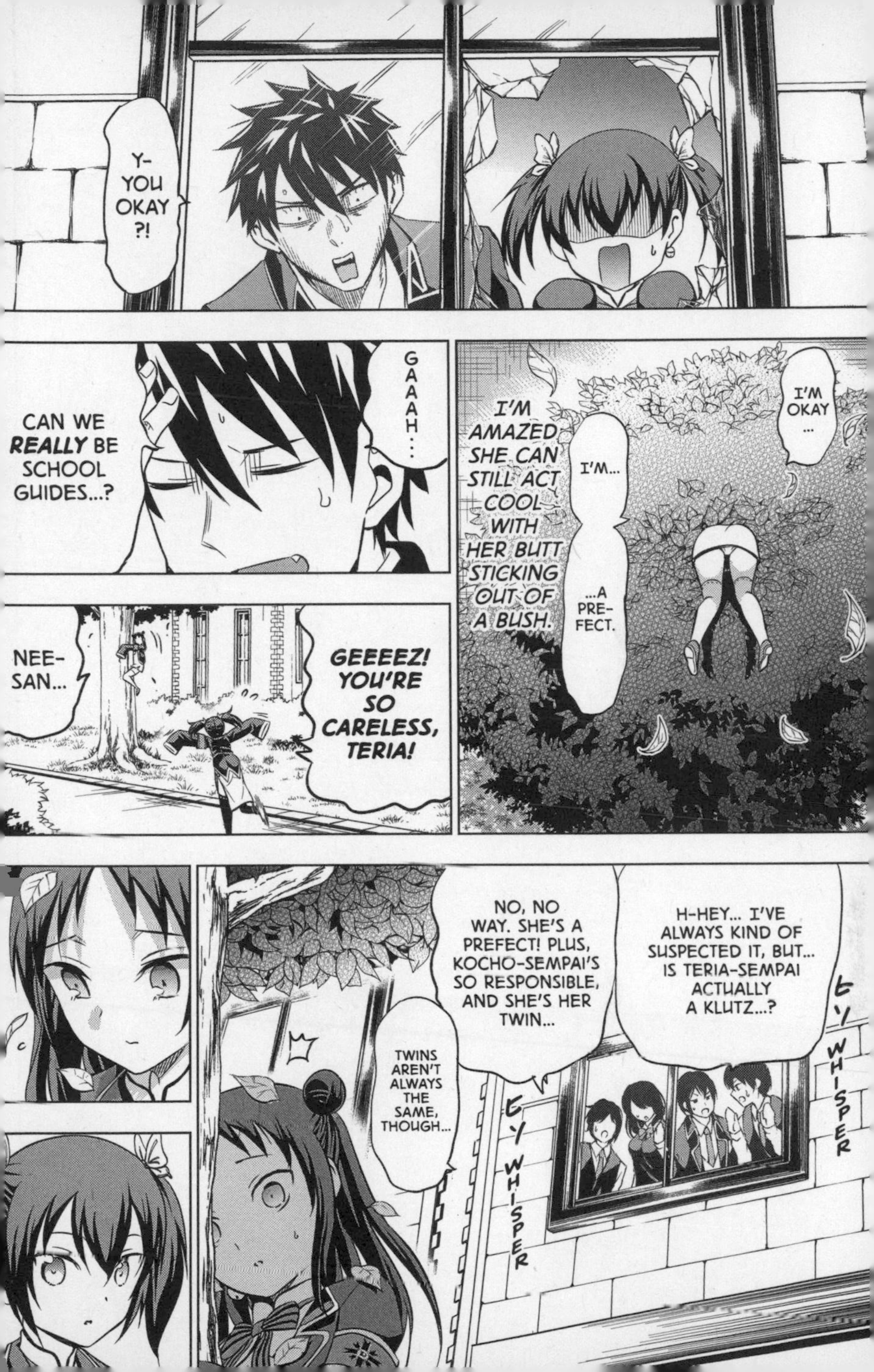
Y-YOU OKAY?!
I'M OKAY...
I'M... ...A PREFECT.
I'M AMAZED SHE CAN STILL ACT COOL WITH HER BUTT STICKING OUT OF A BUSH.
GAAAH...
CAN WE REALLY BE SCHOOL GUIDES...?
GEEEEZ! YOU'RE SO CARELESS, TERIA!
NEE-SAN...
H-HEY... I'VE ALWAYS KIND OF SUSPECTED IT, BUT... IS TERIA-SEMPAI ACTUALLY A KLUTZ...?
ヒソ WHISPER
NO, NO WAY. SHE'S A PREFECT! PLUS, KOCHO-SEMPAI'S SO RESPONSIBLE, AND SHE'S HER TWIN...
TWINS AREN'T ALWAYS THE SAME, THOUGH...
ヒソ WHISPER

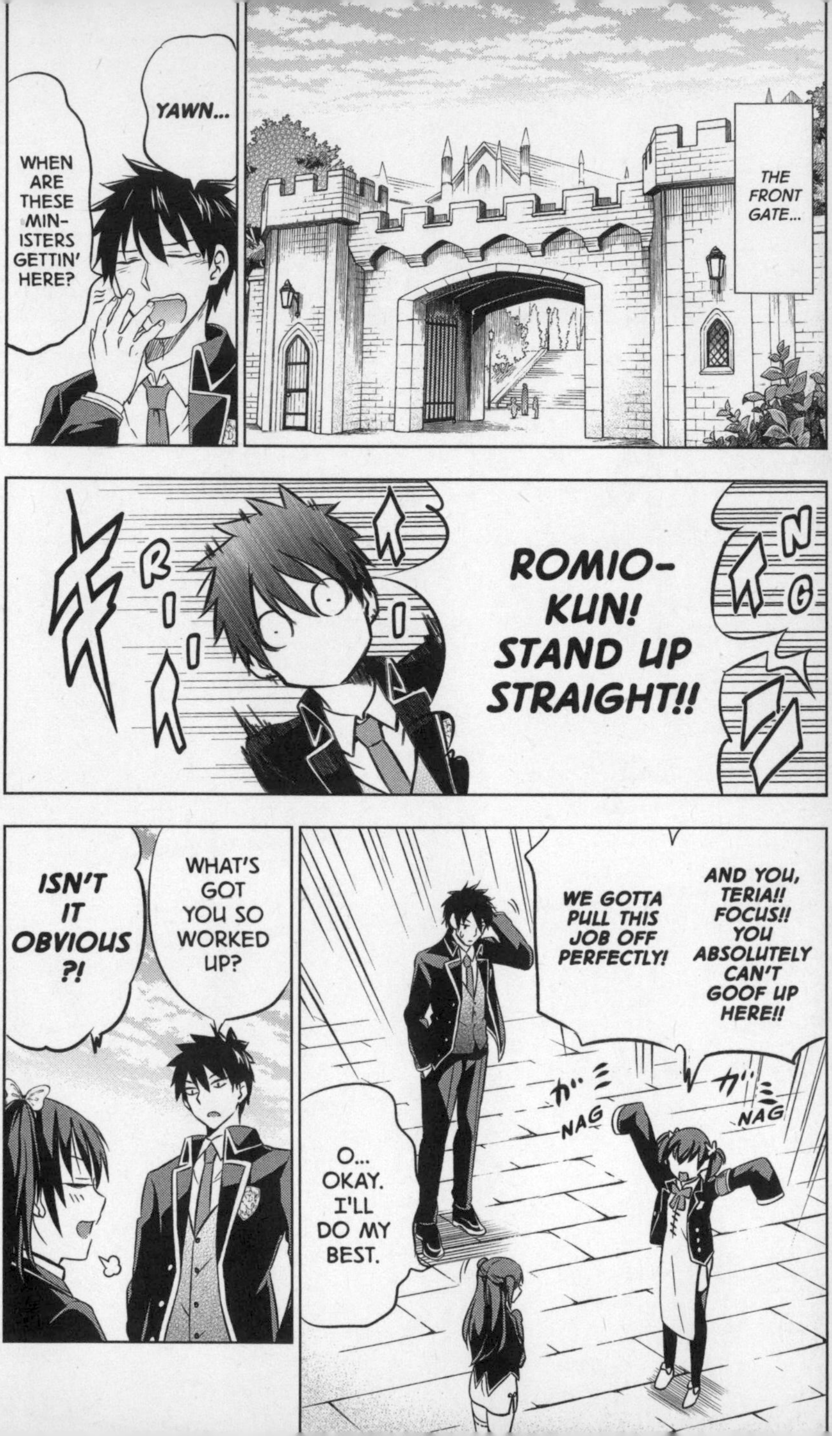
THE FRONT GATE...
YAWN...
WHEN ARE THESE MIN-ISTERS GETTIN' HERE?
ROMIO-KUN! STAND UP STRAIGHT!!
AND YOU, TERIA!! FOCUS!! YOU ABSOLUTELY CAN'T GOOF UP HERE!!
WE GOTTA PULL THIS JOB OFF PERFECTLY!
NAG
NAG
O... OKAY. I'LL DO MY BEST.
WHAT'S GOT YOU SO WORKED UP?
ISN'T IT OBVIOUS?!

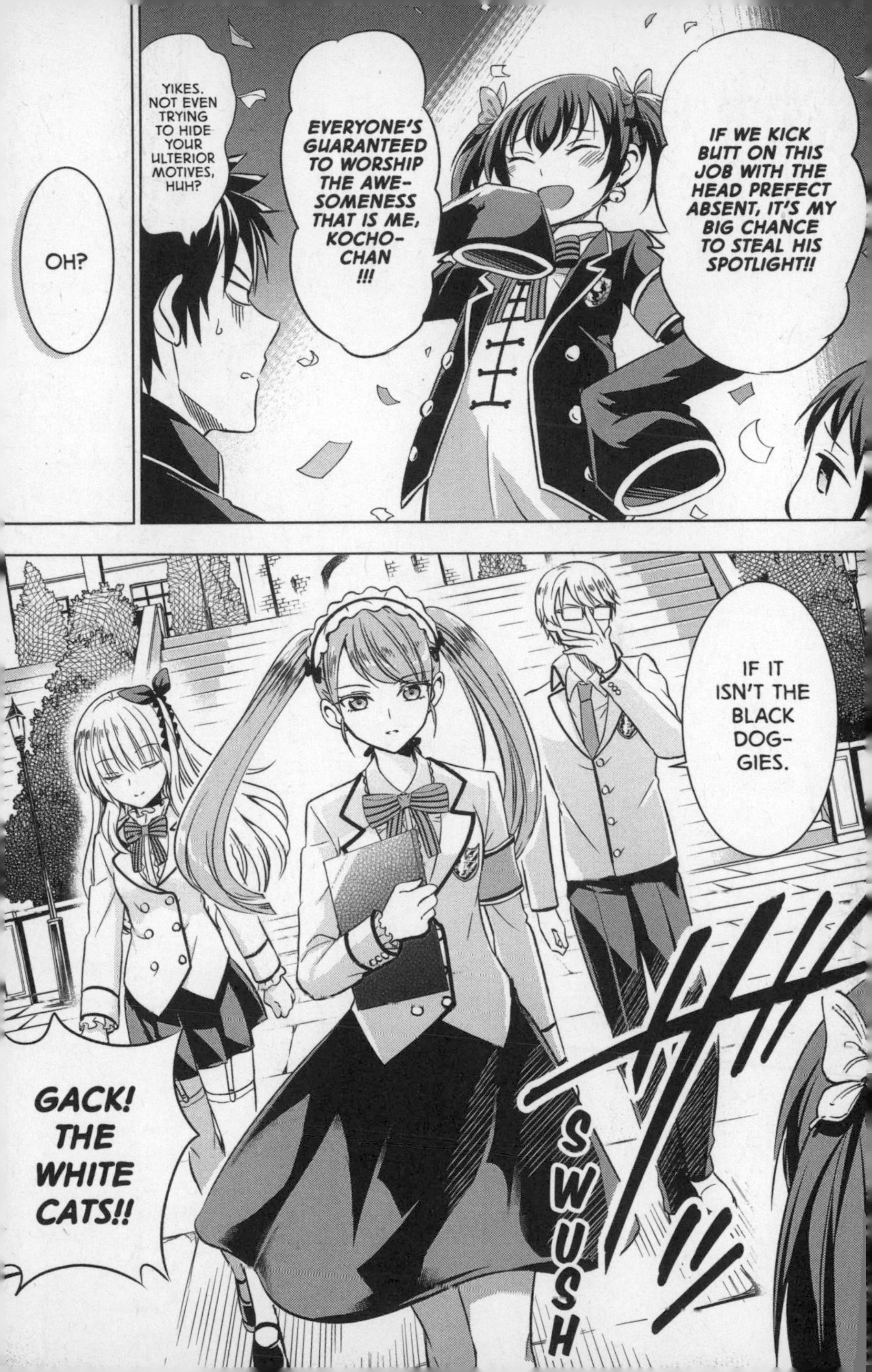
IF WE KICK BUTT ON THIS JOB WITH THE HEAD PREFECT ABSENT, IT'S MY BIG CHANCE TO STEAL HIS SPOTLIGHT!!
EVERYONE'S GUARANTEED TO WORSHIP THE AWE-SOMENESS THAT IS ME, KOCHO-CHAN !!!
YIKES. NOT EVEN TRYING TO HIDE YOUR ULTERIOR MOTIVES, HUH?
OH?
IF IT ISN'T THE BLACK DOG-GIES.
SWUSH
GACK! THE WHITE CATS!!

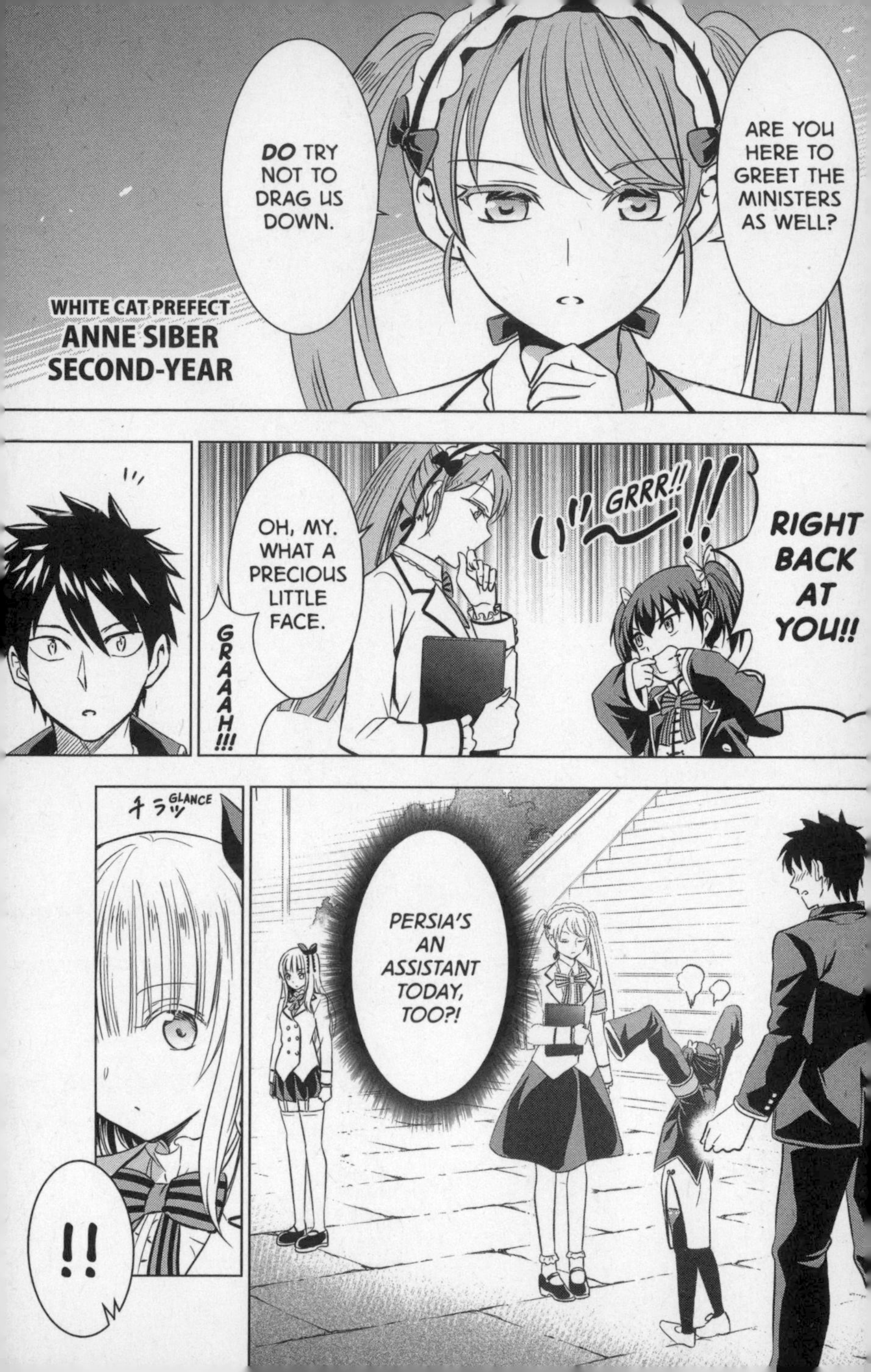
ARE YOU HERE TO GREET THE MINISTERS AS WELL?
DO TRY NOT TO DRAG US DOWN.
WHITE CAT PREFECT ANNE SIBER SECOND-YEAR
RIGHT BACK AT YOU!!
GRRR!!
OH, MY. WHAT A PRECIOUS LITTLE FACE.
GRAAAAH!!!
PERSIA'S AN ASSISTANT TODAY, TOO?!
チラッ GLANCE
!!

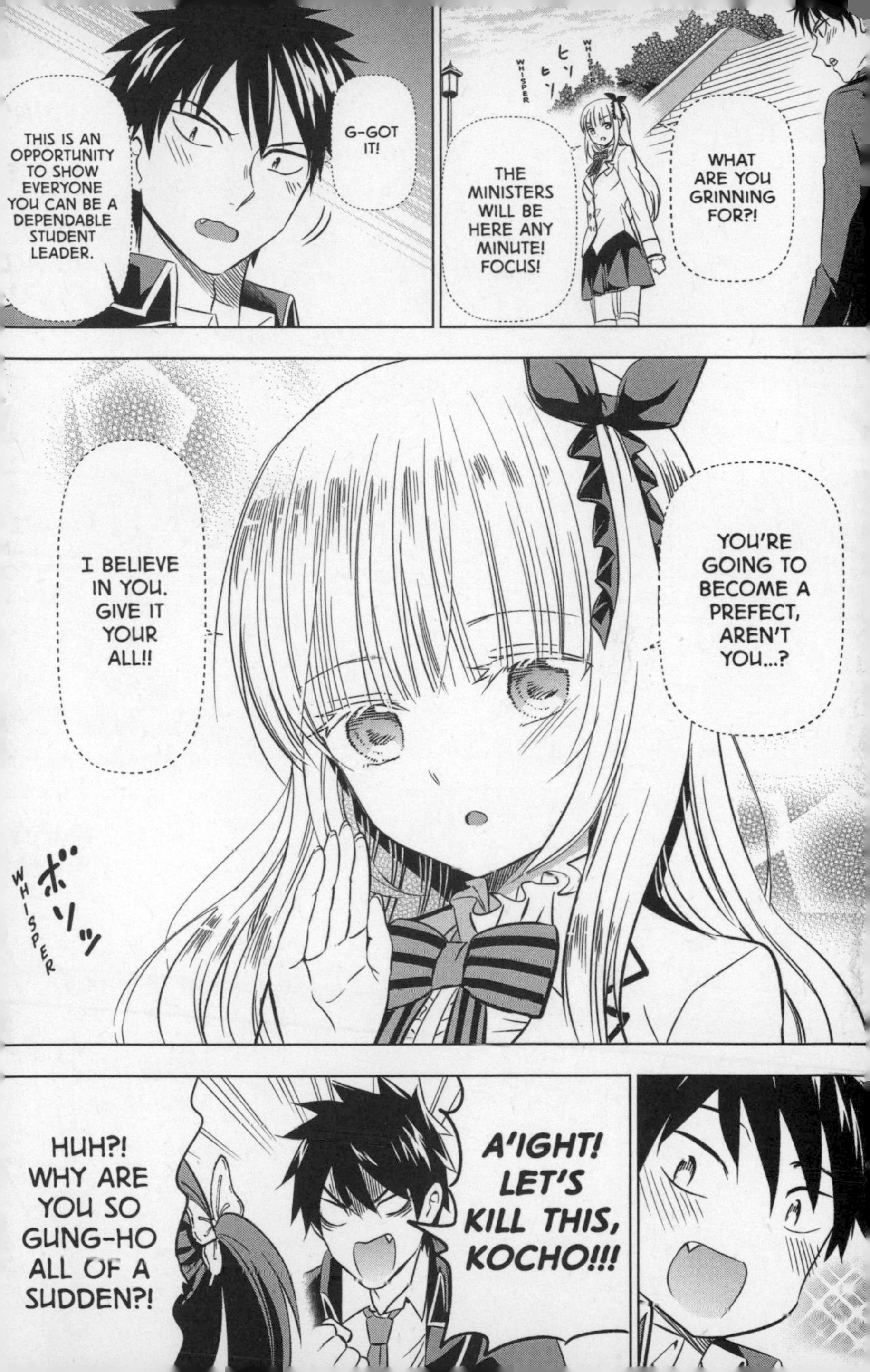
WHISPER ヒソ
WHISPER ヒソ
WHAT ARE YOU GRINNING FOR?!
THE MINISTERS WILL BE HERE ANY MINUTE! FOCUS!
G-GOT IT!
THIS IS AN OPPORTUNITY TO SHOW EVERYONE YOU CAN BE A DEPENDABLE STUDENT LEADER.
YOU'RE GOING TO BECOME A PREFECT, AREN'T YOU...?
I BELIEVE IN YOU. GIVE IT YOUR ALL!!
WHISPER ボソッ
A'IGHT! LET'S KILL THIS, KOCHO!!!
HUH?! WHY ARE YOU SO GUNG-HO ALL OF A SUDDEN?!

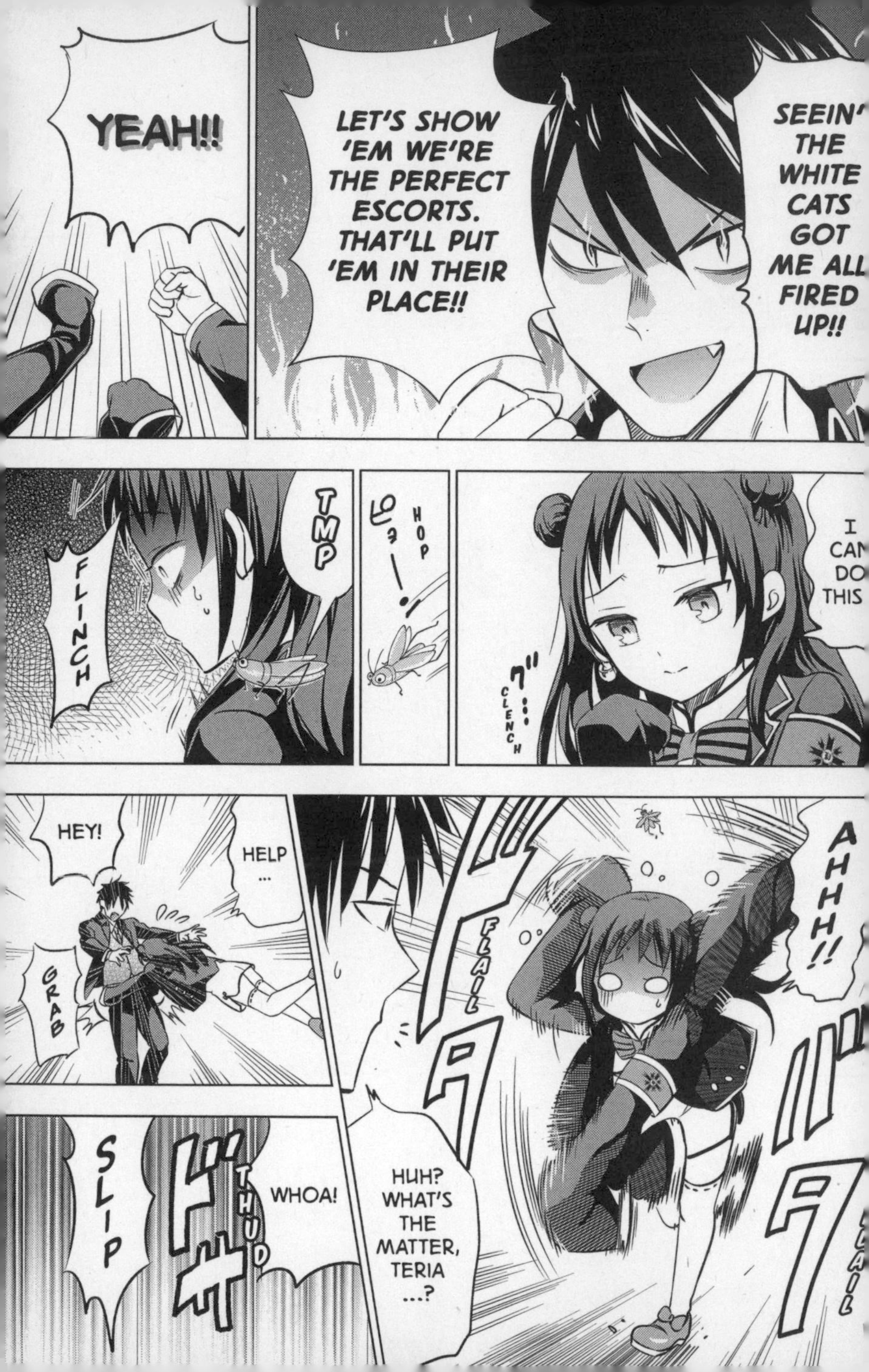

SEEIN' THE WHITE CATS GOT ME ALL FIRED UP!!
LET'S SHOW 'EM WE'RE THE PERFECT ESCORTS. THAT'LL PUT 'EM IN THEIR PLACE!!
YEAH!!
I CAN DO THIS
CLENCH
HOP
TMP
FLINCH
AHHHH!!
FLAIL
FLAIL
HUH? WHAT'S THE MATTER, TERIA ...?
HELP ...
HEY!
GRAB
WHOA!
THUD
SLIP

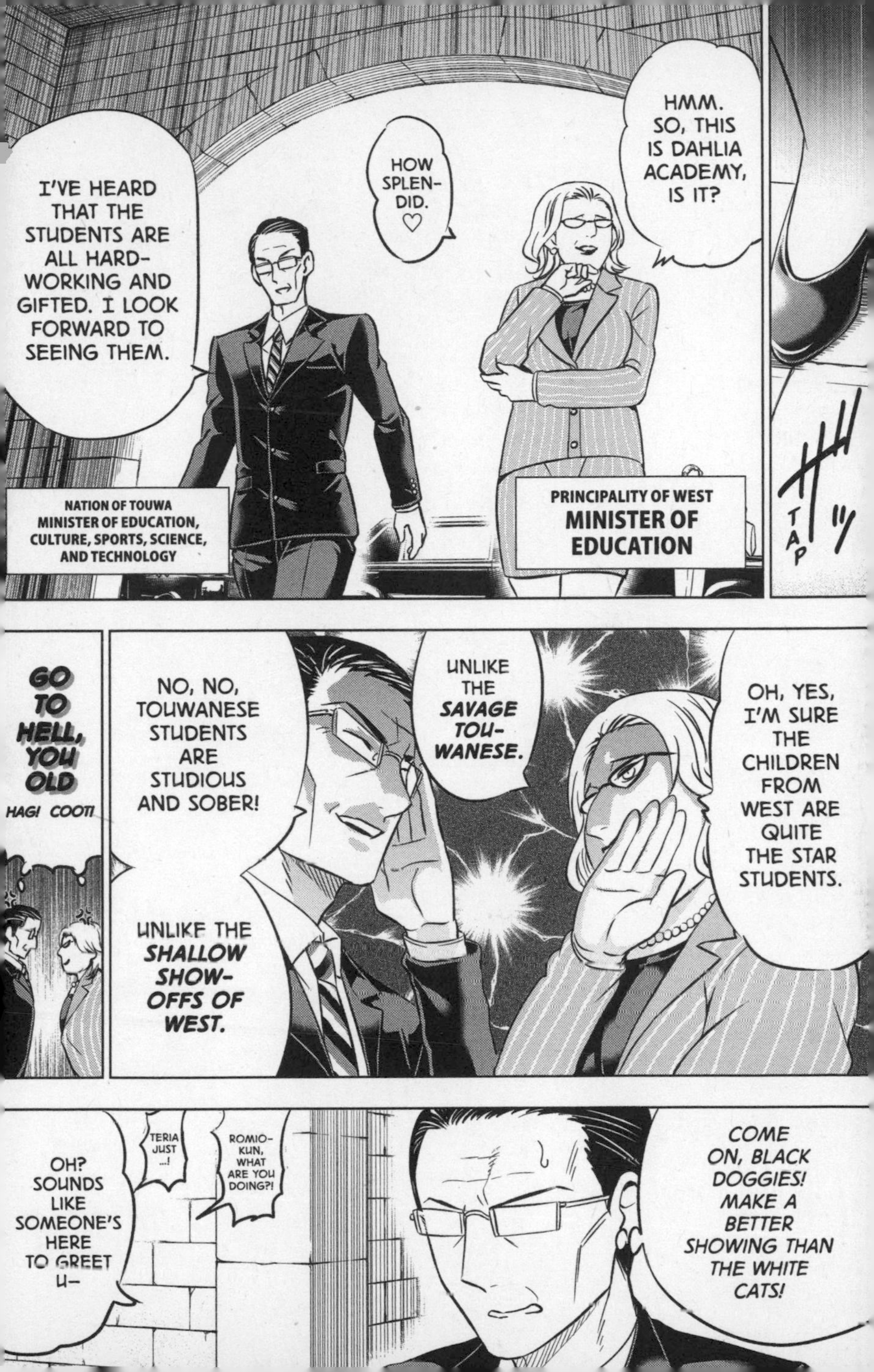
TAP
HMM. SO, THIS IS DAHLIA ACADEMY, IS IT?
HOW SPLENDID. ♡
I'VE HEARD THAT THE STUDENTS ARE ALL HARD-WORKING AND GIFTED. I LOOK FORWARD TO SEEING THEM.
PRINCIPALITY OF WEST MINISTER OF EDUCATION
NATION OF TOUWA MINISTER OF EDUCATION, CULTURE, SPORTS, SCIENCE, AND TECHNOLOGY
OH, YES, I'M SURE THE CHILDREN FROM WEST ARE QUITE THE STAR STUDENTS.
UNLIKE THE *SAVAGE TOU-WANESE.*
NO, NO, TOUWANESE STUDENTS ARE STUDIOUS AND SOBER!
UNLIKE THE *SHALLOW SHOW-OFFS OF WEST.*
GO TO HELL, YOU OLD
HAG! COOT!
COME ON, BLACK DOGGIES! MAKE A BETTER SHOWING THAN THE WHITE CATS!
ROMIO-KUN, WHAT ARE YOU DOING?!
TERIA JUST ...!
OH? SOUNDS LIKE SOMEONE'S HERE TO GREET U–

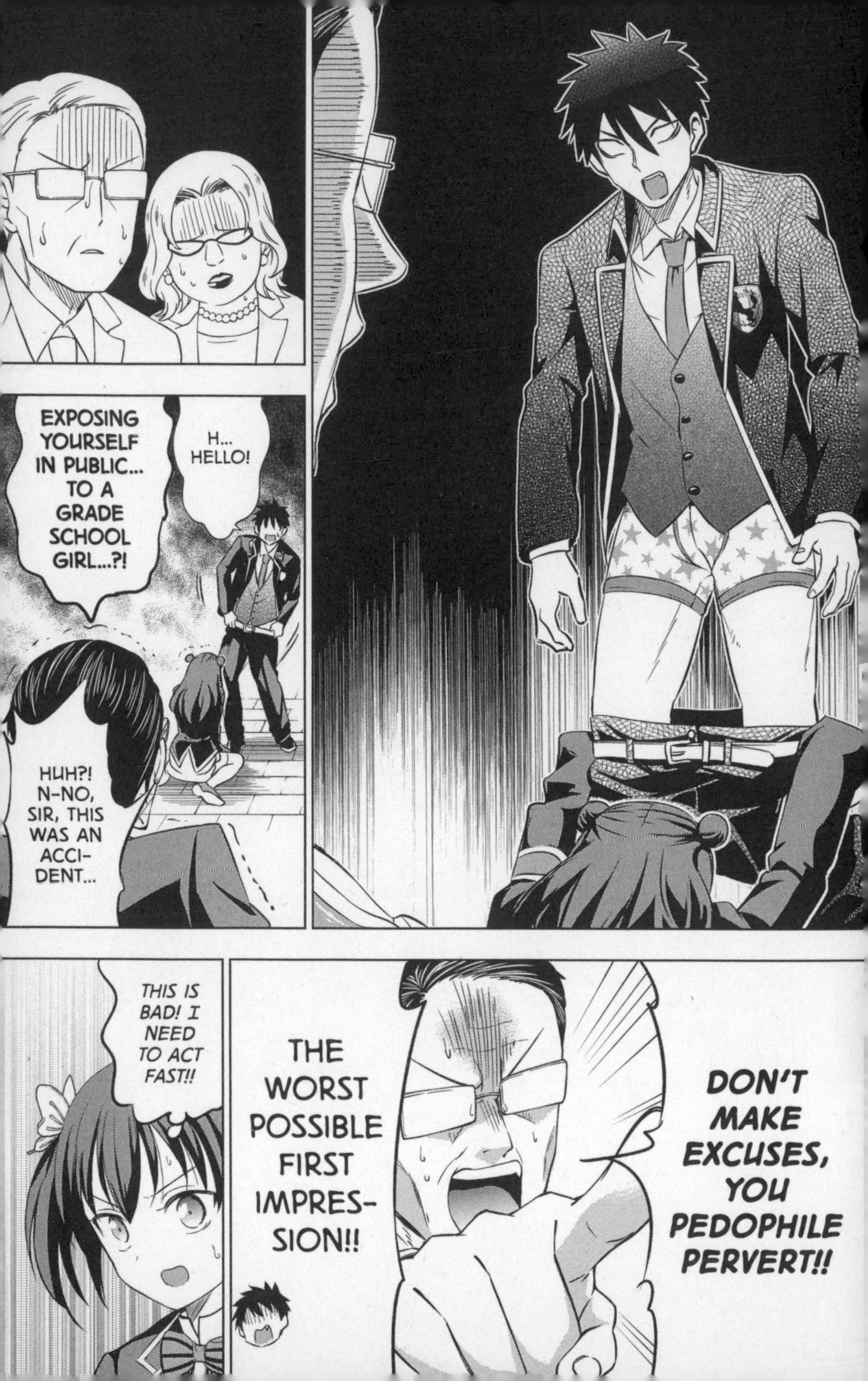
H... HELLO!
EXPOSING YOURSELF IN PUBLIC... TO A GRADE SCHOOL GIRL...?!
HUH?! N-NO, SIR, THIS WAS AN ACCI-DENT...
DON'T MAKE EXCUSES, YOU PEDOPHILE PERVERT!!
THE WORST POSSIBLE FIRST IMPRES-SION!!
THIS IS BAD! I NEED TO ACT FAST!!

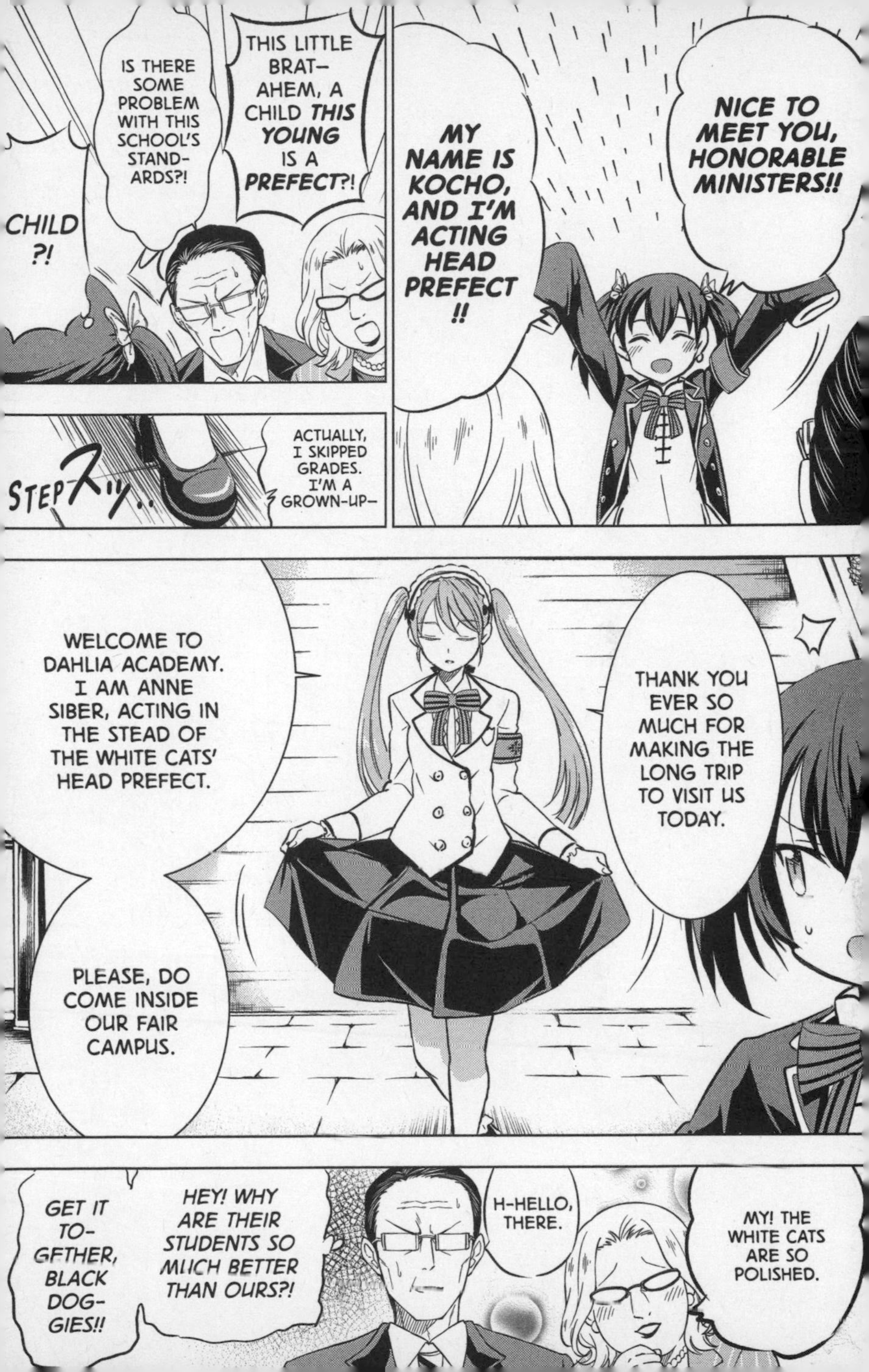
NICE TO MEET YOU, HONORABLE MINISTERS!!
MY NAME IS KOCHO, AND I'M ACTING HEAD PREFECT!!
THIS LITTLE BRAT—AHEM, A CHILD THIS YOUNG IS A PREFECT?!
IS THERE SOME PROBLEM WITH THIS SCHOOL'S STAND-ARDS?!
CHILD ?!
ACTUALLY, I SKIPPED GRADES. I'M A GROWN-UP—
STEP
THANK YOU EVER SO MUCH FOR MAKING THE LONG TRIP TO VISIT US TODAY.
WELCOME TO DAHLIA ACADEMY. I AM ANNE SIBER, ACTING IN THE STEAD OF THE WHITE CATS' HEAD PREFECT.
PLEASE, DO COME INSIDE OUR FAIR CAMPUS.
MY! THE WHITE CATS ARE SO POLISHED.
H-HELLO, THERE.
HEY! WHY ARE THEIR STUDENTS SO MUCH BETTER THAN OURS?!
GET IT TO-GETHER, BLACK DOG-GIES!!

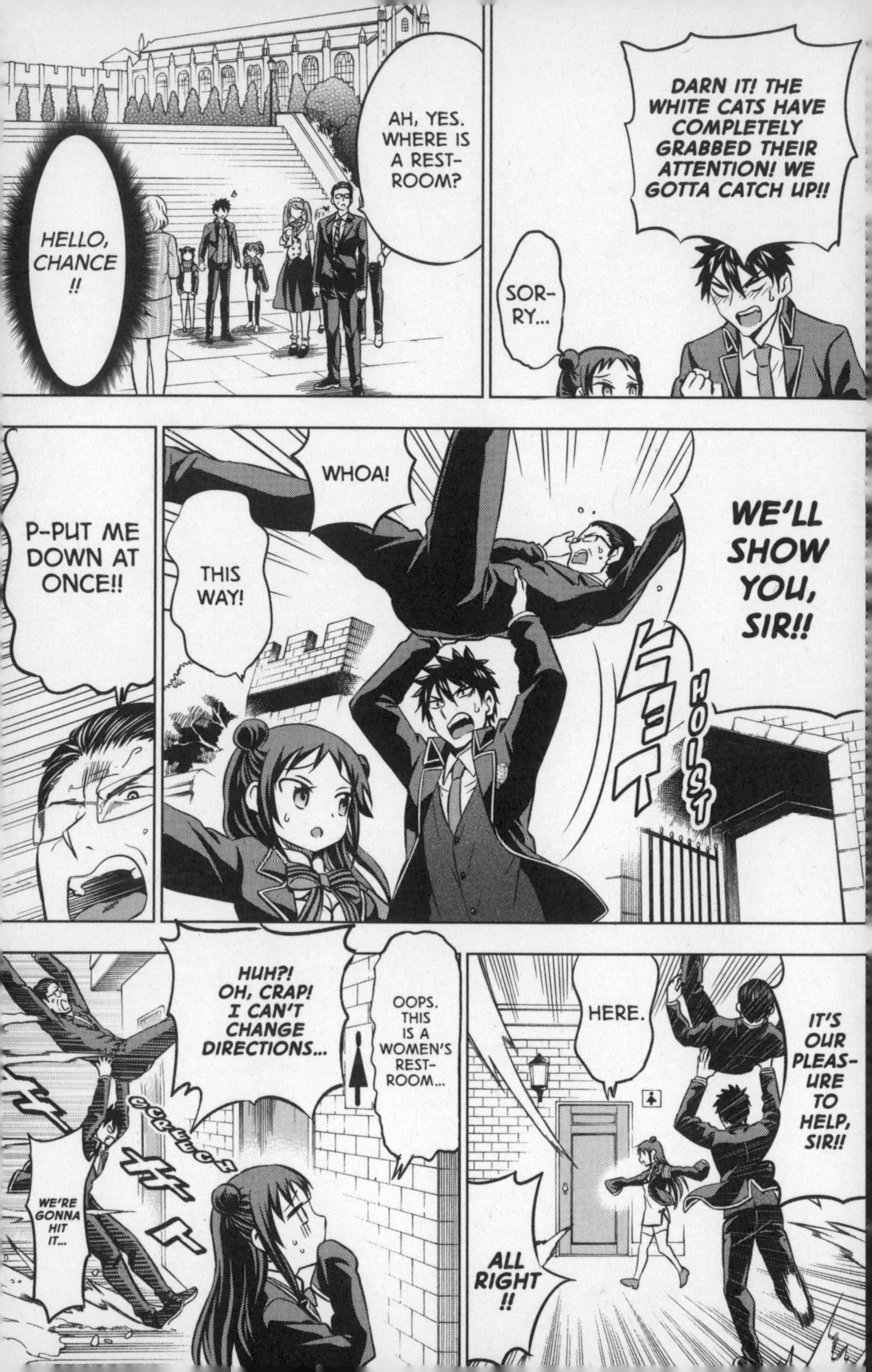

DARN IT! THE WHITE CATS HAVE COMPLETELY GRABBED THEIR ATTENTION! WE GOTTA CATCH UP!!
SOR-RY...
AH, YES. WHERE IS A REST-ROOM?
HELLO, CHANCE!!
WE'LL SHOW YOU, SIR!!
HOIST
WHOA!
THIS WAY!
P-PUT ME DOWN AT ONCE!!
IT'S OUR PLEASURE TO HELP, SIR!!
HERE.
ALL RIGHT!!
OOPS. THIS IS A WOMEN'S REST-ROOM...
HUH?! OH, CRAP! I CAN'T CHANGE DIRECTIONS...
SCREECH
WE'RE GONNA HIT IT...

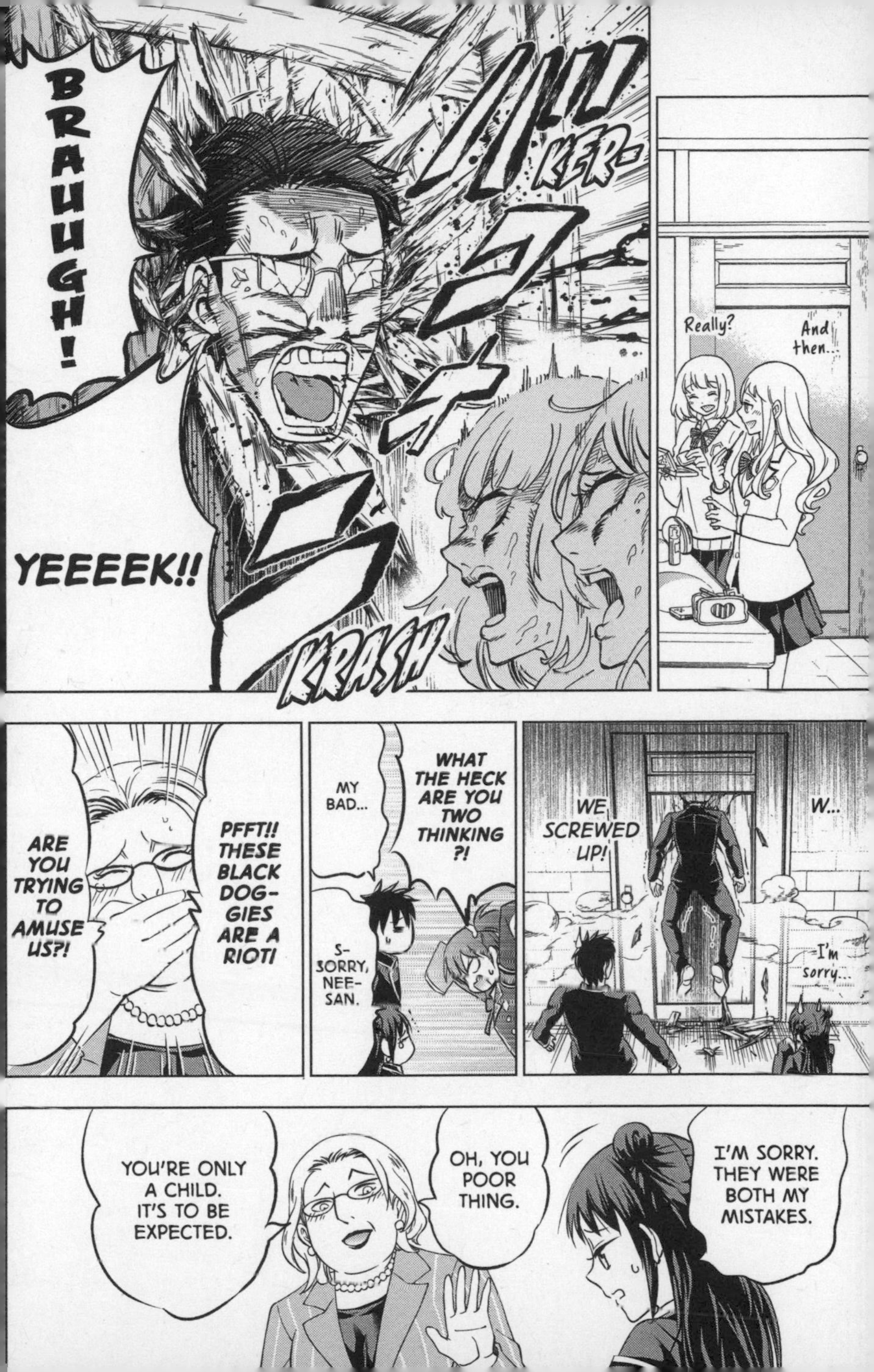

And then...
Really?
KER-
BRAUUGH!
YEEEEK!!
KRASH
W...
WE SCREWED UP!
I'm sorry...
WHAT THE HECK ARE YOU TWO THINKING?!
MY BAD...
S-SORRY, NEE-SAN.
PFFT!! THESE BLACK DOGGIES ARE A RIOT!
ARE YOU TRYING TO AMUSE US?!
I'M SORRY. THEY WERE BOTH MY MISTAKES.
OH, YOU POOR THING.
YOU'RE ONLY A CHILD. IT'S TO BE EXPECTED.

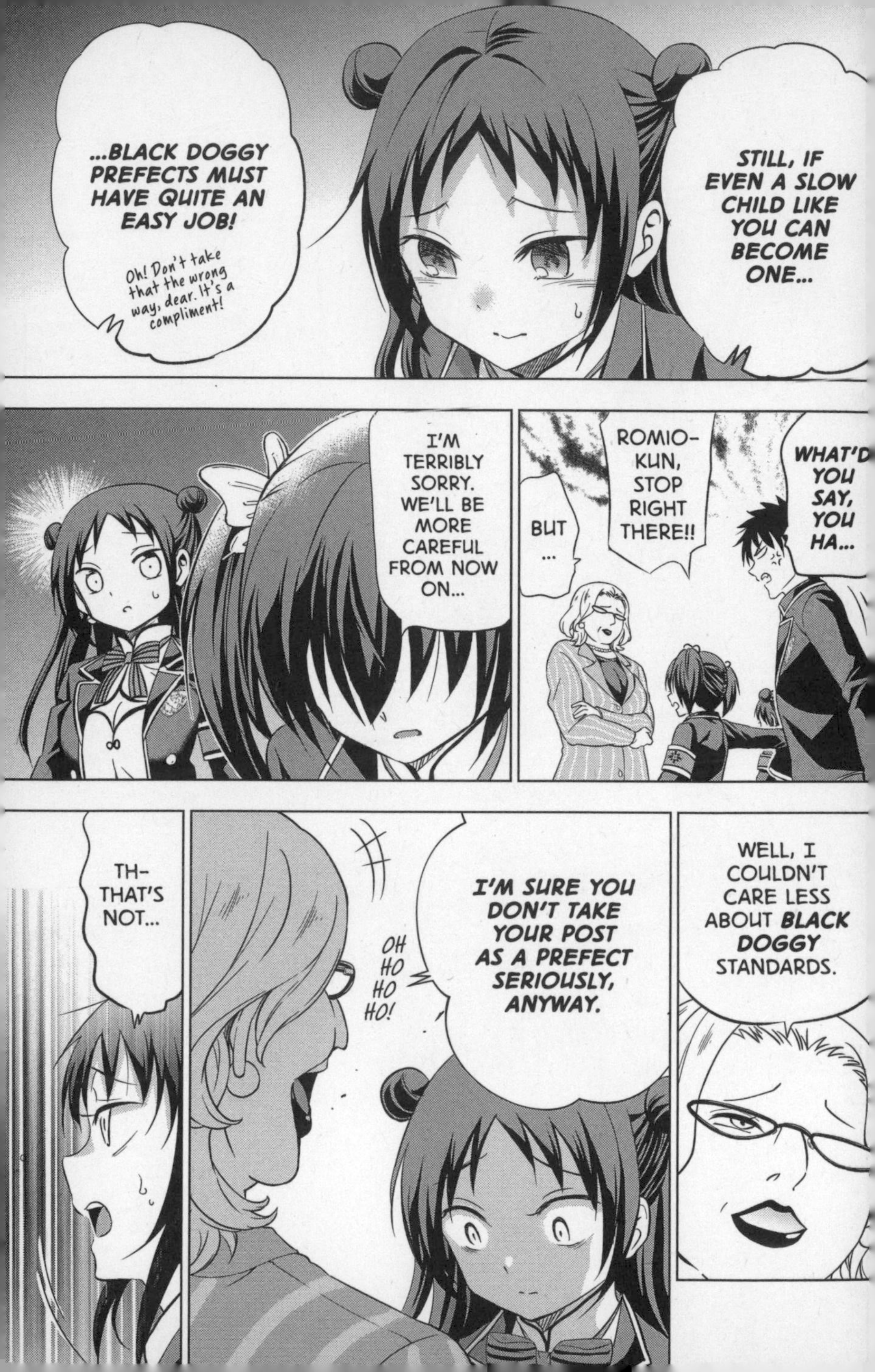
STILL, IF EVEN A SLOW CHILD LIKE YOU CAN BECOME ONE...
...BLACK DOGGY PREFECTS MUST HAVE QUITE AN EASY JOB!
Oh! Don't take that the wrong way, dear. It's a compliment!
WHAT'D YOU SAY, YOU HA...
ROMIO-KUN, STOP RIGHT THERE!!
BUT ...
I'M TERRIBLY SORRY. WE'LL BE MORE CAREFUL FROM NOW ON...
WELL, I COULDN'T CARE LESS ABOUT BLACK DOGGY STANDARDS.
I'M SURE YOU DON'T TAKE YOUR POST AS A PREFECT SERIOUSLY, ANYWAY.
OH HO HO HO!
TH- THAT'S NOT...

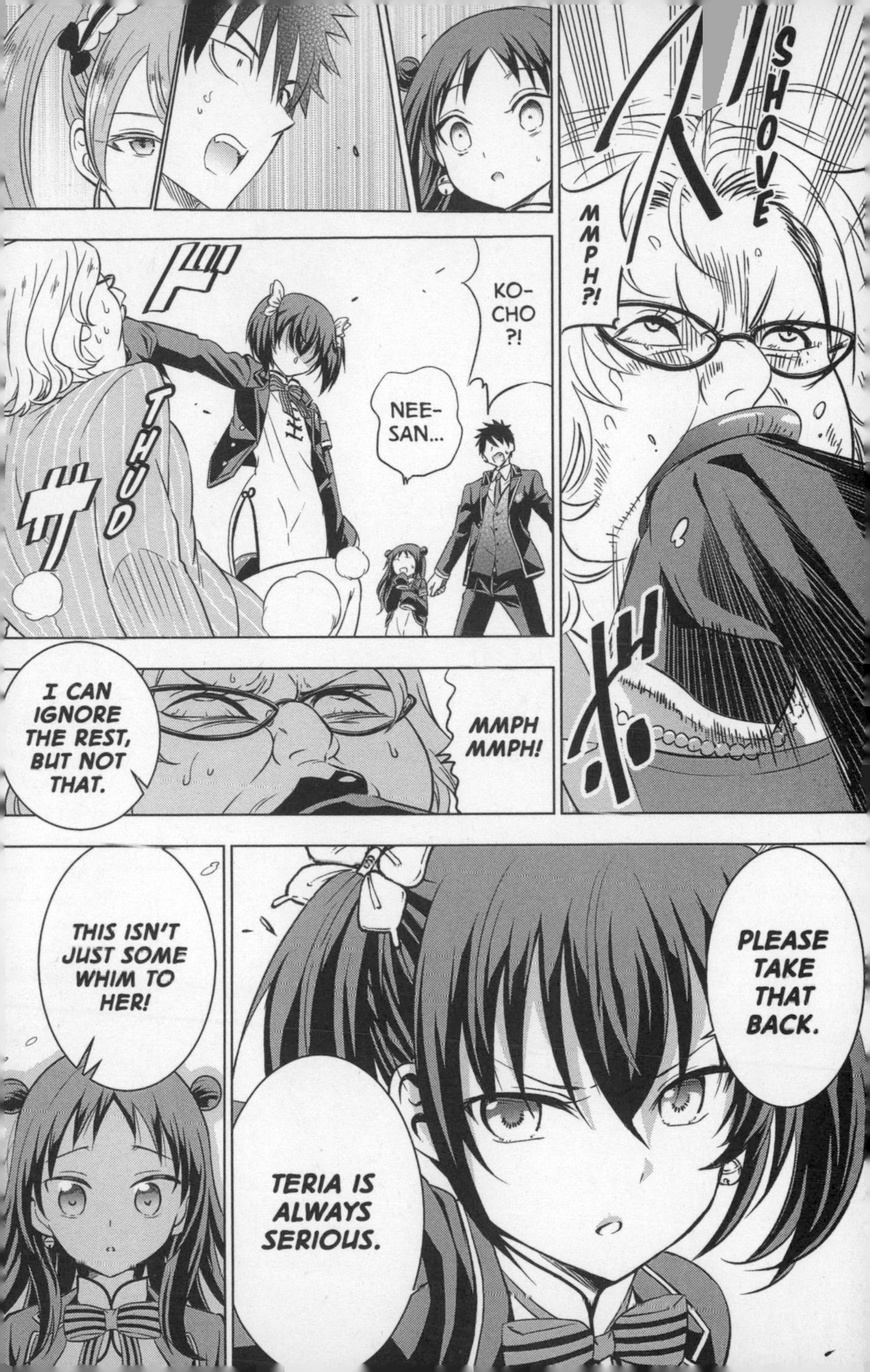
SHOVE
MMPH?!
KO-CHO?!
NEE-SAN...
THUD
MMPH MMPH!
I CAN IGNORE THE REST, BUT NOT THAT.
PLEASE TAKE THAT BACK.
TERIA IS ALWAYS SERIOUS.
THIS ISN'T JUST SOME WHIM TO HER!

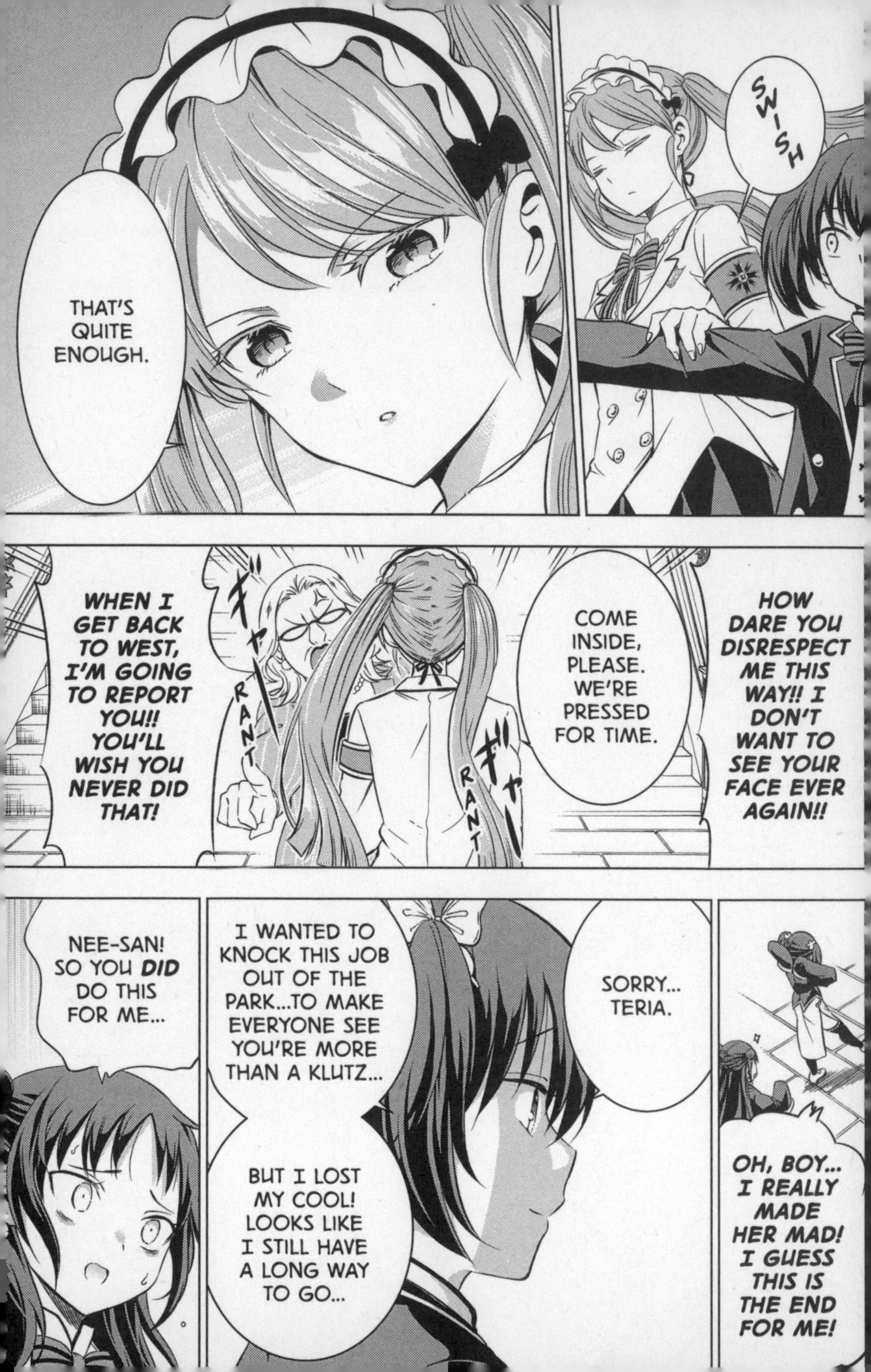
SWISH
THAT'S QUITE ENOUGH.
HOW DARE YOU DISRESPECT ME THIS WAY!! I DON'T WANT TO SEE YOUR FACE EVER AGAIN!!
COME INSIDE, PLEASE. WE'RE PRESSED FOR TIME.
RANT
RANT
WHEN I GET BACK TO WEST, I'M GOING TO REPORT YOU!! YOU'LL WISH YOU NEVER DID THAT!
OH, BOY... I REALLY MADE HER MAD! I GUESS THIS IS THE END FOR ME!
SORRY... TERIA.
I WANTED TO KNOCK THIS JOB OUT OF THE PARK...TO MAKE EVERYONE SEE YOU'RE MORE THAN A KLUTZ...
BUT I LOST MY COOL! LOOKS LIKE I STILL HAVE A LONG WAY TO GO...
NEE-SAN! SO YOU DID DO THIS FOR ME...

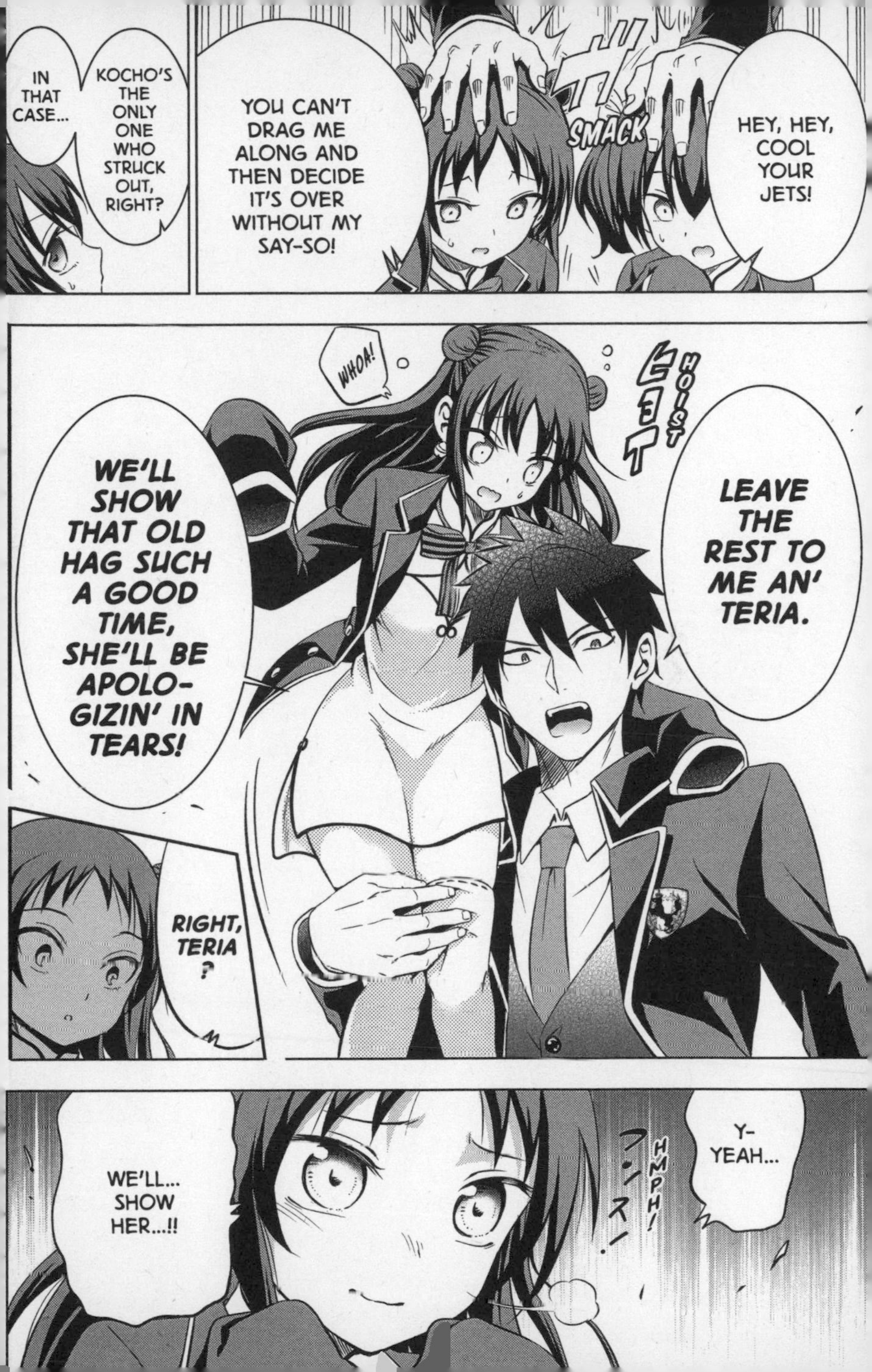
HEY, HEY, COOL YOUR JETS!
SMACK
YOU CAN'T DRAG ME ALONG AND THEN DECIDE IT'S OVER WITHOUT MY SAY-SO!
KOCHO'S THE ONLY ONE WHO STRUCK OUT, RIGHT?
IN THAT CASE...
WHOA!
HOIST
LEAVE THE REST TO ME AN' TERIA.
WE'LL SHOW THAT OLD HAG SUCH A GOOD TIME, SHE'LL BE APOLO-GIZIN' IN TEARS!
RIGHT, TERIA?
Y-YEAH...
HMPH!
WE'LL... SHOW HER...!!

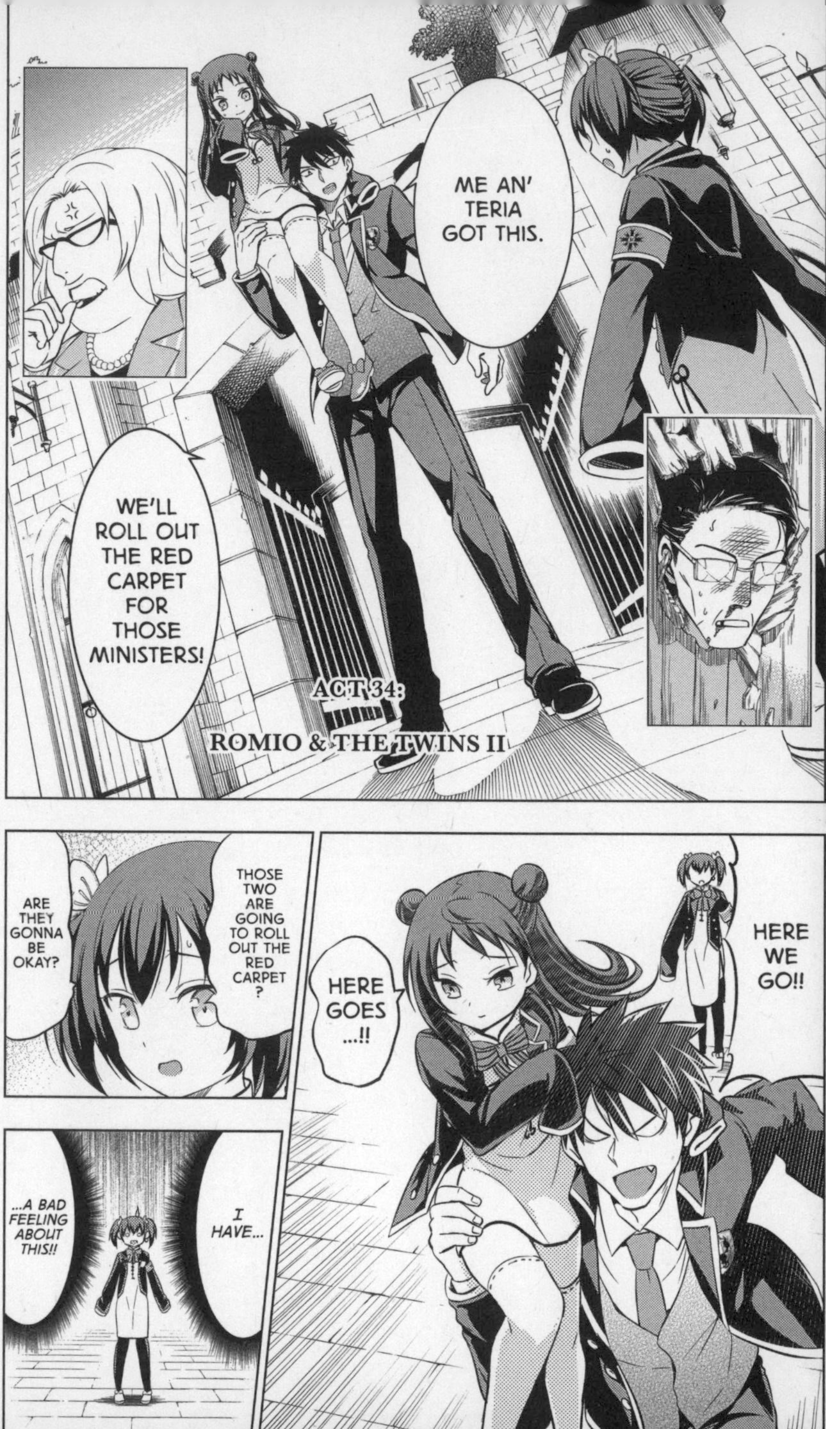
ME AN' TERIA GOT THIS.
WE'LL ROLL OUT THE RED CARPET FOR THOSE MINISTERS!
ACT 34:
ROMIO & THE TWINS II
HERE WE GO!!
HERE GOES ...!!
THOSE TWO ARE GOING TO ROLL OUT THE RED CARPET?
ARE THEY GONNA BE OKAY?
I HAVE...
...A BAD FEELING ABOUT THIS!!

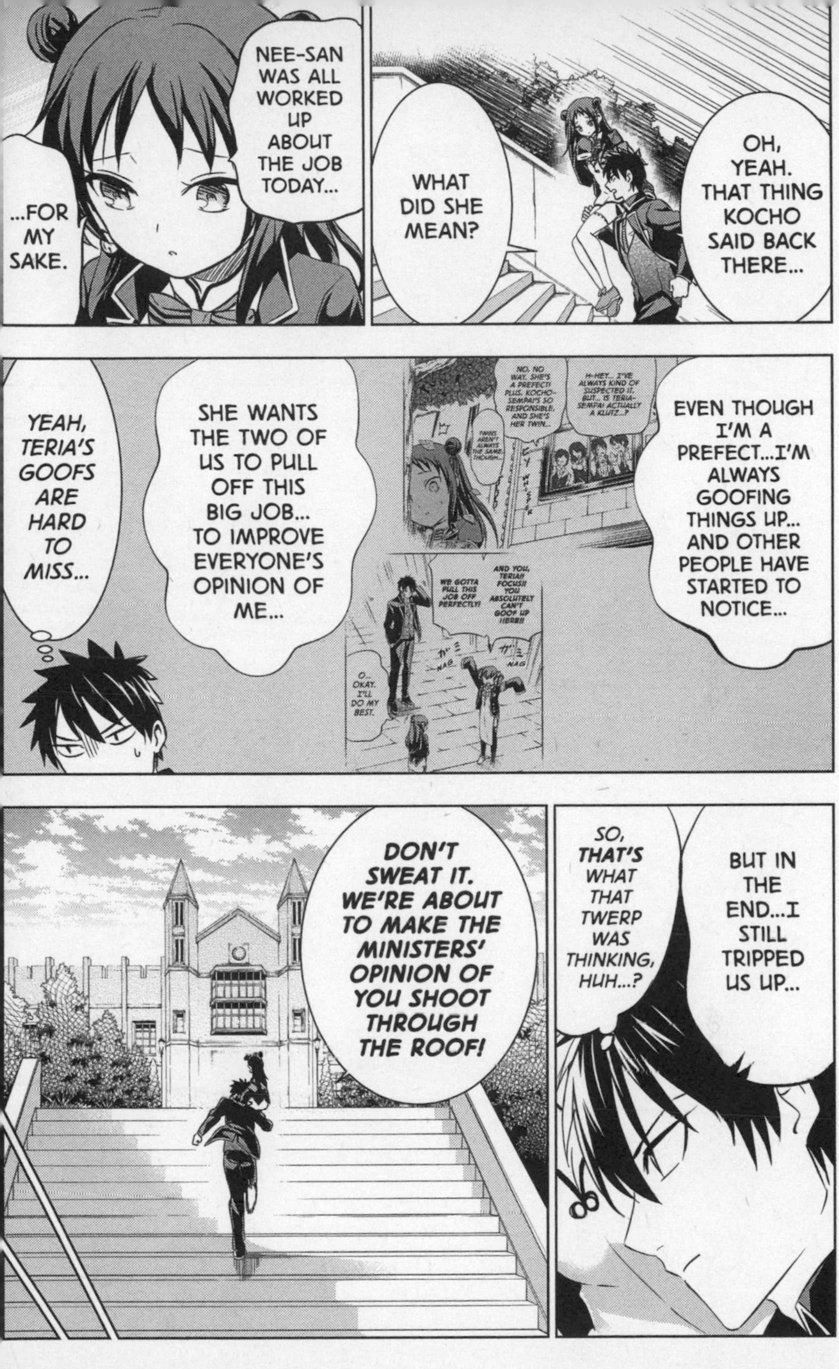
OH, YEAH. THAT THING KOCHO SAID BACK THERE...
WHAT DID SHE MEAN?
NEE-SAN WAS ALL WORKED UP ABOUT THE JOB TODAY...
...FOR MY SAKE.
EVEN THOUGH I'M A PREFECT...I'M ALWAYS GOOFING THINGS UP... AND OTHER PEOPLE HAVE STARTED TO NOTICE...
H-HEY... I'VE ALWAYS KIND OF SUSPECTED IT, BUT... IS TERIA-SEMPAI ACTUALLY A KLUTZ...?
NO, NO WAY. SHE'S A PREFECT! PLUS, KOCHO-SEMPAI'S SO RESPONSIBLE, AND SHE'S HER TWIN...
TWINS AREN'T ALWAYS THE SAME, THOUGH...
WHISPER
AND YOU, TERIA!! FOCUS!! YOU ABSOLUTELY CAN'T GOOF UP HERE!!
WE GOTTA PULL THIS JOB OFF PERFECTLY!
NAG
NAG
O... OKAY. I'LL DO MY BEST.
SHE WANTS THE TWO OF US TO PULL OFF THIS BIG JOB... TO IMPROVE EVERYONE'S OPINION OF ME...
YEAH, TERIA'S GOOFS ARE HARD TO MISS...
BUT IN THE END...I STILL TRIPPED US UP...
SO, THAT'S WHAT THAT TWERP WAS THINKING, HUH...?
DON'T SWEAT IT. WE'RE ABOUT TO MAKE THE MINISTERS' OPINION OF YOU SHOOT THROUGH THE ROOF!

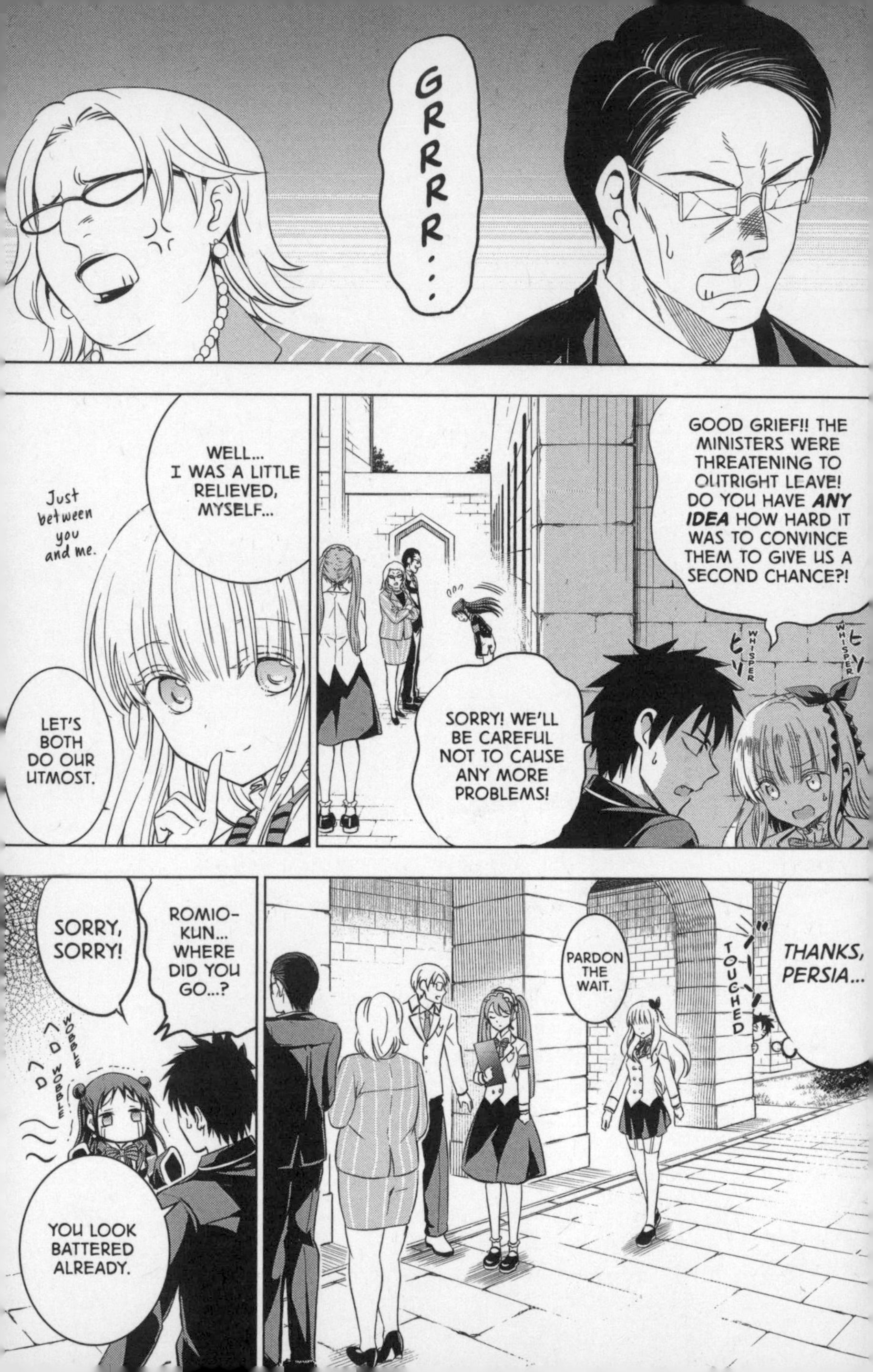
GRRRR...
GOOD GRIEF!! THE MINISTERS WERE THREATENING TO OUTRIGHT LEAVE! DO YOU HAVE ***ANY IDEA*** HOW HARD IT WAS TO CONVINCE THEM TO GIVE US A SECOND CHANCE?!
WHISPER
WHISPER
SORRY! WE'LL BE CAREFUL NOT TO CAUSE ANY MORE PROBLEMS!
WELL... I WAS A LITTLE RELIEVED, MYSELF...
Just between you and me.
LET'S BOTH DO OUR UTMOST.
THANKS, PERSIA...
TOUCHED
PARDON THE WAIT.
ROMIO-KUN... WHERE DID YOU GO...?
SORRY, SORRY!
WOBBLE
WOBBLE
YOU LOOK BATTERED ALREADY.

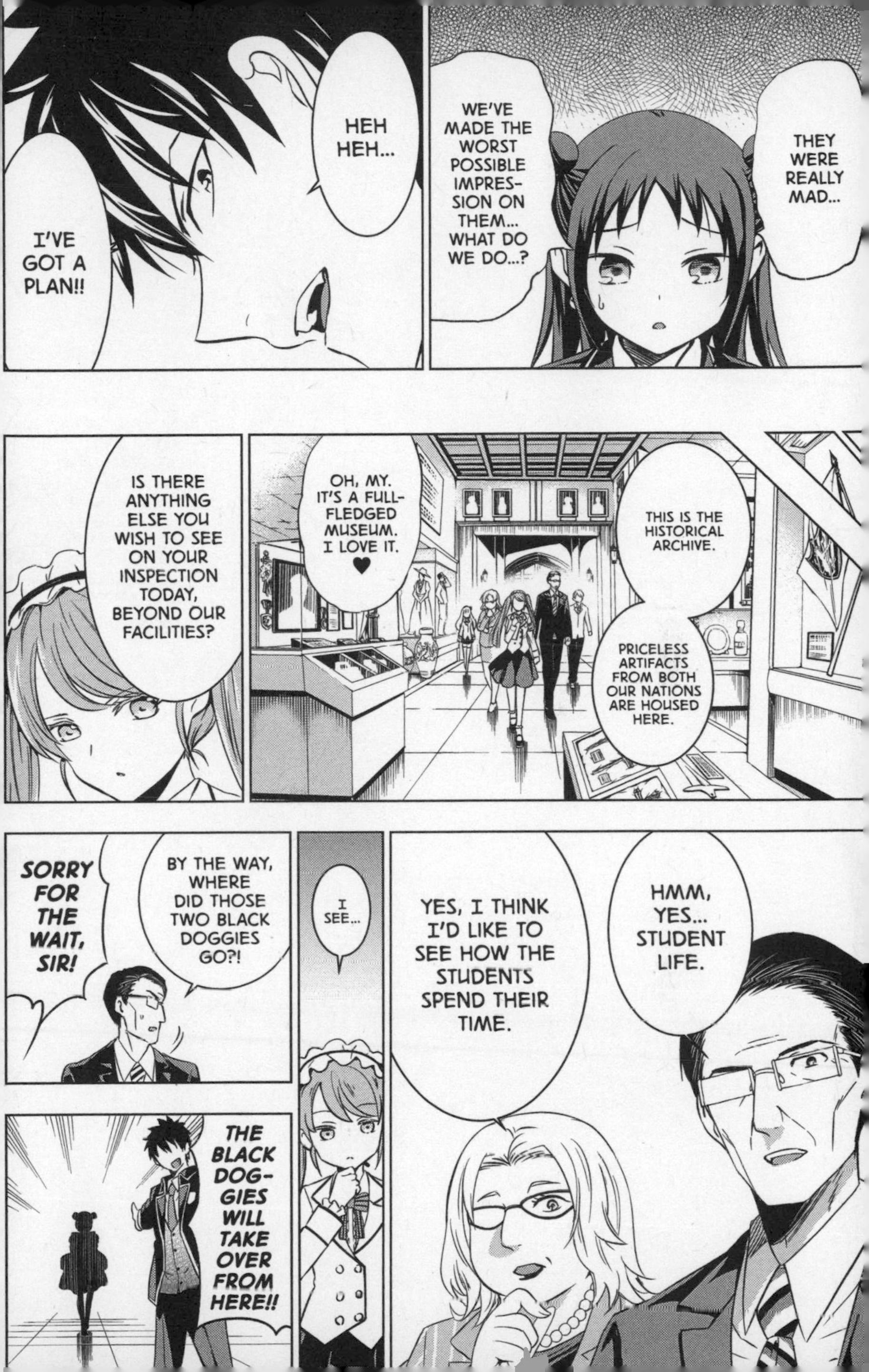
THEY WERE REALLY MAD...
WE'VE MADE THE WORST POSSIBLE IMPRESSION ON THEM... WHAT DO WE DO...?
HEH HEH...
I'VE GOT A PLAN!!
THIS IS THE HISTORICAL ARCHIVE.
PRICELESS ARTIFACTS FROM BOTH OUR NATIONS ARE HOUSED HERE.
OH, MY. IT'S A FULL-FLEDGED MUSEUM. I LOVE IT. ♥
IS THERE ANYTHING ELSE YOU WISH TO SEE ON YOUR INSPECTION TODAY, BEYOND OUR FACILITIES?
HMM, YES... STUDENT LIFE.
YES, I THINK I'D LIKE TO SEE HOW THE STUDENTS SPEND THEIR TIME.
I SEE...
BY THE WAY, WHERE DID THOSE TWO BLACK DOGGIES GO?!
SORRY FOR THE WAIT, SIR!
THE BLACK DOGGIES WILL TAKE OVER FROM HERE!!

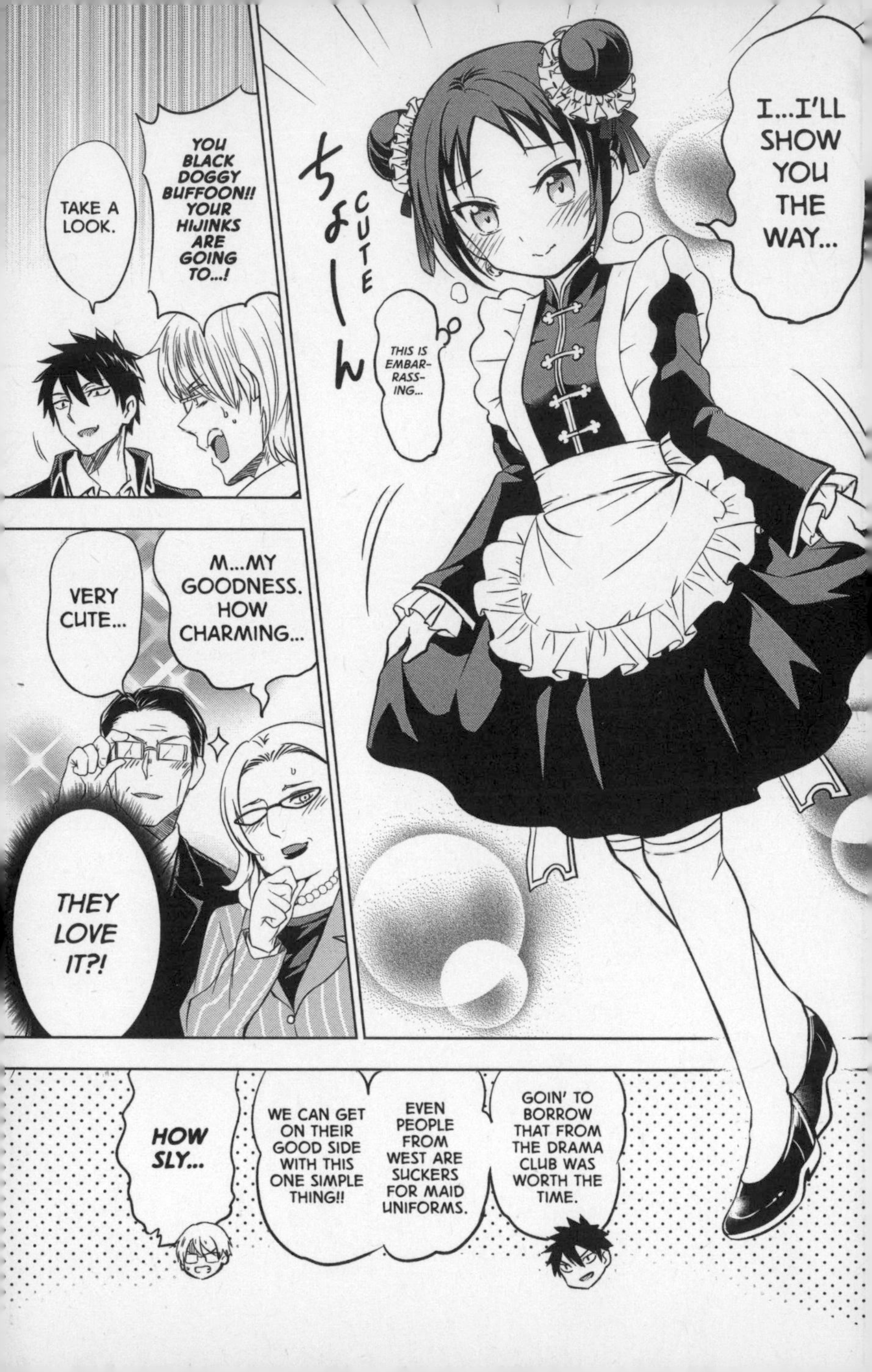
I...I'LL SHOW YOU THE WAY...
ちょーん
CUTE
THIS IS EMBARRASSING...
YOU BLACK DOGGY BUFFOON!! YOUR HIJINKS ARE GOING TO...!
TAKE A LOOK.
M...MY GOODNESS. HOW CHARMING...
VERY CUTE...
THEY LOVE IT?!
GOIN' TO BORROW THAT FROM THE DRAMA CLUB WAS WORTH THE TIME.
EVEN PEOPLE FROM WEST ARE SUCKERS FOR MAID UNIFORMS.
WE CAN GET ON THEIR GOOD SIDE WITH THIS ONE SIMPLE THING!!
HOW SLY...

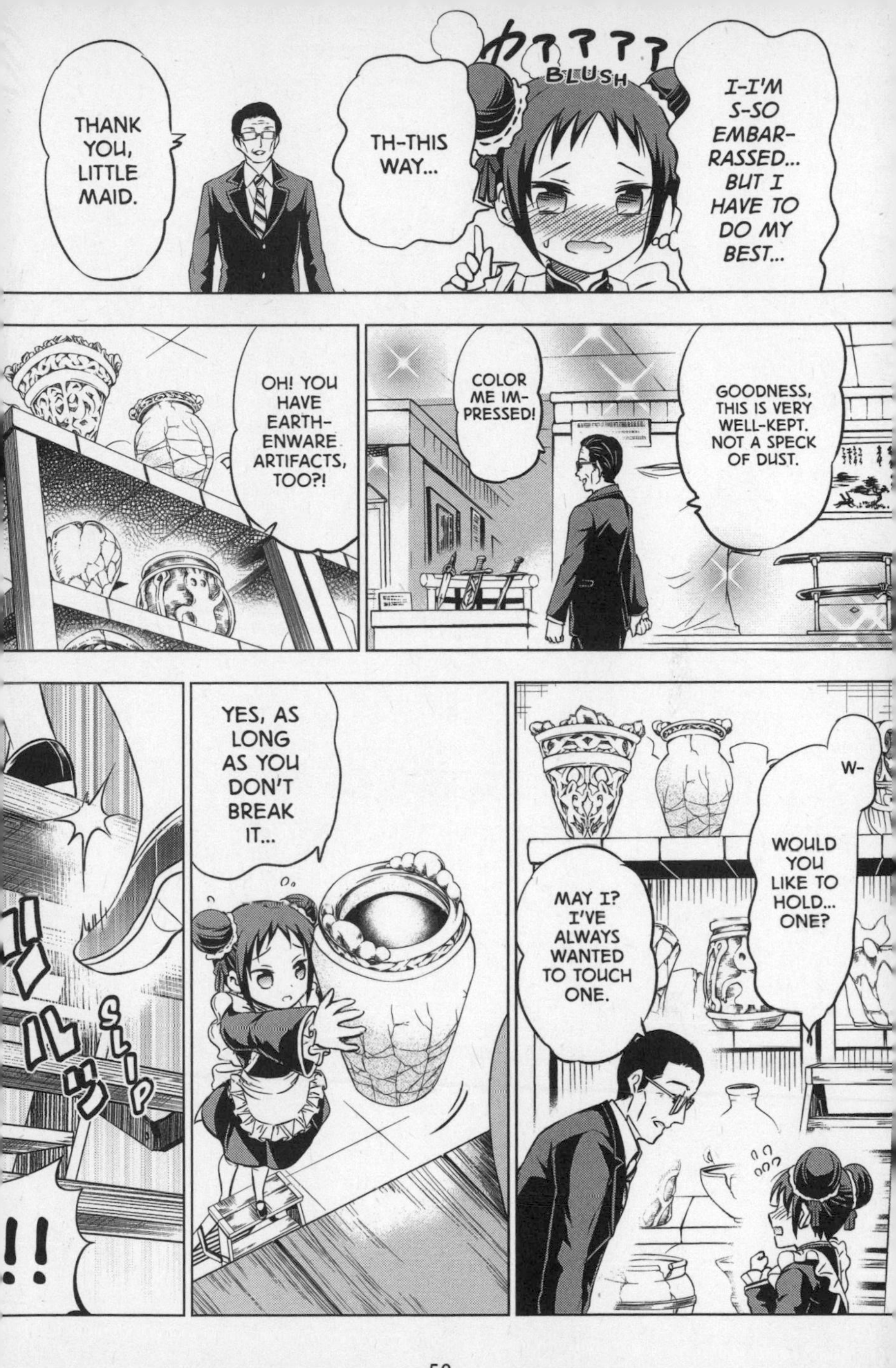
BLUSH
I-I'M S-SO EMBARRASSED... BUT I HAVE TO DO MY BEST...
TH-THIS WAY...
THANK YOU, LITTLE MAID.
GOODNESS, THIS IS VERY WELL-KEPT. NOT A SPECK OF DUST.
COLOR ME IMPRESSED!
OH! YOU HAVE EARTHENWARE ARTIFACTS, TOO?!
W-
WOULD YOU LIKE TO HOLD... ONE?
MAY I? I'VE ALWAYS WANTED TO TOUCH ONE.
YES, AS LONG AS YOU DON'T BREAK IT...
SLIP
!!

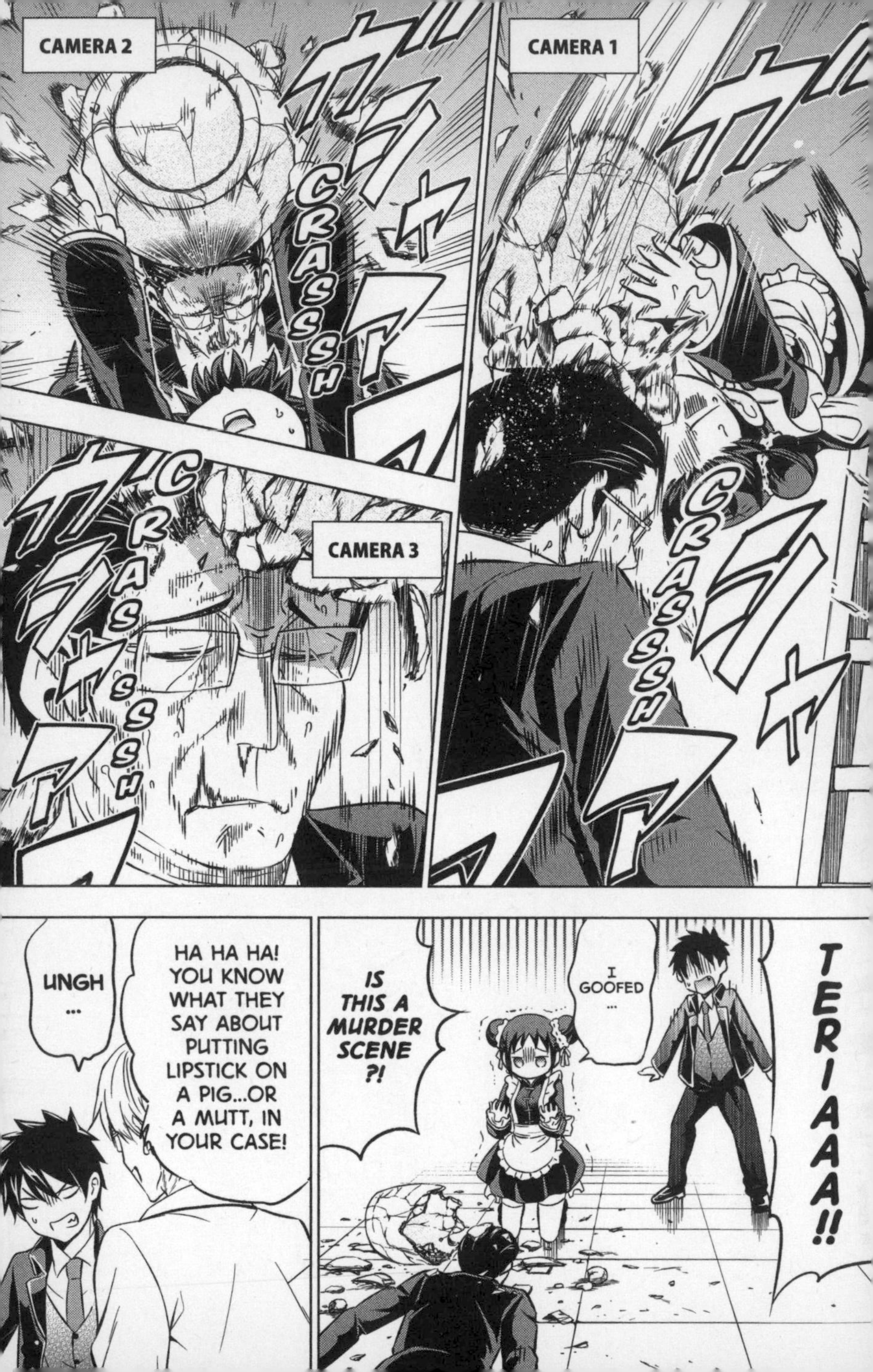
CAMERA 1
CRASSSSH
CAMERA 2
CRASSSH
CAMERA 3
CRASSSSH
TERIAAAA!!
I GOOFED ...
IS THIS A MURDER SCENE ?!
HA HA HA! YOU KNOW WHAT THEY SAY ABOUT PUTTING LIPSTICK ON A PIG...OR A MUTT, IN YOUR CASE!
UNGH ...

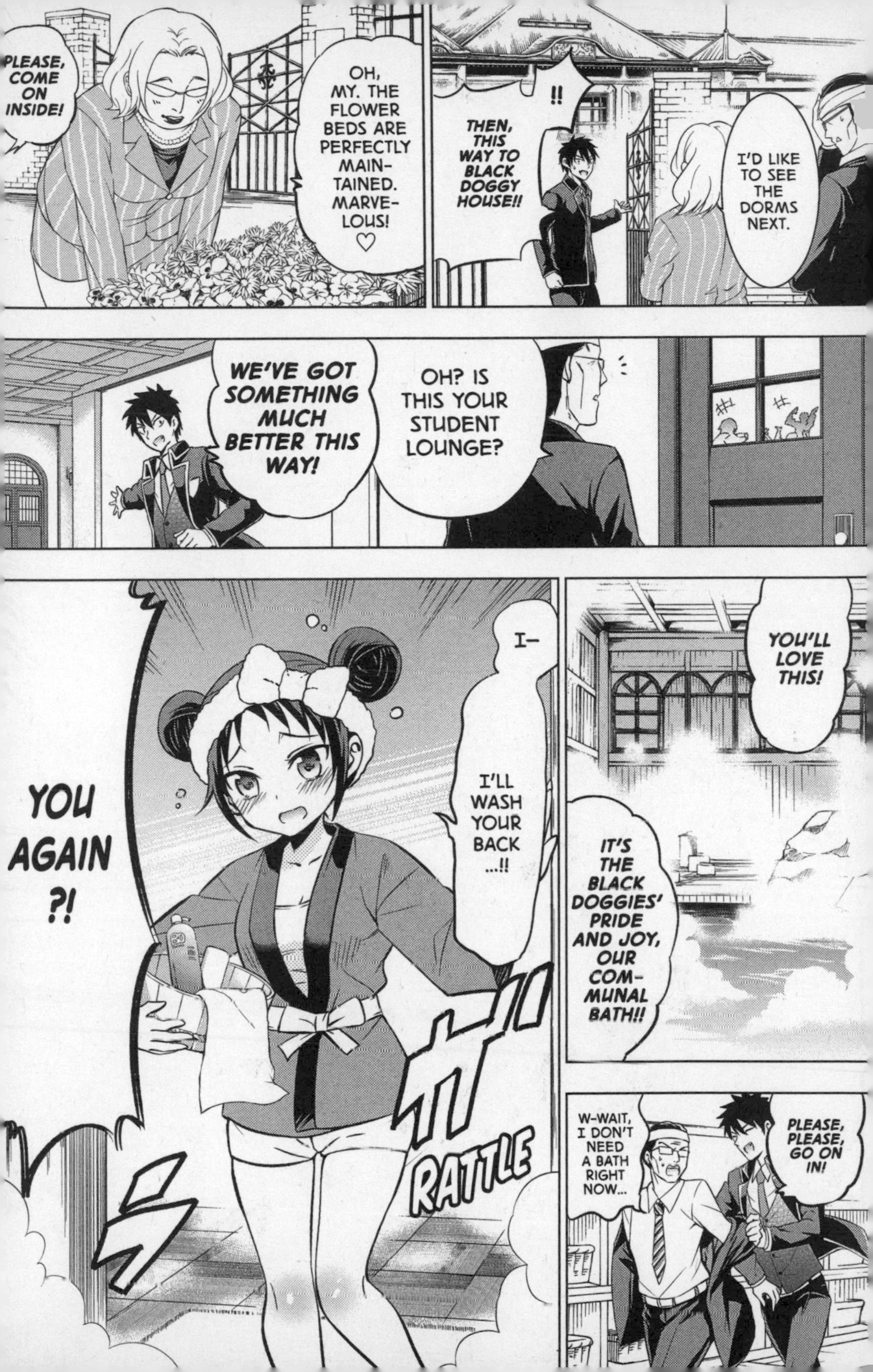
I'D LIKE TO SEE THE DORMS NEXT.
!!
THEN, THIS WAY TO BLACK DOGGY HOUSE!!
OH, MY. THE FLOWER BEDS ARE PERFECTLY MAIN-TAINED. MARVE-LOUS! ♡
PLEASE, COME ON INSIDE!
OH? IS THIS YOUR STUDENT LOUNGE?
WE'VE GOT SOMETHING MUCH BETTER THIS WAY!
YOU'LL LOVE THIS!
IT'S THE BLACK DOGGIES' PRIDE AND JOY, OUR COM-MUNAL BATH!!
PLEASE, PLEASE, GO ON IN!
W-WAIT, I DON'T NEED A BATH RIGHT NOW...
I–
I'LL WASH YOUR BACK ...!!
RATTLE
YOU AGAIN ?!

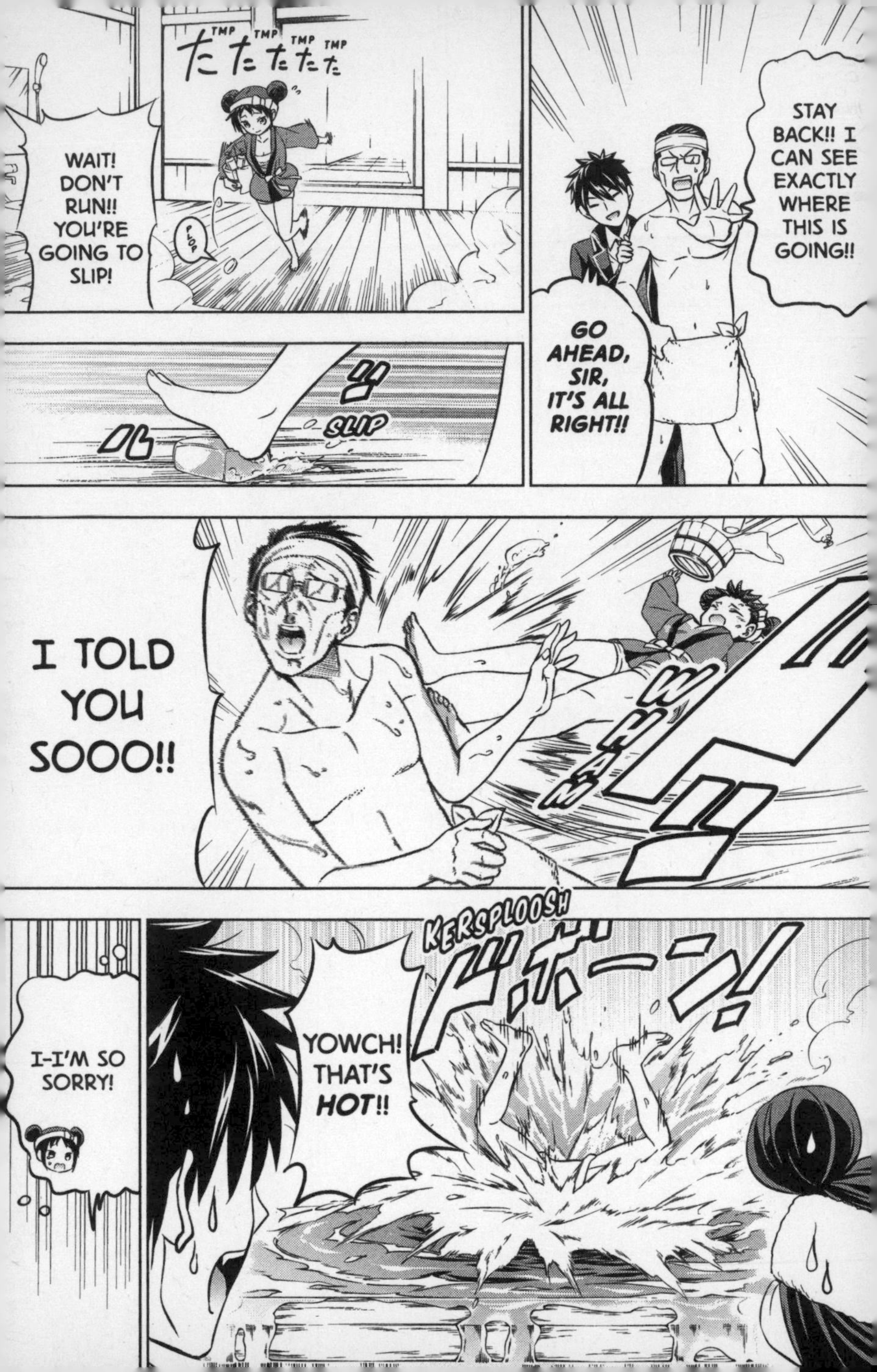
STAY BACK!! I CAN SEE EXACTLY WHERE THIS IS GOING!!
GO AHEAD, SIR, IT'S ALL RIGHT!!
TMP TMP TMP TMP
たたたたた
WAIT! DON'T RUN!! YOU'RE GOING TO SLIP!
FLOP
SLIP
WHAM
I TOLD YOU SOOO!!
KERSPLOOSH
ドボーン!
YOWCH! THAT'S HOT!!
I-I'M SO SORRY!

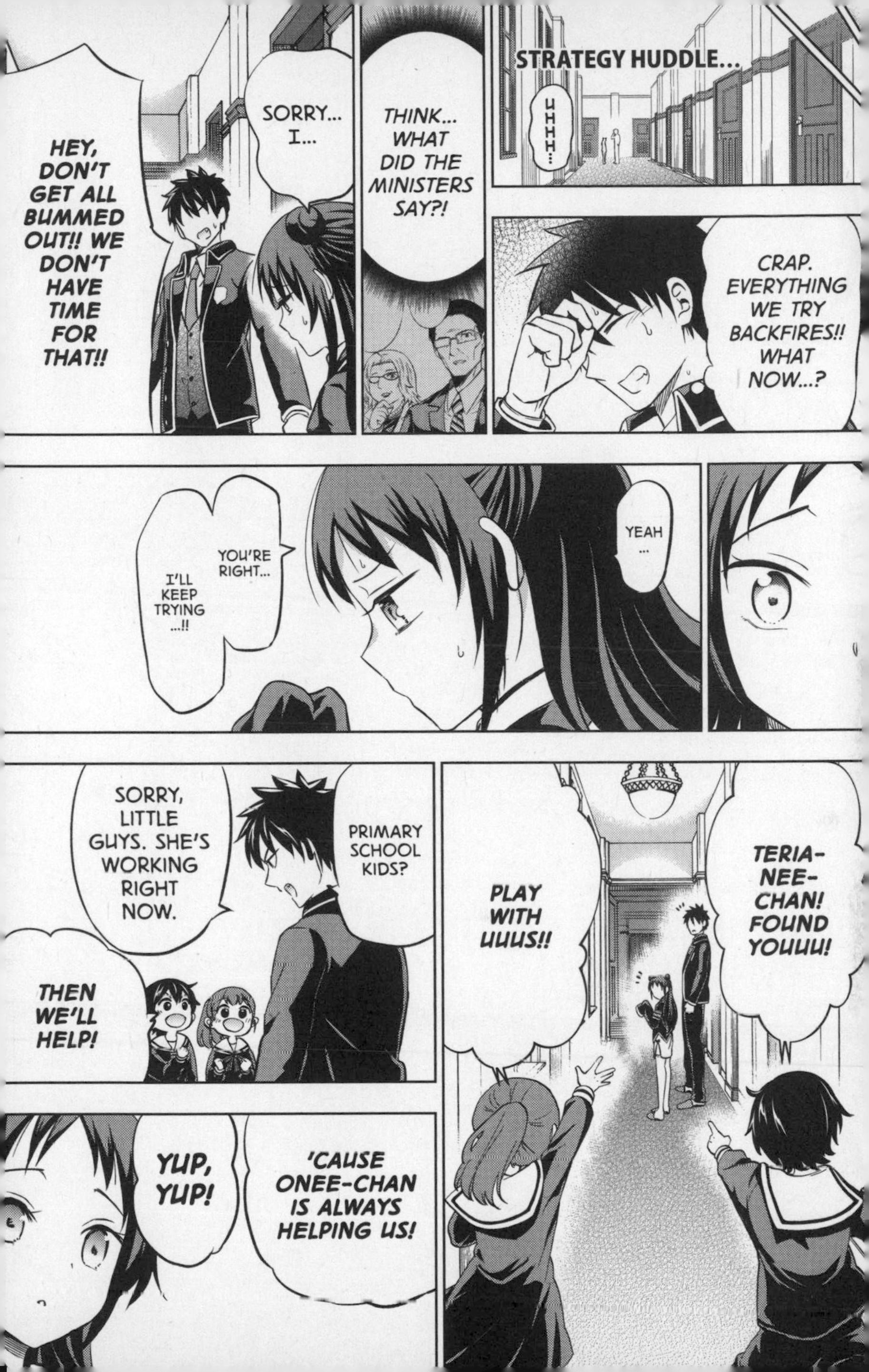
STRATEGY HUDDLE...
UHHH...
CRAP. EVERYTHING WE TRY BACKFIRES!! WHAT NOW...?
THINK... WHAT DID THE MINISTERS SAY?!
SORRY... I...
HEY, DON'T GET ALL BUMMED OUT!! WE DON'T HAVE TIME FOR THAT!!
YEAH ...
YOU'RE RIGHT... I'LL KEEP TRYING ...!!
TERIA-NEE-CHAN! FOUND YOUUU!
PLAY WITH UUUS!!
PRIMARY SCHOOL KIDS?
SORRY, LITTLE GUYS. SHE'S WORKING RIGHT NOW.
THEN WE'LL HELP!
'CAUSE ONEE-CHAN IS ALWAYS HELPING US!
YUP, YUP!

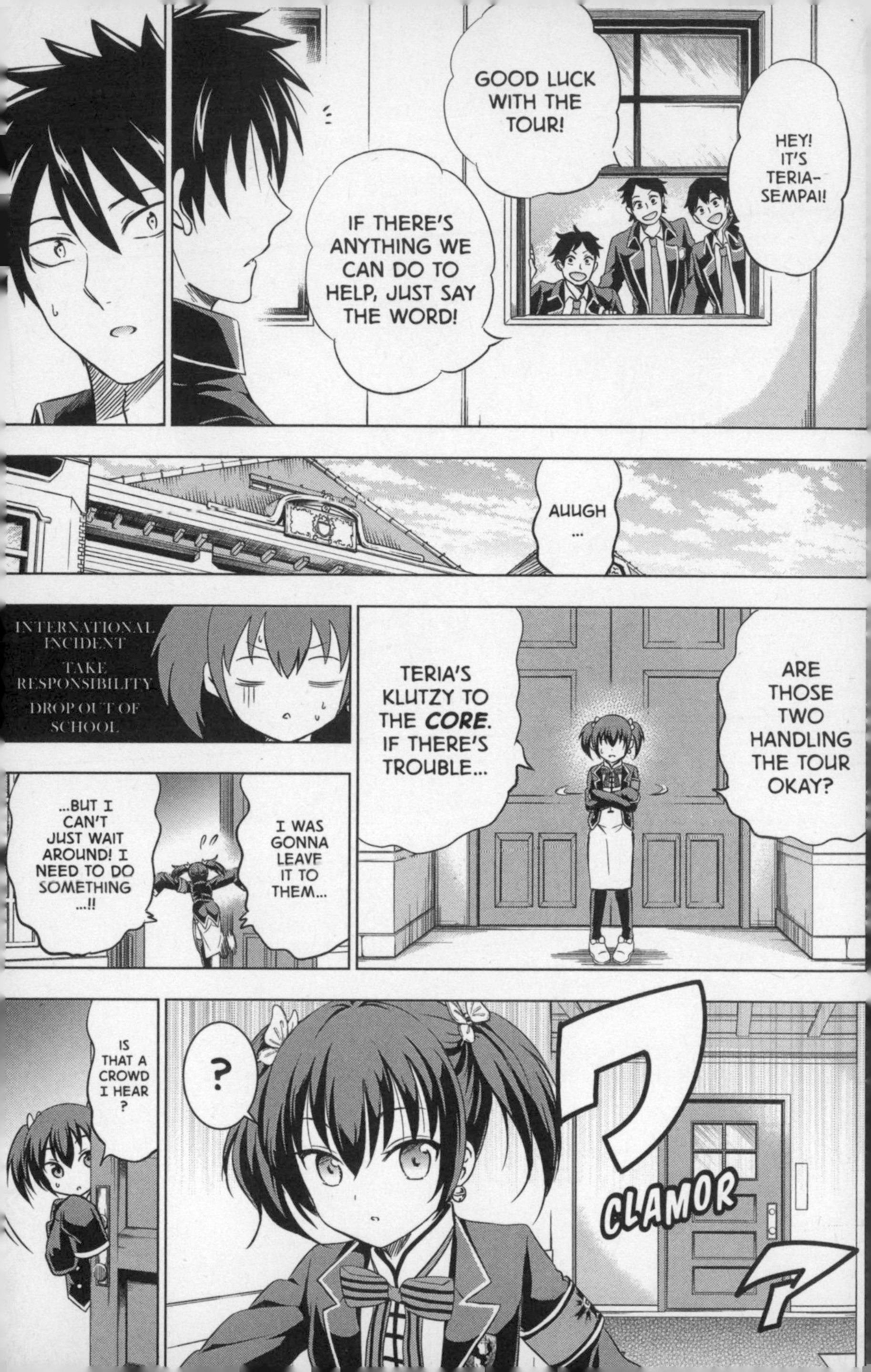
HEY! IT'S TERIA-SEMPAI!
GOOD LUCK WITH THE TOUR!
IF THERE'S ANYTHING WE CAN DO TO HELP, JUST SAY THE WORD!
AUUGH ...
ARE THOSE TWO HANDLING THE TOUR OKAY?
TERIA'S KLUTZY TO THE *CORE*. IF THERE'S TROUBLE...
INTERNATIONAL INCIDENT
TAKE RESPONSIBILITY
DROP OUT OF SCHOOL
I WAS GONNA LEAVE IT TO THEM...
...BUT I CAN'T JUST WAIT AROUND! I NEED TO DO SOMETHING ...!!
CLAMOR
?
IS THAT A CROWD I HEAR ?

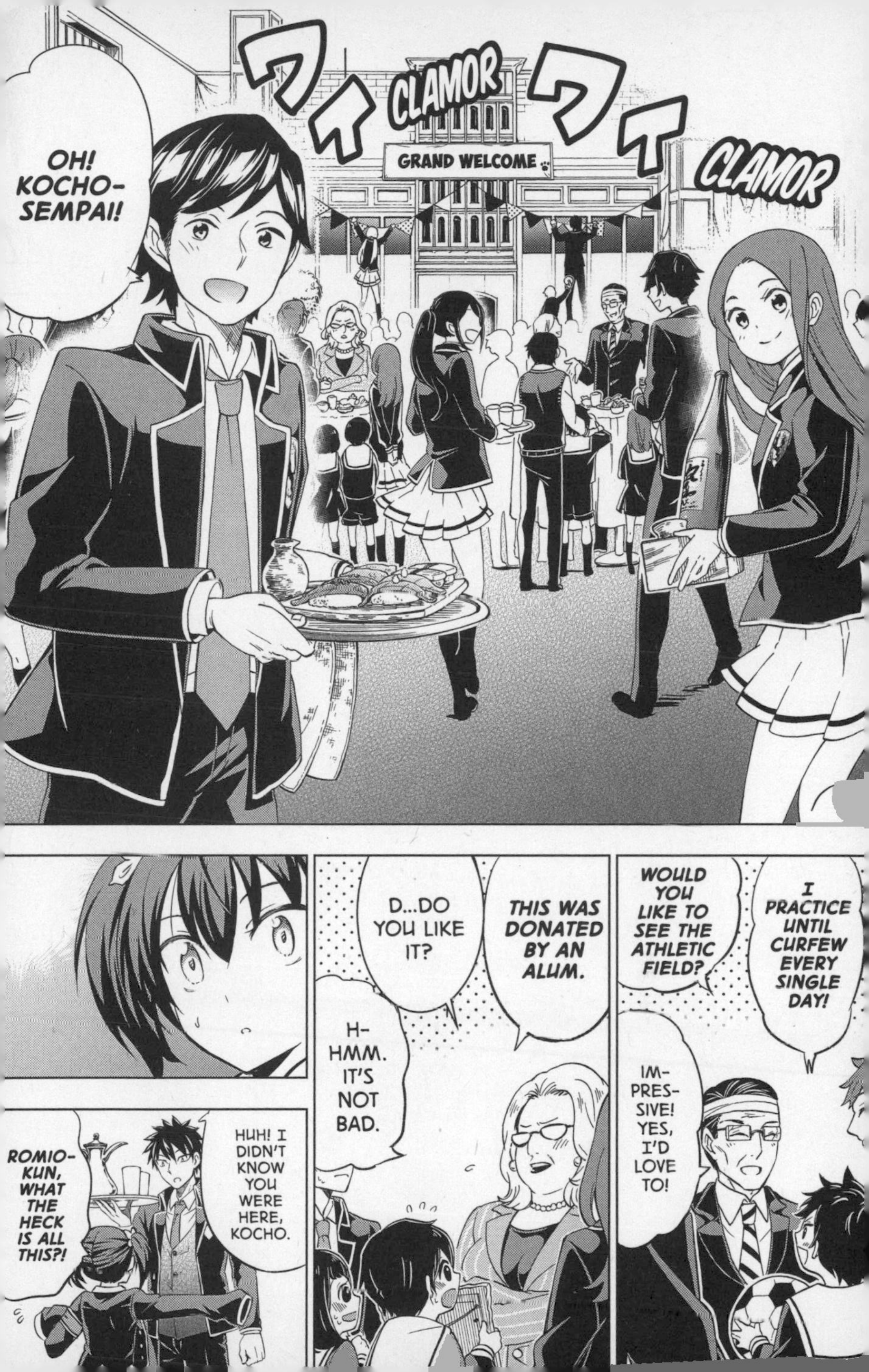
ワイ
CLAMOR
GRAND WELCOME
ワイ
CLAMOR
OH! KOCHO-SEMPAI!
I PRACTICE UNTIL CURFEW EVERY SINGLE DAY!
WOULD YOU LIKE TO SEE THE ATHLETIC FIELD?
IM-PRES-SIVE! YES, I'D LOVE TO!
THIS WAS DONATED BY AN ALUM.
D...DO YOU LIKE IT?
H-HMM. IT'S NOT BAD.
HUH! I DIDN'T KNOW YOU WERE HERE, KOCHO.
ROMIO-KUN, WHAT THE HECK IS ALL THIS?!

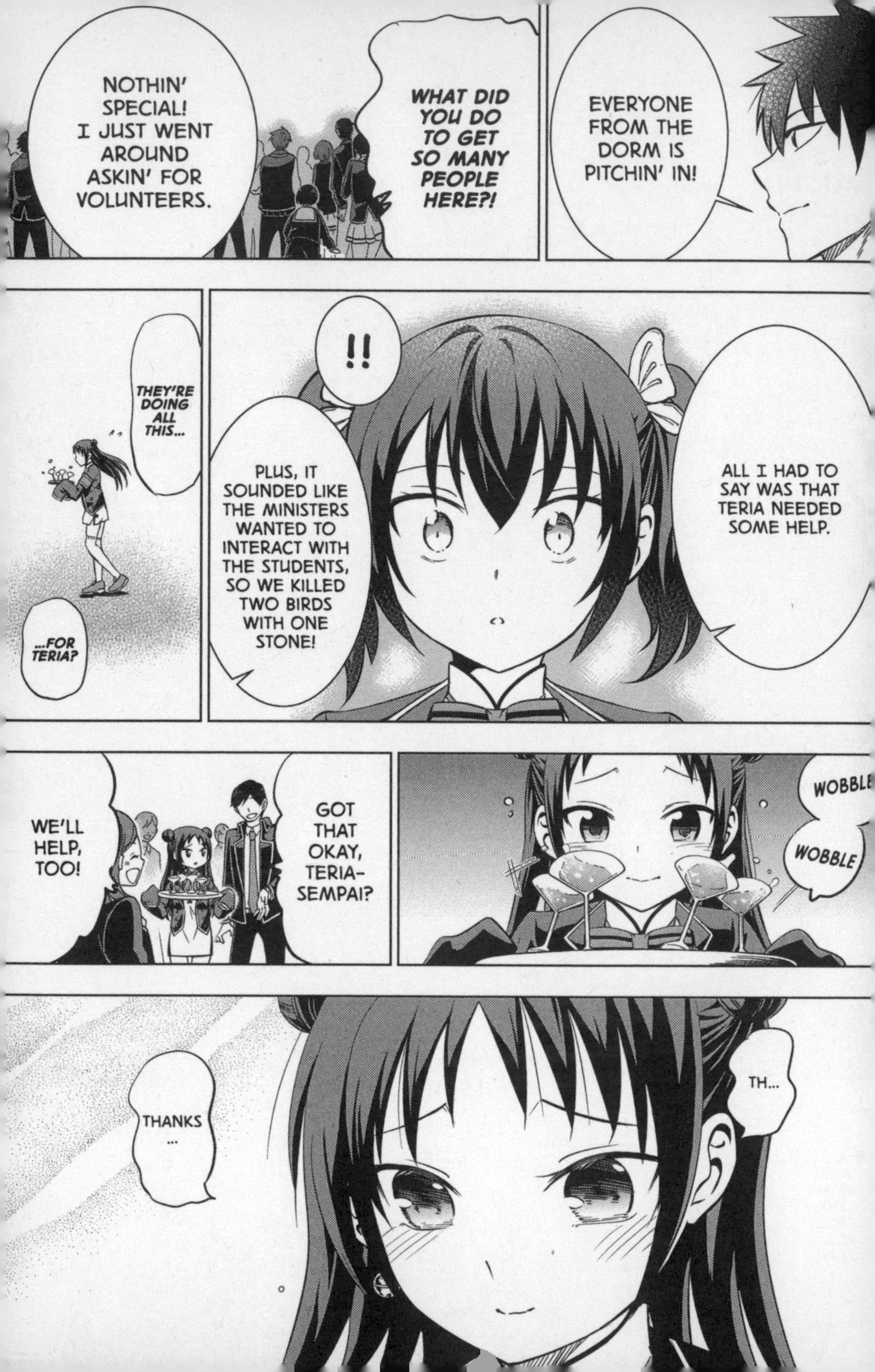
EVERYONE FROM THE DORM IS PITCHIN' IN!
WHAT DID YOU DO TO GET SO MANY PEOPLE HERE?!
NOTHIN' SPECIAL! I JUST WENT AROUND ASKIN' FOR VOLUNTEERS.
ALL I HAD TO SAY WAS THAT TERIA NEEDED SOME HELP.
!!
PLUS, IT SOUNDED LIKE THE MINISTERS WANTED TO INTERACT WITH THE STUDENTS, SO WE KILLED TWO BIRDS WITH ONE STONE!
THEY'RE DOING ALL THIS...
...FOR TERIA?
WOBBLE
WOBBLE
GOT THAT OKAY, TERIA-SEMPAI?
WE'LL HELP, TOO!
TH...
THANKS ...

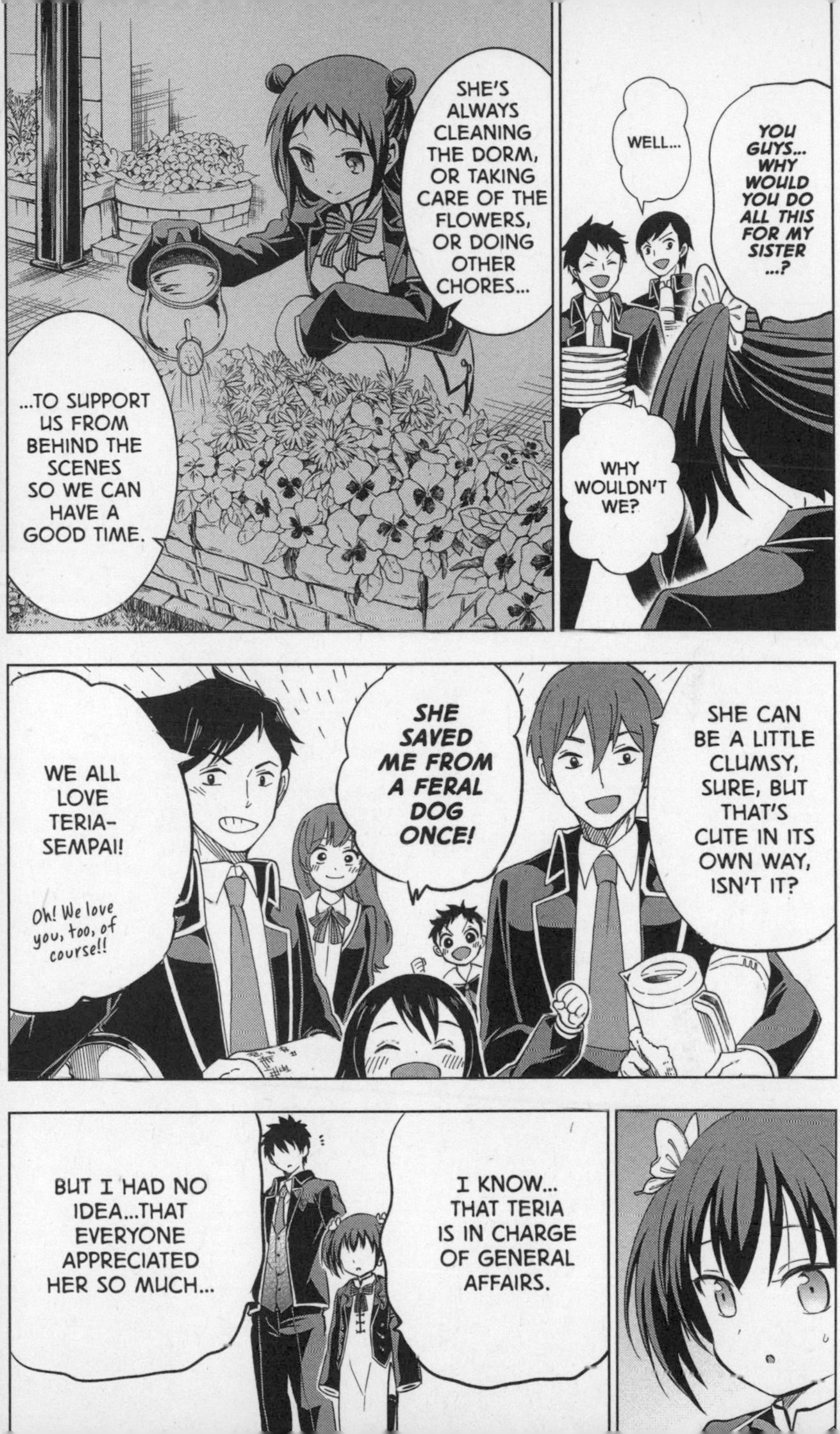
YOU GUYS... WHY WOULD YOU DO ALL THIS FOR MY SISTER ...?
WELL...
WHY WOULDN'T WE?
SHE'S ALWAYS CLEANING THE DORM, OR TAKING CARE OF THE FLOWERS, OR DOING OTHER CHORES...
...TO SUPPORT US FROM BEHIND THE SCENES SO WE CAN HAVE A GOOD TIME.
SHE CAN BE A LITTLE CLUMSY, SURE, BUT THAT'S CUTE IN ITS OWN WAY, ISN'T IT?
SHE SAVED ME FROM A FERAL DOG ONCE!
WE ALL LOVE TERIA-SEMPAI!
Oh! We love you, too, of course!!
I KNOW... THAT TERIA IS IN CHARGE OF GENERAL AFFAIRS.
BUT I HAD NO IDEA...THAT EVERYONE APPRECIATED HER SO MUCH...

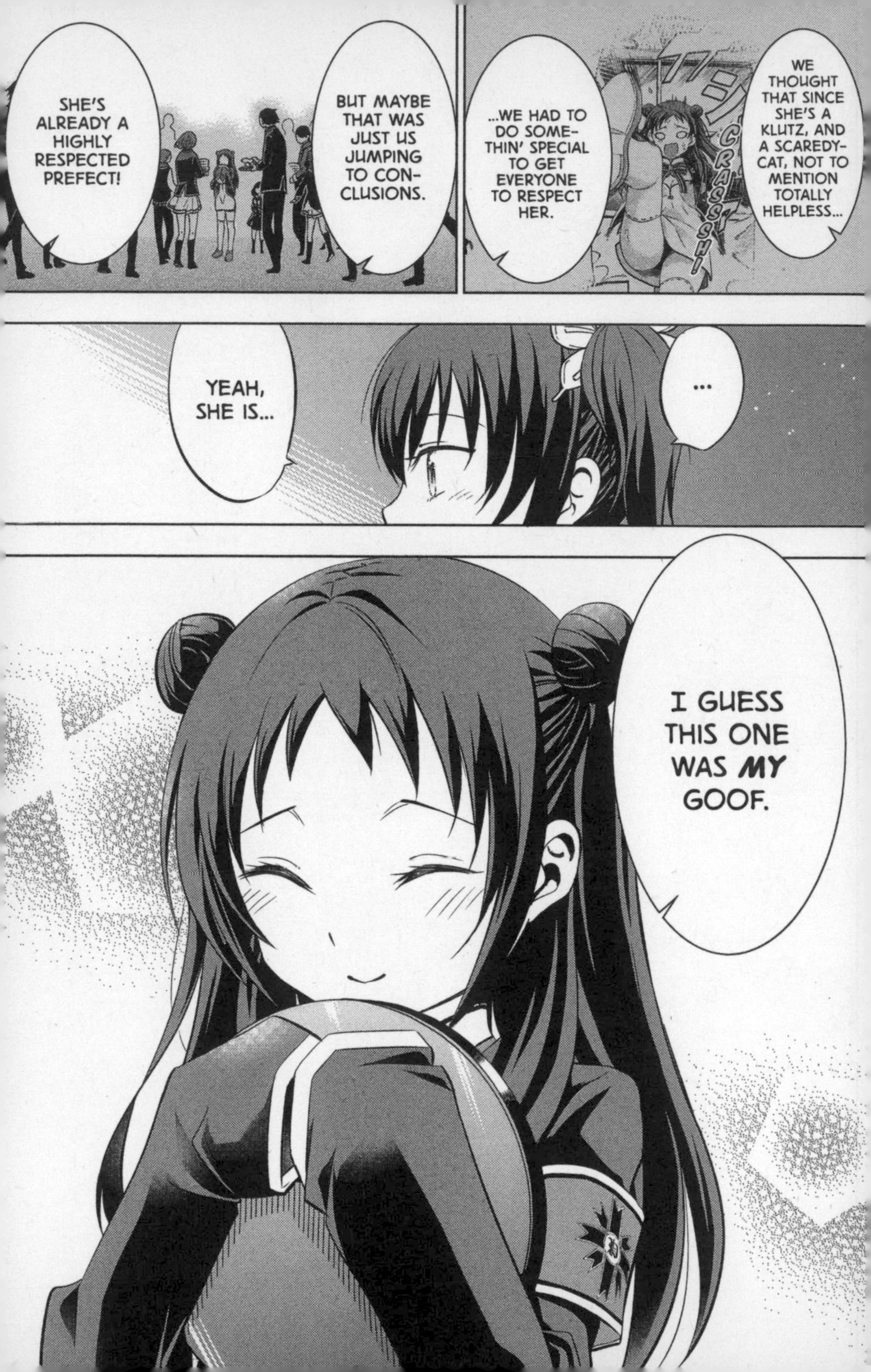
WE THOUGHT THAT SINCE SHE'S A KLUTZ, AND A SCAREDY-CAT, NOT TO MENTION TOTALLY HELPLESS...
CRASSSH!
...WE HAD TO DO SOME-THIN' SPECIAL TO GET EVERYONE TO RESPECT HER.
BUT MAYBE THAT WAS JUST US JUMPING TO CON-CLUSIONS.
SHE'S ALREADY A HIGHLY RESPECTED PREFECT!
...
YEAH, SHE IS...
I GUESS THIS ONE WAS *MY* GOOF.

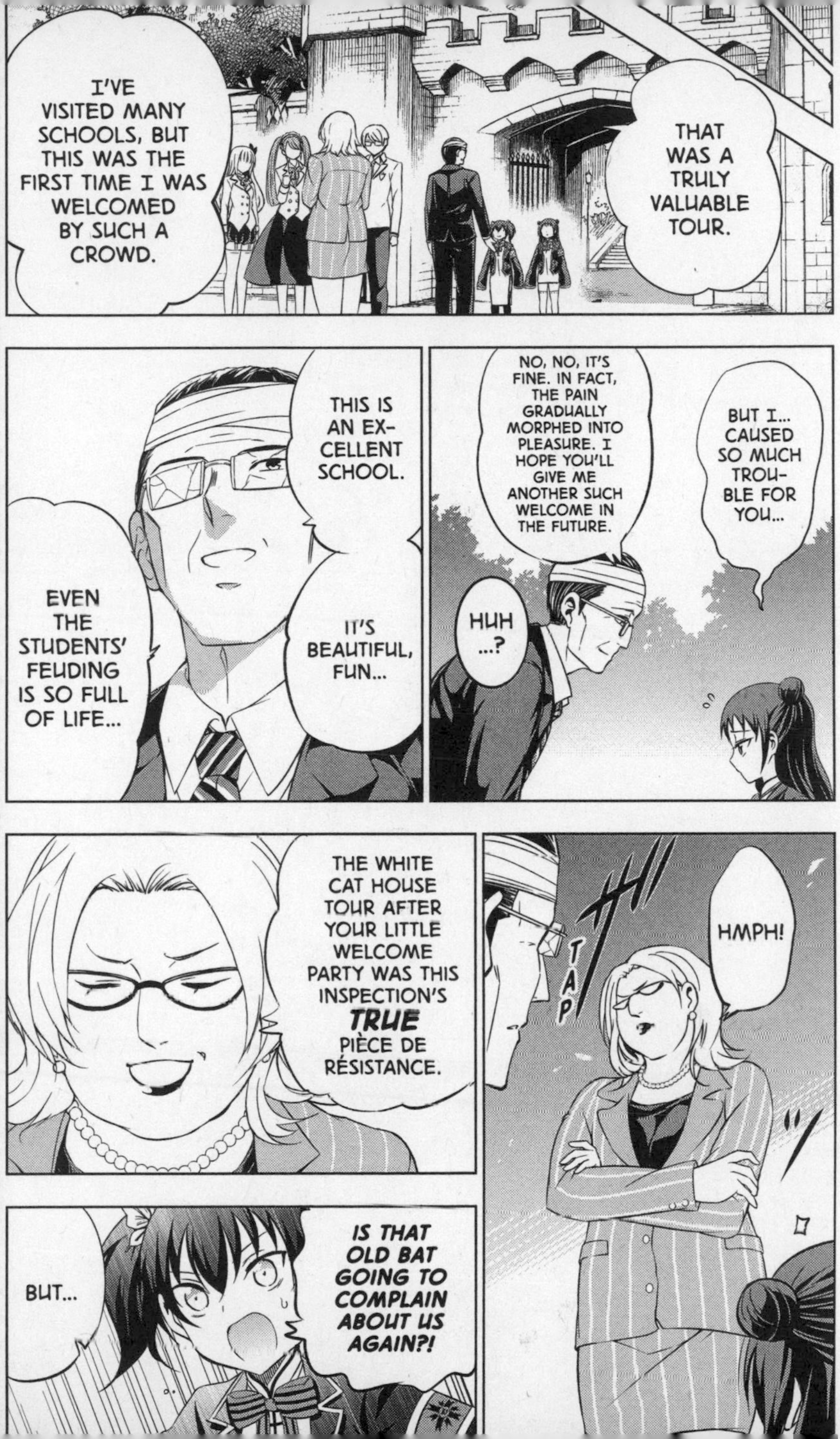
THAT WAS A TRULY VALUABLE TOUR.
I'VE VISITED MANY SCHOOLS, BUT THIS WAS THE FIRST TIME I WAS WELCOMED BY SUCH A CROWD.
BUT I... CAUSED SO MUCH TROUBLE FOR YOU...
NO, NO, IT'S FINE. IN FACT, THE PAIN GRADUALLY MORPHED INTO PLEASURE. I HOPE YOU'LL GIVE ME ANOTHER SUCH WELCOME IN THE FUTURE.
HUH ...?
THIS IS AN EX-CELLENT SCHOOL.
IT'S BEAUTIFUL, FUN...
EVEN THE STUDENTS' FEUDING IS SO FULL OF LIFE...
HMPH!
TAP TAP
THE WHITE CAT HOUSE TOUR AFTER YOUR LITTLE WELCOME PARTY WAS THIS INSPECTION'S TRUE PIÈCE DE RÉSISTANCE.
IS THAT OLD BAT GOING TO COMPLAIN ABOUT US AGAIN?!
BUT...

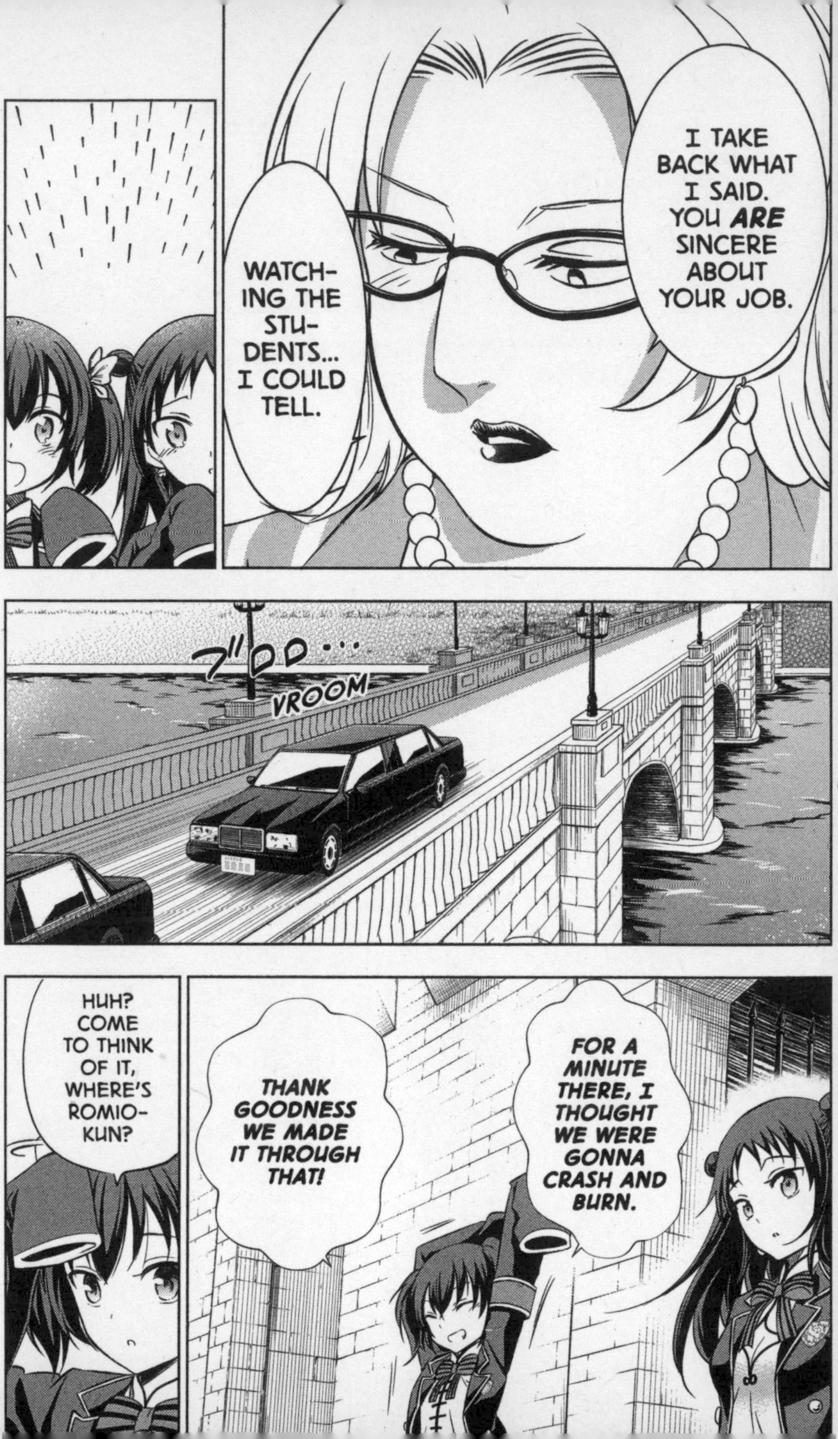
I TAKE BACK WHAT I SAID. YOU ARE SINCERE ABOUT YOUR JOB.
WATCHING THE STUDENTS... I COULD TELL.
ブロロ・・・
VROOM
FOR A MINUTE THERE, I THOUGHT WE WERE GONNA CRASH AND BURN.
THANK GOODNESS WE MADE IT THROUGH THAT!
HUH? COME TO THINK OF IT, WHERE'S ROMIO-KUN?

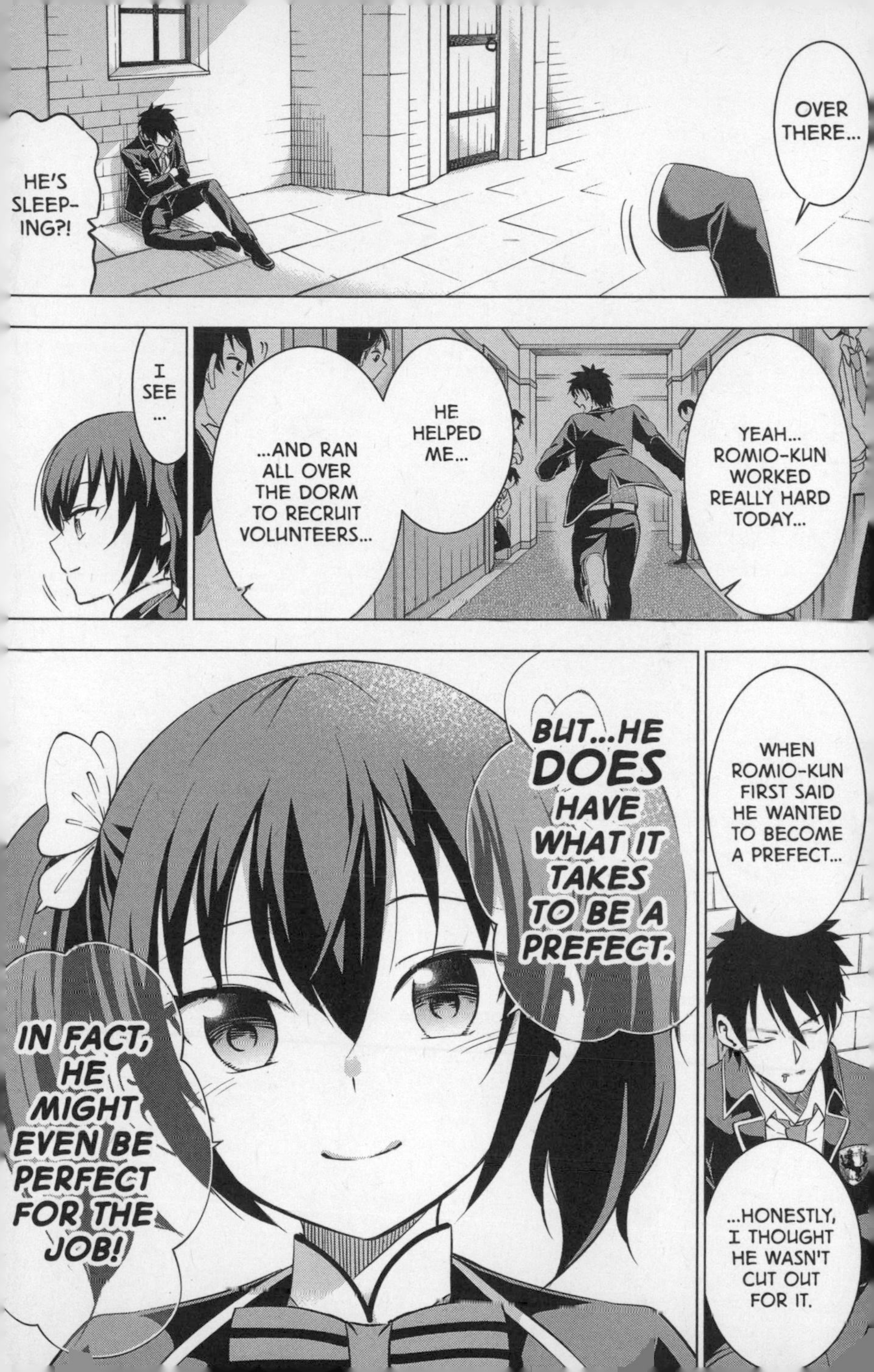
OVER THERE...
HE'S SLEEP-ING?!
YEAH... ROMIO-KUN WORKED REALLY HARD TODAY...
HE HELPED ME...
...AND RAN ALL OVER THE DORM TO RECRUIT VOLUNTEERS...
I SEE ...
WHEN ROMIO-KUN FIRST SAID HE WANTED TO BECOME A PREFECT...
...HONESTLY, I THOUGHT HE WASN'T CUT OUT FOR IT.
BUT...HE DOES HAVE WHAT IT TAKES TO BE A PREFECT.
IN FACT, HE MIGHT EVEN BE PERFECT FOR THE JOB!

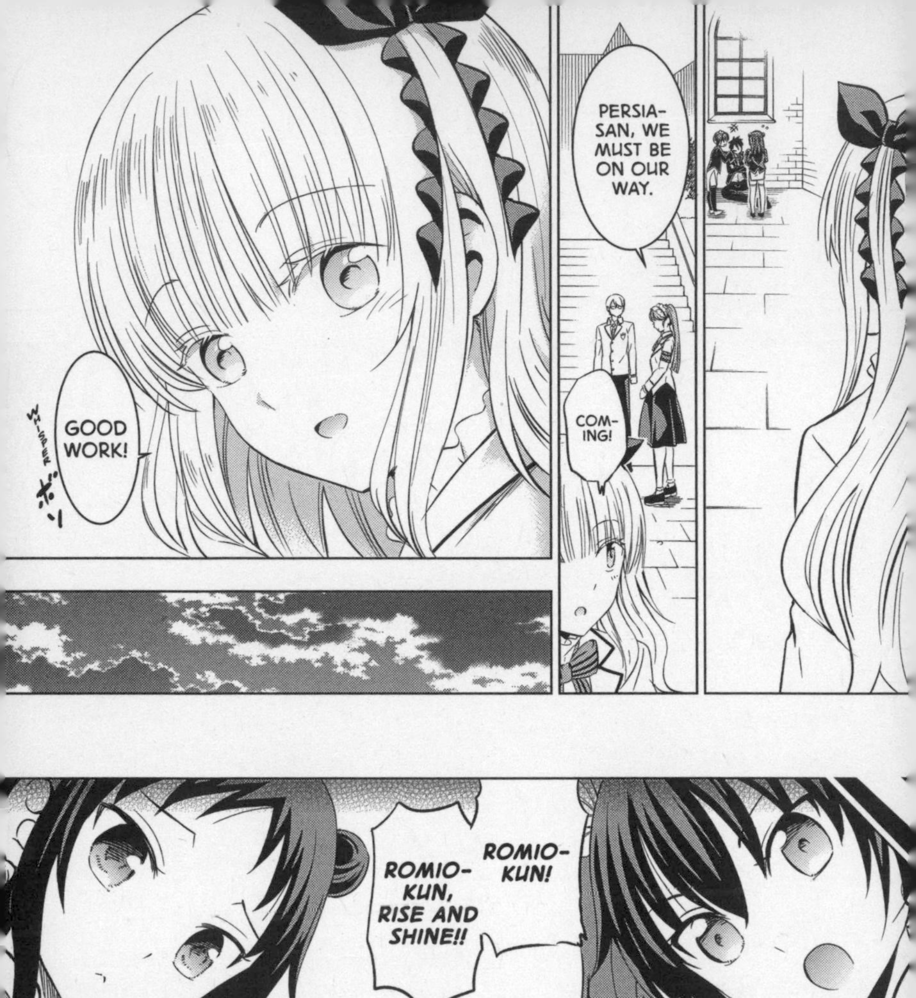
PERSIA-SAN, WE MUST BE ON OUR WAY.
COMING!
WHISPER
GOOD WORK!
ROMIO-KUN!
ROMIO-KUN, RISE AND SHINE!!

Translator's Note: "Meat" as forehead graffiti originated in the *Kinnikuman* manga/anime series and was popularized by the *Sugoi yo!! Masaru-san* manga/anime series.

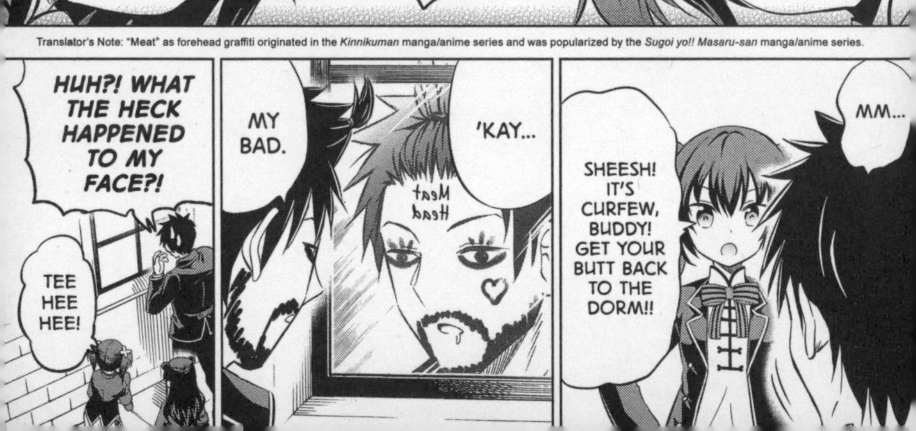
MM...
SHEESH! IT'S CURFEW, BUDDY! GET YOUR BUTT BACK TO THE DORM!!
'KAY...
MY BAD.
Meat Head
HUH?! WHAT THE HECK HAPPENED TO MY FACE?!
TEE HEE HEE!

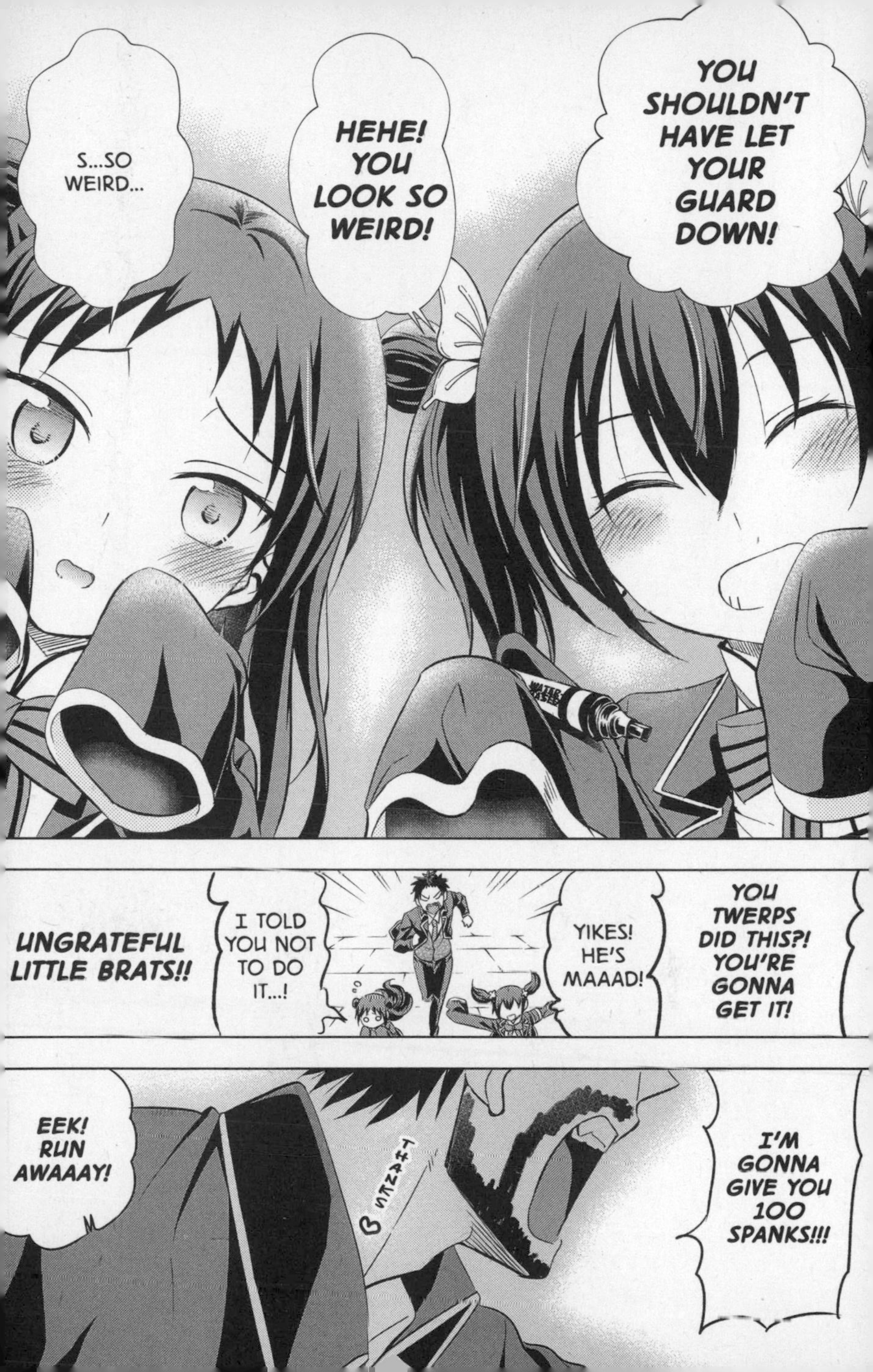
YOU SHOULDN'T HAVE LET YOUR GUARD DOWN!
HEHE! YOU LOOK SO WEIRD!
S...SO WEIRD...
YOU TWERPS DID THIS?! YOU'RE GONNA GET IT!
YIKES! HE'S MAAAD!
I TOLD YOU NOT TO DO IT...!
UNGRATEFUL LITTLE BRATS!!
I'M GONNA GIVE YOU 100 SPANKS!!!
THANKS ♡
EEK! RUN AWAAAY!

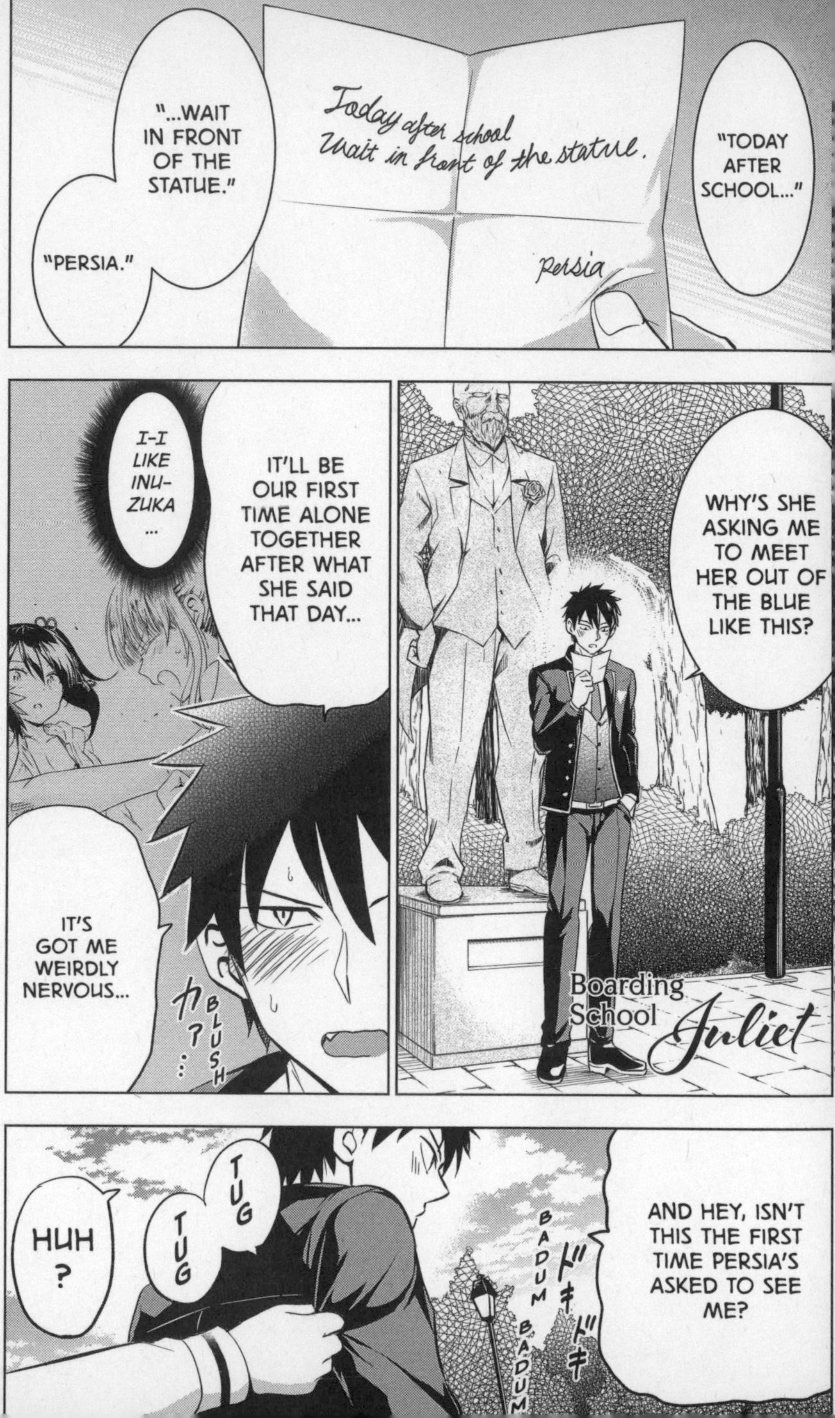
"TODAY AFTER SCHOOL..."
Today after school
Wait in front of the statue.
persia
"...WAIT IN FRONT OF THE STATUE."
"PERSIA."
WHY'S SHE ASKING ME TO MEET HER OUT OF THE BLUE LIKE THIS?
Boarding School Juliet
IT'LL BE OUR FIRST TIME ALONE TOGETHER AFTER WHAT SHE SAID THAT DAY...
I-I LIKE INU-ZUKA...
IT'S GOT ME WEIRDLY NERVOUS...
カァ…
BLUSH
AND HEY, ISN'T THIS THE FIRST TIME PERSIA'S ASKED TO SEE ME?
ドキドキ
BADUM BADUM
TUG
TUG
HUH?

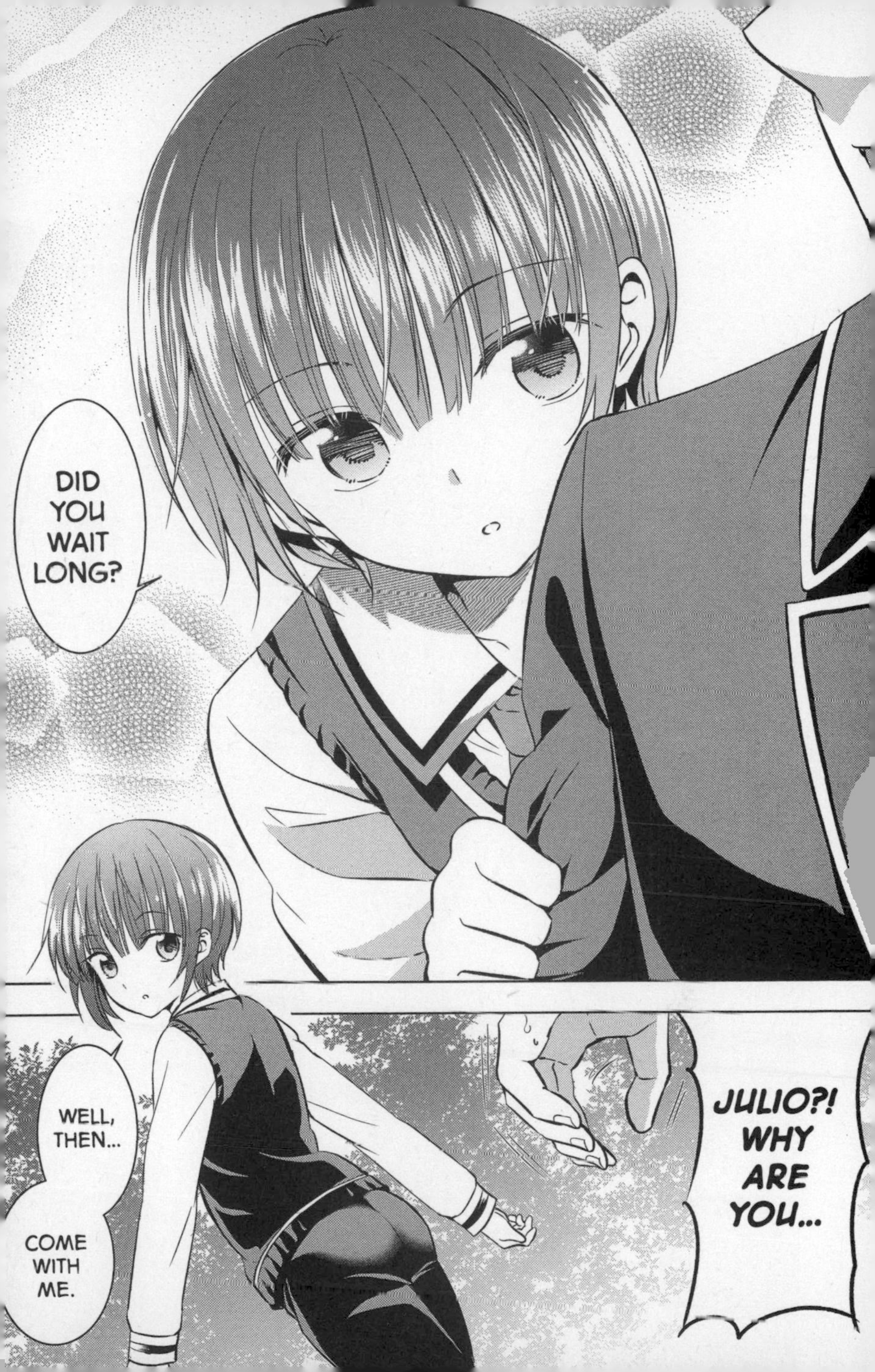
DID YOU WAIT LONG?
JULIO?! WHY ARE YOU...
WELL, THEN...
COME WITH ME.

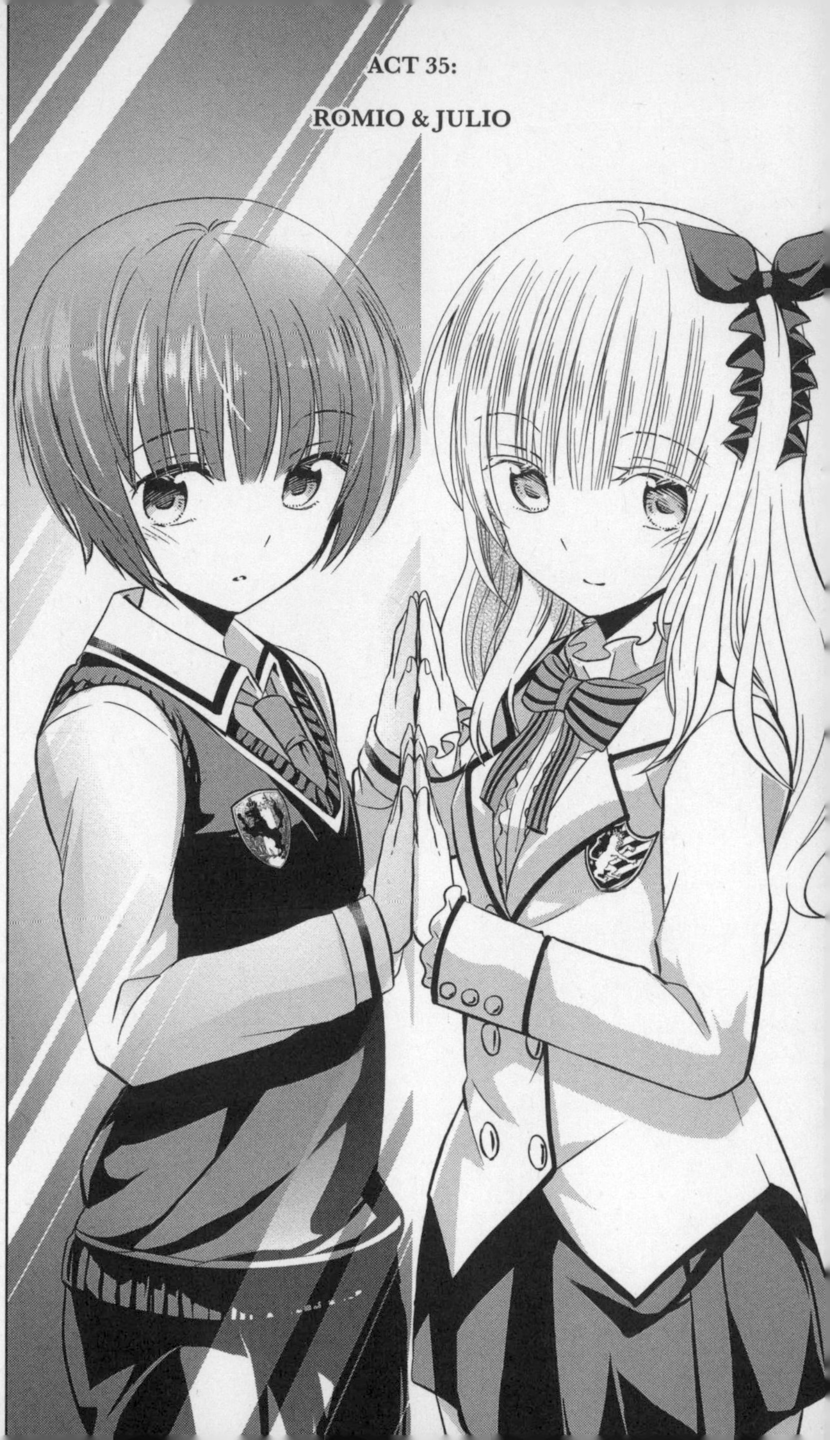
ACT 35:
ROMIO & JULIO

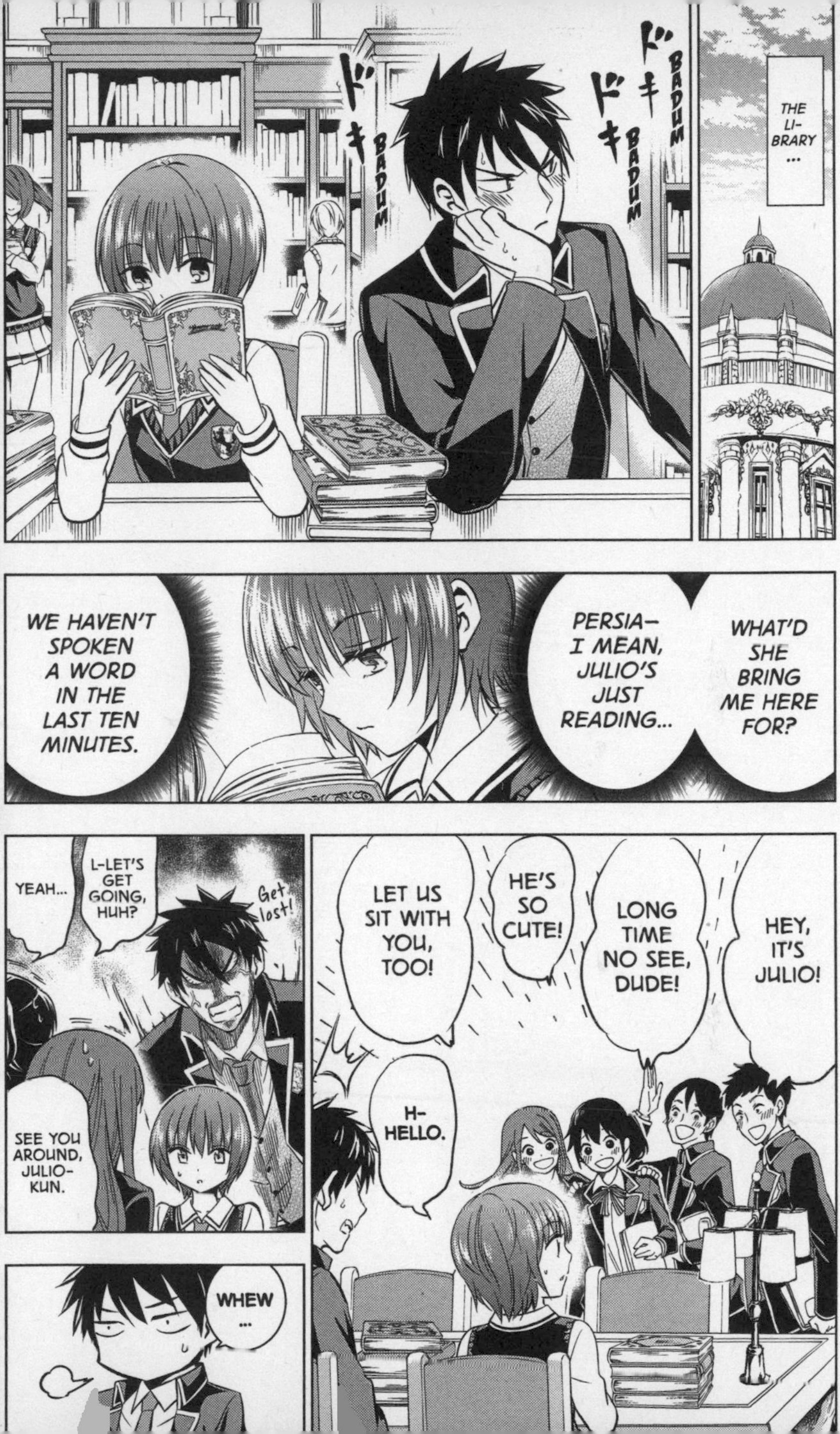
THE LI-BRARY ...
ドキ ドキ
BADUM BADUM
ドキ ドキ
BADUM BADUM
WHAT'D SHE BRING ME HERE FOR?
PERSIA— I MEAN, JULIO'S JUST READING...
WE HAVEN'T SPOKEN A WORD IN THE LAST TEN MINUTES.
HEY, IT'S JULIO!
LONG TIME NO SEE, DUDE!
HE'S SO CUTE!
LET US SIT WITH YOU, TOO!
H-HELLO.
L-LET'S GET GOING, HUH?
Get lost!
YEAH...
SEE YOU AROUND, JULIO-KUN.
WHEW ...

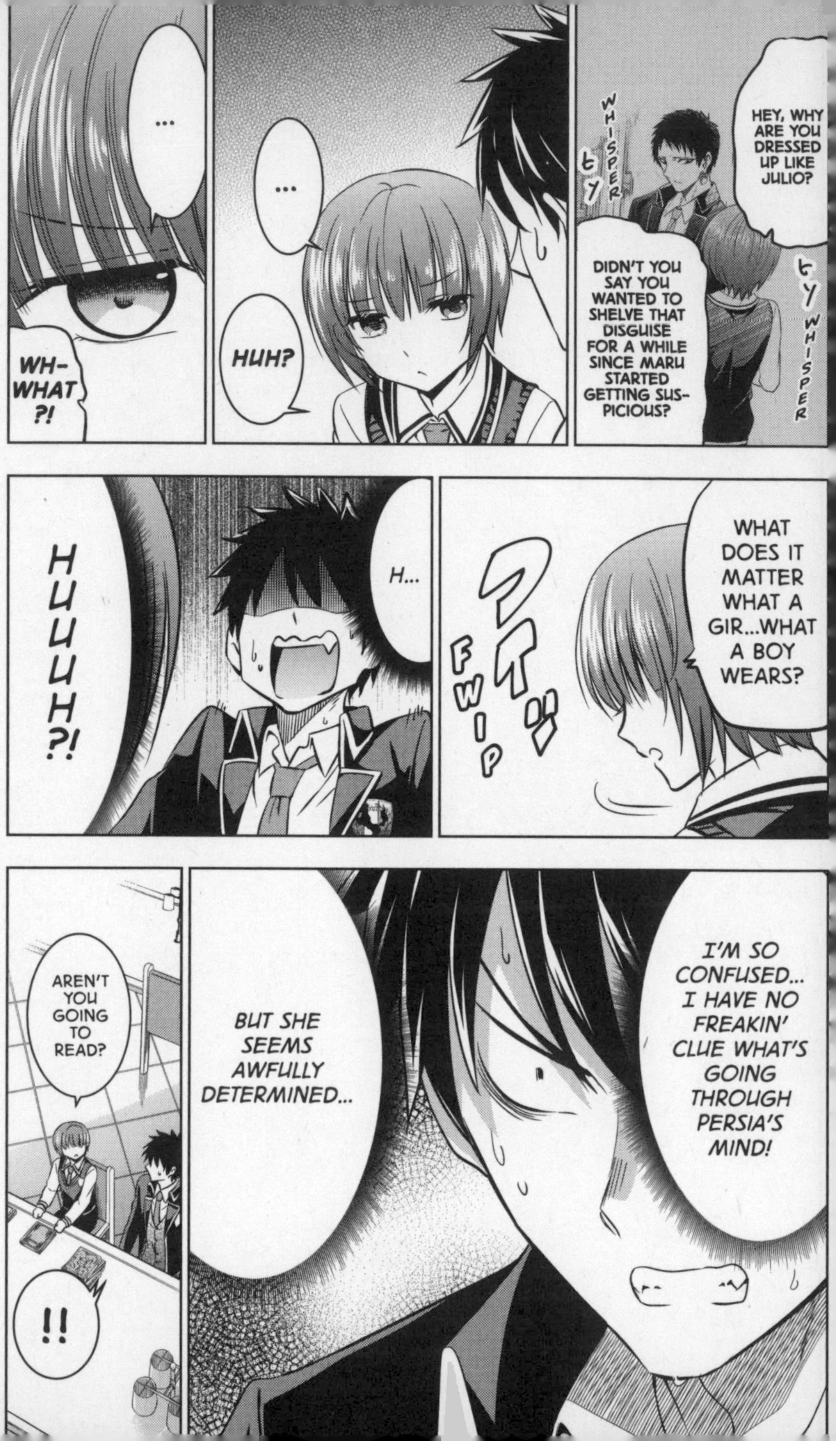
HEY, WHY ARE YOU DRESSED UP LIKE JULIO?
WHISPER
WHISPER
DIDN'T YOU SAY YOU WANTED TO SHELVE THAT DISGUISE FOR A WHILE SINCE MARU STARTED GETTING SUS-PICIOUS?
...
HUH?
...
WH-WHAT?!
WHAT DOES IT MATTER WHAT A GIR...WHAT A BOY WEARS?
FWIP
H...
HUUUUH?!
I'M SO CONFUSED... I HAVE NO FREAKIN' CLUE WHAT'S GOING THROUGH PERSIA'S MIND!
BUT SHE SEEMS AWFULLY DETERMINED...
AREN'T YOU GOING TO READ?
!!

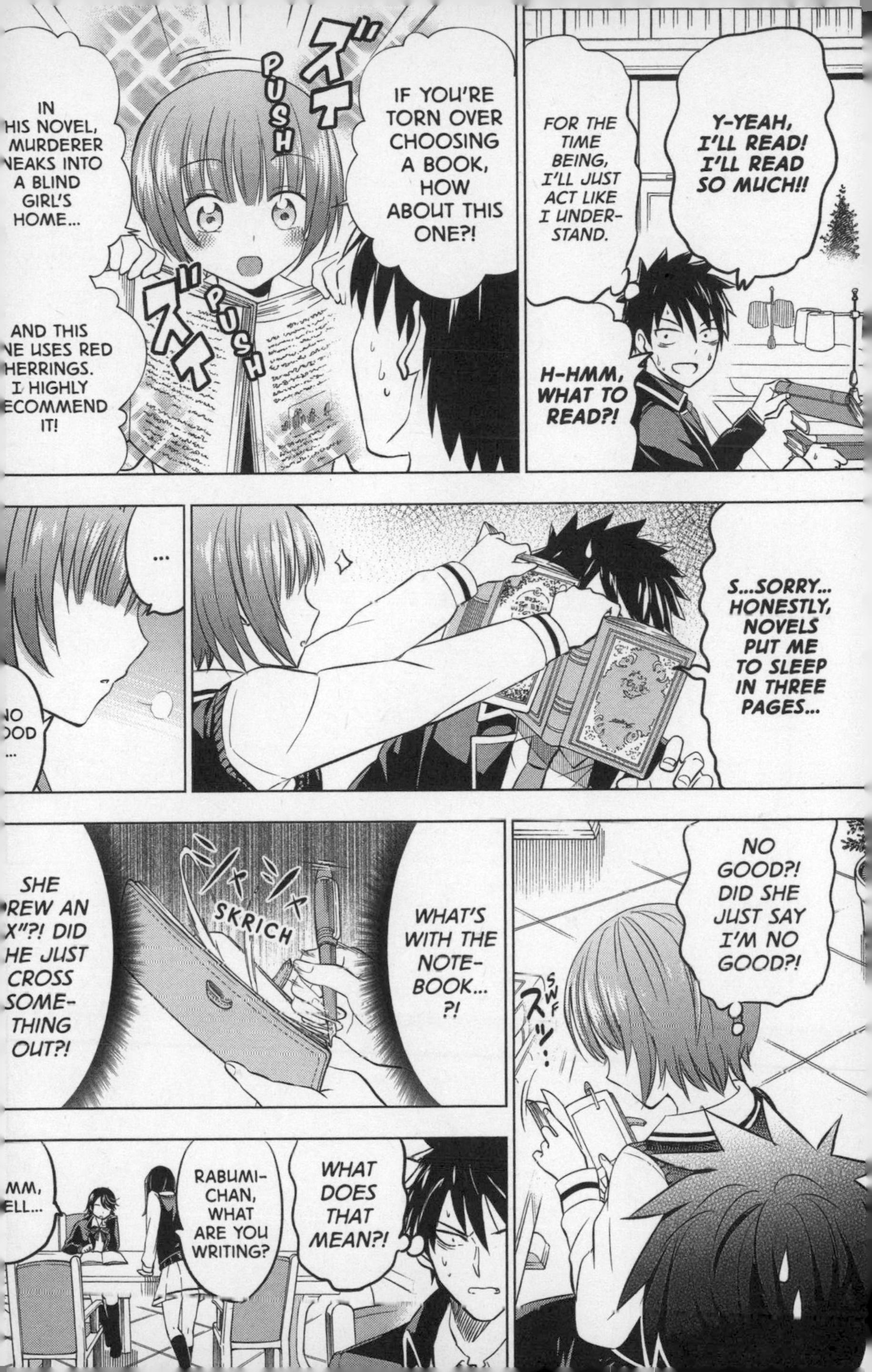
Y-YEAH, I'LL READ! I'LL READ SO MUCH!!
FOR THE TIME BEING, I'LL JUST ACT LIKE I UNDER-STAND.
H-HMM, WHAT TO READ?!
PUSH
IF YOU'RE TORN OVER CHOOSING A BOOK, HOW ABOUT THIS ONE?!
IN HIS NOVEL, MURDERER NEAKS INTO A BLIND GIRL'S HOME...
PUSH
AND THIS NE USES RED HERRINGS. I HIGHLY ECOMMEND IT!
S...SORRY... HONESTLY, NOVELS PUT ME TO SLEEP IN THREE PAGES...
...
NO OOD ...
NO GOOD?! DID SHE JUST SAY I'M NO GOOD?!
SWF
WHAT'S WITH THE NOTE-BOOK... ?!
SKRICH
SHE REW AN X"?! DID HE JUST CROSS SOME-THING OUT?!
WHAT DOES THAT MEAN?!
RABUMI-CHAN, WHAT ARE YOU WRITING?
MM, ELL...

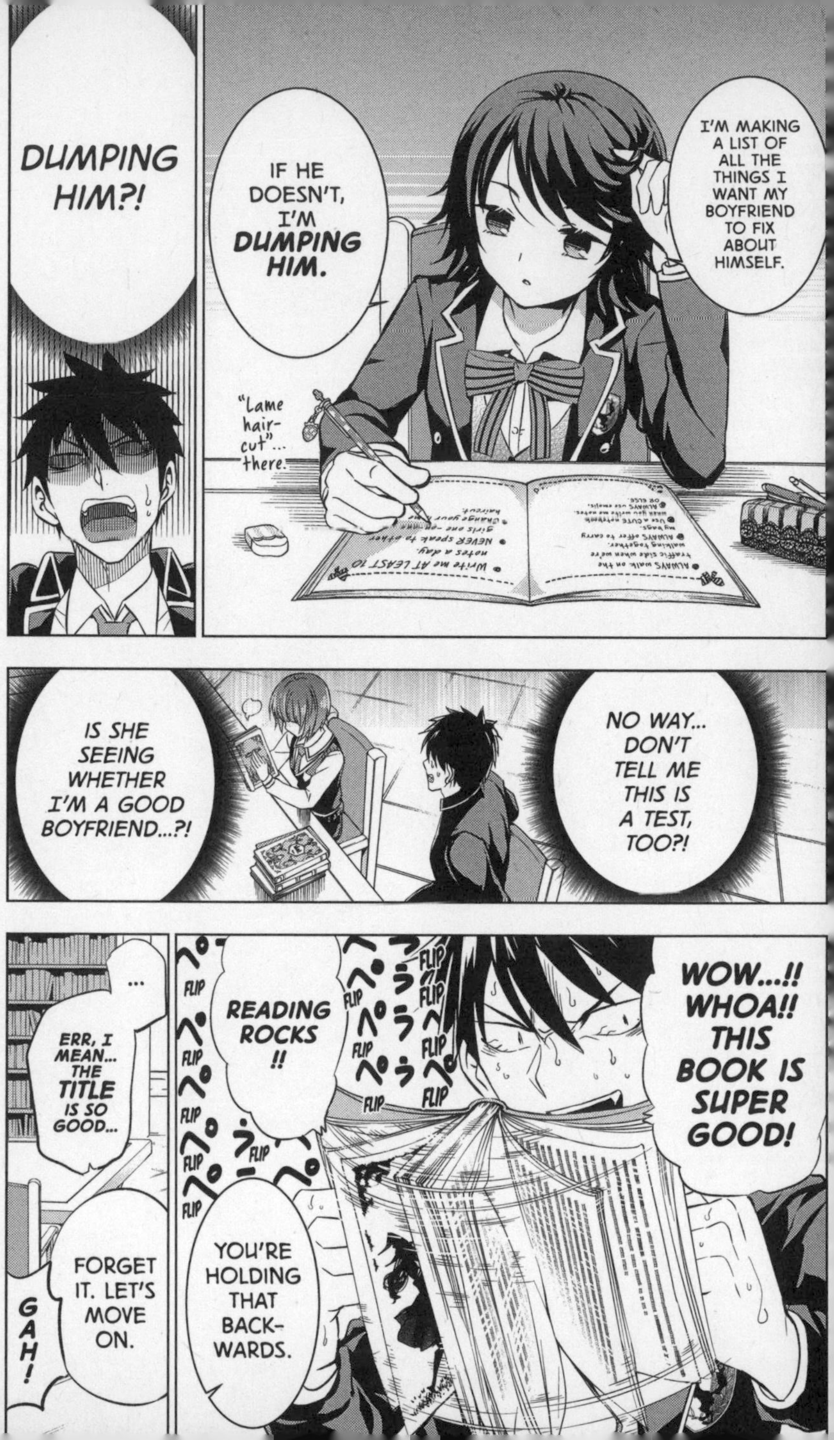
I'M MAKING A LIST OF ALL THE THINGS I WANT MY BOYFRIEND TO FIX ABOUT HIMSELF.
IF HE DOESN'T, I'M **DUMPING HIM.**
"Lame hair-cut"... there.
DUMPING HIM?!
NO WAY... DON'T TELL ME THIS IS A TEST, TOO?!
IS SHE SEEING WHETHER I'M A GOOD BOYFRIEND...?!
WOW...!! WHOA!! THIS BOOK IS SUPER GOOD!
READING ROCKS!!
FLIP FLIP FLIP FLIP FLIP FLIP FLIP
YOU'RE HOLDING THAT BACK-WARDS.
...
ERR, I MEAN... THE TITLE IS SO GOOD...
GAH!
FORGET IT. LET'S MOVE ON.

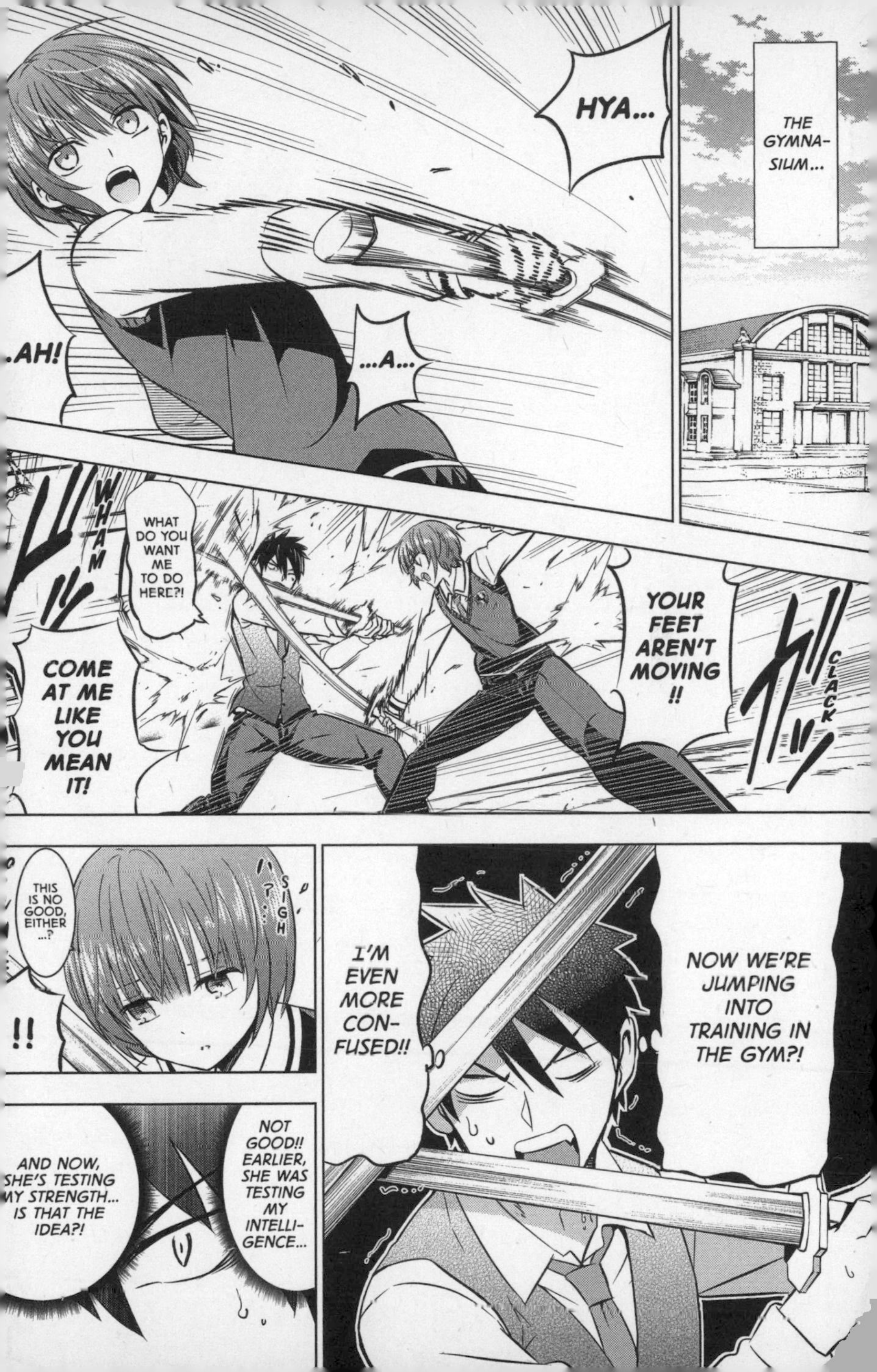
THE GYMNA-SIUM...
HYA...
...A...
...AH!
CLACK
YOUR FEET AREN'T MOVING!!
WHAT DO YOU WANT ME TO DO HERE?!
WHAM
COME AT ME LIKE YOU MEAN IT!
NOW WE'RE JUMPING INTO TRAINING IN THE GYM?!
I'M EVEN MORE CON-FUSED!!
SIGH
THIS IS NO GOOD, EITHER ...?
!!
NOT GOOD!! EARLIER, SHE WAS TESTING MY INTELLI-GENCE...
AND NOW, SHE'S TESTING MY STRENGTH... IS THAT THE IDEA?!

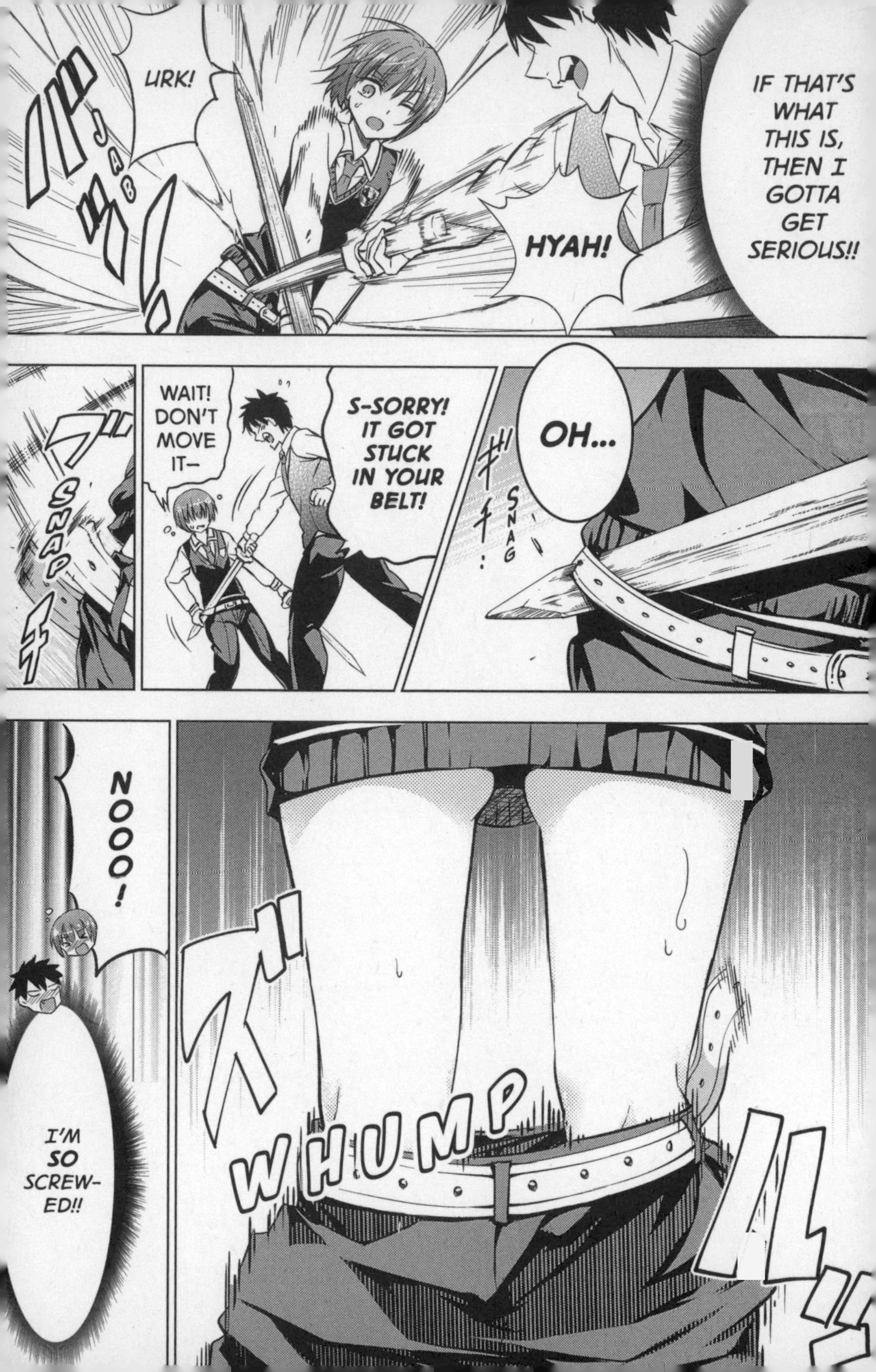
IF THAT'S WHAT THIS IS, THEN I GOTTA GET SERIOUS!!
HYAH!
URK!
JAB
OH...
SNAG
S-SORRY! IT GOT STUCK IN YOUR BELT!
WAIT! DON'T MOVE IT–
SNAP
WHUMP
NOOOO!
I'M SO SCREW-ED!!

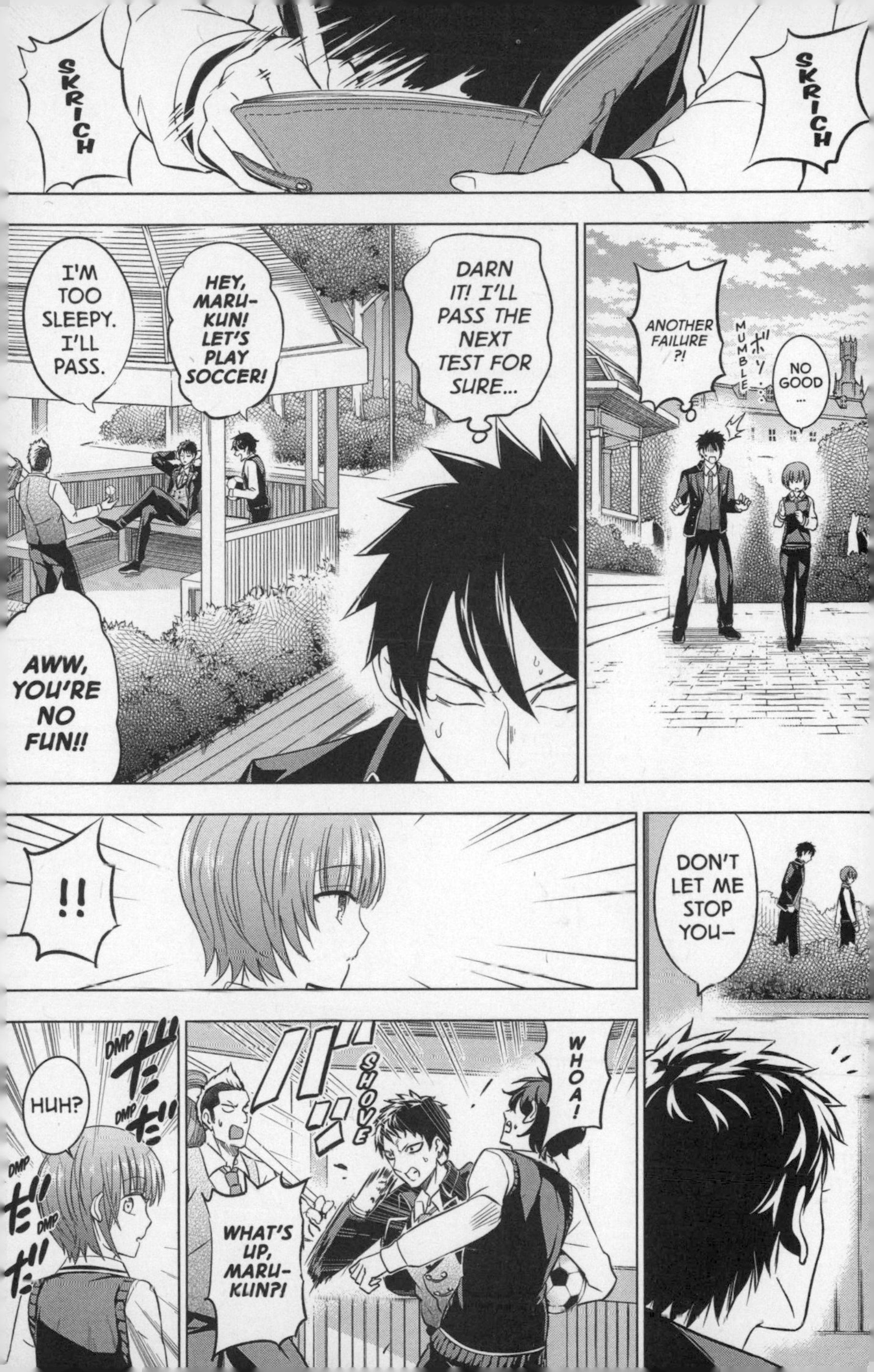
SKRICH
SKRICH
NO GOOD...
MUMBLE
ANOTHER FAILURE?!
DARN IT! I'LL PASS THE NEXT TEST FOR SURE...
HEY, MARU-KUN! LET'S PLAY SOCCER!
I'M TOO SLEEPY. I'LL PASS.
AWW, YOU'RE NO FUN!!
DON'T LET ME STOP YOU—
!!
WHOA!
SHOVE
WHAT'S UP, MARU-KUN?!
DMP
HUH?
DMP
DMP
DMP

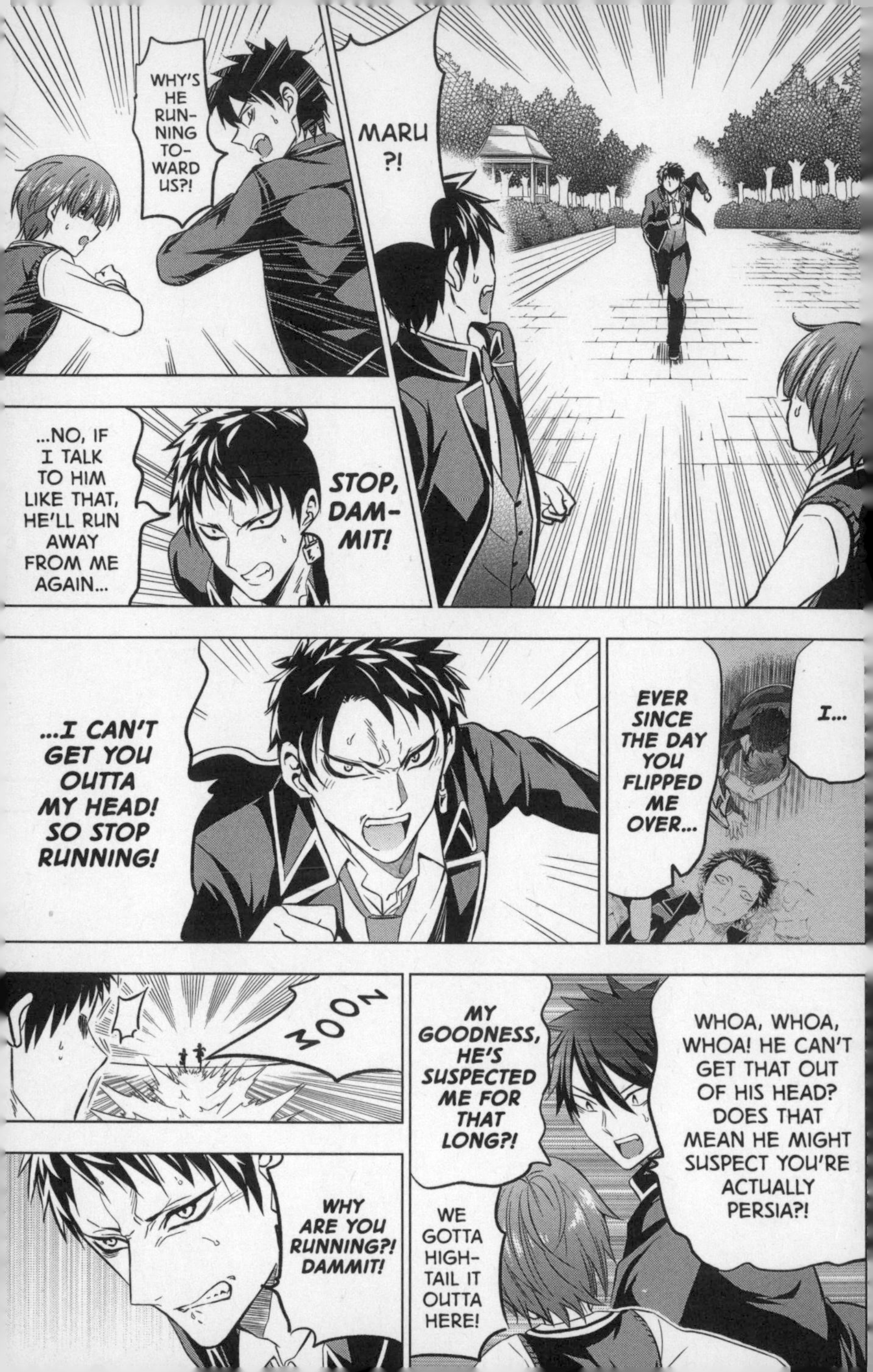
MARU ?!
WHY'S HE RUNNING TOWARD US?!
STOP, DAMMIT!
...NO, IF I TALK TO HIM LIKE THAT, HE'LL RUN AWAY FROM ME AGAIN...
I...
EVER SINCE THE DAY YOU FLIPPED ME OVER...
...I CAN'T GET YOU OUTTA MY HEAD! SO STOP RUNNING!
WHOA, WHOA, WHOA! HE CAN'T GET THAT OUT OF HIS HEAD? DOES THAT MEAN HE MIGHT SUSPECT YOU'RE ACTUALLY PERSIA?!
MY GOODNESS, HE'S SUSPECTED ME FOR THAT LONG?!
WE GOTTA HIGHTAIL IT OUTTA HERE!
ZOOM
WHY ARE YOU RUNNING?! DAMMIT!

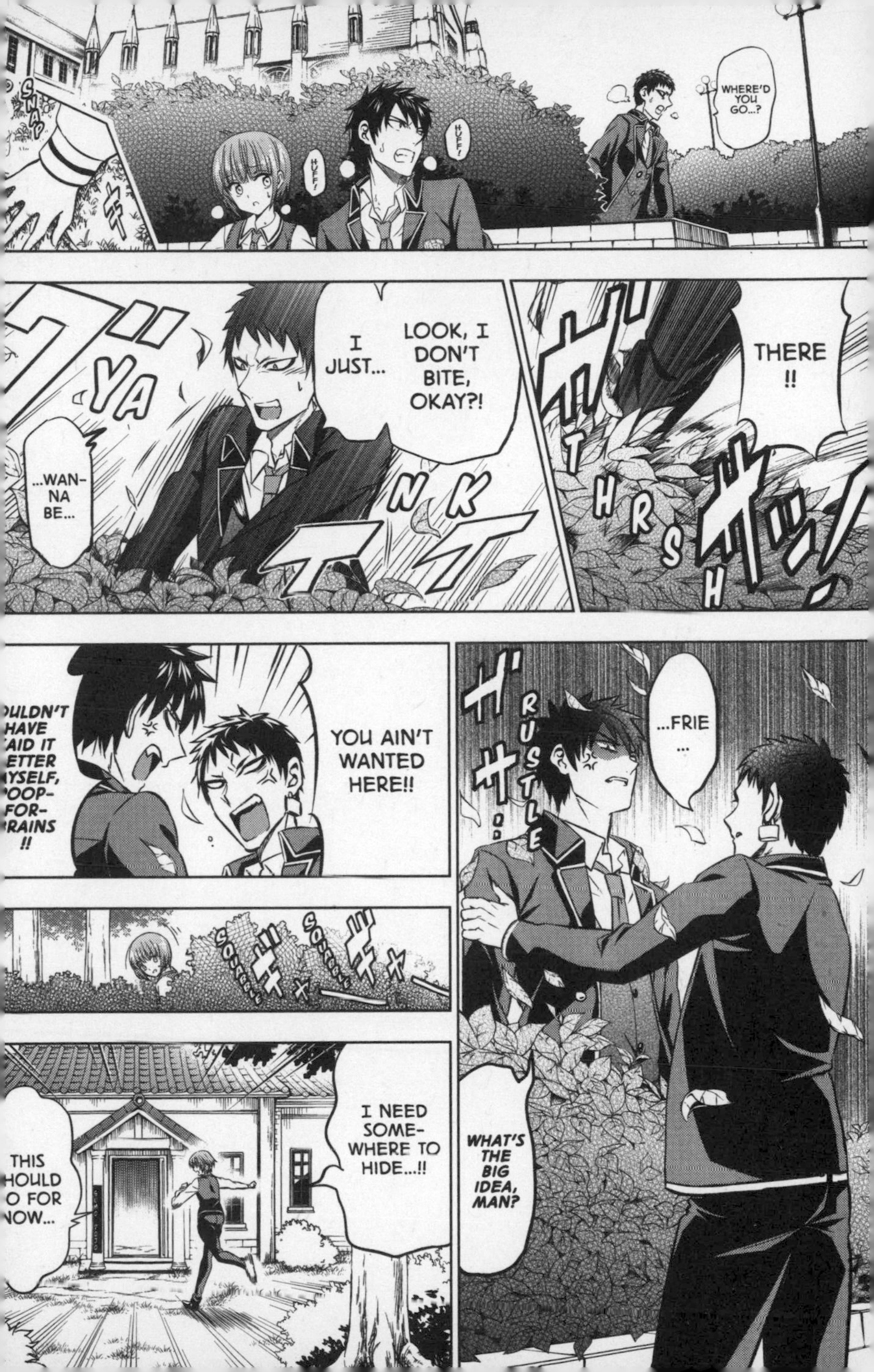
WHERE'D YOU GO...?
HUFF!
HUFF!
SNAP
THERE !!
THRSSH
LOOK, I DON'T BITE, OKAY?!
I JUST...
...WAN-NA BE...
YANK
RUSTLE
...FRIE ...
WHAT'S THE BIG IDEA, MAN?
YOU AIN'T WANTED HERE!!
OULDN'T HAVE AID IT ETTER YSELF, POOP-FOR-RAINS !!
SQUABBLE
SQUABBLE
I NEED SOME-WHERE TO HIDE...!!
THIS HOULD O FOR NOW...

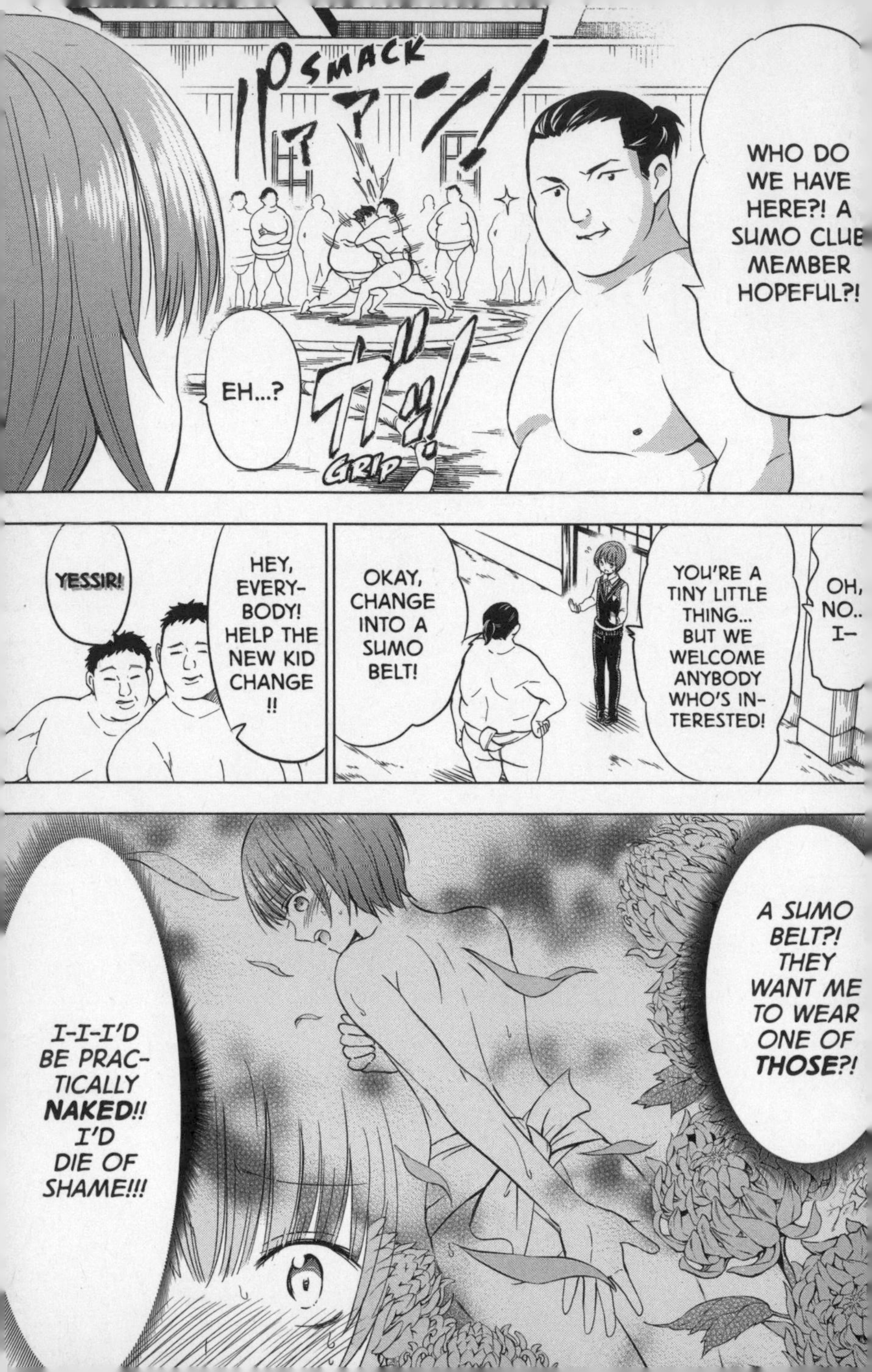
WHO DO WE HAVE HERE?! A SUMO CLUB MEMBER HOPEFUL?!
SMACK
GRIP
EH...?
OH, NO.. I—
YOU'RE A TINY LITTLE THING... BUT WE WELCOME ANYBODY WHO'S INTERESTED!
OKAY, CHANGE INTO A SUMO BELT!
HEY, EVERYBODY! HELP THE NEW KID CHANGE !!
YESSIR!
A SUMO BELT?! THEY WANT ME TO WEAR ONE OF THOSE?!
I-I-I'D BE PRACTICALLY NAKED!! I'D DIE OF SHAME!!!

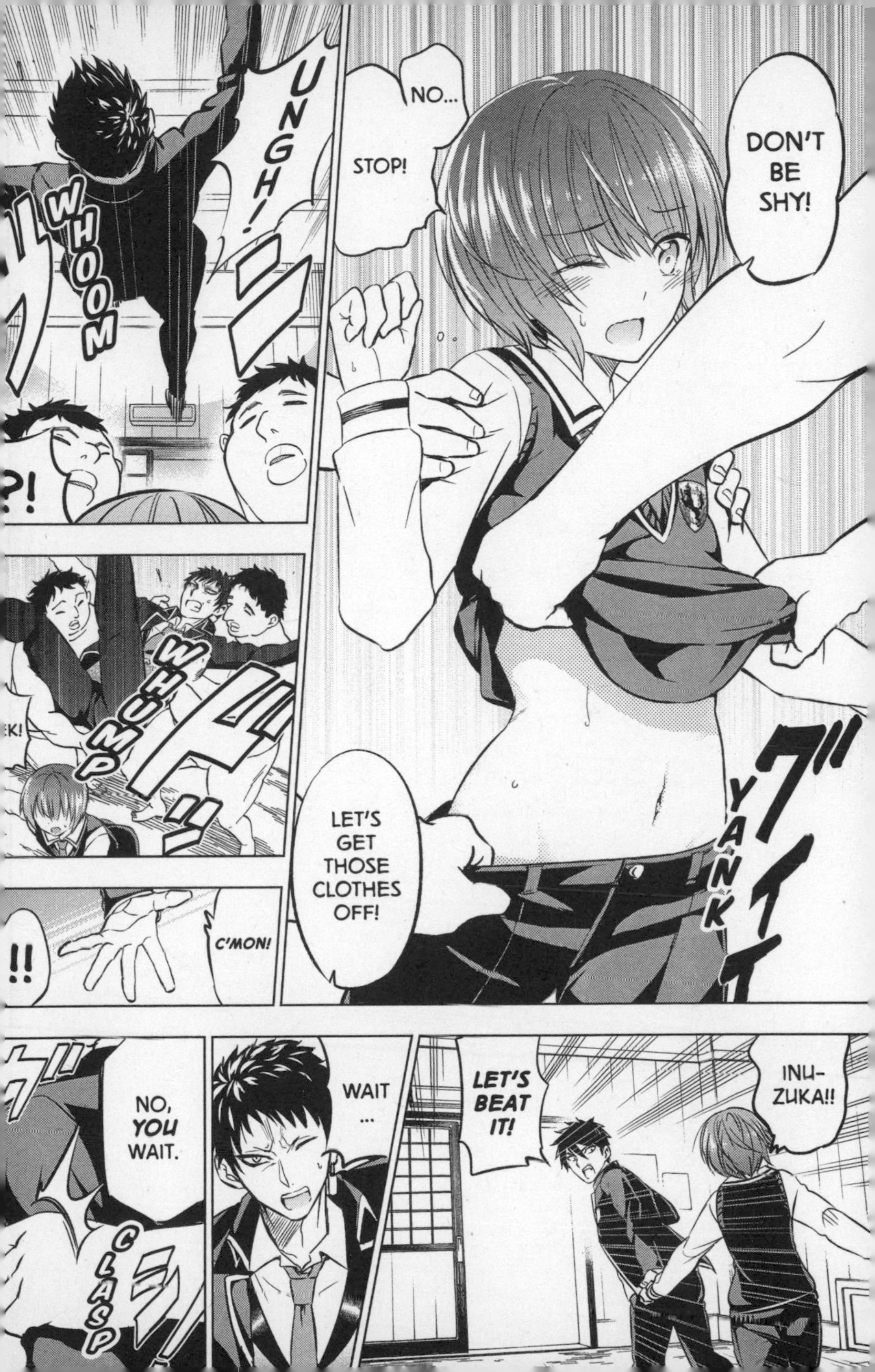
DON'T BE SHY!
NO... STOP!
YANK
LET'S GET THOSE CLOTHES OFF!
UNGH!
WHOOM
?!
WHUMP
EK!
C'MON!
!!
INU-ZUKA!!
LET'S BEAT IT!
WAIT ...
NO, YOU WAIT.
CLASP

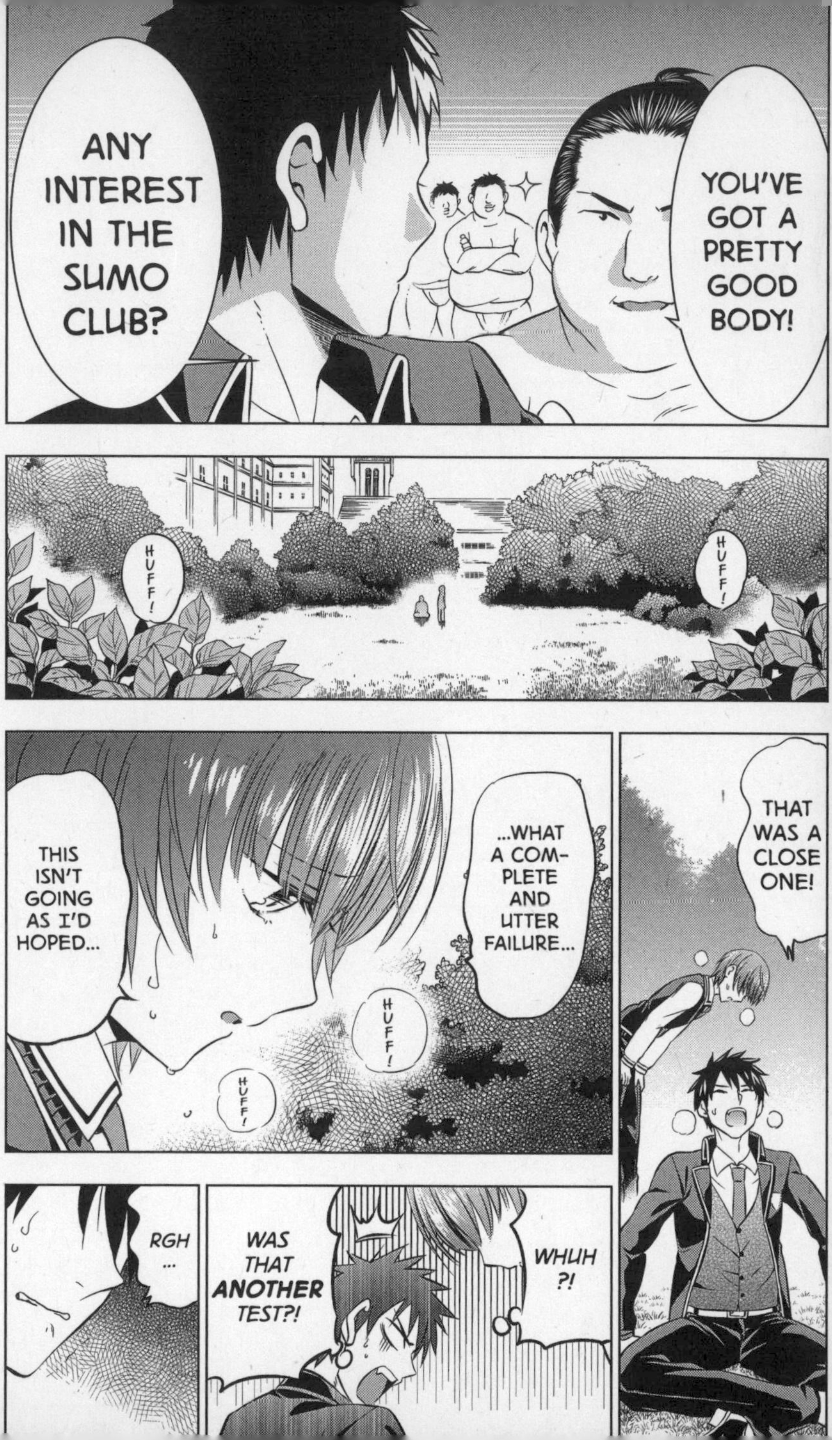
YOU'VE GOT A PRETTY GOOD BODY!
ANY INTEREST IN THE SUMO CLUB?
HUFF!
HUFF!
THAT WAS A CLOSE ONE!
...WHAT A COMPLETE AND UTTER FAILURE...
THIS ISN'T GOING AS I'D HOPED...
HUFF!
HUFF!
WHUH?!
WAS THAT ANOTHER TEST?!
RGH...

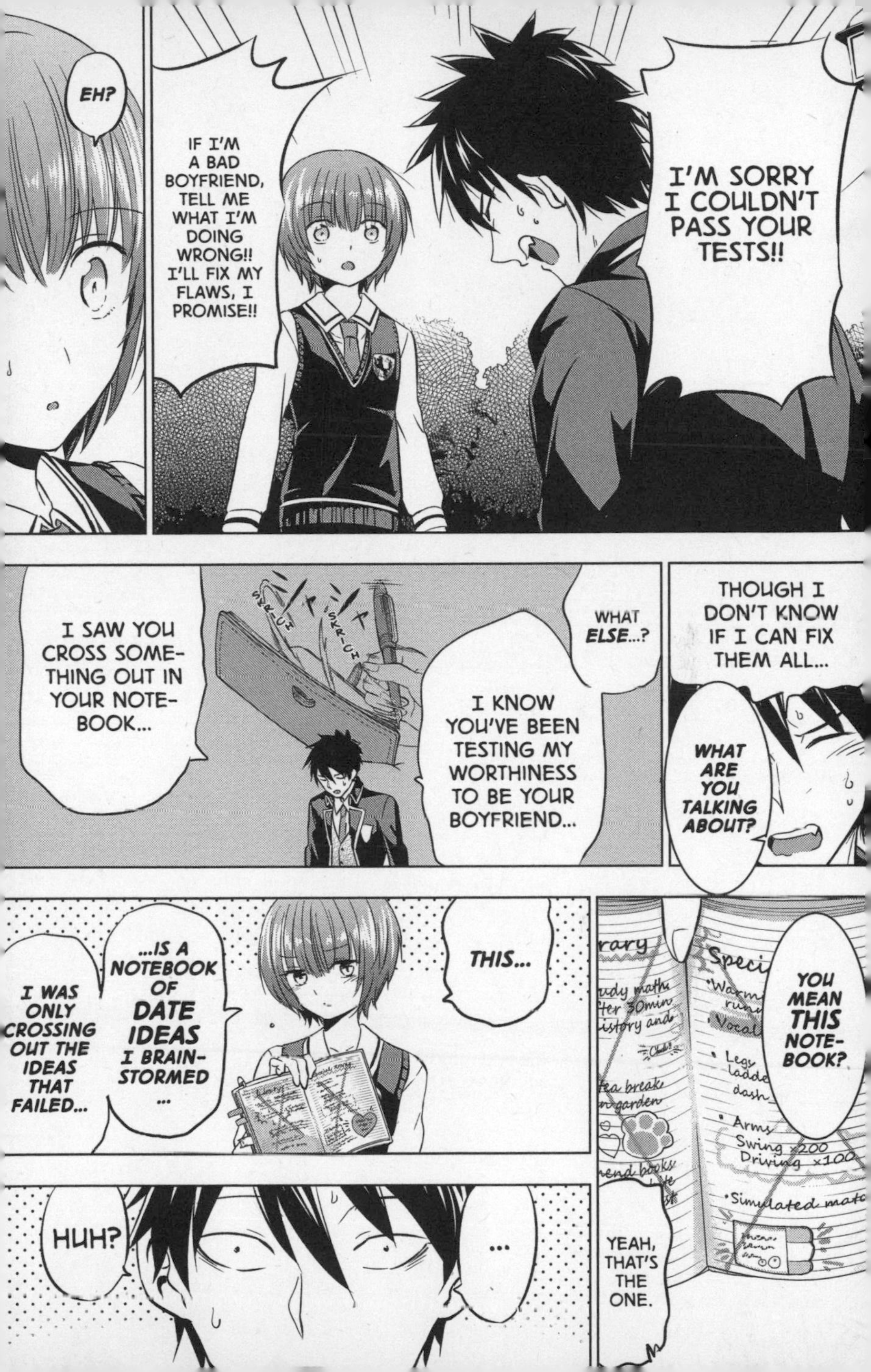
I'M SORRY I COULDN'T PASS YOUR TESTS!!
IF I'M A BAD BOYFRIEND, TELL ME WHAT I'M DOING WRONG!! I'LL FIX MY FLAWS, I PROMISE!!
EH?
THOUGH I DON'T KNOW IF I CAN FIX THEM ALL...
WHAT ARE YOU TALKING ABOUT?
WHAT ELSE...?
I KNOW YOU'VE BEEN TESTING MY WORTHINESS TO BE YOUR BOYFRIEND...
I SAW YOU CROSS SOME-THING OUT IN YOUR NOTE-BOOK...
YOU MEAN THIS NOTE-BOOK?
YEAH, THAT'S THE ONE.
THIS...
...IS A NOTEBOOK OF DATE IDEAS I BRAIN-STORMED ...
I WAS ONLY CROSSING OUT THE IDEAS THAT FAILED...
...
HUH?

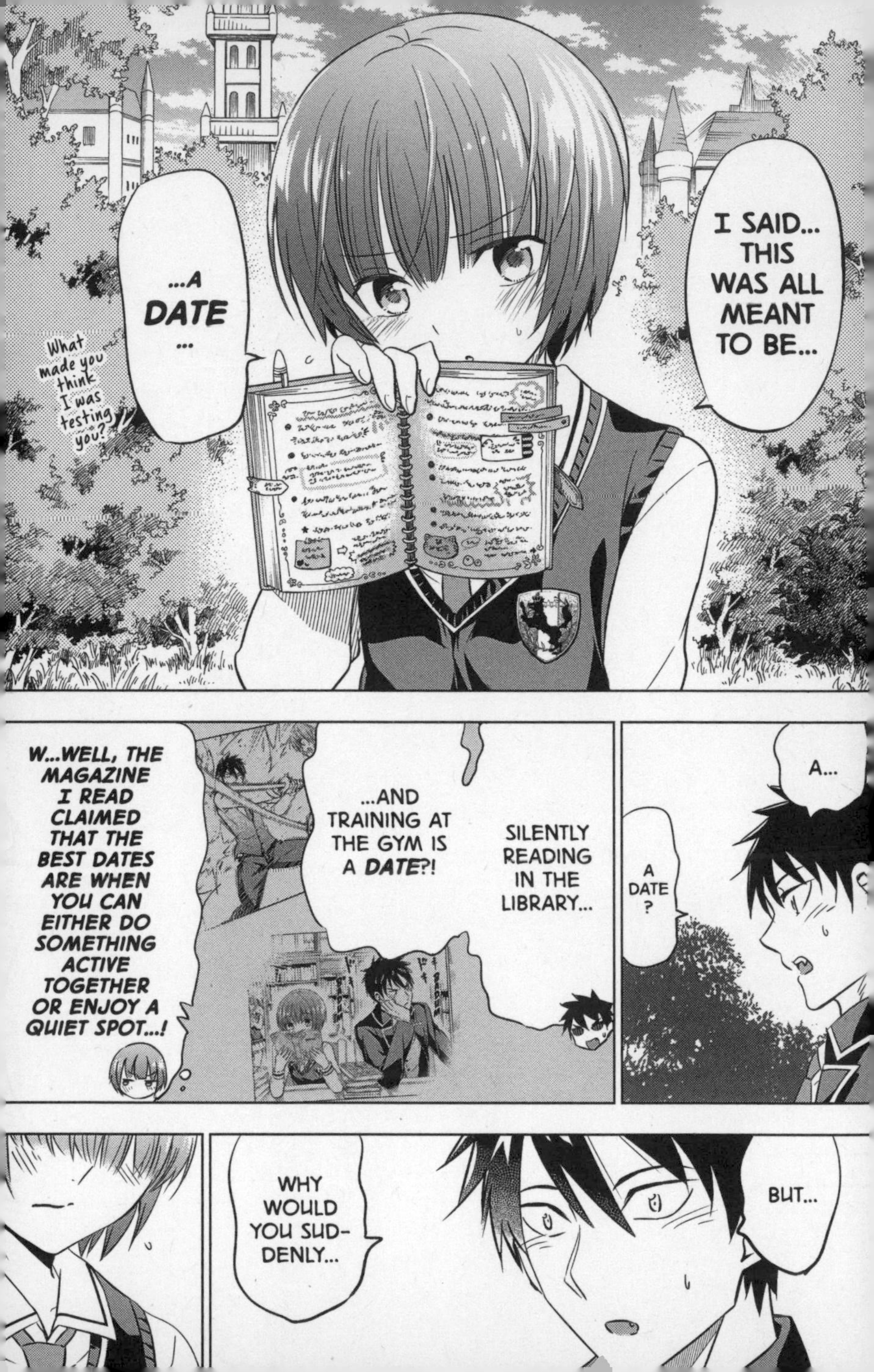
I SAID... THIS WAS ALL MEANT TO BE...
...A DATE ...
What made you think I was testing you?
A...
A DATE ?
SILENTLY READING IN THE LIBRARY...
...AND TRAINING AT THE GYM IS A DATE?!
W...WELL, THE MAGAZINE I READ CLAIMED THAT THE BEST DATES ARE WHEN YOU CAN EITHER DO SOMETHING ACTIVE TOGETHER OR ENJOY A QUIET SPOT...!
BUT...
WHY WOULD YOU SUD-DENLY...

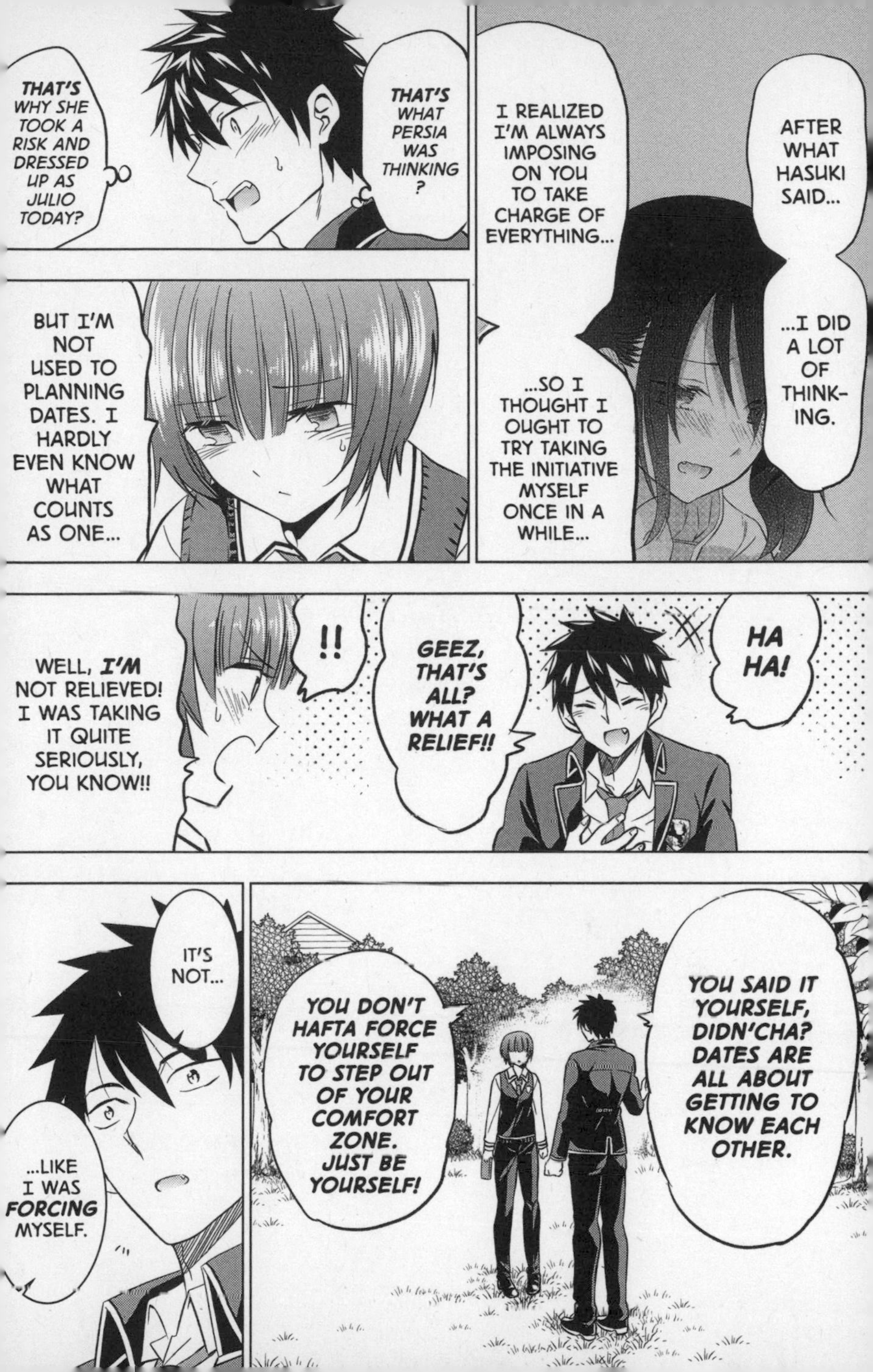
AFTER WHAT HASUKI SAID...
...I DID A LOT OF THINK-ING.
I REALIZED I'M ALWAYS IMPOSING ON YOU TO TAKE CHARGE OF EVERYTHING...
...SO I THOUGHT I OUGHT TO TRY TAKING THE INITIATIVE MYSELF ONCE IN A WHILE...
THAT'S WHAT PERSIA WAS THINKING?
THAT'S WHY SHE TOOK A RISK AND DRESSED UP AS JULIO TODAY?
BUT I'M NOT USED TO PLANNING DATES. I HARDLY EVEN KNOW WHAT COUNTS AS ONE...
HA HA!
GEEZ, THAT'S ALL? WHAT A RELIEF!!
!!
WELL, I'M NOT RELIEVED! I WAS TAKING IT QUITE SERIOUSLY, YOU KNOW!!
YOU SAID IT YOURSELF, DIDN'CHA? DATES ARE ALL ABOUT GETTING TO KNOW EACH OTHER.
YOU DON'T HAFTA FORCE YOURSELF TO STEP OUT OF YOUR COMFORT ZONE. JUST BE YOURSELF!
IT'S NOT...
...LIKE I WAS FORCING MYSELF.

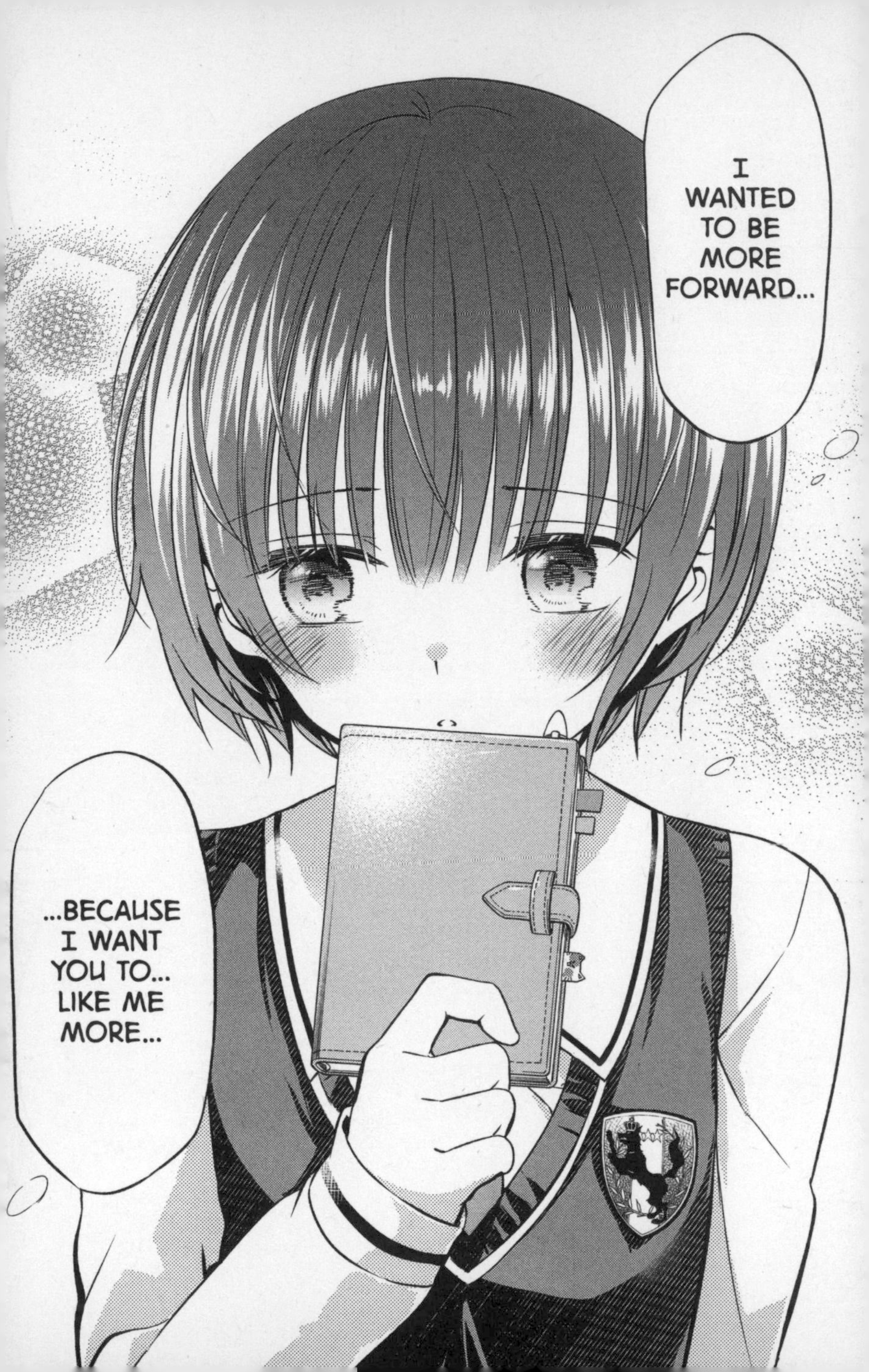
I WANTED TO BE MORE FORWARD...
...BECAUSE I WANT YOU TO... LIKE ME MORE...

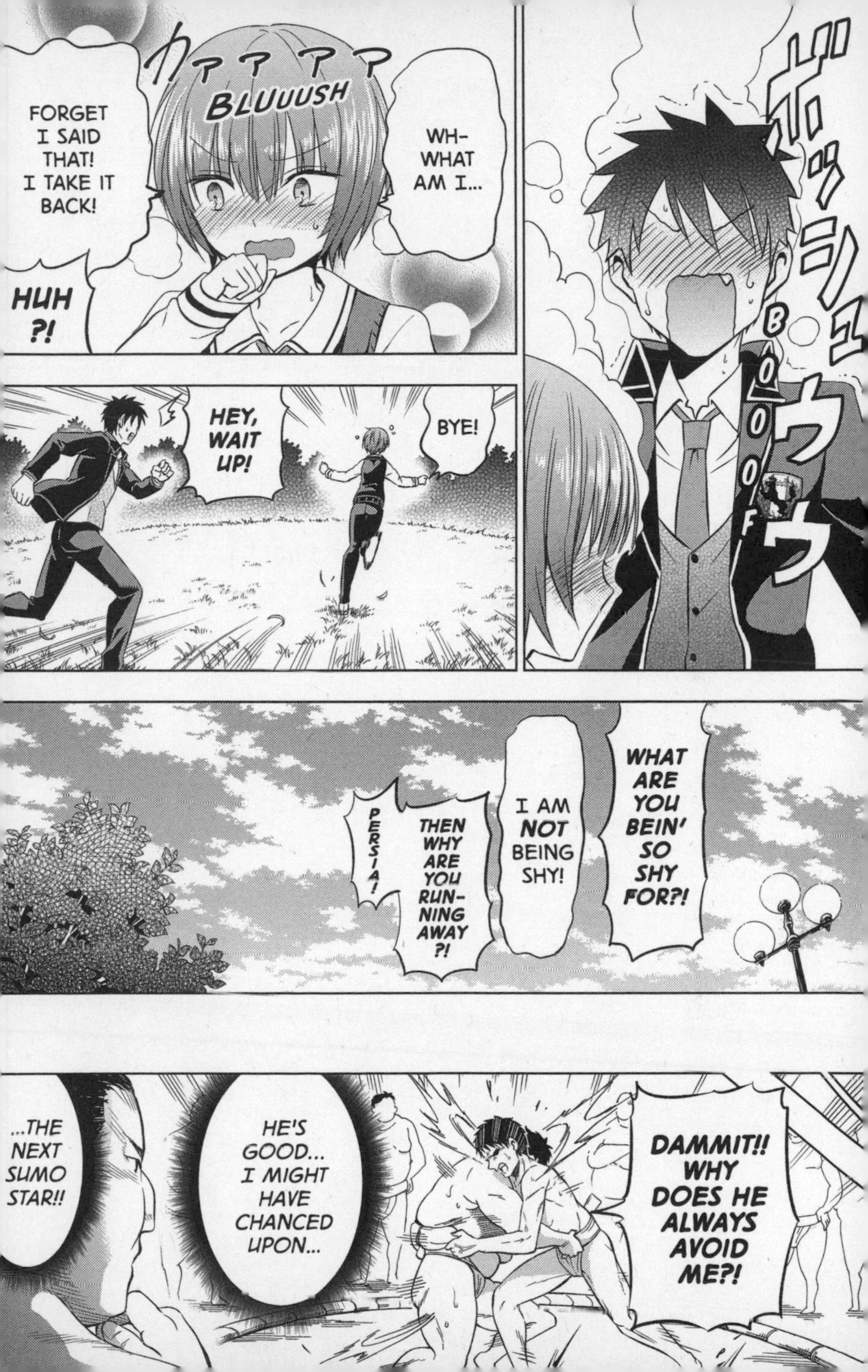
ボッシュウウ
BOOOF
WH-WHAT AM I...
カァァァァ
BLUUUSH
FORGET I SAID THAT! I TAKE IT BACK!
HUH?!
BYE!
HEY, WAIT UP!
WHAT ARE YOU BEIN' SO SHY FOR?!
I AM NOT BEING SHY!
THEN WHY ARE YOU RUNNING AWAY?!
PERSIA!
DAMMIT!! WHY DOES HE ALWAYS AVOID ME?!
HE'S GOOD... I MIGHT HAVE CHANCED UPON...
...THE NEXT SUMO STAR!!

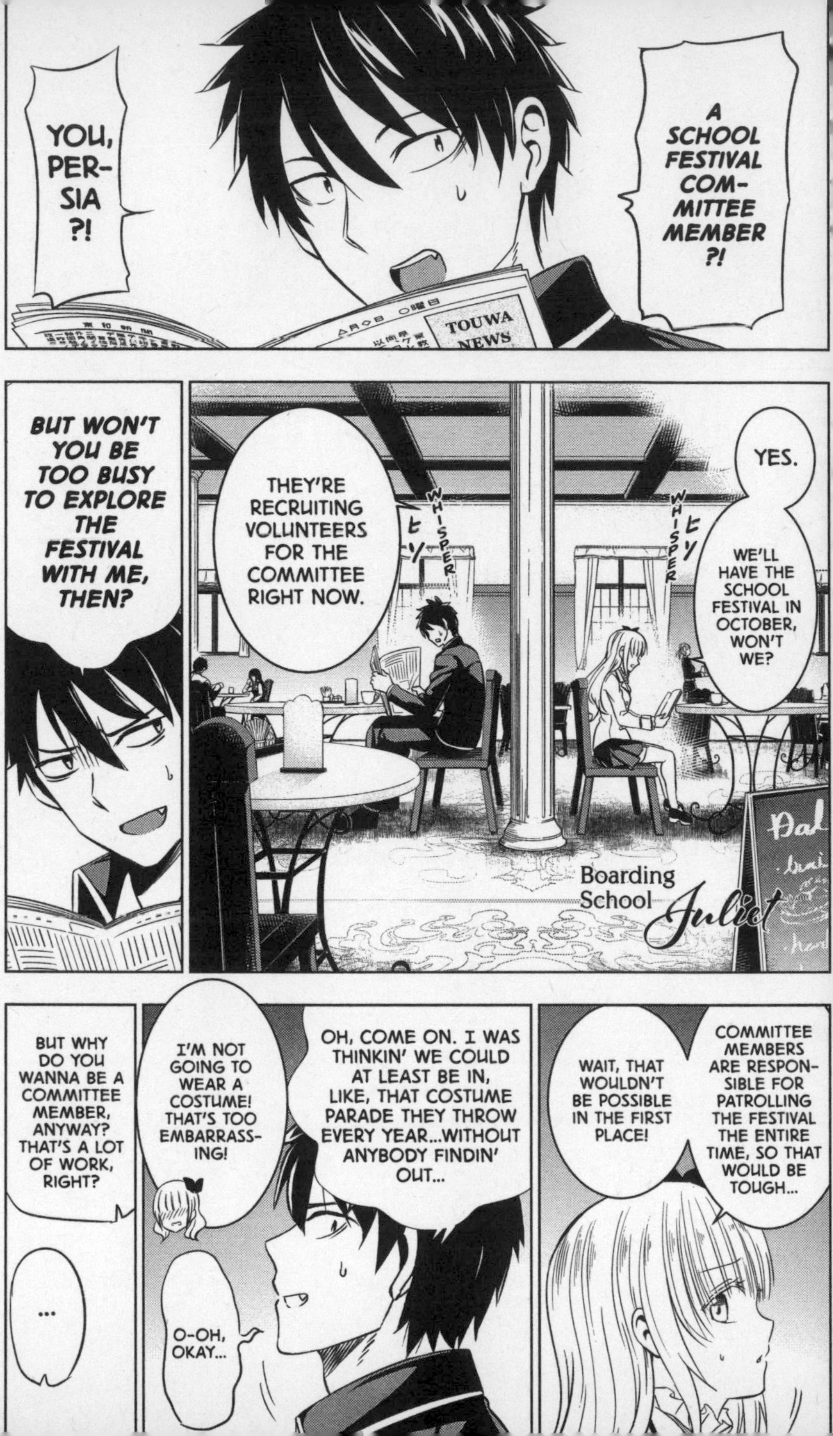
A SCHOOL FESTIVAL COMMITTEE MEMBER?!
YOU, PERSIA?!
TOUWA NEWS
YES.
WE'LL HAVE THE SCHOOL FESTIVAL IN OCTOBER, WON'T WE?
WHISPER
THEY'RE RECRUITING VOLUNTEERS FOR THE COMMITTEE RIGHT NOW.
WHISPER
Boarding School Juliet
BUT WON'T YOU BE TOO BUSY TO EXPLORE THE FESTIVAL WITH ME, THEN?
COMMITTEE MEMBERS ARE RESPONSIBLE FOR PATROLLING THE FESTIVAL THE ENTIRE TIME, SO THAT WOULD BE TOUGH...
WAIT, THAT WOULDN'T BE POSSIBLE IN THE FIRST PLACE!
OH, COME ON. I WAS THINKIN' WE COULD AT LEAST BE IN, LIKE, THAT COSTUME PARADE THEY THROW EVERY YEAR...WITHOUT ANYBODY FINDIN' OUT...
I'M NOT GOING TO WEAR A COSTUME! THAT'S TOO EMBARRASSING!
O-OH, OKAY...
BUT WHY DO YOU WANNA BE A COMMITTEE MEMBER, ANYWAY? THAT'S A LOT OF WORK, RIGHT?
...

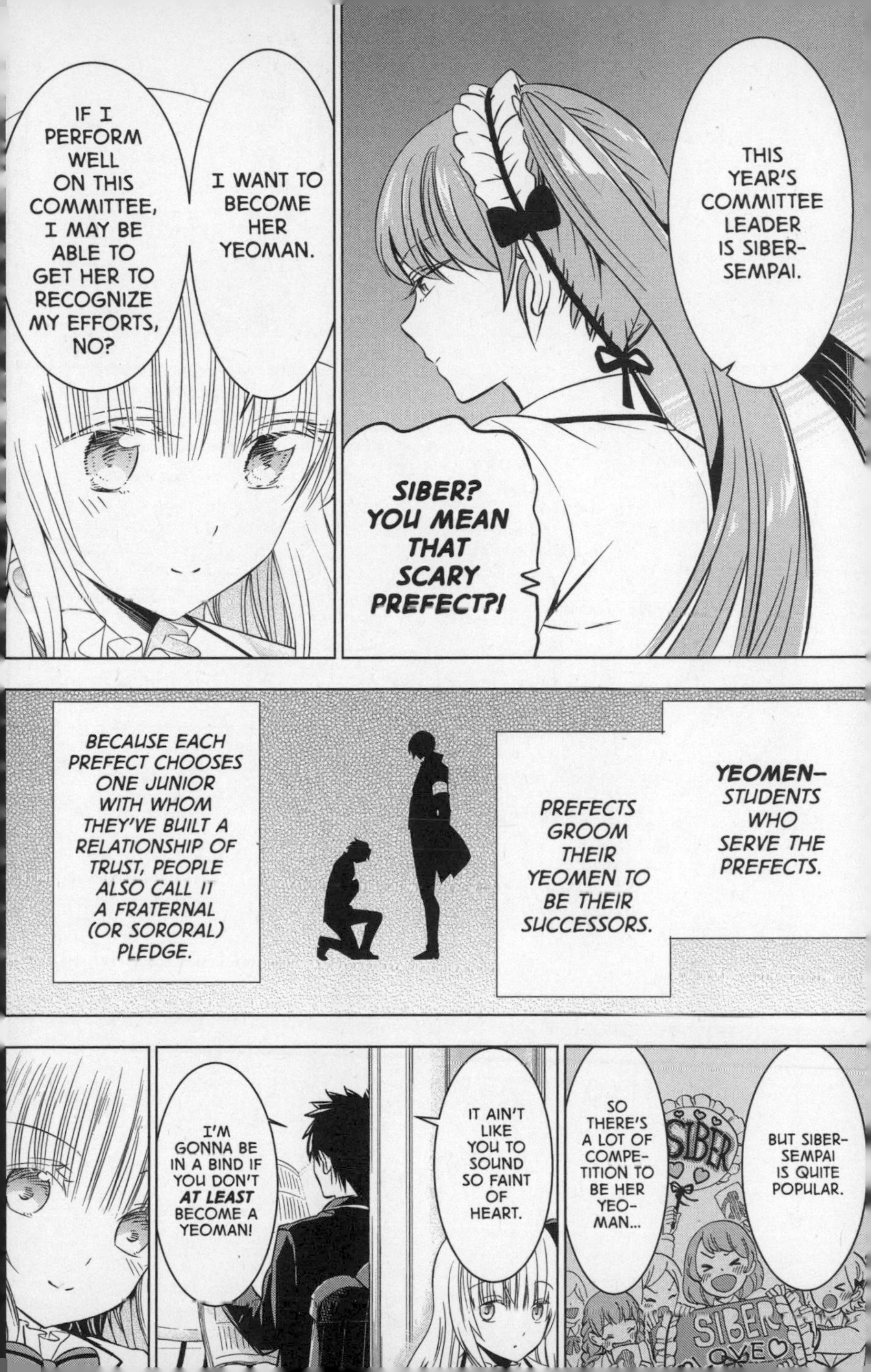
THIS YEAR'S COMMITTEE LEADER IS SIBER-SEMPAI.
SIBER? YOU MEAN THAT SCARY PREFECT?!
I WANT TO BECOME HER YEOMAN.
IF I PERFORM WELL ON THIS COMMITTEE, I MAY BE ABLE TO GET HER TO RECOGNIZE MY EFFORTS, NO?
YEOMEN—STUDENTS WHO SERVE THE PREFECTS.
PREFECTS GROOM THEIR YEOMEN TO BE THEIR SUCCESSORS.
BECAUSE EACH PREFECT CHOOSES ONE JUNIOR WITH WHOM THEY'VE BUILT A RELATIONSHIP OF TRUST, PEOPLE ALSO CALL IT A FRATERNAL (OR SORORAL) PLEDGE.
BUT SIBER-SEMPAI IS QUITE POPULAR.
SIBER
SIBER
SO THERE'S A LOT OF COMPETITION TO BE HER YEOMAN...
IT AIN'T LIKE YOU TO SOUND SO FAINT OF HEART.
I'M GONNA BE IN A BIND IF YOU DON'T **AT LEAST** BECOME A YEOMAN!

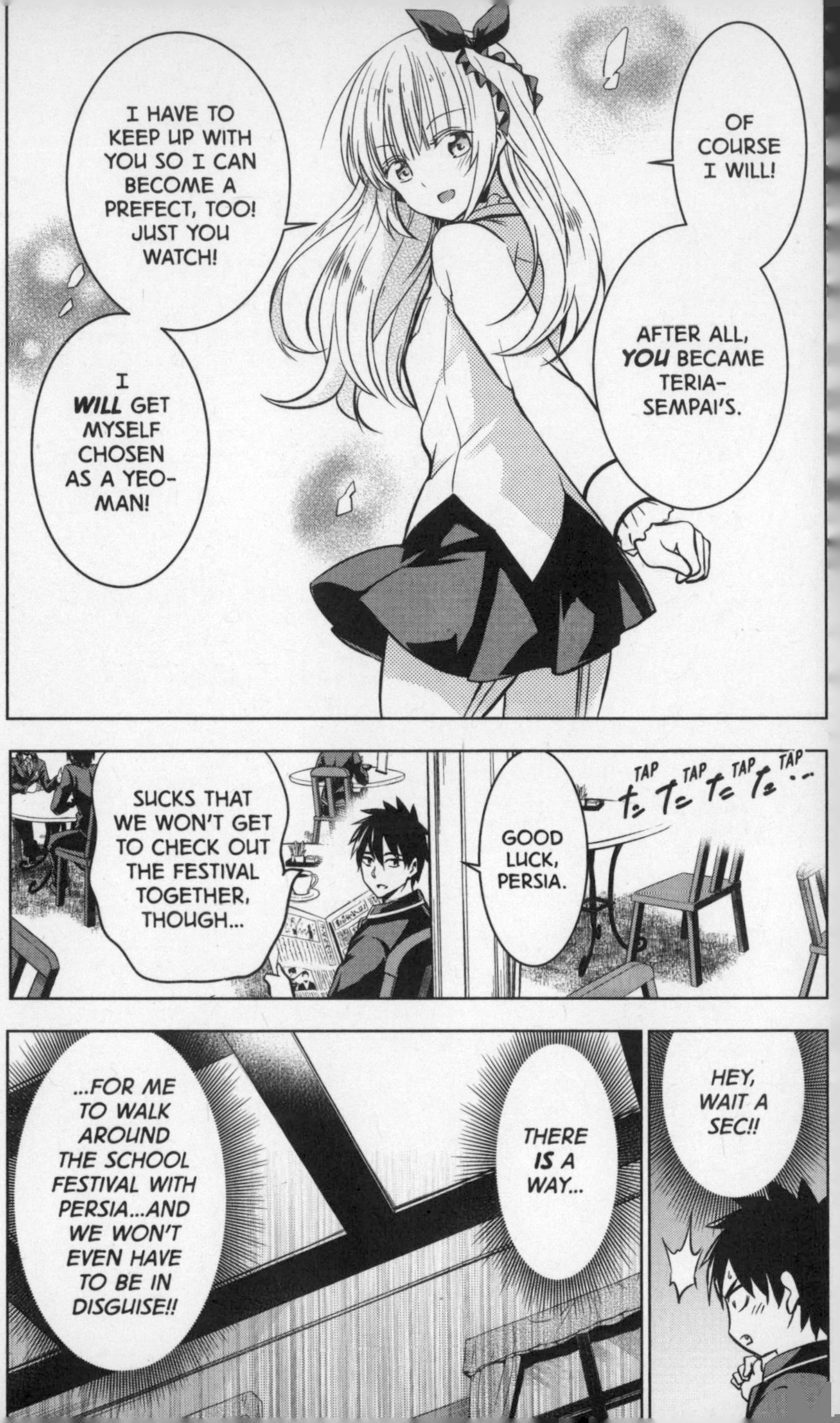
OF COURSE I WILL!
AFTER ALL, YOU BECAME TERIA-SEMPAI'S.
I HAVE TO KEEP UP WITH YOU SO I CAN BECOME A PREFECT, TOO! JUST YOU WATCH!
I WILL GET MYSELF CHOSEN AS A YEO-MAN!
TAP TAP TAP TAP
GOOD LUCK, PERSIA.
SUCKS THAT WE WON'T GET TO CHECK OUT THE FESTIVAL TOGETHER, THOUGH...
HEY, WAIT A SEC!!
THERE IS A WAY...
...FOR ME TO WALK AROUND THE SCHOOL FESTIVAL WITH PERSIA...AND WE WON'T EVEN HAVE TO BE IN DISGUISE!!

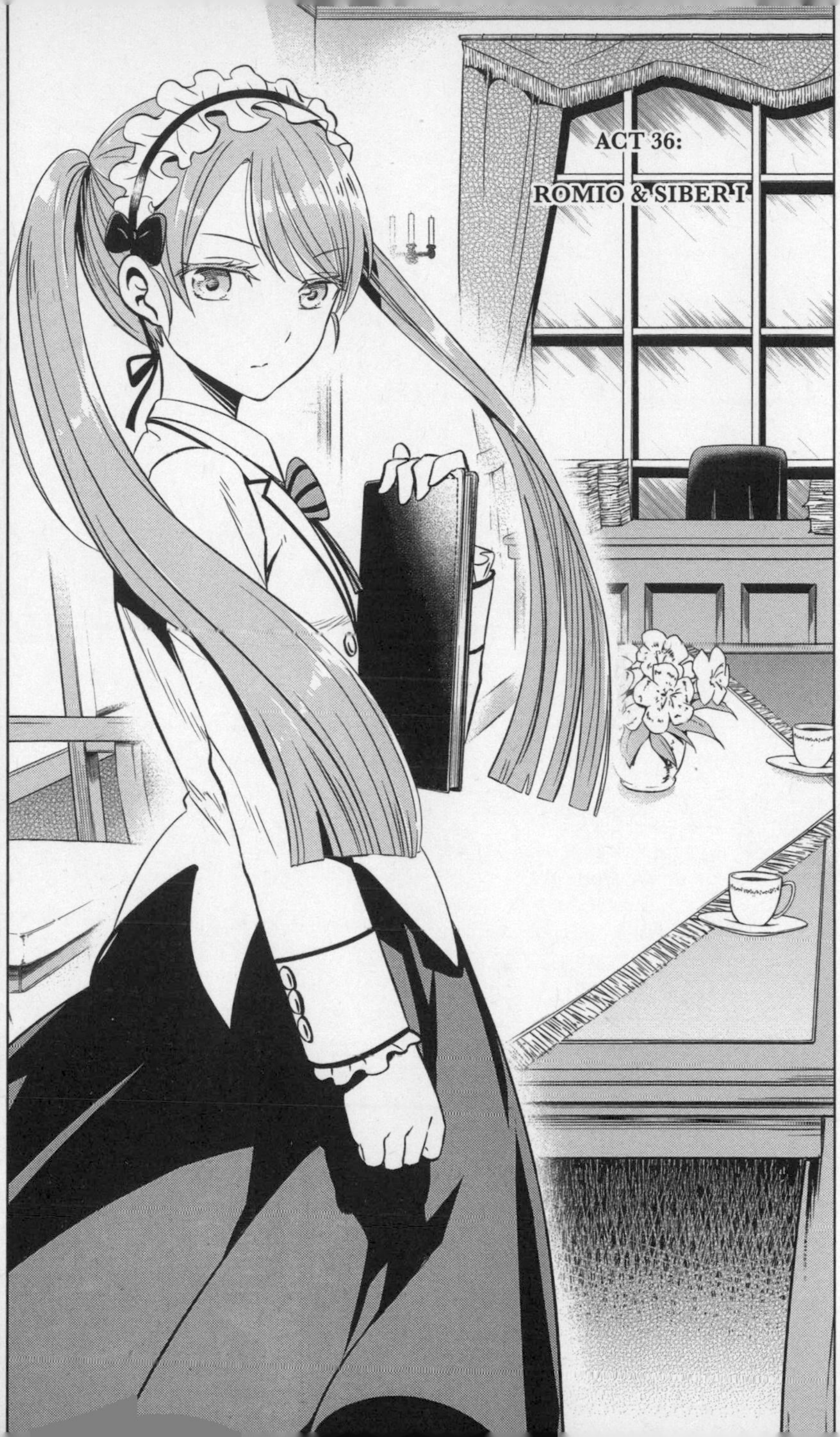
ACT 36:
ROMIO & SIBER I

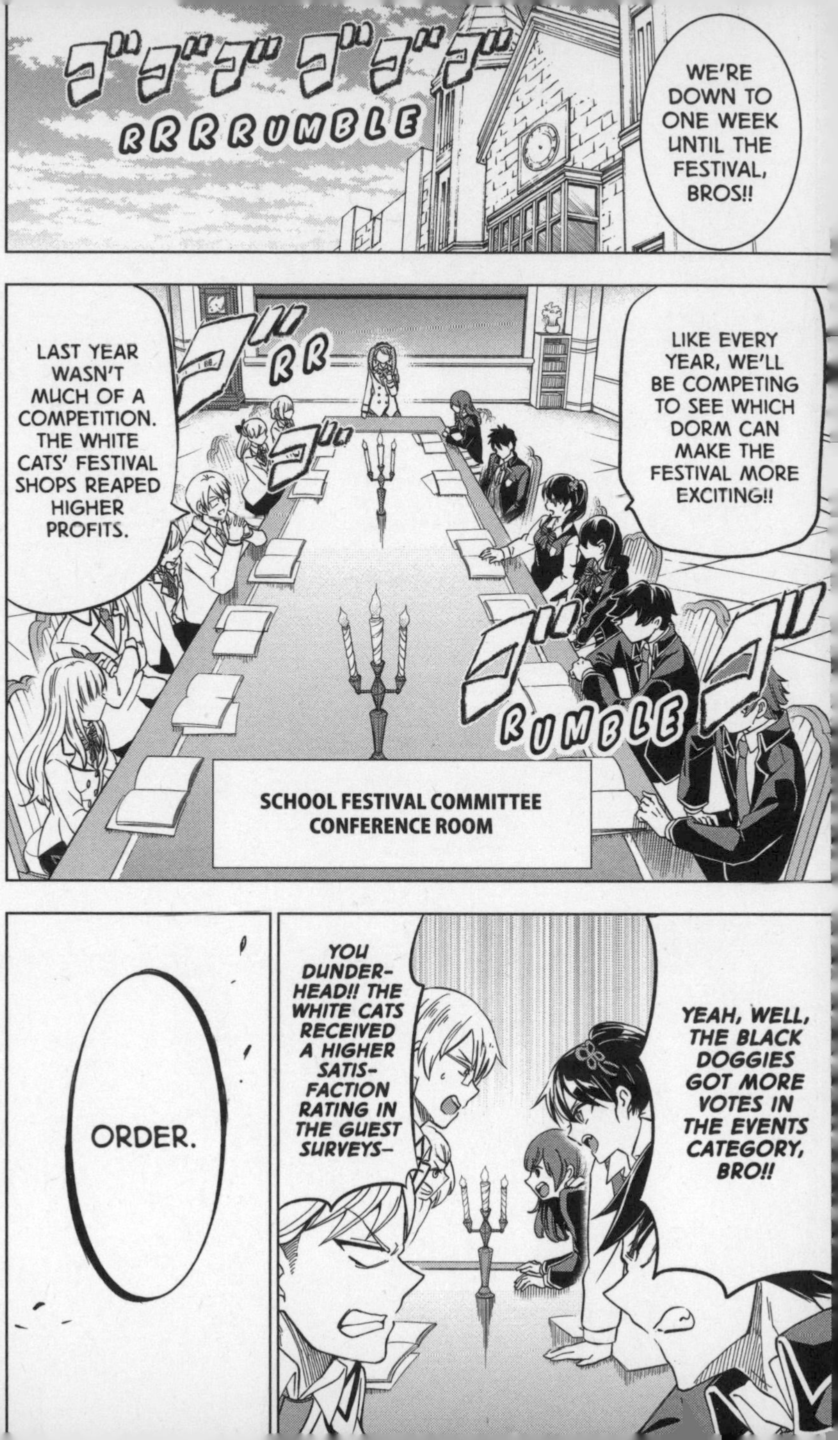
WE'RE DOWN TO ONE WEEK UNTIL THE FESTIVAL, BROS!!
ゴゴゴゴゴゴ
RRRRUMBLE
LIKE EVERY YEAR, WE'LL BE COMPETING TO SEE WHICH DORM CAN MAKE THE FESTIVAL MORE EXCITING!!
LAST YEAR WASN'T MUCH OF A COMPETITION. THE WHITE CATS' FESTIVAL SHOPS REAPED HIGHER PROFITS.
RR
RUMBLE
SCHOOL FESTIVAL COMMITTEE CONFERENCE ROOM
YEAH, WELL, THE BLACK DOGGIES GOT MORE VOTES IN THE EVENTS CATEGORY, BRO!!
YOU DUNDER-HEAD!! THE WHITE CATS RECEIVED A HIGHER SATIS-FACTION RATING IN THE GUEST SURVEYS–
ORDER.

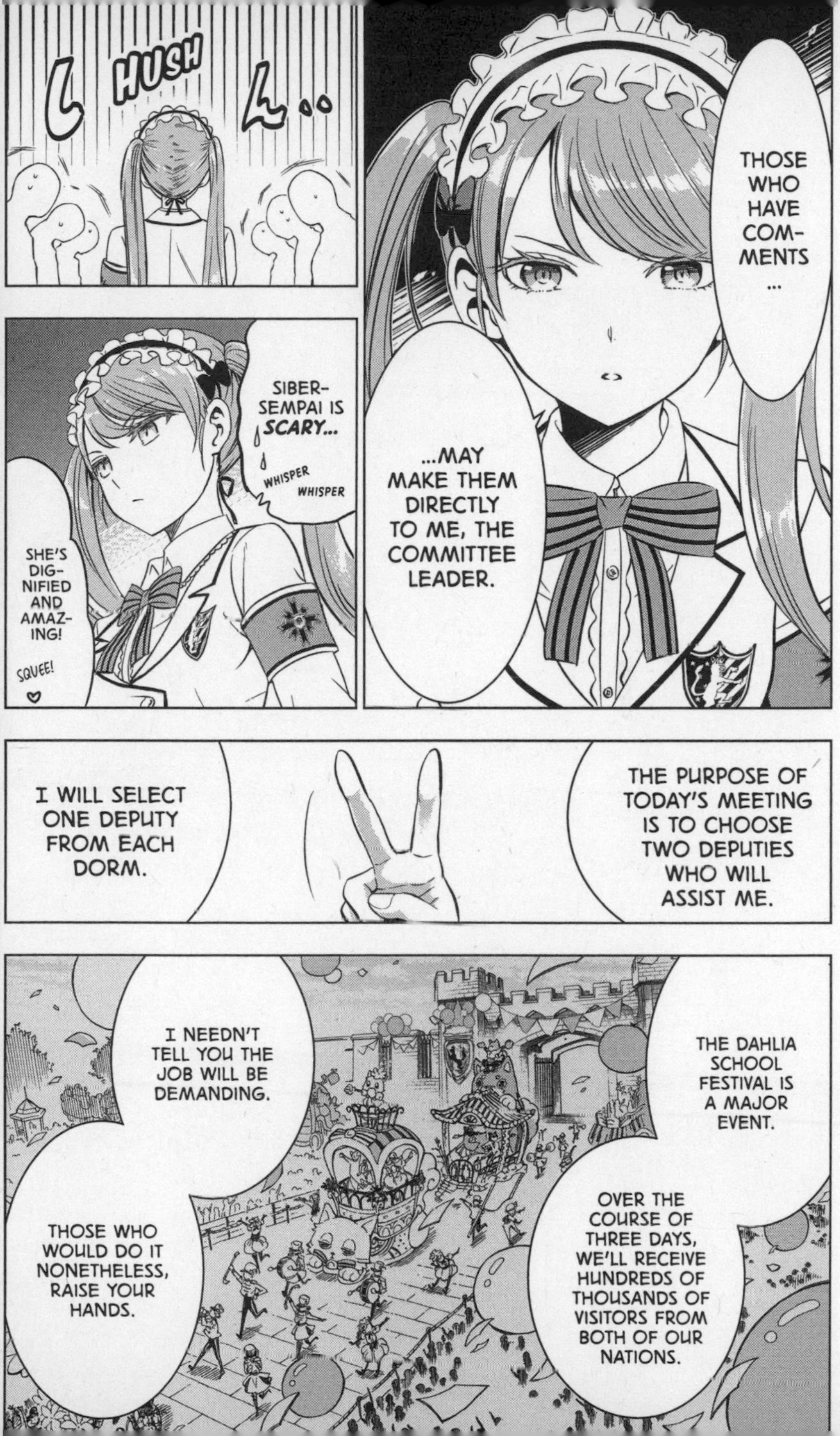
THOSE WHO HAVE COMMENTS ...
...MAY MAKE THEM DIRECTLY TO ME, THE COMMITTEE LEADER.
HUSH
SIBER-SEMPAI IS SCARY...
WHISPER WHISPER
SHE'S DIGNIFIED AND AMAZING!
SQUEE!
THE PURPOSE OF TODAY'S MEETING IS TO CHOOSE TWO DEPUTIES WHO WILL ASSIST ME.
I WILL SELECT ONE DEPUTY FROM EACH DORM.
THE DAHLIA SCHOOL FESTIVAL IS A MAJOR EVENT.
OVER THE COURSE OF THREE DAYS, WE'LL RECEIVE HUNDREDS OF THOUSANDS OF VISITORS FROM BOTH OF OUR NATIONS.
I NEEDN'T TELL YOU THE JOB WILL BE DEMANDING.
THOSE WHO WOULD DO IT NONETHELESS, RAISE YOUR HANDS.

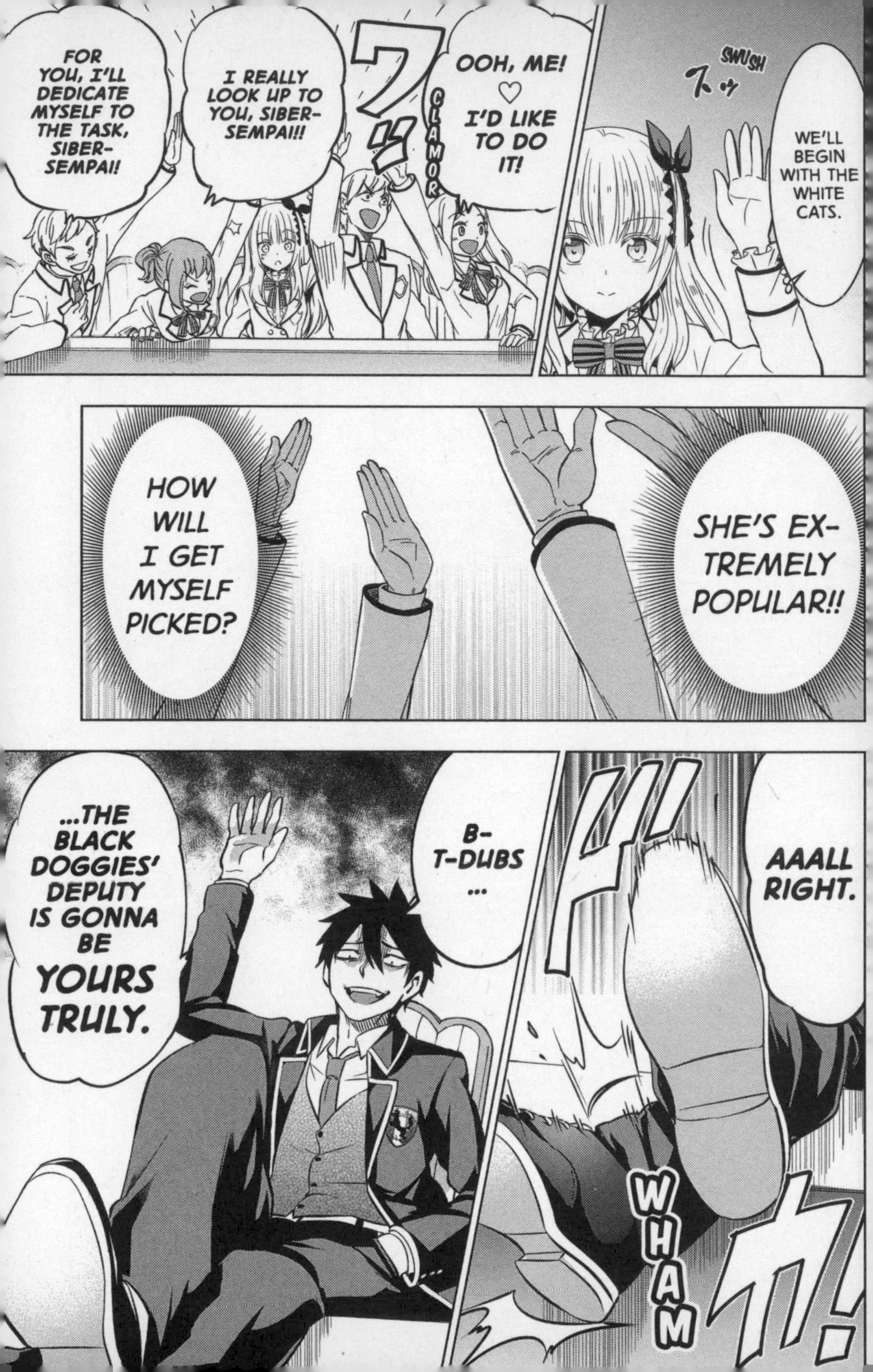
SWUSH
WE'LL BEGIN WITH THE WHITE CATS.
OOH, ME! ♡ I'D LIKE TO DO IT!
CLAMOR
I REALLY LOOK UP TO YOU, SIBER-SEMPAI!!
FOR YOU, I'LL DEDICATE MYSELF TO THE TASK, SIBER-SEMPAI!
SHE'S EX-TREMELY POPULAR!!
HOW WILL I GET MYSELF PICKED?
AAALL RIGHT.
WHAM
B-T-DUBS...
...THE BLACK DOGGIES' DEPUTY IS GONNA BE YOURS TRULY.

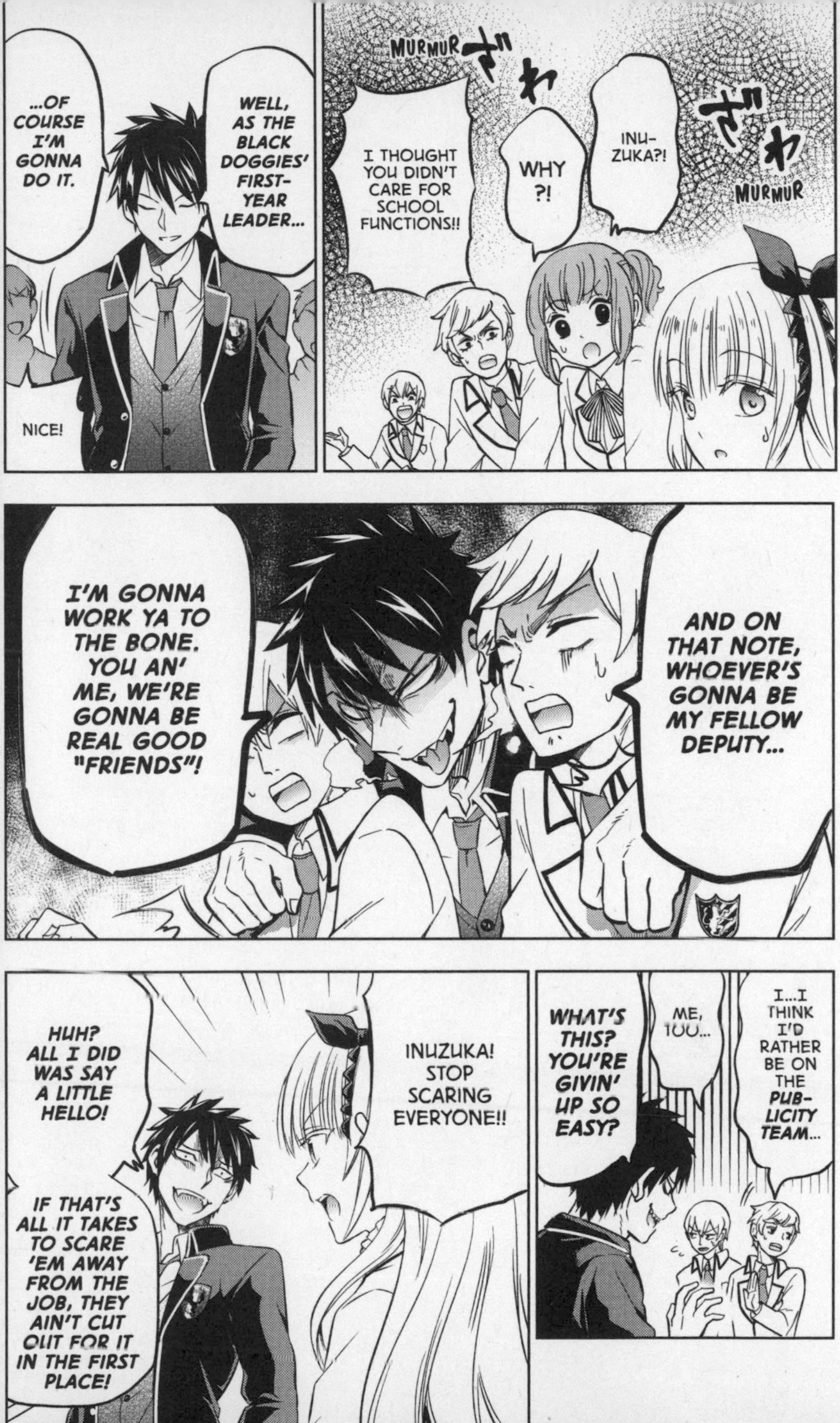
ざわ
MURMUR
MURMUR
ざわ
INU-ZUKA?!
WHY?!
I THOUGHT YOU DIDN'T CARE FOR SCHOOL FUNCTIONS!!
WELL, AS THE BLACK DOGGIES' FIRST-YEAR LEADER...
...OF COURSE I'M GONNA DO IT.
NICE!
AND ON THAT NOTE, WHOEVER'S GONNA BE MY FELLOW DEPUTY...
I'M GONNA WORK YA TO THE BONE. YOU AN' ME, WE'RE GONNA BE REAL GOOD "FRIENDS"!
I...I THINK I'D RATHER BE ON THE PUBLICITY TEAM...
ME, TOO...
WHAT'S THIS? YOU'RE GIVIN' UP SO EASY?
INUZUKA! STOP SCARING EVERYONE!!
HUH? ALL I DID WAS SAY A LITTLE HELLO!
IF THAT'S ALL IT TAKES TO SCARE 'EM AWAY FROM THE JOB, THEY AIN'T CUT OUT FOR IT IN THE FIRST PLACE!

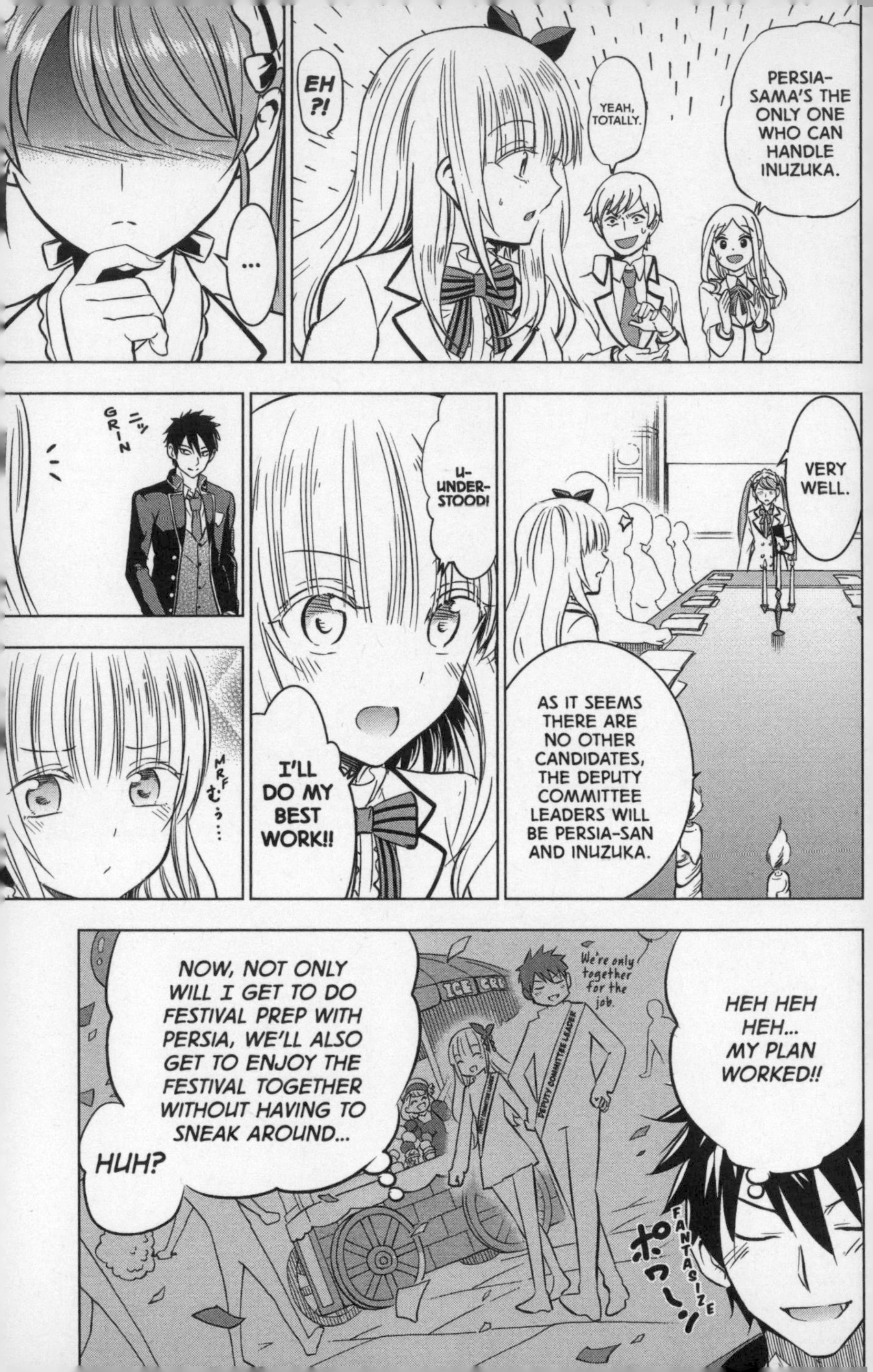
PERSIA-SAMA'S THE ONLY ONE WHO CAN HANDLE INUZUKA.
YEAH, TOTALLY.
EH?!
...
VERY WELL.
AS IT SEEMS THERE ARE NO OTHER CANDIDATES, THE DEPUTY COMMITTEE LEADERS WILL BE PERSIA-SAN AND INUZUKA.
U-UNDERSTOOD!
I'LL DO MY BEST WORK!!
GRIN ニッ
MRF むぅ…
HEH HEH HEH... MY PLAN WORKED!!
We're only together for the job.
DEPUTY COMMITTEE LEADER
NOW, NOT ONLY WILL I GET TO DO FESTIVAL PREP WITH PERSIA, WE'LL ALSO GET TO ENJOY THE FESTIVAL TOGETHER WITHOUT HAVING TO SNEAK AROUND...
HUH?
FANTASIZE ポワ～ン

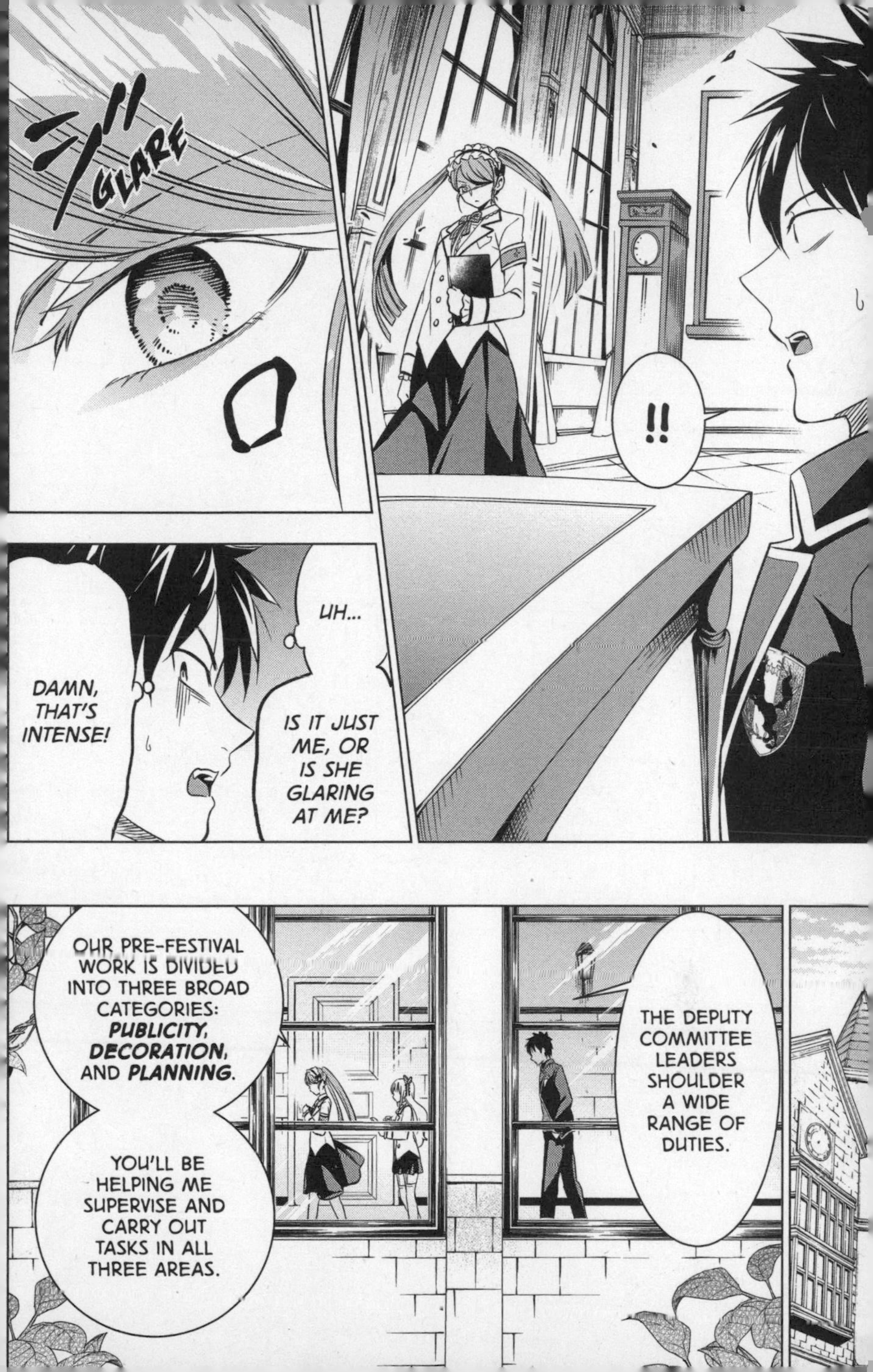
!!
GLARE
UH...
IS IT JUST ME, OR IS SHE GLARING AT ME?
DAMN, THAT'S INTENSE!
THE DEPUTY COMMITTEE LEADERS SHOULDER A WIDE RANGE OF DUTIES.
OUR PRE-FESTIVAL WORK IS DIVIDED INTO THREE BROAD CATEGORIES: **PUBLICITY**, **DECORATION**, AND **PLANNING**.
YOU'LL BE HELPING ME SUPERVISE AND CARRY OUT TASKS IN ALL THREE AREAS.

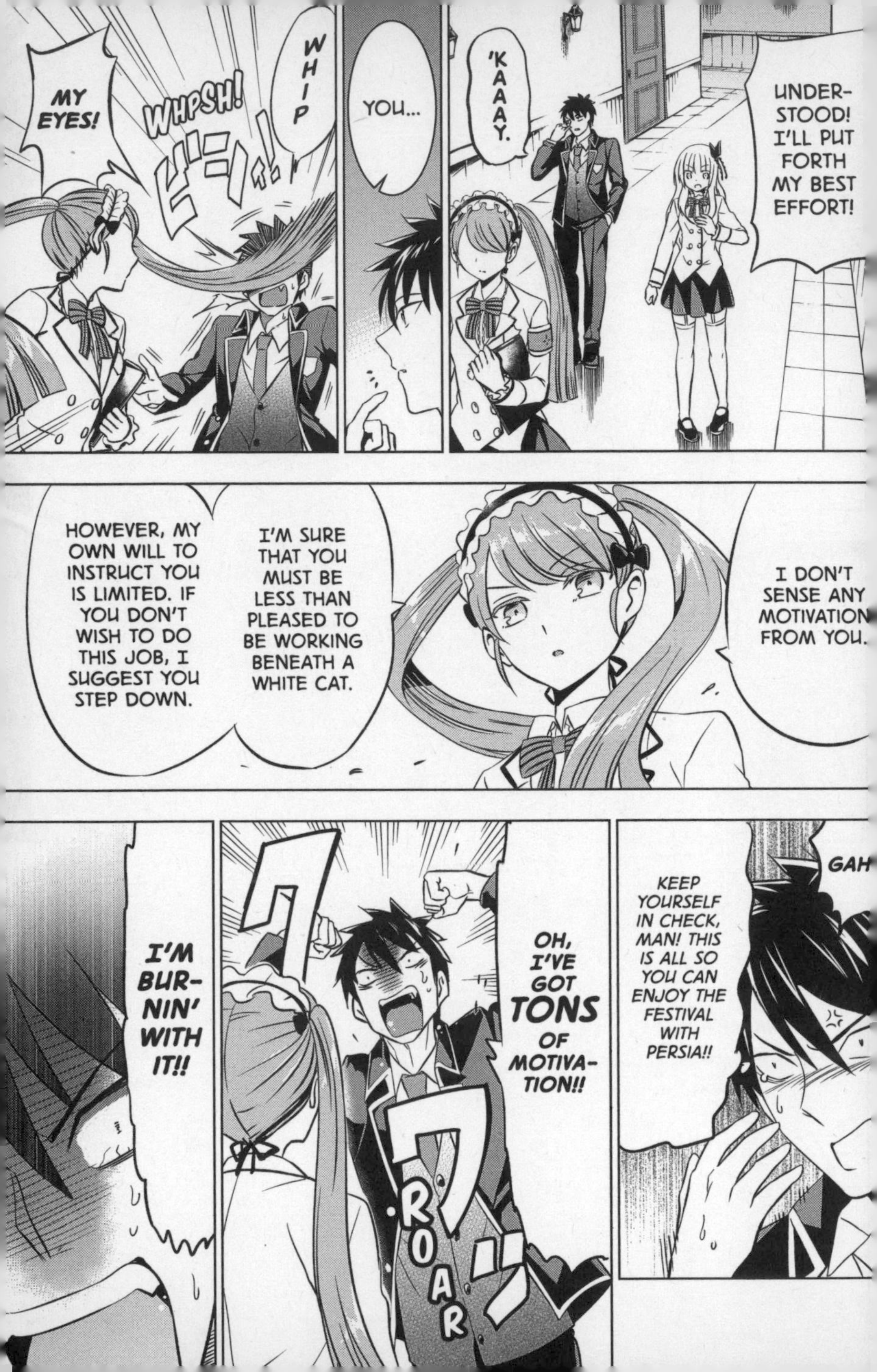
UNDER-STOOD! I'LL PUT FORTH MY BEST EFFORT!
'KAAAAY.
YOU...
WHIP
MY EYES!
WHPSH!
I DON'T SENSE ANY MOTIVATION FROM YOU.
I'M SURE THAT YOU MUST BE LESS THAN PLEASED TO BE WORKING BENEATH A WHITE CAT.
HOWEVER, MY OWN WILL TO INSTRUCT YOU IS LIMITED. IF YOU DON'T WISH TO DO THIS JOB, I SUGGEST YOU STEP DOWN.
GAH
KEEP YOURSELF IN CHECK, MAN! THIS IS ALL SO YOU CAN ENJOY THE FESTIVAL WITH PERSIA!!
OH, I'VE GOT TONS OF MOTIVATION!!
ROAR
I'M BURNIN' WITH IT!!

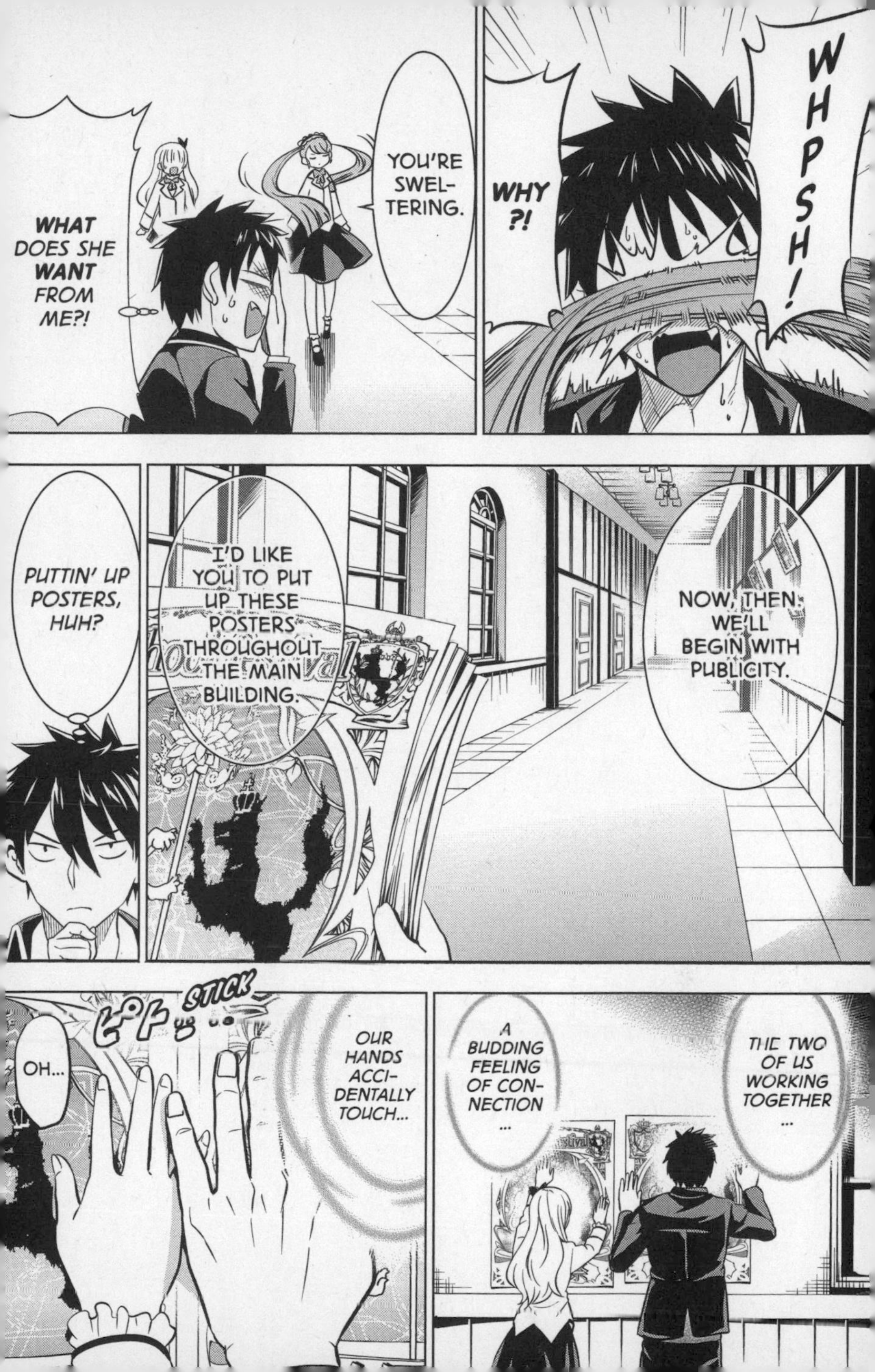
WHPSH!
WHY ?!
YOU'RE SWEL- TERING.
WHAT DOES SHE WANT FROM ME?!
NOW, THEN. WE'LL BEGIN WITH PUBLICITY.
I'D LIKE YOU TO PUT UP THESE POSTERS THROUGHOUT THE MAIN BUILDING.
PUTTIN' UP POSTERS, HUH?
THE TWO OF US WORKING TOGETHER ...
A BUDDING FEELING OF CON- NECTION ...
OUR HANDS ACCI- DENTALLY TOUCH...
STICK
OH...

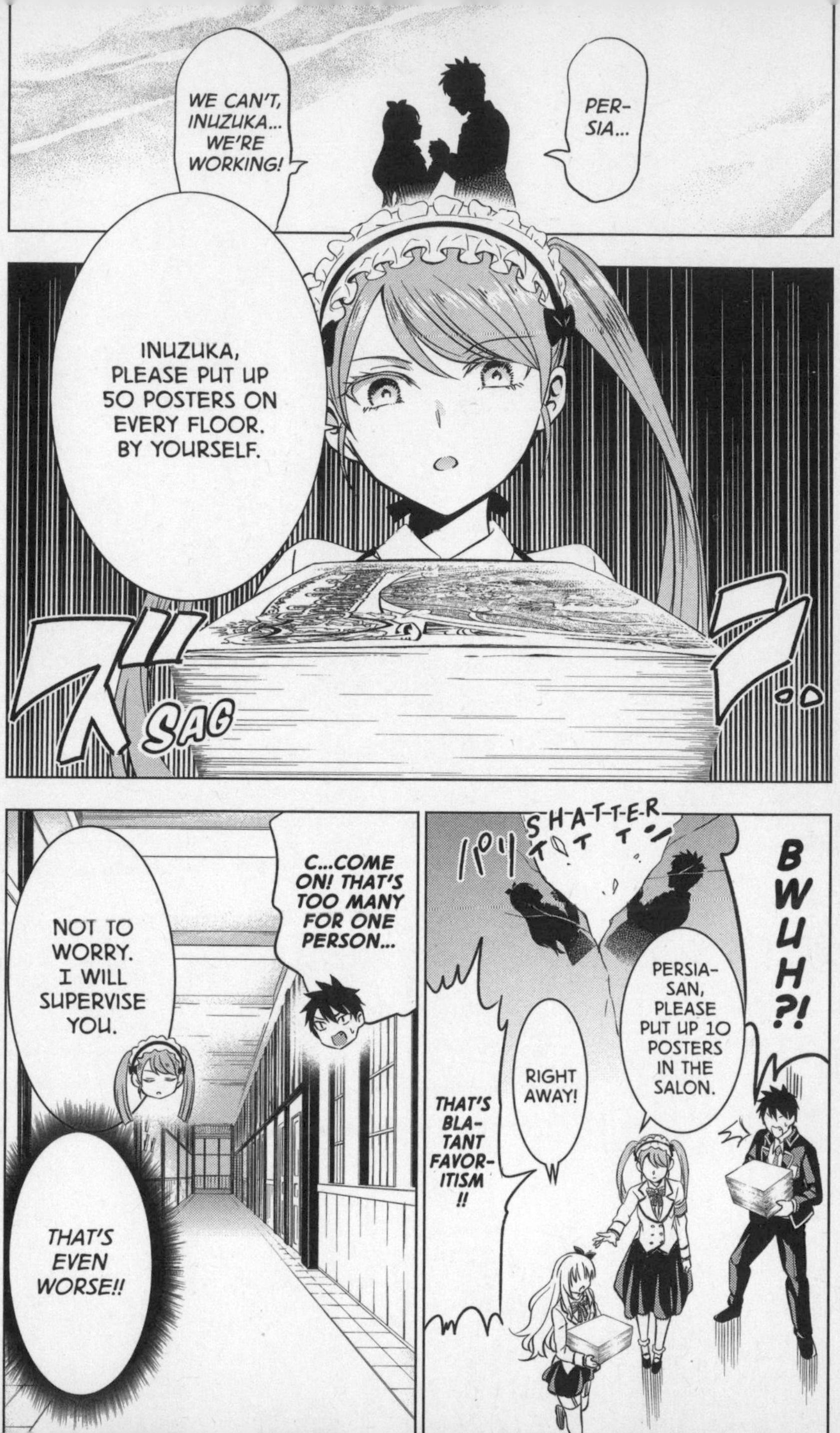
PER-SIA...
WE CAN'T, INUZUKA... WE'RE WORKING!
INUZUKA, PLEASE PUT UP 50 POSTERS ON EVERY FLOOR. BY YOURSELF.
SAG
SHATTER
BWUH?!
PERSIA-SAN, PLEASE PUT UP 10 POSTERS IN THE SALON.
RIGHT AWAY!
THAT'S BLATANT FAVORITISM!!
C...COME ON! THAT'S TOO MANY FOR ONE PERSON...
NOT TO WORRY. I WILL SUPERVISE YOU.
THAT'S EVEN WORSE!!

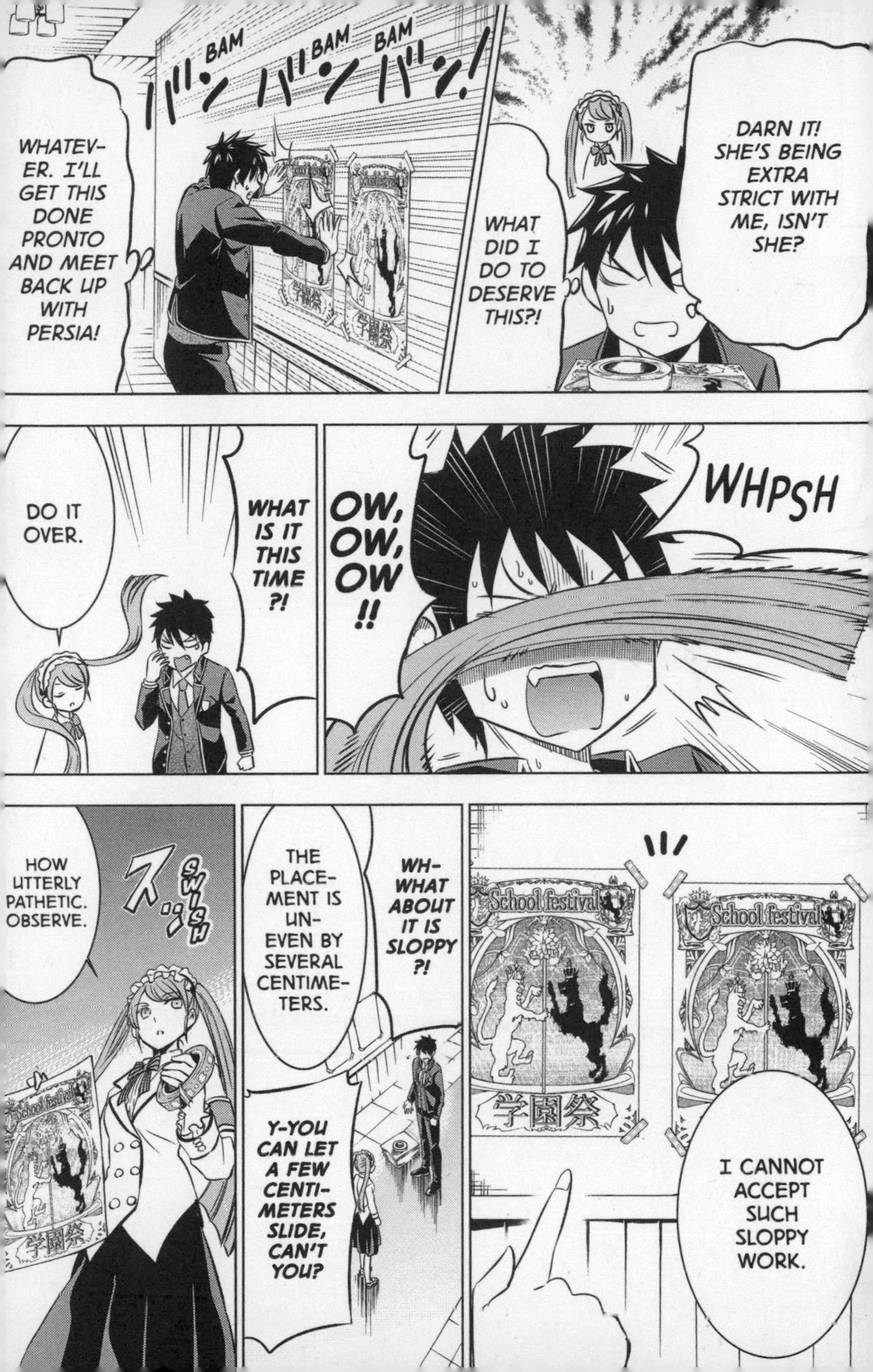
DARN IT! SHE'S BEING EXTRA STRICT WITH ME, ISN'T SHE?
WHAT DID I DO TO DESERVE THIS?!
BAM BAM BAM
WHATEVER. I'LL GET THIS DONE PRONTO AND MEET BACK UP WITH PERSIA!
WHPSH
OW, OW, OW!!
WHAT IS IT THIS TIME?!
DO IT OVER.
School festival
学園祭
School festival
学園祭
I CANNOT ACCEPT SUCH SLOPPY WORK.
WH-WHAT ABOUT IT IS SLOPPY?!
THE PLACEMENT IS UNEVEN BY SEVERAL CENTIMETERS.
Y-YOU CAN LET A FEW CENTIMETERS SLIDE, CAN'T YOU?
SWISH
HOW UTTERLY PATHETIC. OBSERVE.

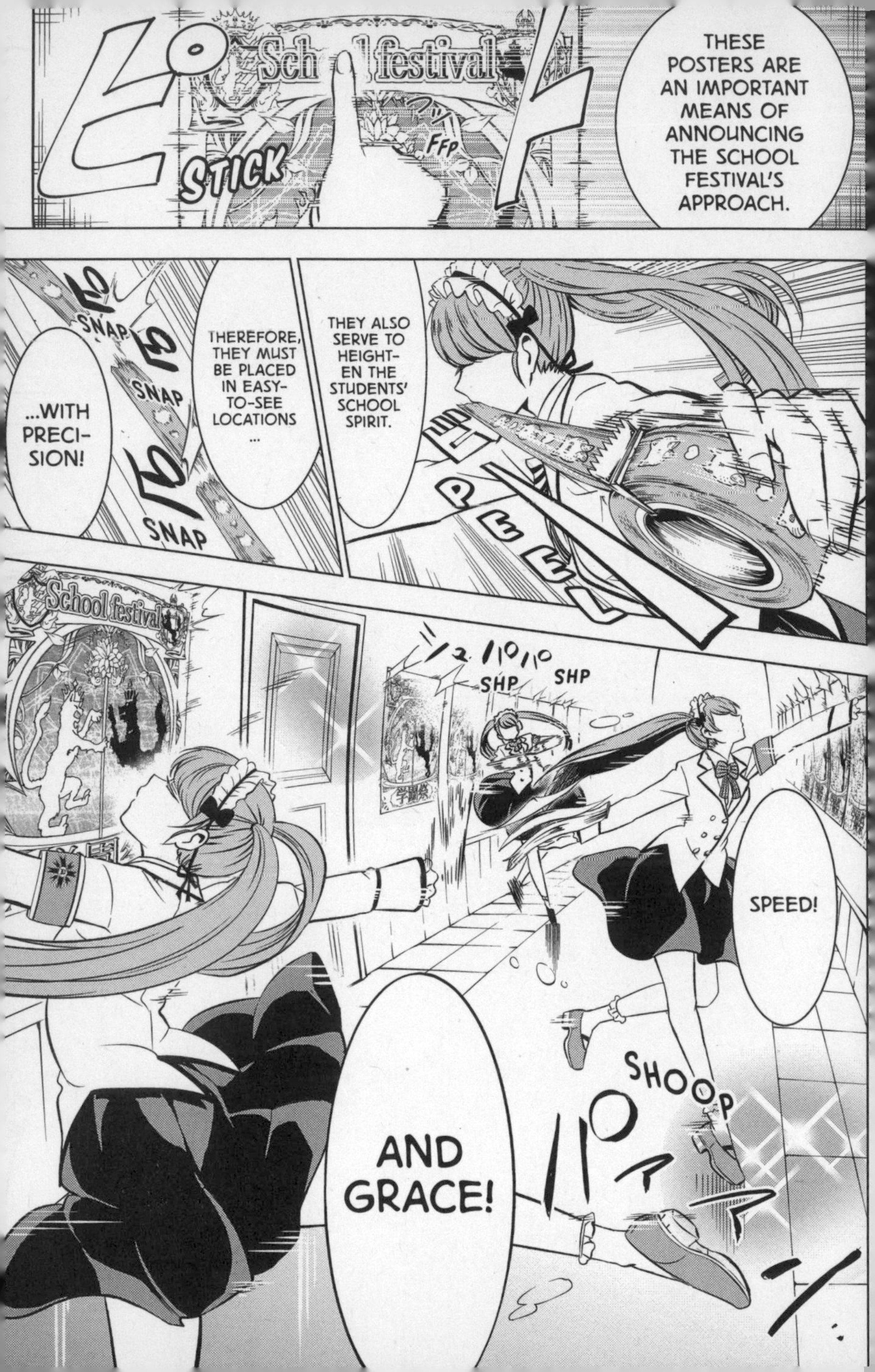
THESE POSTERS ARE AN IMPORTANT MEANS OF ANNOUNCING THE SCHOOL FESTIVAL'S APPROACH.
FFP
STICK
THEY ALSO SERVE TO HEIGHT-EN THE STUDENTS' SCHOOL SPIRIT.
PEEL
THEREFORE, THEY MUST BE PLACED IN EASY-TO-SEE LOCATIONS ...
SNAP
SNAP
SNAP
...WITH PRECI-SION!
SHP SHP
School festival
SPEED!
SHOOP
AND GRACE!

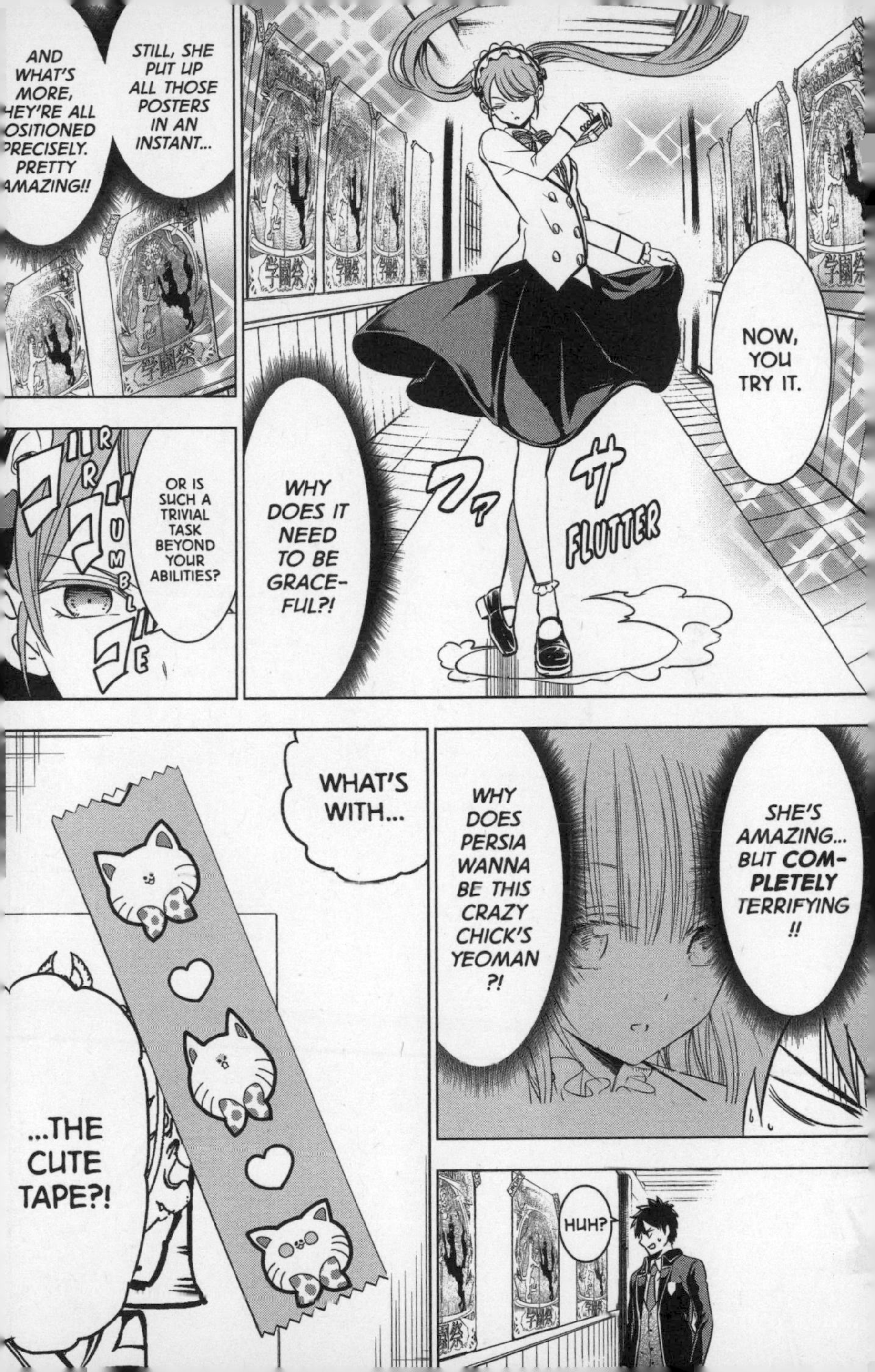
NOW, YOU TRY IT.
FLUTTER
WHY DOES IT NEED TO BE GRACE-FUL?!
STILL, SHE PUT UP ALL THOSE POSTERS IN AN INSTANT...
AND WHAT'S MORE, HEY'RE ALL OSITIONED RECISELY. PRETTY AMAZING!!
OR IS SUCH A TRIVIAL TASK BEYOND YOUR ABILITIES?
RRRUMBLE
SHE'S AMAZING... BUT COMPLETELY TERRIFYING!!
WHY DOES PERSIA WANNA BE THIS CRAZY CHICK'S YEOMAN?!
HUH?
WHAT'S WITH...
...THE CUTE TAPE?!

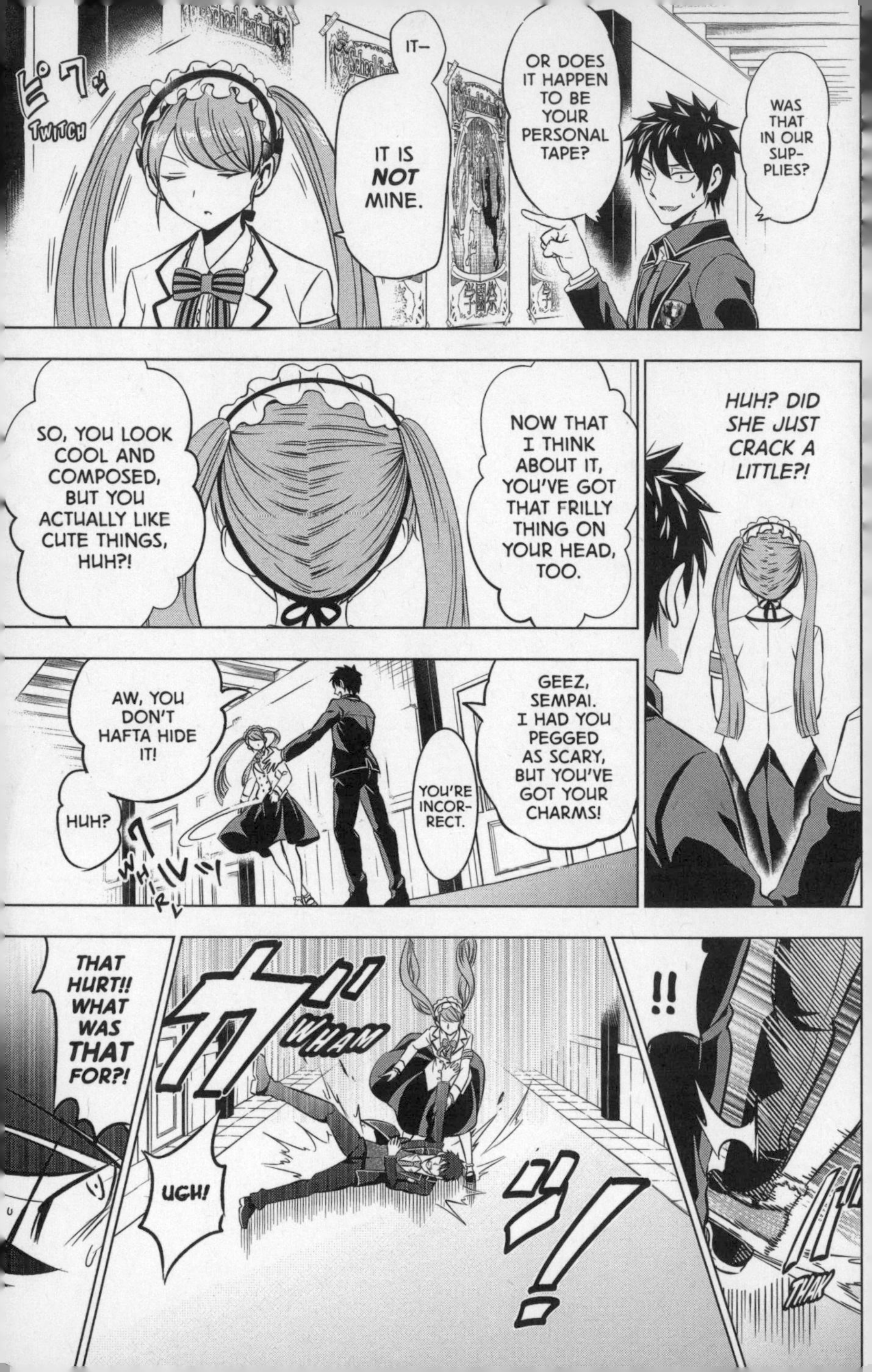
WAS THAT IN OUR SUPPLIES?
OR DOES IT HAPPEN TO BE YOUR PERSONAL TAPE?
IT—
IT IS NOT MINE.
TWITCH
HUH? DID SHE JUST CRACK A LITTLE?!
NOW THAT I THINK ABOUT IT, YOU'VE GOT THAT FRILLY THING ON YOUR HEAD, TOO.
SO, YOU LOOK COOL AND COMPOSED, BUT YOU ACTUALLY LIKE CUTE THINGS, HUH?!
GEEZ, SEMPAI. I HAD YOU PEGGED AS SCARY, BUT YOU'VE GOT YOUR CHARMS!
YOU'RE INCORRECT.
AW, YOU DON'T HAFTA HIDE IT!
HUH?
WHIRL
!!
THAK
WHAM
UGH!
THAT HURT!! WHAT WAS THAT FOR?!

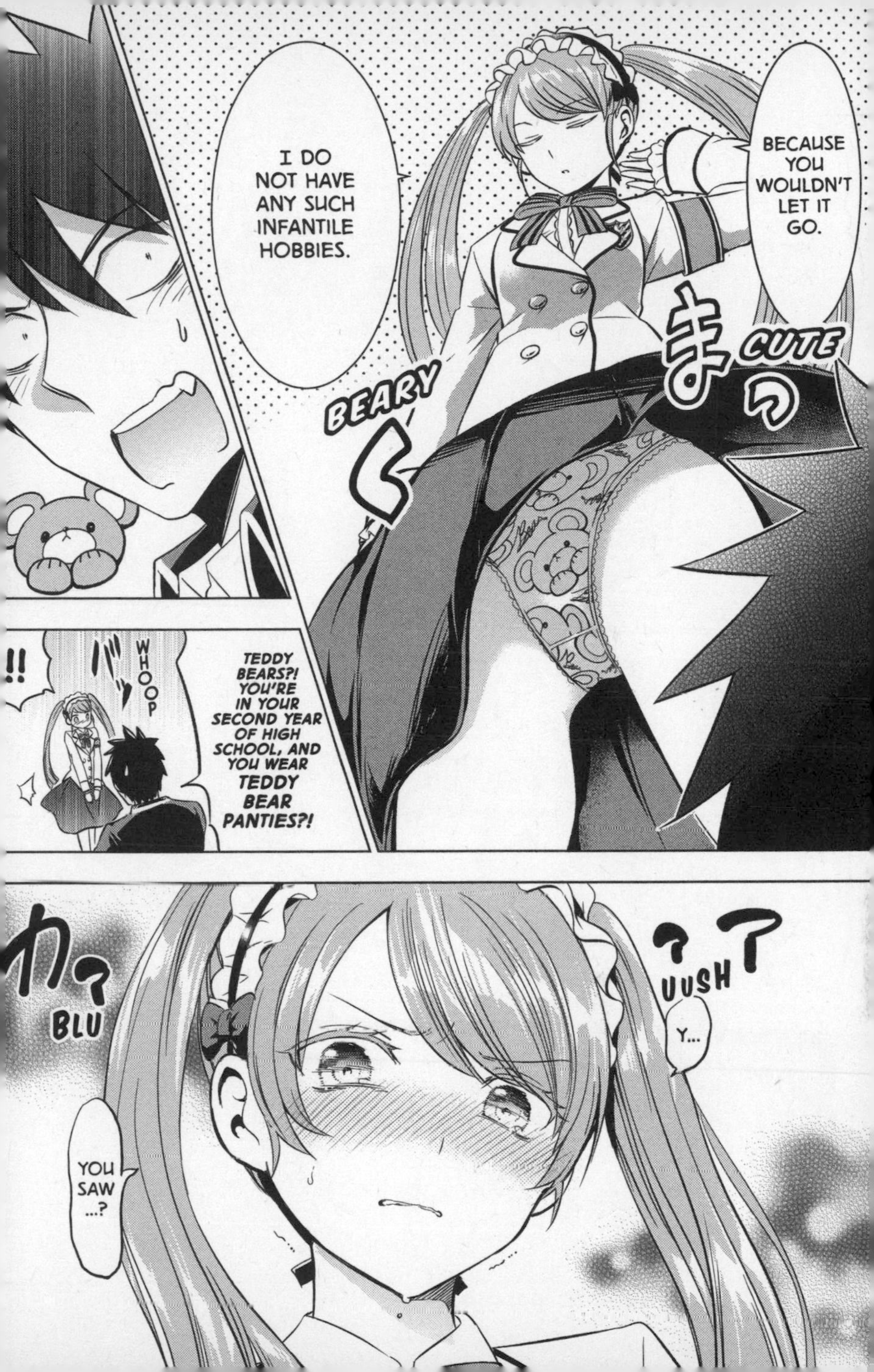
BECAUSE YOU WOULDN'T LET IT GO.
I DO NOT HAVE ANY SUCH INFANTILE HOBBIES.
まっ
CUTE
く
BEARY
TEDDY BEARS?! YOU'RE IN YOUR SECOND YEAR OF HIGH SCHOOL, AND YOU WEAR TEDDY BEAR PANTIES?!
バッ
WHOOP
!!
UUSH
Y...
BLU
YOU SAW ...?

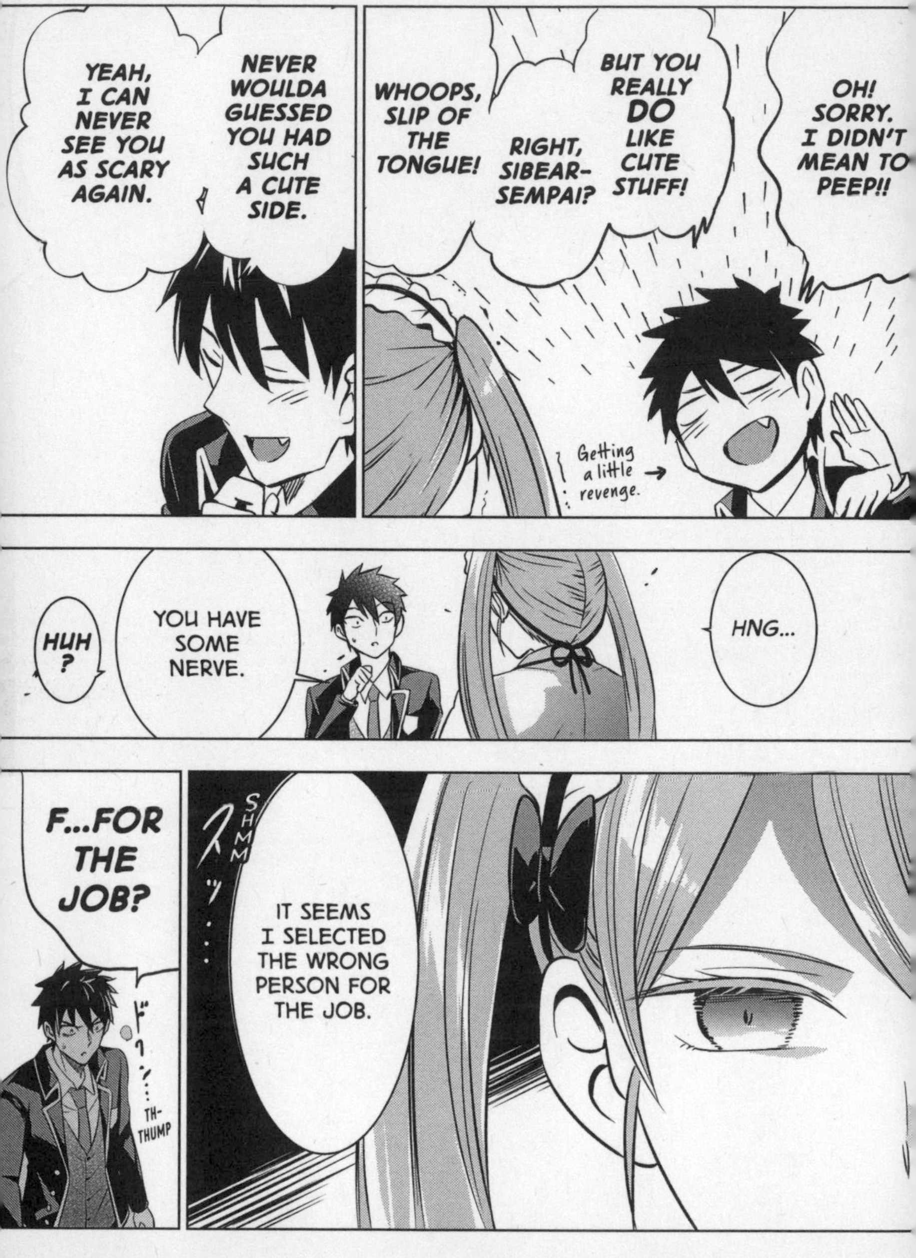
OH! SORRY. I DIDN'T MEAN TO PEEP!!
BUT YOU REALLY DO LIKE CUTE STUFF!
RIGHT, SIBEAR-SEMPAI?
WHOOPS, SLIP OF THE TONGUE!
Getting a little revenge.
NEVER WOULDA GUESSED YOU HAD SUCH A CUTE SIDE.
YEAH, I CAN NEVER SEE YOU AS SCARY AGAIN.
HNG...
YOU HAVE SOME NERVE.
HUH?
SHMM
IT SEEMS I SELECTED THE WRONG PERSON FOR THE JOB.
F...FOR THE JOB?
TH-THUMP

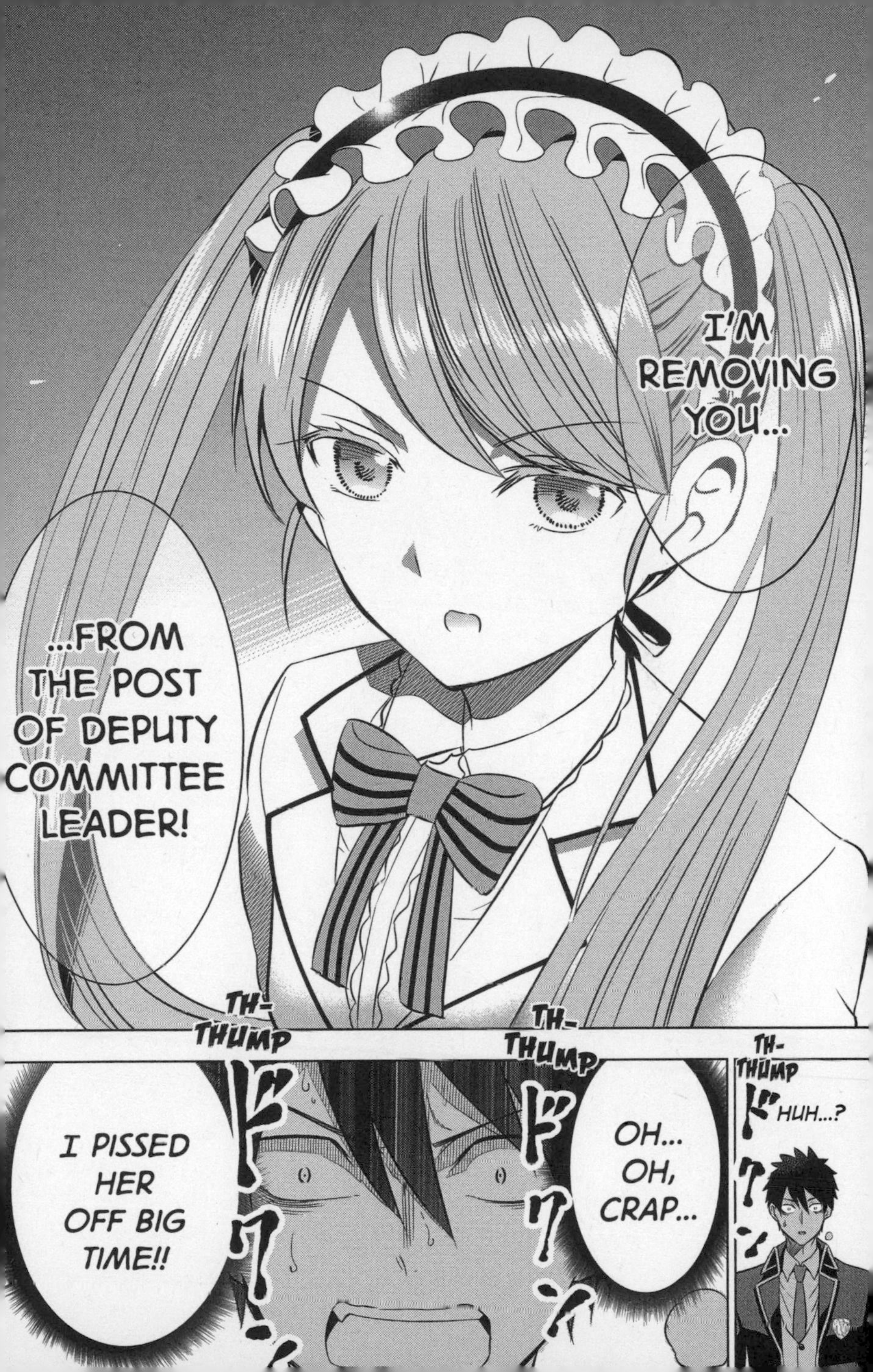
I'M REMOVING YOU...
...FROM THE POST OF DEPUTY COMMITTEE LEADER!
TH-THUMP
HUH...?
TH-THUMP
OH... OH, CRAP...
TH-THUMP
I PISSED HER OFF BIG TIME!!

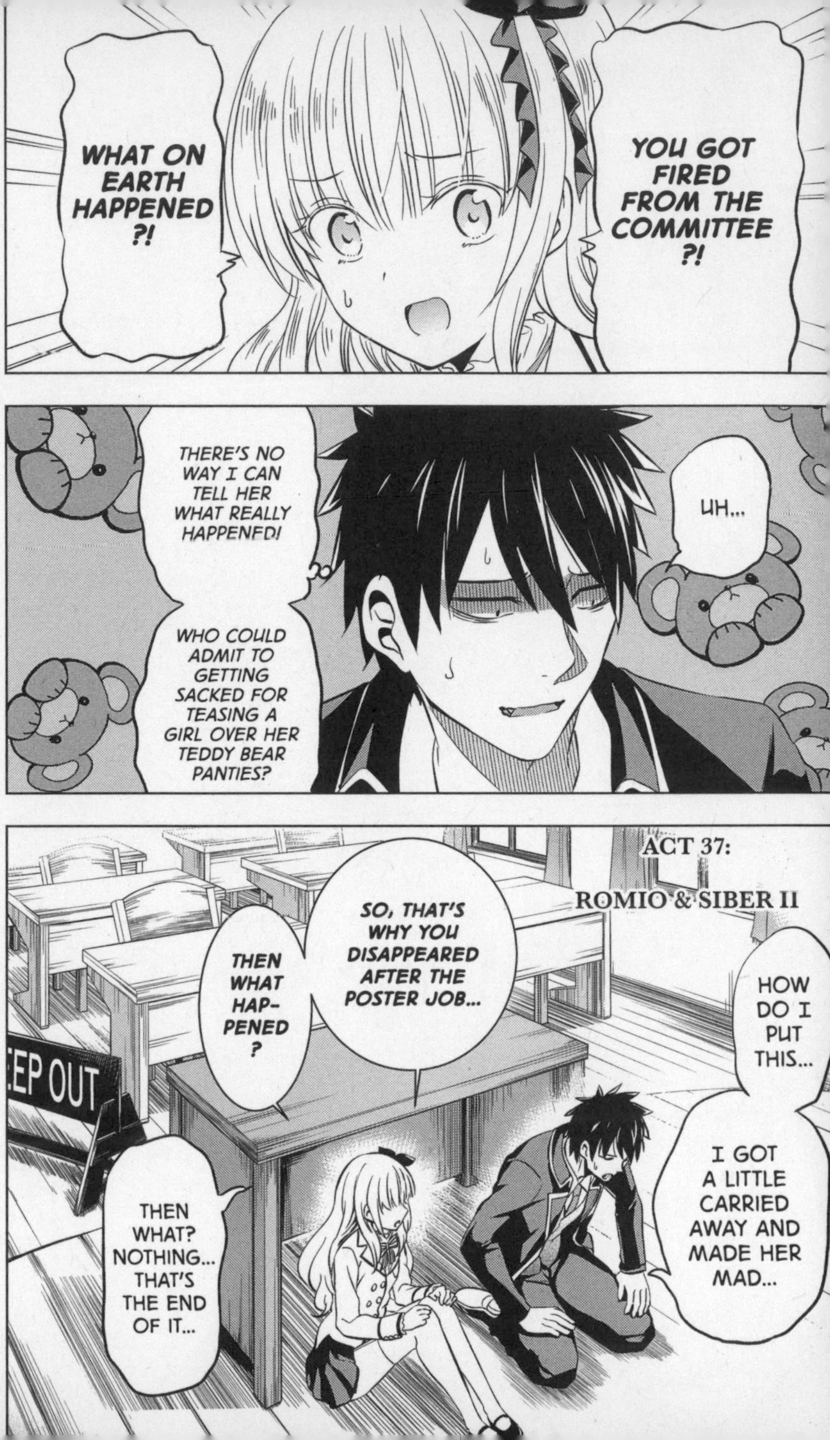
YOU GOT FIRED FROM THE COMMITTEE ?!
WHAT ON EARTH HAPPENED ?!
UH...
THERE'S NO WAY I CAN TELL HER WHAT REALLY HAPPENED!
WHO COULD ADMIT TO GETTING SACKED FOR TEASING A GIRL OVER HER TEDDY BEAR PANTIES?
ACT 37:
ROMIO & SIBER II
HOW DO I PUT THIS...
I GOT A LITTLE CARRIED AWAY AND MADE HER MAD...
SO, THAT'S WHY YOU DISAPPEARED AFTER THE POSTER JOB...
THEN WHAT HAP- PENED ?
THEN WHAT? NOTHING... THAT'S THE END OF IT...

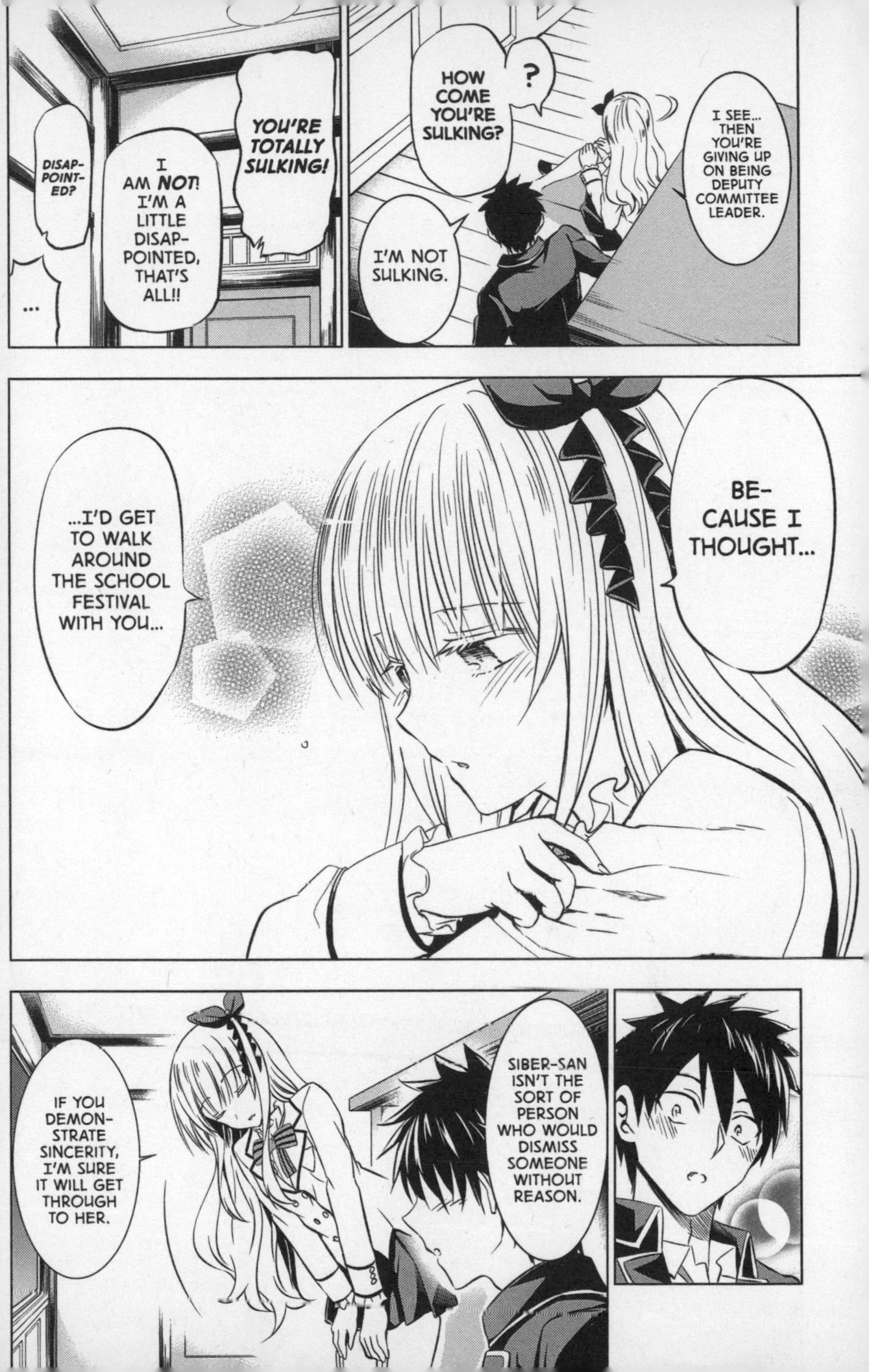
I SEE... THEN YOU'RE GIVING UP ON BEING DEPUTY COMMITTEE LEADER.
?
HOW COME YOU'RE SULKING?
I'M NOT SULKING.
YOU'RE TOTALLY SULKING!
I AM NOT! I'M A LITTLE DISAPPOINTED, THAT'S ALL!!
DISAPPOINTED?
...
BECAUSE I THOUGHT...
...I'D GET TO WALK AROUND THE SCHOOL FESTIVAL WITH YOU...
SIBER-SAN ISN'T THE SORT OF PERSON WHO WOULD DISMISS SOMEONE WITHOUT REASON.
IF YOU DEMONSTRATE SINCERITY, I'M SURE IT WILL GET THROUGH TO HER.

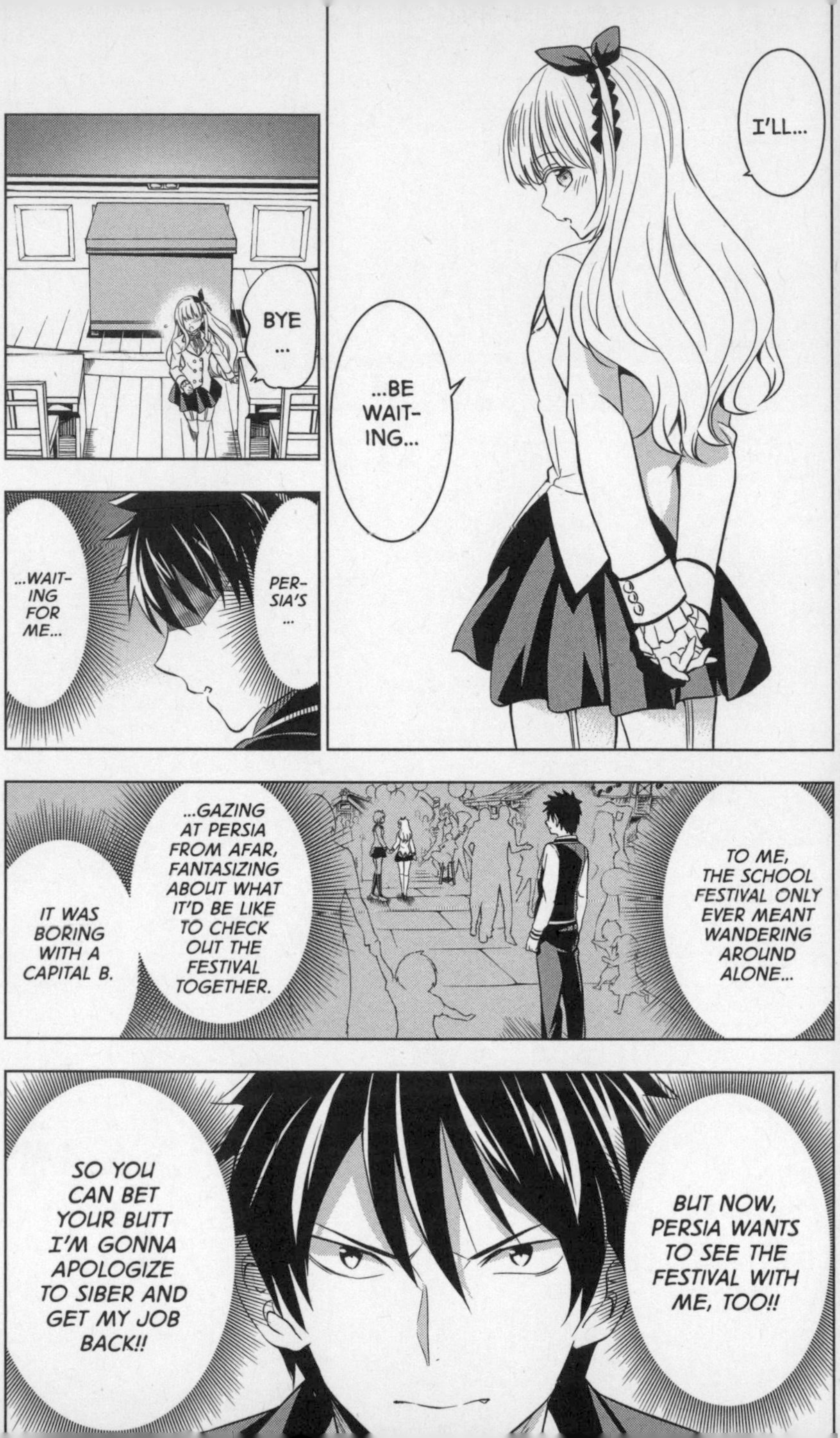
I'LL...
...BE WAITING...
BYE...
PERSIA'S...
...WAITING FOR ME...
TO ME, THE SCHOOL FESTIVAL ONLY EVER MEANT WANDERING AROUND ALONE...
...GAZING AT PERSIA FROM AFAR, FANTASIZING ABOUT WHAT IT'D BE LIKE TO CHECK OUT THE FESTIVAL TOGETHER.
IT WAS BORING WITH A CAPITAL B.
BUT NOW, PERSIA WANTS TO SEE THE FESTIVAL WITH ME, TOO!!
SO YOU CAN BET YOUR BUTT I'M GONNA APOLOGIZE TO SIBER AND GET MY JOB BACK!!

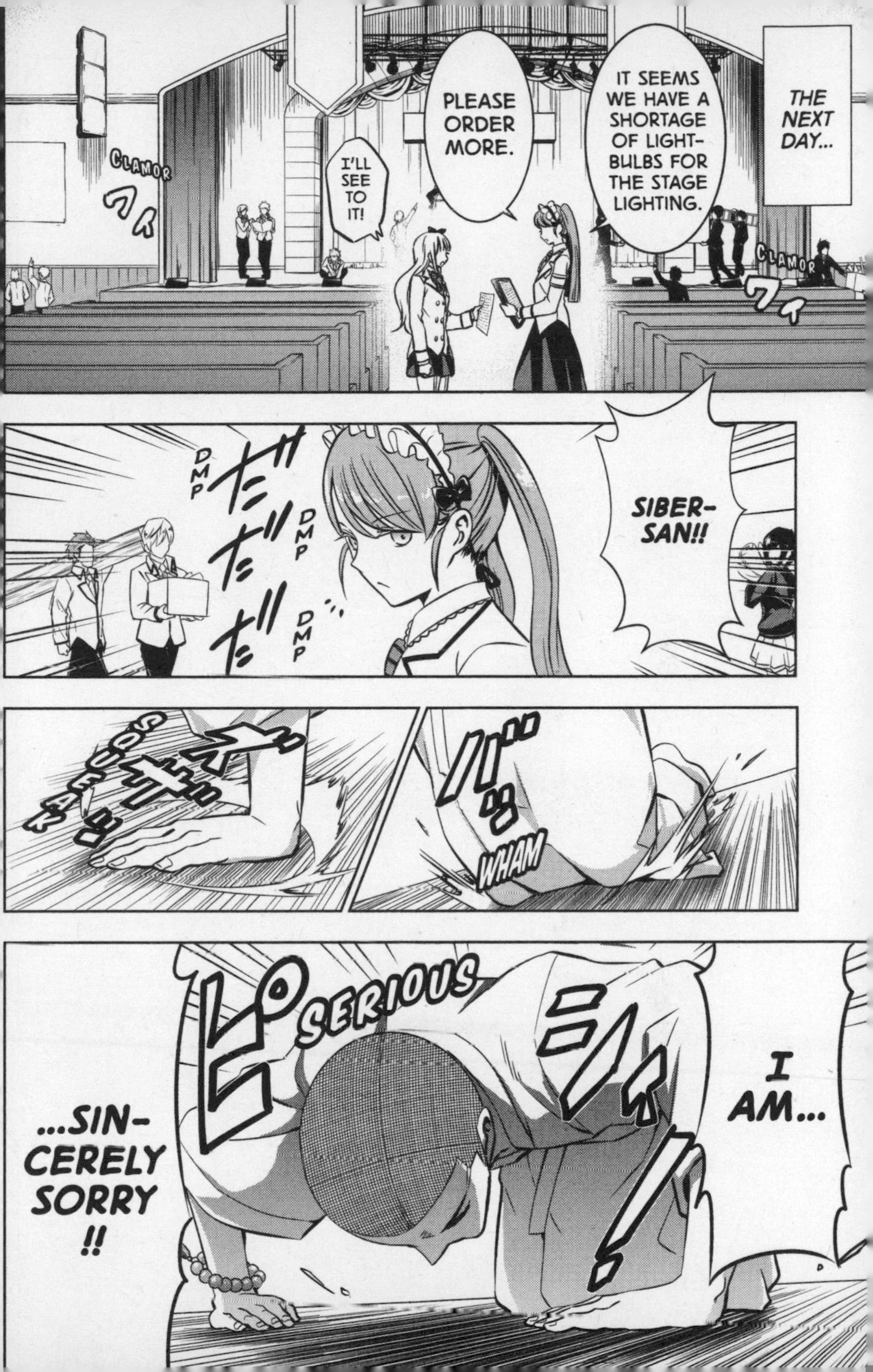
THE NEXT DAY...
IT SEEMS WE HAVE A SHORTAGE OF LIGHT-BULBS FOR THE STAGE LIGHTING.
PLEASE ORDER MORE.
I'LL SEE TO IT!
CLAMOR
CLAMOR
SIBER-SAN!!
DMP
DMP
DMP
WHAM
SQUEAK!!
I AM...
SERIOUS
...SIN-CERELY SORRY!!

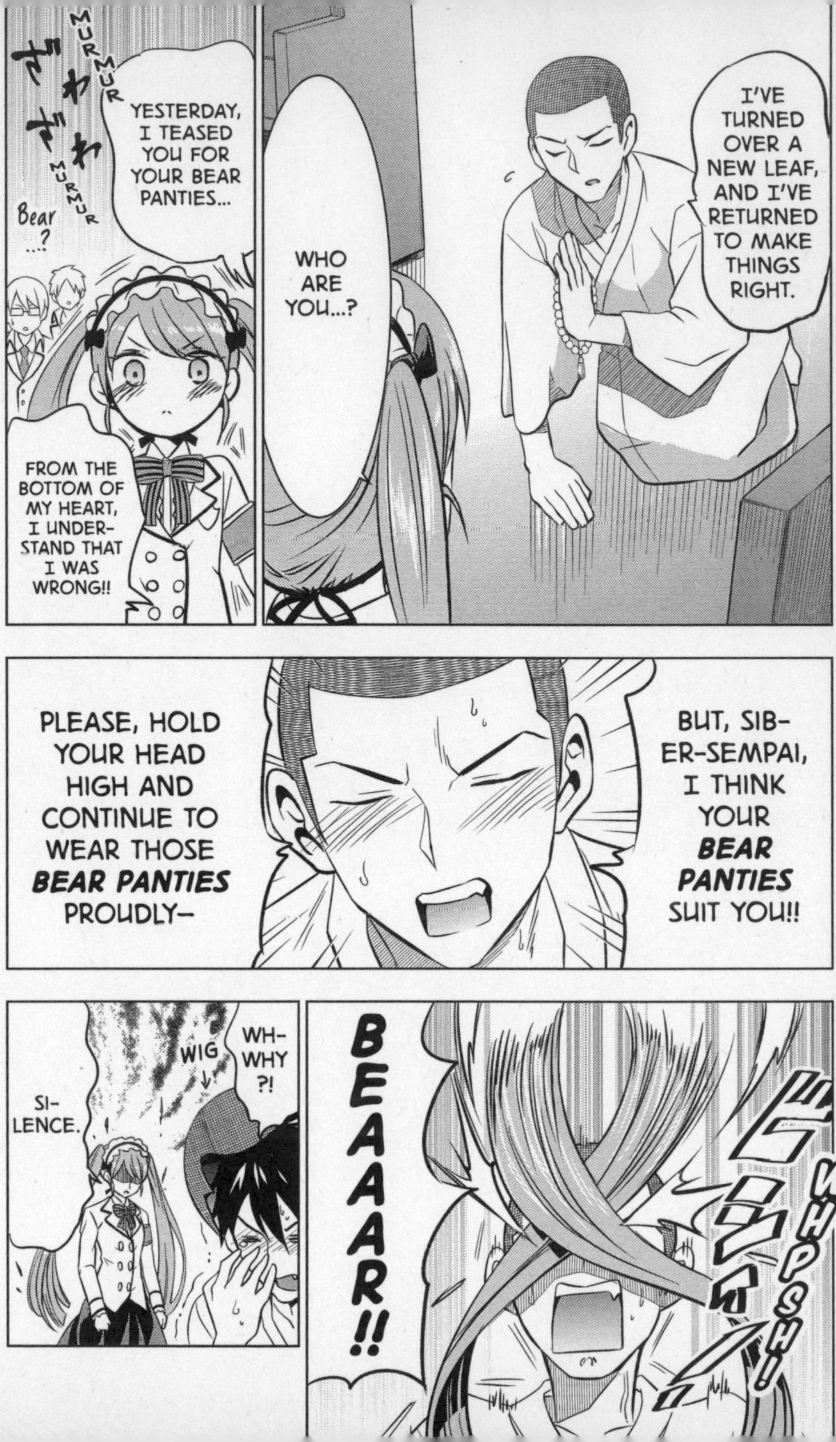
I'VE TURNED OVER A NEW LEAF, AND I'VE RETURNED TO MAKE THINGS RIGHT.
WHO ARE YOU...?
ざわざわ
MURMUR MURMUR
YESTERDAY, I TEASED YOU FOR YOUR BEAR PANTIES...
Bear ...?
FROM THE BOTTOM OF MY HEART, I UNDERSTAND THAT I WAS WRONG!!
BUT, SIBER-SEMPAI, I THINK YOUR BEAR PANTIES SUIT YOU!!
PLEASE, HOLD YOUR HEAD HIGH AND CONTINUE TO WEAR THOSE BEAR PANTIES PROUDLY–
WHPSH!
BEAAAAR!!
WH-WHY?!
WIG
SI-LENCE.

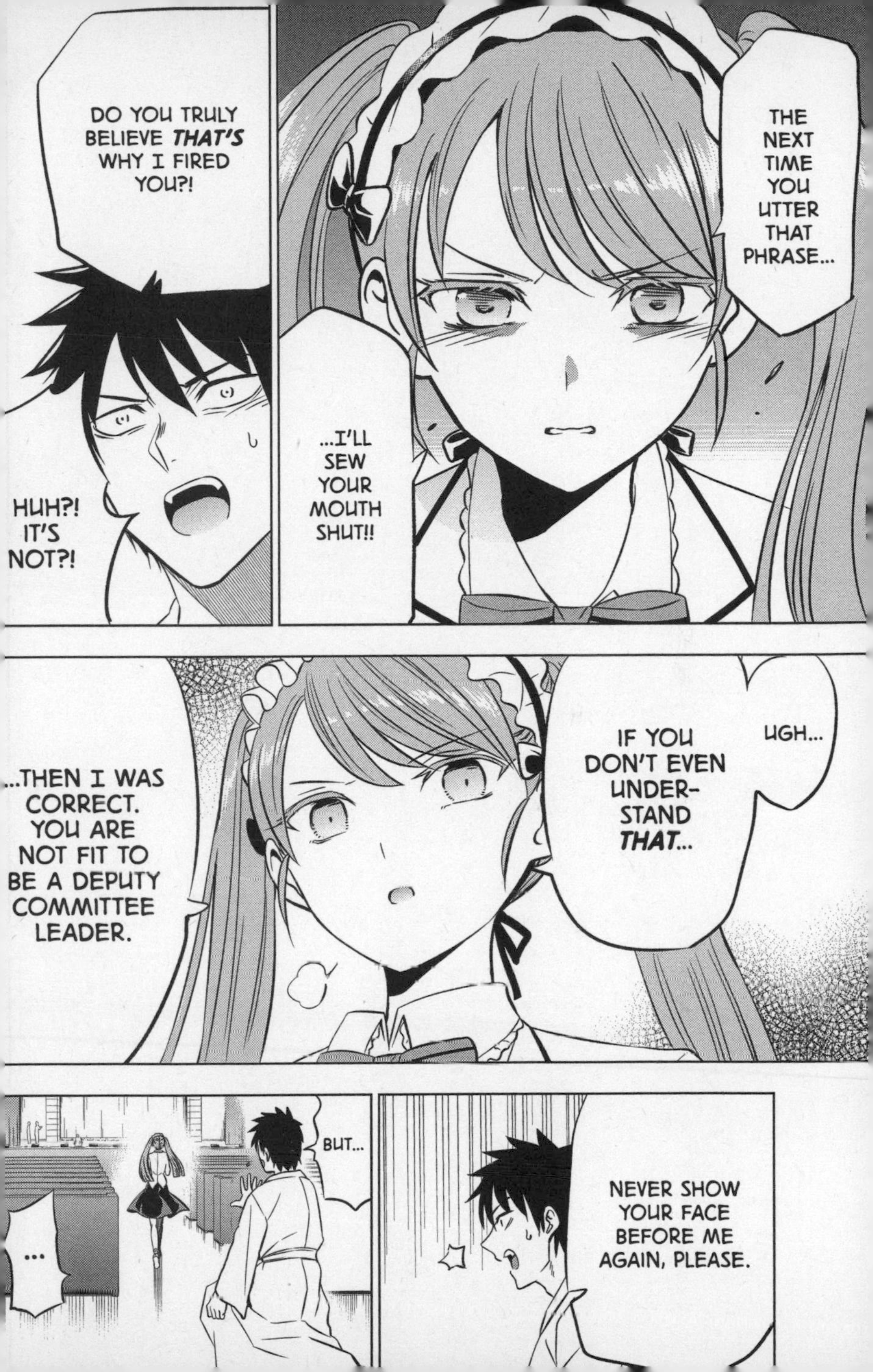
THE NEXT TIME YOU UTTER THAT PHRASE...
...I'LL SEW YOUR MOUTH SHUT!!
DO YOU TRULY BELIEVE *THAT'S* WHY I FIRED YOU?!
HUH?! IT'S NOT?!
UGH...
IF YOU DON'T EVEN UNDER-STAND *THAT*...
...THEN I WAS CORRECT. YOU ARE NOT FIT TO BE A DEPUTY COMMITTEE LEADER.
NEVER SHOW YOUR FACE BEFORE ME AGAIN, PLEASE.
BUT...
...

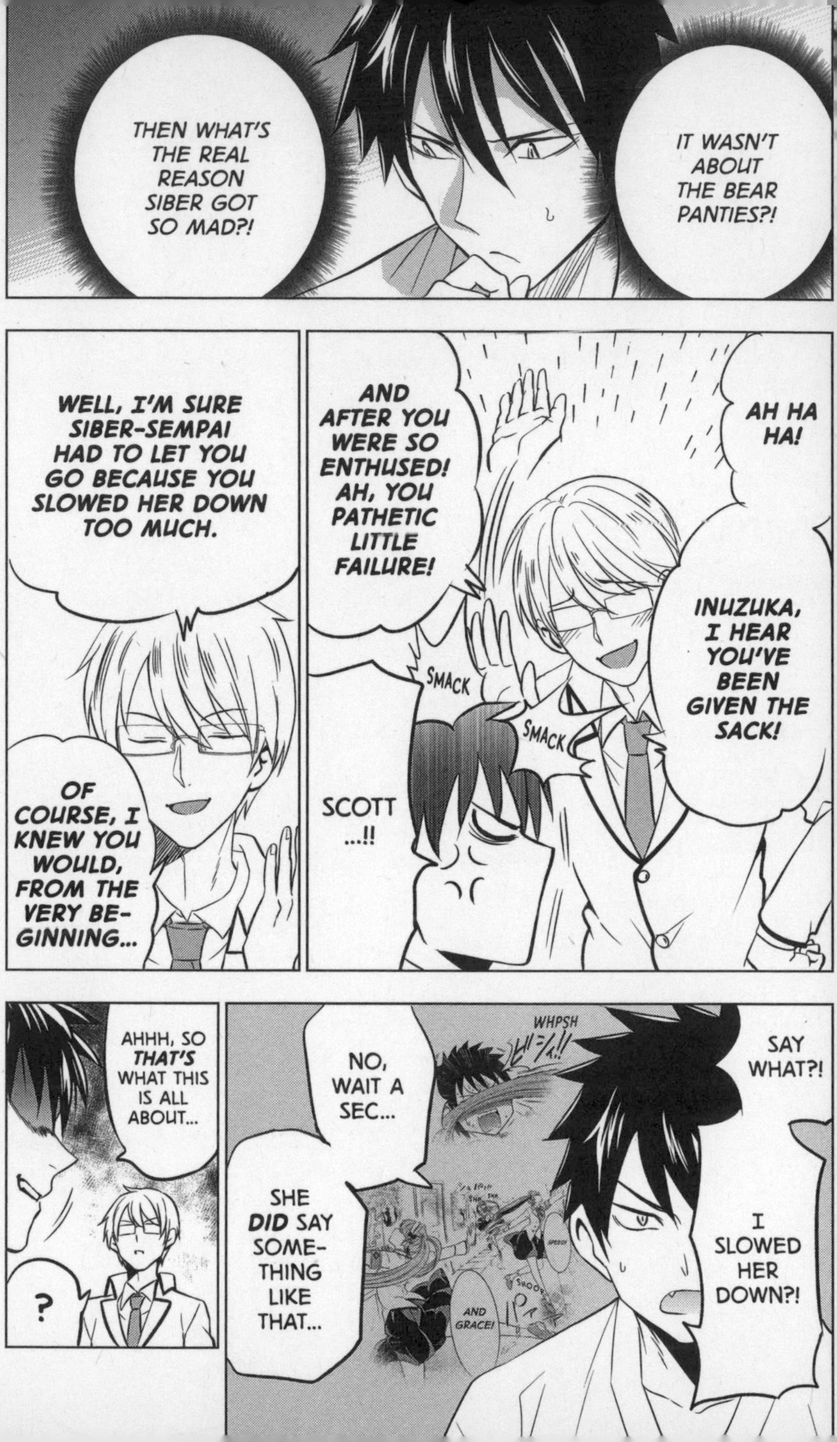
IT WASN'T ABOUT THE BEAR PANTIES?!
THEN WHAT'S THE REAL REASON SIBER GOT SO MAD?!
AH HA HA!
INUZUKA, I HEAR YOU'VE BEEN GIVEN THE SACK!
AND AFTER YOU WERE SO ENTHUSED! AH, YOU PATHETIC LITTLE FAILURE!
SMACK
SMACK
SCOTT ...!!
WELL, I'M SURE SIBER-SEMPAI HAD TO LET YOU GO BECAUSE YOU SLOWED HER DOWN TOO MUCH.
OF COURSE, I KNEW YOU WOULD, FROM THE VERY BE-GINNING...
SAY WHAT?!
I SLOWED HER DOWN?!
WHPSH
NO, WAIT A SEC...
SHE DID SAY SOMETHING LIKE THAT...
AND GRACE!
AHHH, SO THAT'S WHAT THIS IS ALL ABOUT...
?

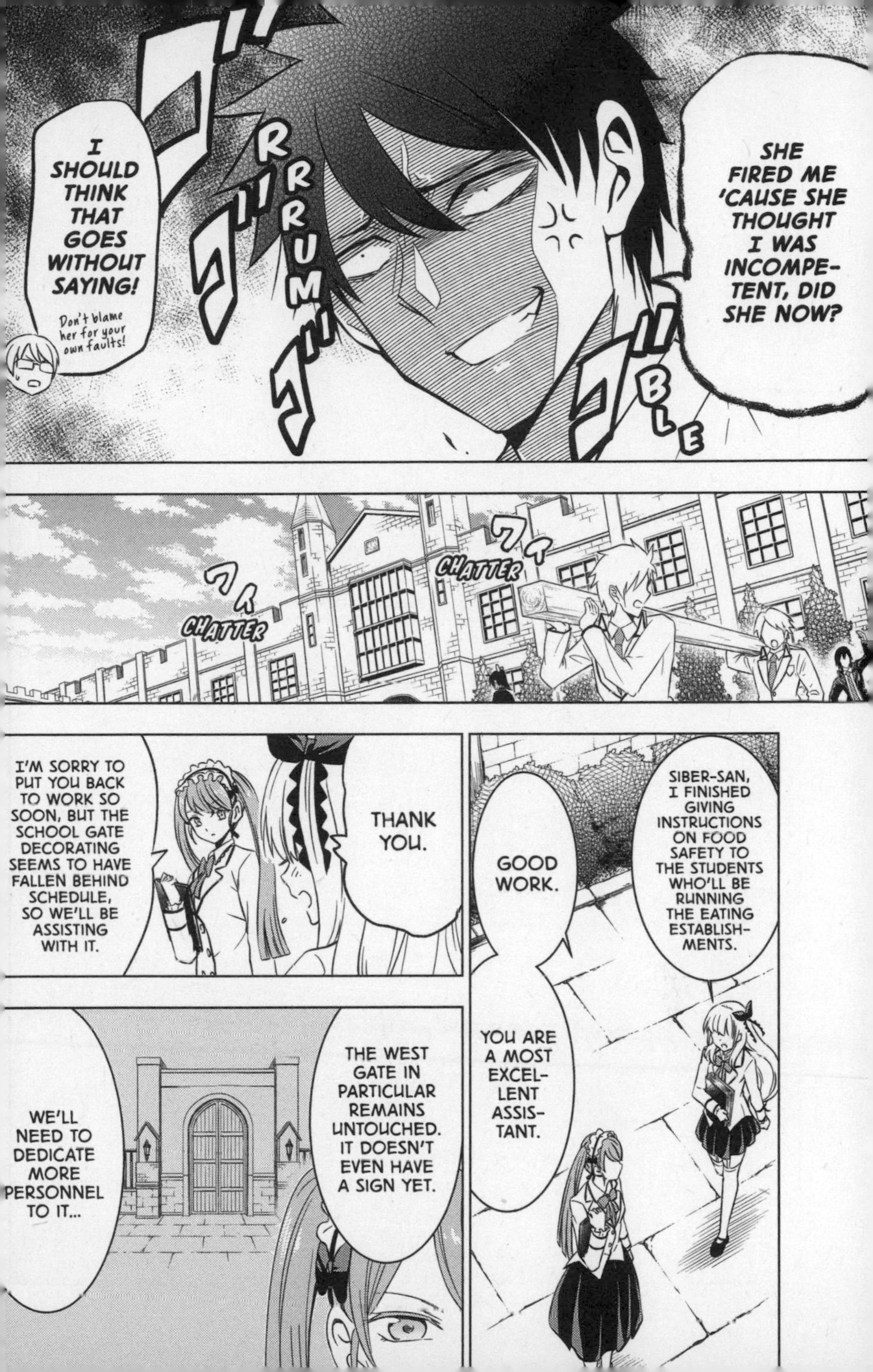
SHE FIRED ME 'CAUSE SHE THOUGHT I WAS INCOMPETENT, DID SHE NOW?
RRRUM
BLE
I SHOULD THINK THAT GOES WITHOUT SAYING!
Don't blame her for your own faults!
CHATTER
CHATTER
SIBER-SAN, I FINISHED GIVING INSTRUCTIONS ON FOOD SAFETY TO THE STUDENTS WHO'LL BE RUNNING THE EATING ESTABLISHMENTS.
GOOD WORK.
YOU ARE A MOST EXCELLENT ASSISTANT.
THANK YOU.
I'M SORRY TO PUT YOU BACK TO WORK SO SOON, BUT THE SCHOOL GATE DECORATING SEEMS TO HAVE FALLEN BEHIND SCHEDULE, SO WE'LL BE ASSISTING WITH IT.
THE WEST GATE IN PARTICULAR REMAINS UNTOUCHED. IT DOESN'T EVEN HAVE A SIGN YET.
WE'LL NEED TO DEDICATE MORE PERSONNEL TO IT...

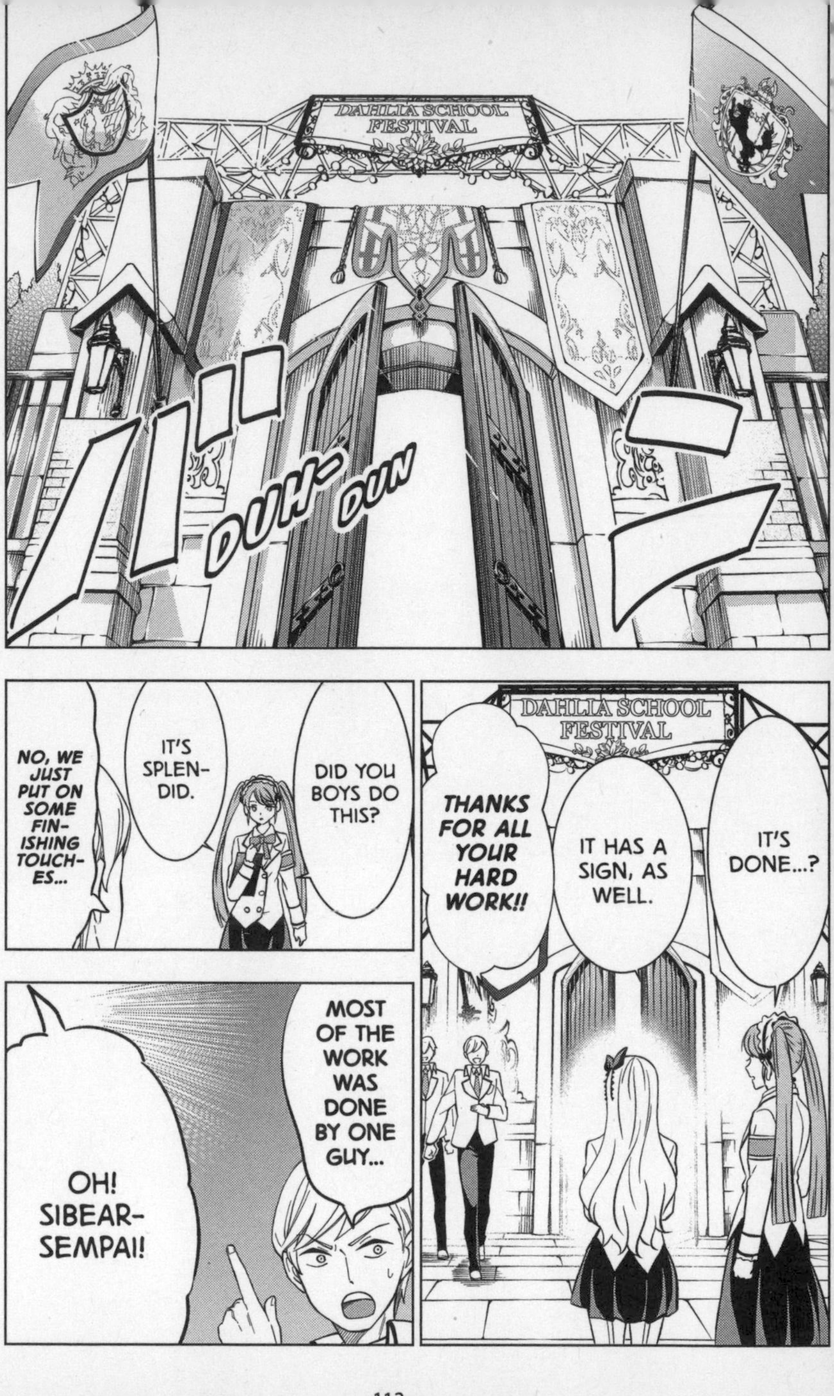
DAHLIA SCHOOL FESTIVAL
DUH-DUN
DAHLIA SCHOOL FESTIVAL
IT'S DONE...?
IT HAS A SIGN, AS WELL.
THANKS FOR ALL YOUR HARD WORK!!
DID YOU BOYS DO THIS?
IT'S SPLEN-DID.
NO, WE JUST PUT ON SOME FIN-ISHING TOUCH-ES...
MOST OF THE WORK WAS DONE BY ONE GUY...
OH! SIBEAR-SEMPAI!

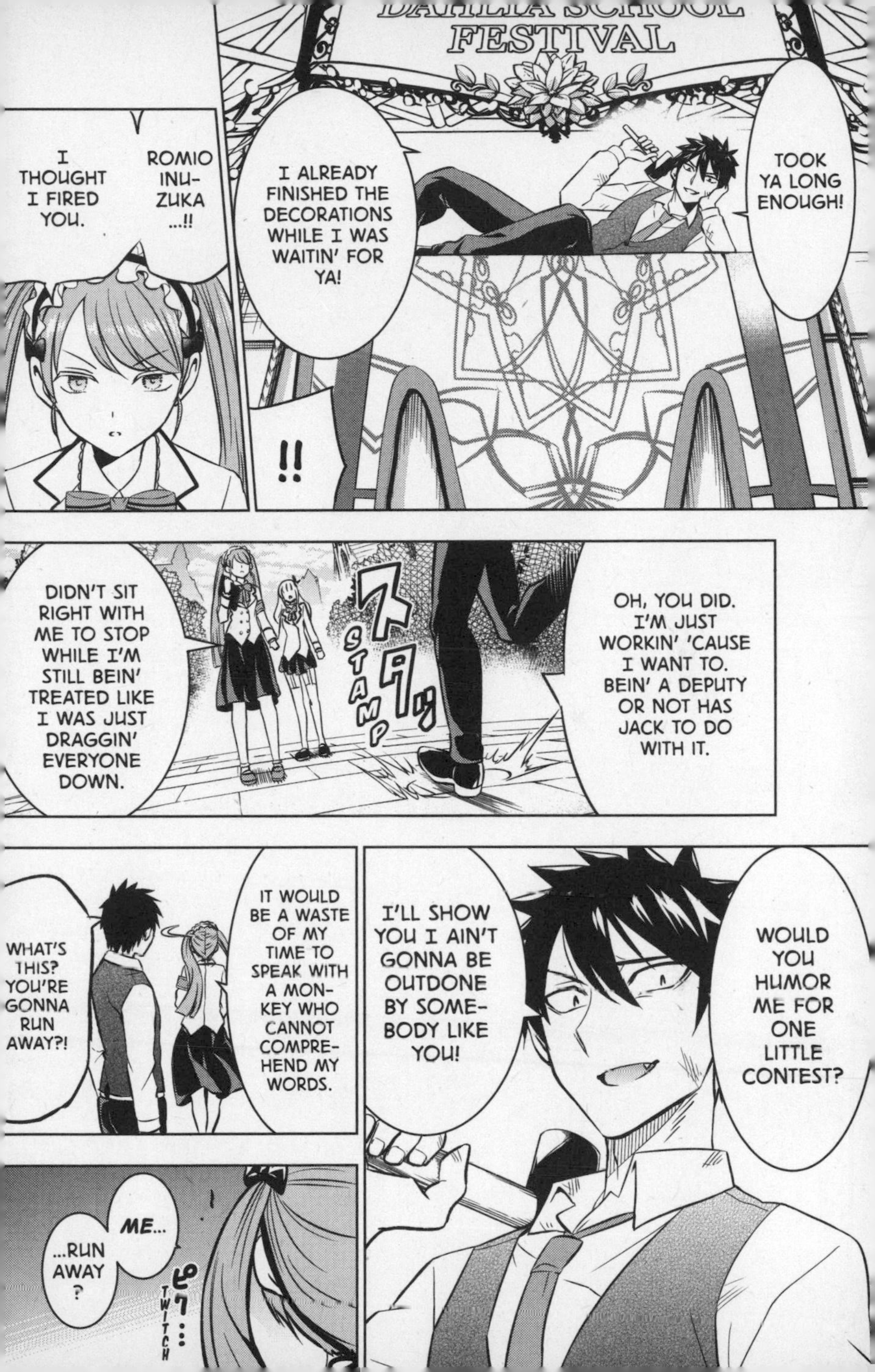
DAHLIA SCHOOL FESTIVAL
TOOK YA LONG ENOUGH!
I ALREADY FINISHED THE DECORATIONS WHILE I WAS WAITIN' FOR YA!
!!
ROMIO INU-ZUKA ...!!
I THOUGHT I FIRED YOU.
OH, YOU DID. I'M JUST WORKIN' 'CAUSE I WANT TO. BEIN' A DEPUTY OR NOT HAS JACK TO DO WITH IT.
STAMP
DIDN'T SIT RIGHT WITH ME TO STOP WHILE I'M STILL BEIN' TREATED LIKE I WAS JUST DRAGGIN' EVERYONE DOWN.
WOULD YOU HUMOR ME FOR ONE LITTLE CONTEST?
I'LL SHOW YOU I AIN'T GONNA BE OUTDONE BY SOMEBODY LIKE YOU!
IT WOULD BE A WASTE OF MY TIME TO SPEAK WITH A MONKEY WHO CANNOT COMPREHEND MY WORDS.
WHAT'S THIS? YOU'RE GONNA RUN AWAY?!
ME... ...RUN AWAY?
TWITCH

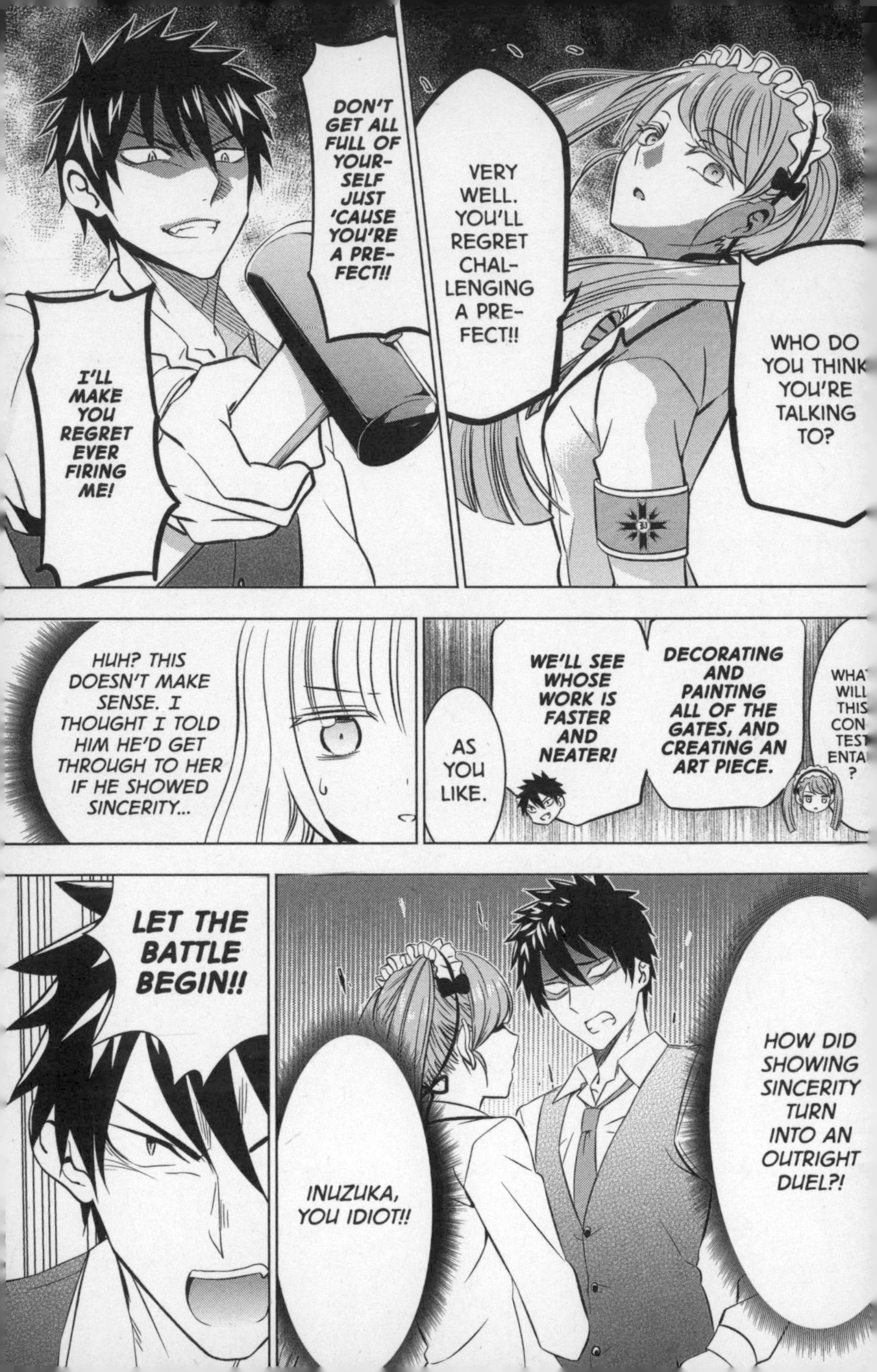
WHO DO YOU THINK YOU'RE TALKING TO?
VERY WELL. YOU'LL REGRET CHAL-LENGING A PRE-FECT!!
DON'T GET ALL FULL OF YOUR-SELF JUST 'CAUSE YOU'RE A PRE-FECT!!
I'LL MAKE YOU REGRET EVER FIRING ME!
WHA WILL THIS CON-TEST ENTA ?
DECORATING AND PAINTING ALL OF THE GATES, AND CREATING AN ART PIECE.
WE'LL SEE WHOSE WORK IS FASTER AND NEATER!
AS YOU LIKE.
HUH? THIS DOESN'T MAKE SENSE. I THOUGHT I TOLD HIM HE'D GET THROUGH TO HER IF HE SHOWED SINCERITY...
HOW DID SHOWING SINCERITY TURN INTO AN OUTRIGHT DUEL?!
INUZUKA, YOU IDIOT!!
LET THE BATTLE BEGIN!!

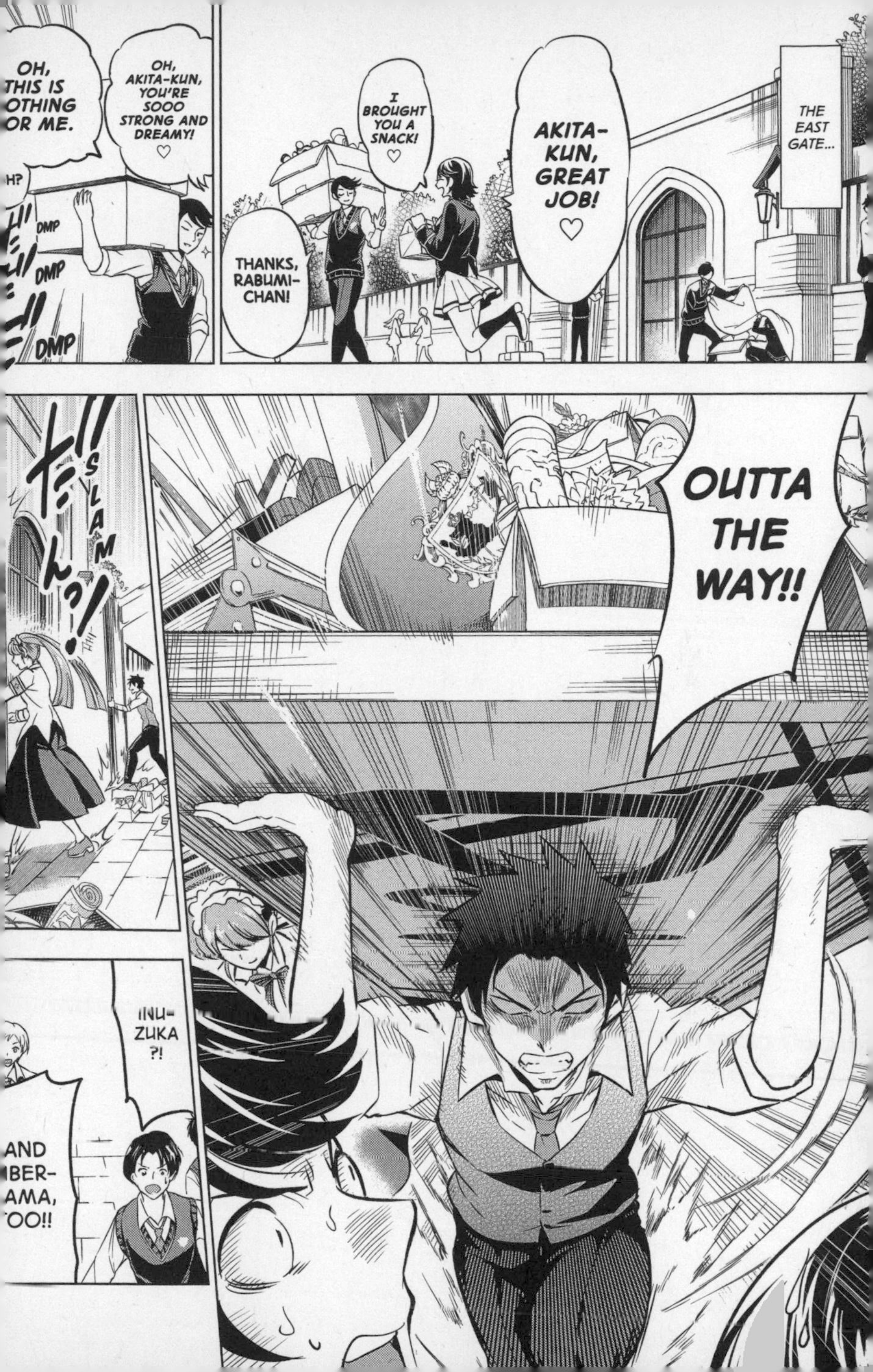
THE EAST GATE...
AKITA-KUN, GREAT JOB! ♡
I BROUGHT YOU A SNACK! ♡
THANKS, RABUMI-CHAN!
OH, AKITA-KUN, YOU'RE SOOO STRONG AND DREAMY! ♡
OH, THIS IS OTHING OR ME.
H?
DMP
DMP
DMP
OUTTA THE WAY!!
SLAM
INU-ZUKA ?!
AND IBER-AMA, OO!!

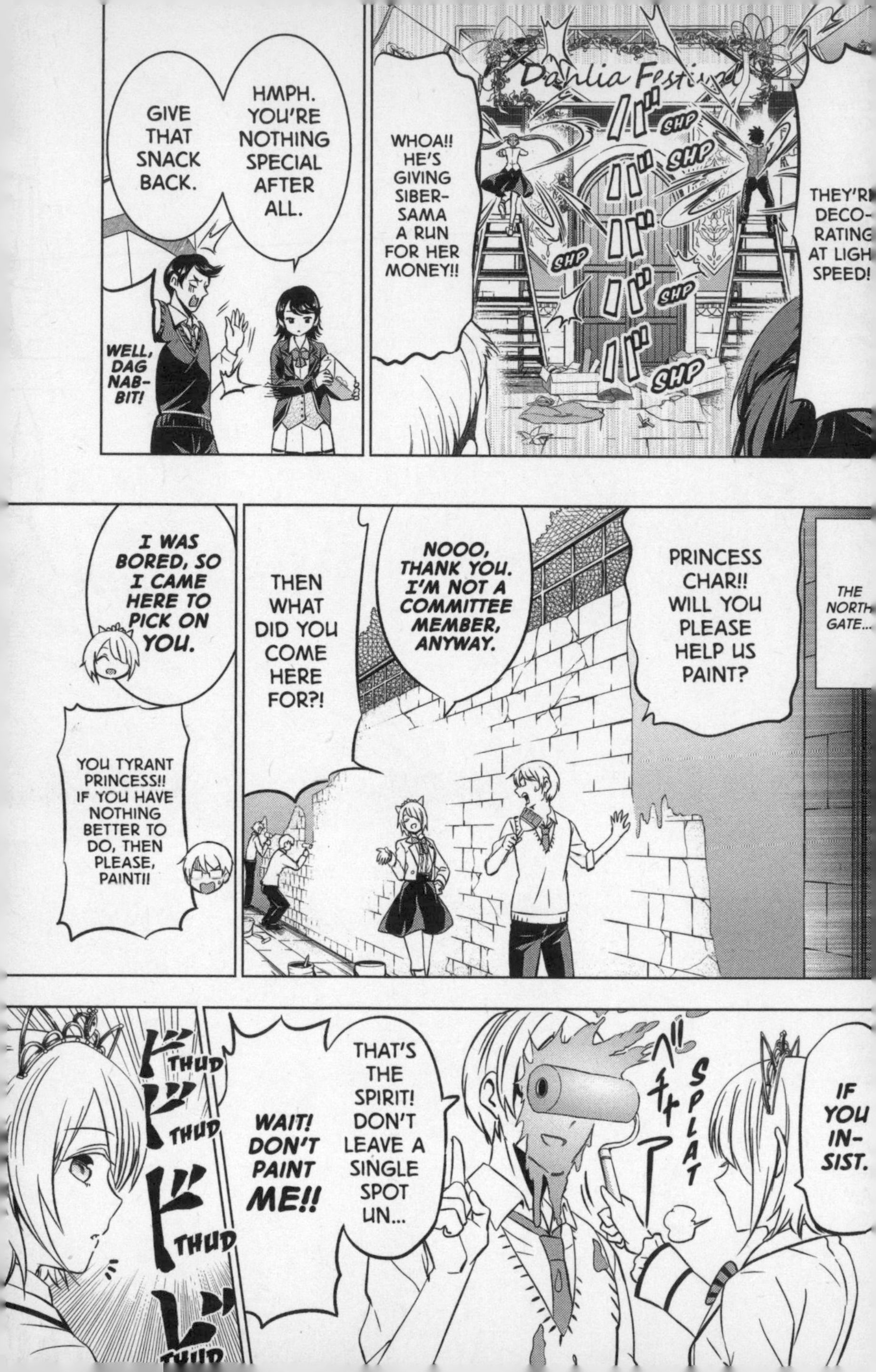
THEY'R DECO-RATING AT LIGH SPEED!
Dahlia Festi
SHP
SHP
SHP
SHP
SHP
WHOA!! HE'S GIVING SIBER-SAMA A RUN FOR HER MONEY!!
HMPH. YOU'RE NOTHING SPECIAL AFTER ALL.
GIVE THAT SNACK BACK.
WELL, DAG NAB-BIT!
THE NORTH GATE...
PRINCESS CHAR!! WILL YOU PLEASE HELP US PAINT?
NOOO, THANK YOU. I'M NOT A COMMITTEE MEMBER, ANYWAY.
THEN WHAT DID YOU COME HERE FOR?!
I WAS BORED, SO I CAME HERE TO PICK ON YOU.
YOU TYRANT PRINCESS!! IF YOU HAVE NOTHING BETTER TO DO, THEN PLEASE, PAINT!!
IF YOU IN-SIST.
SPLAT
THAT'S THE SPIRIT! DON'T LEAVE A SINGLE SPOT UN...
WAIT! DON'T PAINT ME!!
THUD
THUD
THUD

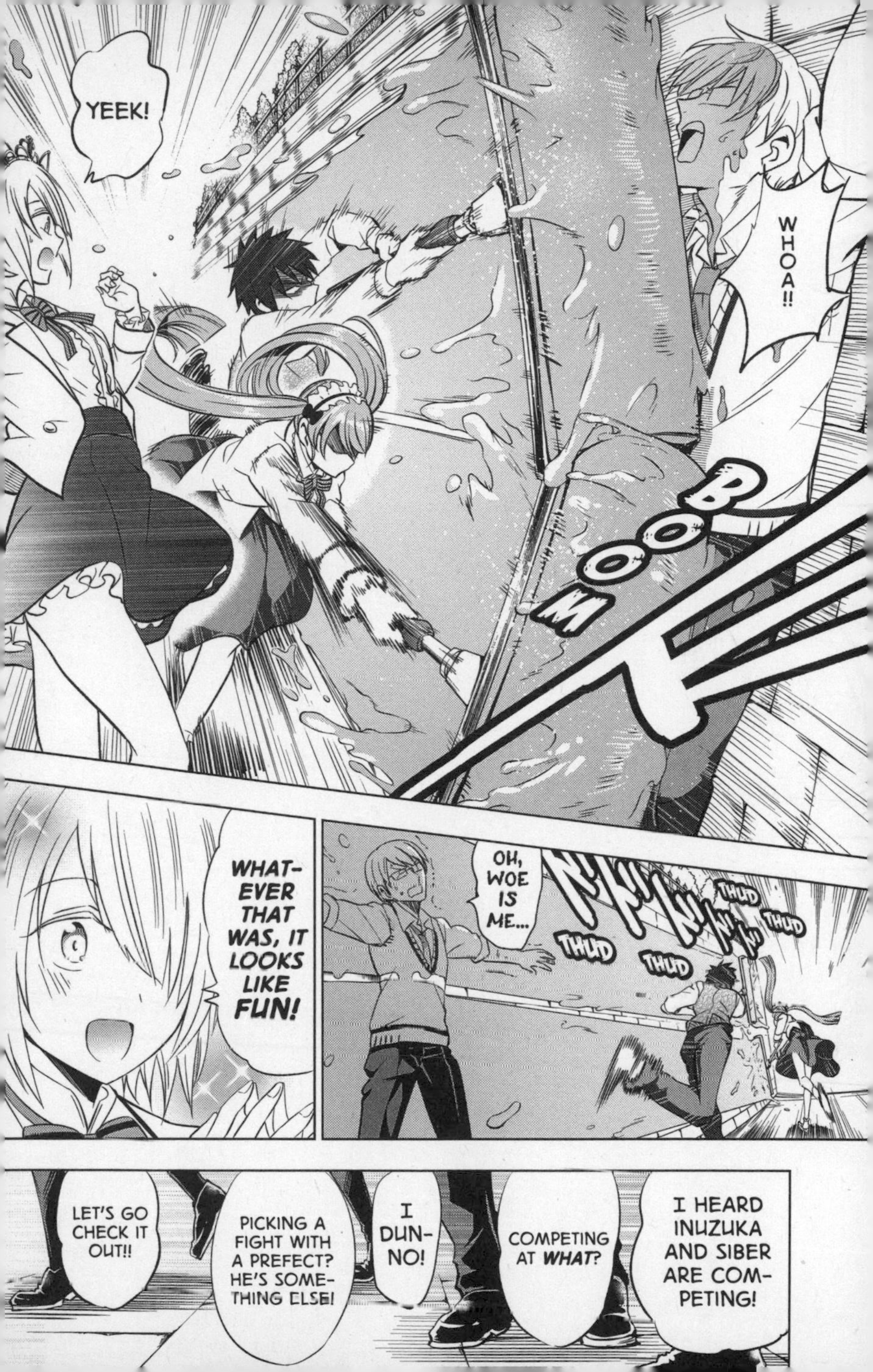
WHOA!!
BOOM
YEEK!
OH, WOE IS ME...
THUD THUD THUD THUD
WHATEVER THAT WAS, IT LOOKS LIKE FUN!
I HEARD INUZUKA AND SIBER ARE COMPETING!
COMPETING AT WHAT?
I DUNNO!
PICKING A FIGHT WITH A PREFECT? HE'S SOMETHING ELSE!
LET'S GO CHECK IT OUT!!

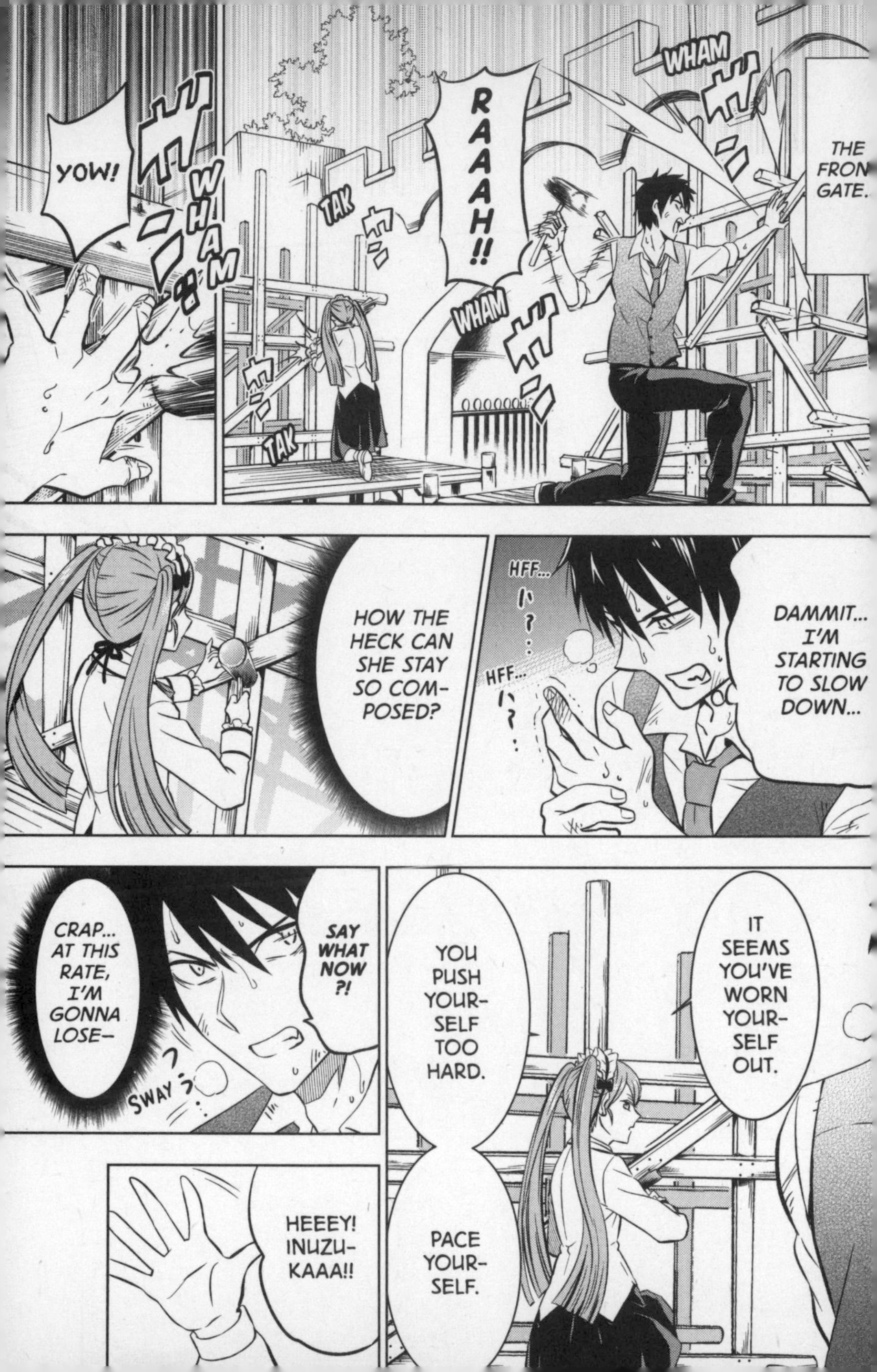
THE FRON GATE.
WHAM
RAAAAH!!
TAK
WHAM
TAK
YOW!
WHAM
DAMMIT... I'M STARTING TO SLOW DOWN...
HFF...
HFF...
HOW THE HECK CAN SHE STAY SO COM-POSED?
IT SEEMS YOU'VE WORN YOUR-SELF OUT.
YOU PUSH YOUR-SELF TOO HARD.
PACE YOUR-SELF.
SAY WHAT NOW?!
CRAP... AT THIS RATE, I'M GONNA LOSE–
SWAY
HEEEY! INUZU-KAAA!!

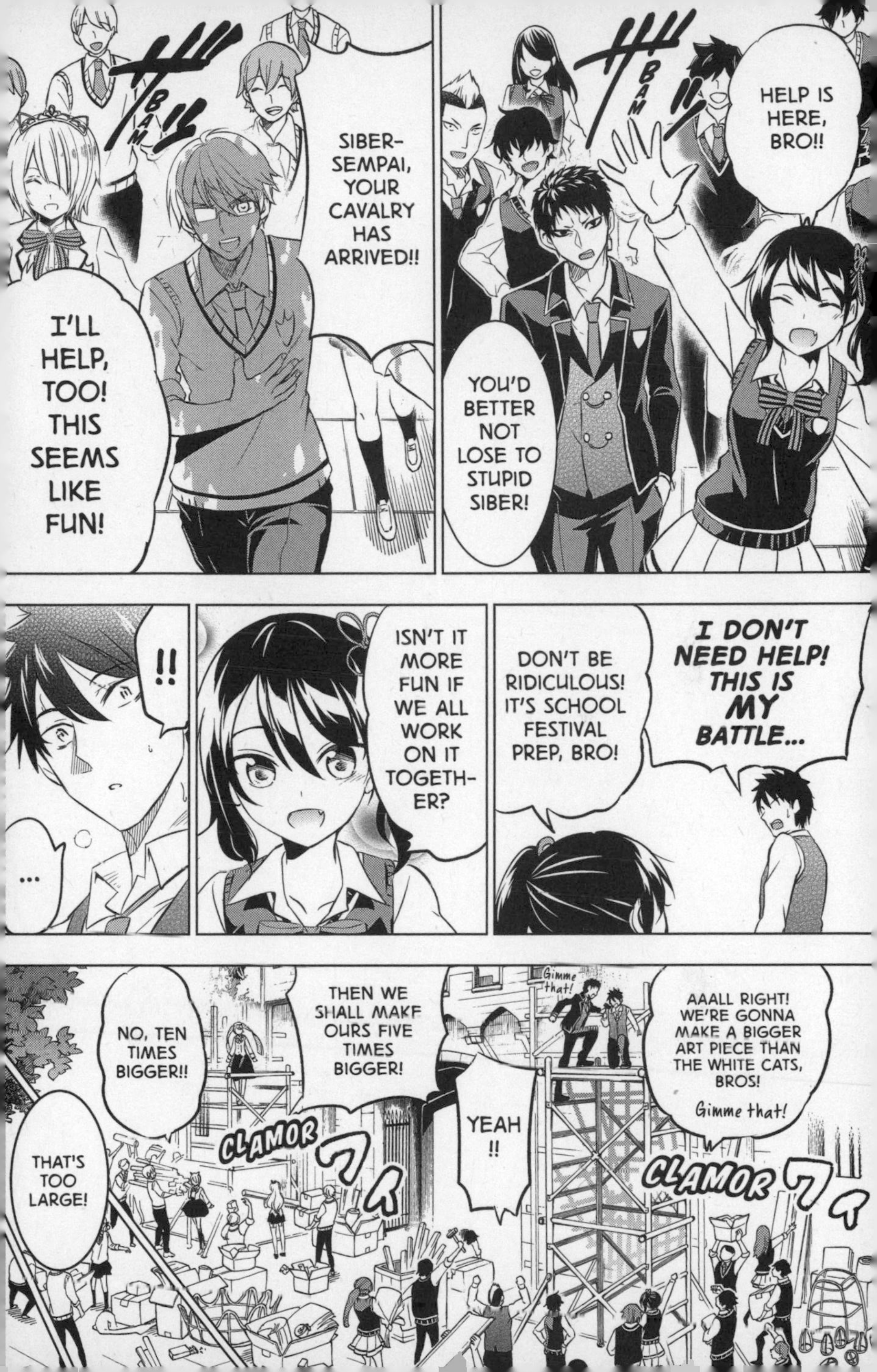
BAM
HELP IS HERE, BRO!!
YOU'D BETTER NOT LOSE TO STUPID SIBER!
BAM
SIBER-SEMPAI, YOUR CAVALRY HAS ARRIVED!!
I'LL HELP, TOO! THIS SEEMS LIKE FUN!
I DON'T NEED HELP! THIS IS MY BATTLE...
DON'T BE RIDICULOUS! IT'S SCHOOL FESTIVAL PREP, BRO!
ISN'T IT MORE FUN IF WE ALL WORK ON IT TOGETH-ER?
!!
...
Gimme that!
AAALL RIGHT! WE'RE GONNA MAKE A BIGGER ART PIECE THAN THE WHITE CATS, BROS!
Gimme that!
YEAH!!
CLAMOR
THEN WE SHALL MAKE OURS FIVE TIMES BIGGER!
NO, TEN TIMES BIGGER!!
CLAMOR
THAT'S TOO LARGE!

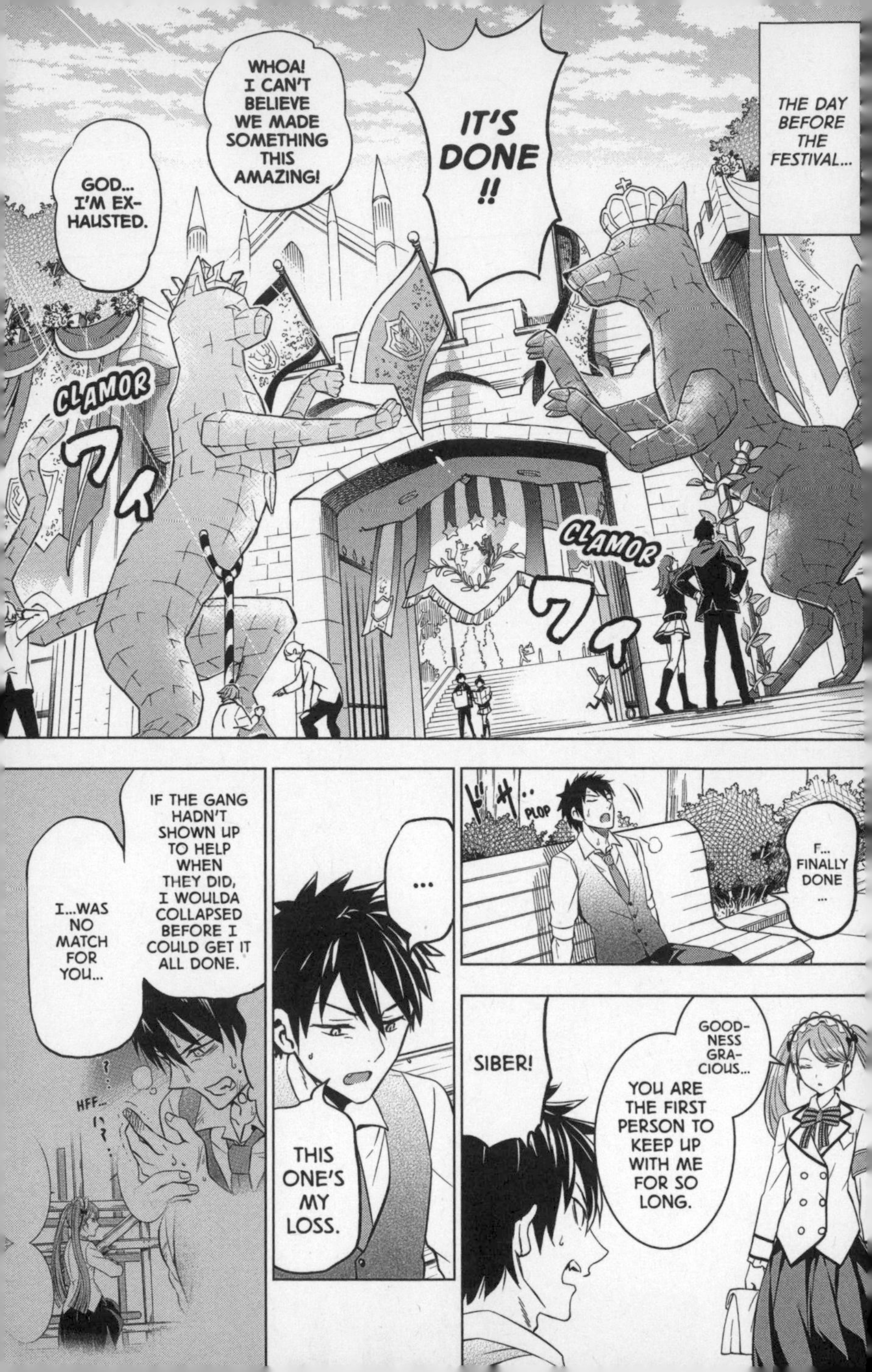
THE DAY BEFORE THE FESTIVAL...
IT'S DONE!!
WHOA! I CAN'T BELIEVE WE MADE SOMETHING THIS AMAZING!
GOD... I'M EXHAUSTED.
CLAMOR
CLAMOR
PLOP
F... FINALLY DONE...
GOODNESS GRACIOUS...
YOU ARE THE FIRST PERSON TO KEEP UP WITH ME FOR SO LONG.
SIBER!
...
THIS ONE'S MY LOSS.
IF THE GANG HADN'T SHOWN UP TO HELP WHEN THEY DID, I WOULDA COLLAPSED BEFORE I COULD GET IT ALL DONE.
I...WAS NO MATCH FOR YOU...
HFF...

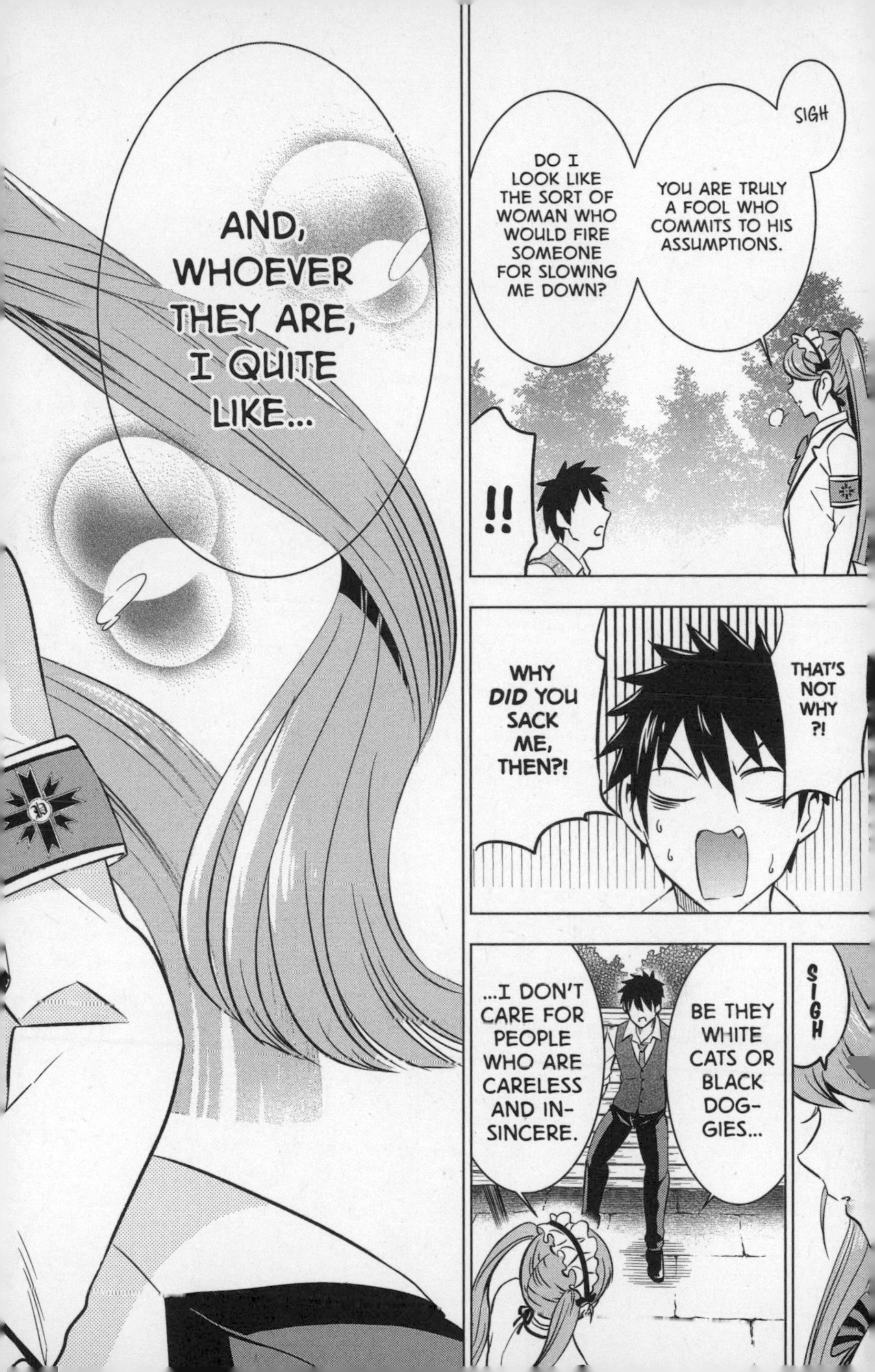
SIGH
YOU ARE TRULY A FOOL WHO COMMITS TO HIS ASSUMPTIONS.
DO I LOOK LIKE THE SORT OF WOMAN WHO WOULD FIRE SOMEONE FOR SLOWING ME DOWN?
!!
THAT'S NOT WHY?!
WHY *DID* YOU SACK ME, THEN?!
SIGH
BE THEY WHITE CATS OR BLACK DOGGIES...
...I DON'T CARE FOR PEOPLE WHO ARE CARELESS AND INSINCERE.
AND, WHOEVER THEY ARE, I QUITE LIKE...

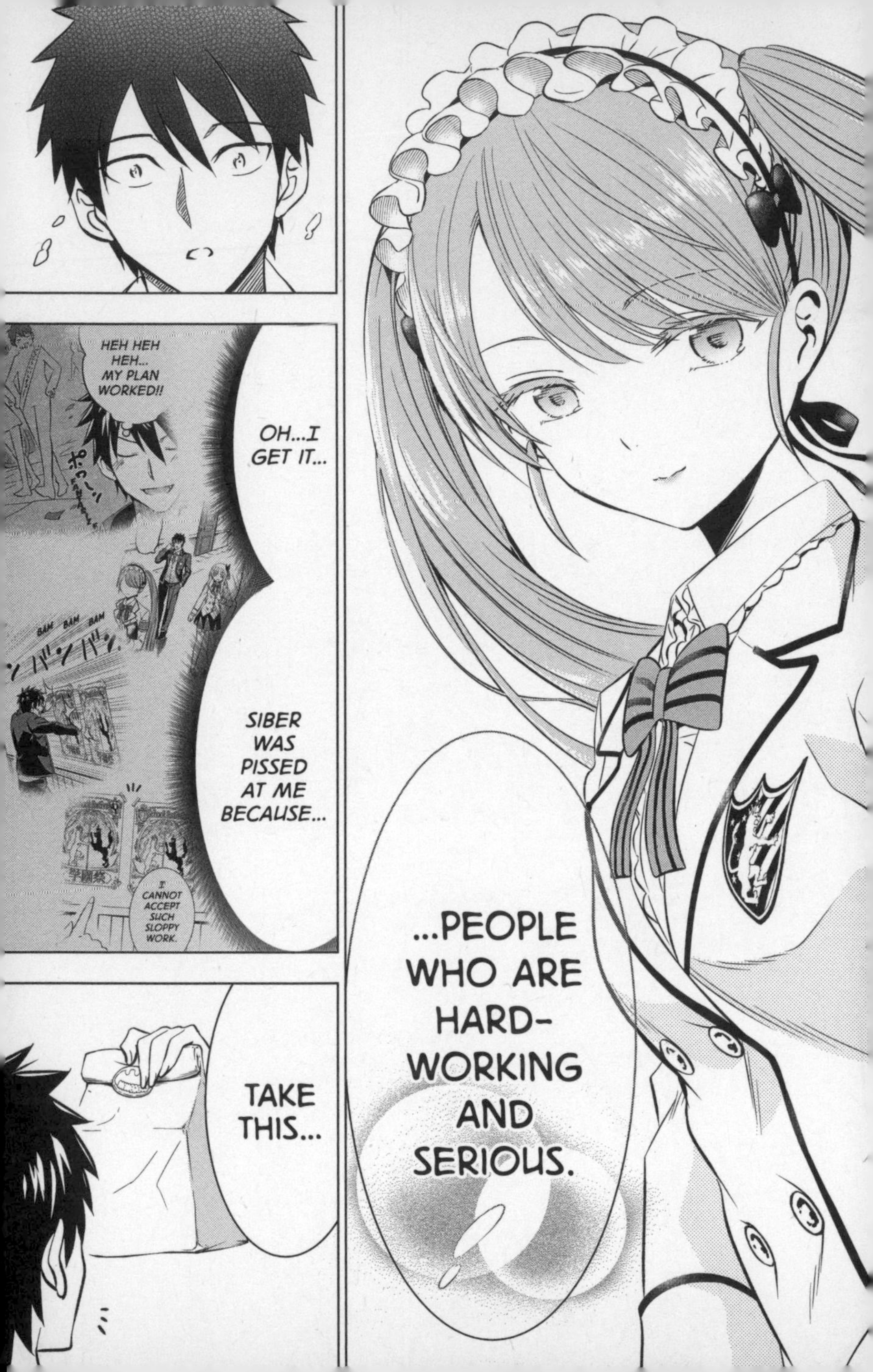
...PEOPLE WHO ARE HARD-WORKING AND SERIOUS.
OH...I GET IT...
SIBER WAS PISSED AT ME BECAUSE...
HEH HEH HEH... MY PLAN WORKED!!
BAM BAM BAM
I CANNOT ACCEPT SUCH SLOPPY WORK.
TAKE THIS...

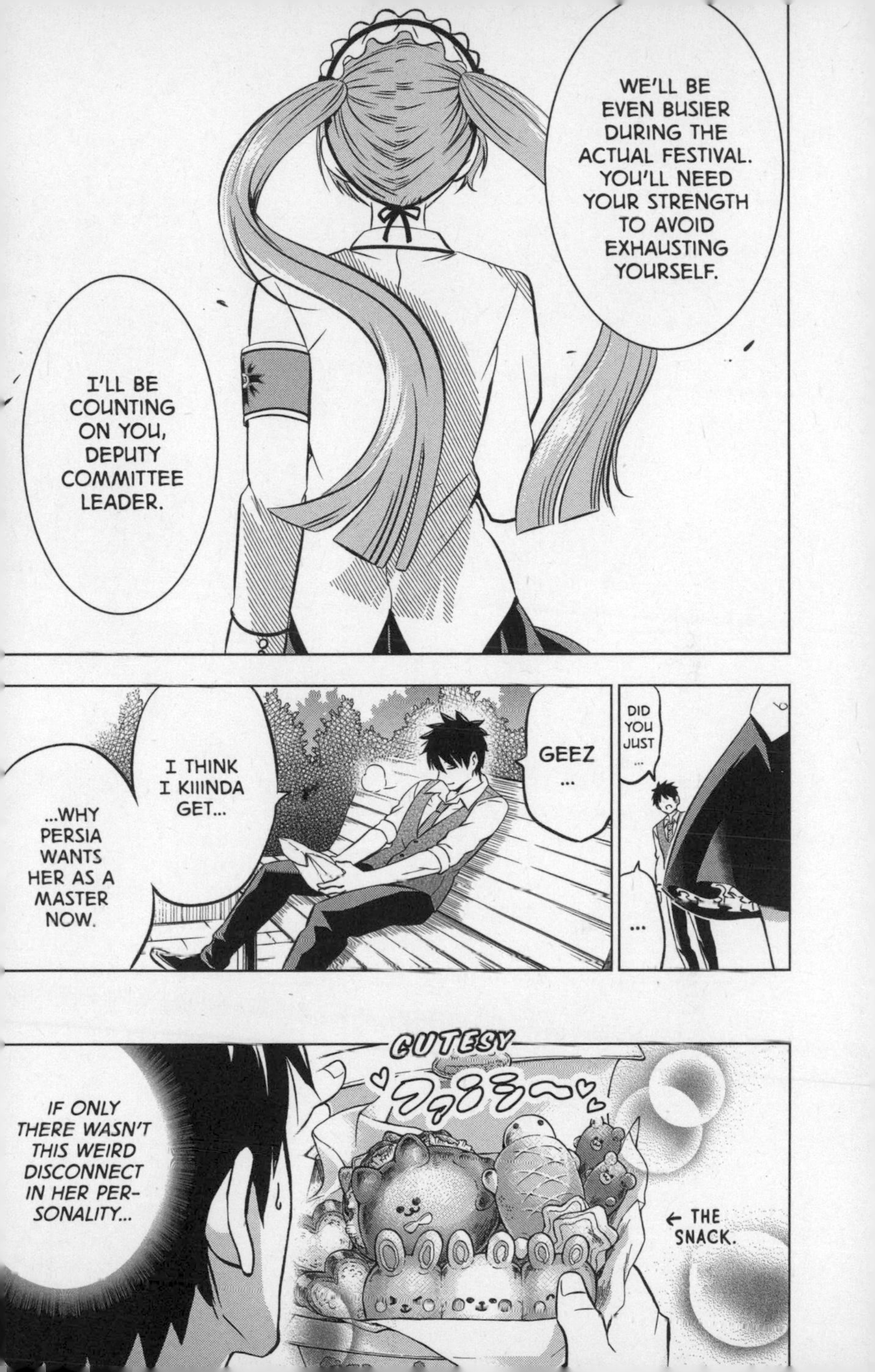
WE'LL BE EVEN BUSIER DURING THE ACTUAL FESTIVAL. YOU'LL NEED YOUR STRENGTH TO AVOID EXHAUSTING YOURSELF.
I'LL BE COUNTING ON YOU, DEPUTY COMMITTEE LEADER.
DID YOU JUST ...
...
GEEZ ...
I THINK I KIIINDA GET...
...WHY PERSIA WANTS HER AS A MASTER NOW.
CUTESY
← THE SNACK.
IF ONLY THERE WASN'T THIS WEIRD DISCONNECT IN HER PER- SONALITY...

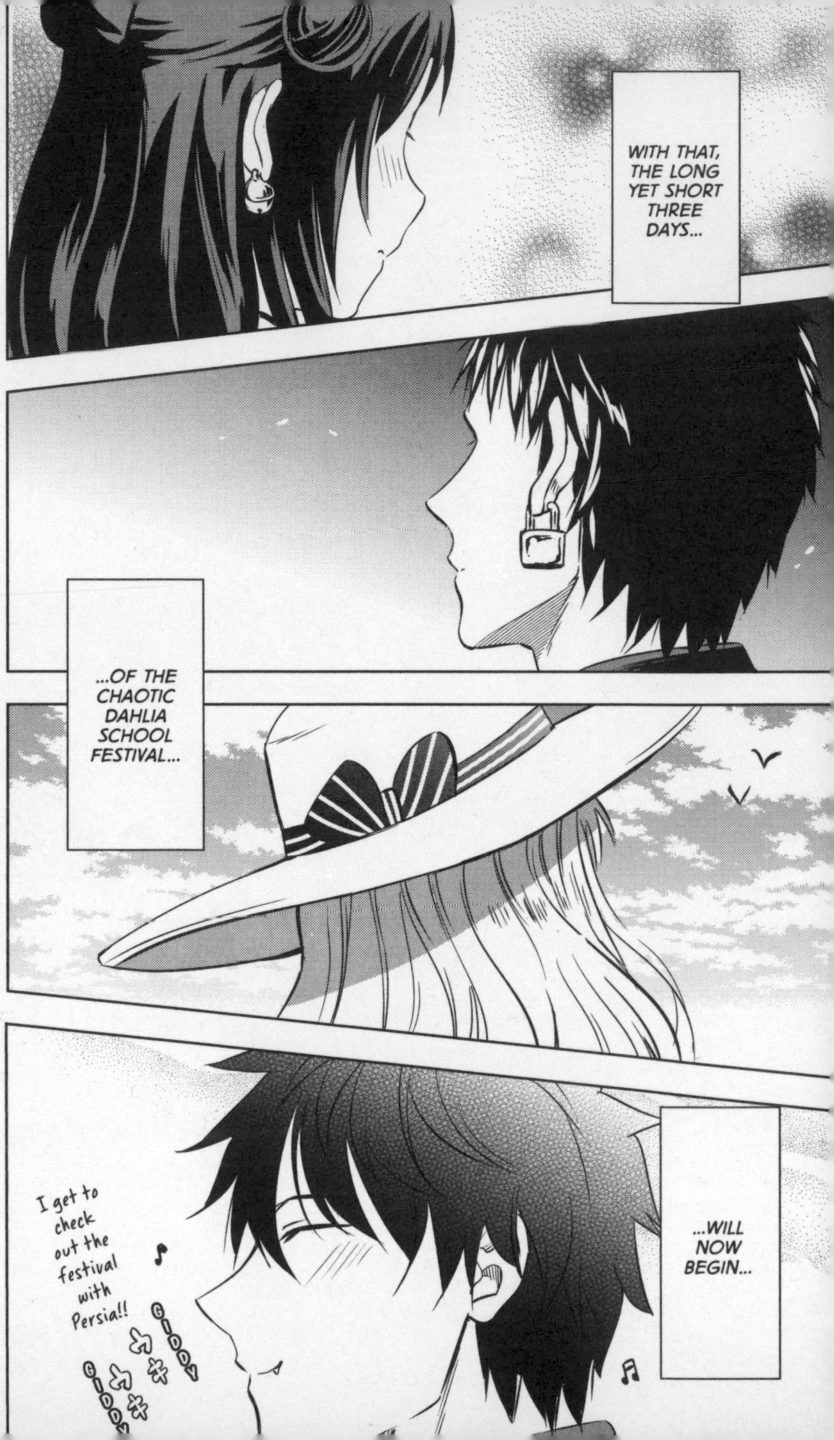
WITH THAT, THE LONG YET SHORT THREE DAYS...
...OF THE CHAOTIC DAHLIA SCHOOL FESTIVAL...
...WILL NOW BEGIN...
I get to check out the festival with Persia!!
GIDDY
GIDDY

EXTRAS SPOTLIGHT

AKITA-KUN

A romantic who dreams of the big city. Since he comes from the countryside, he slips into an accent when he gets emotional. A super-pure and innocent boy.

RABUMI-CHAN

A girl who only has romance on the brain. She changes her hairstyle and clothing depending on her boyfriend. If she doesn't get enough attention, she quickly goes psycho.

SHIZUKA SHISHI

Hasuki's friend. Loves sweets, fashion, and chatting about romance. Three cheers for normalness.

NIA POMERA

Hasuki's friend. Loves girl talk and singing. A normal girl at a school where they're in short supply.

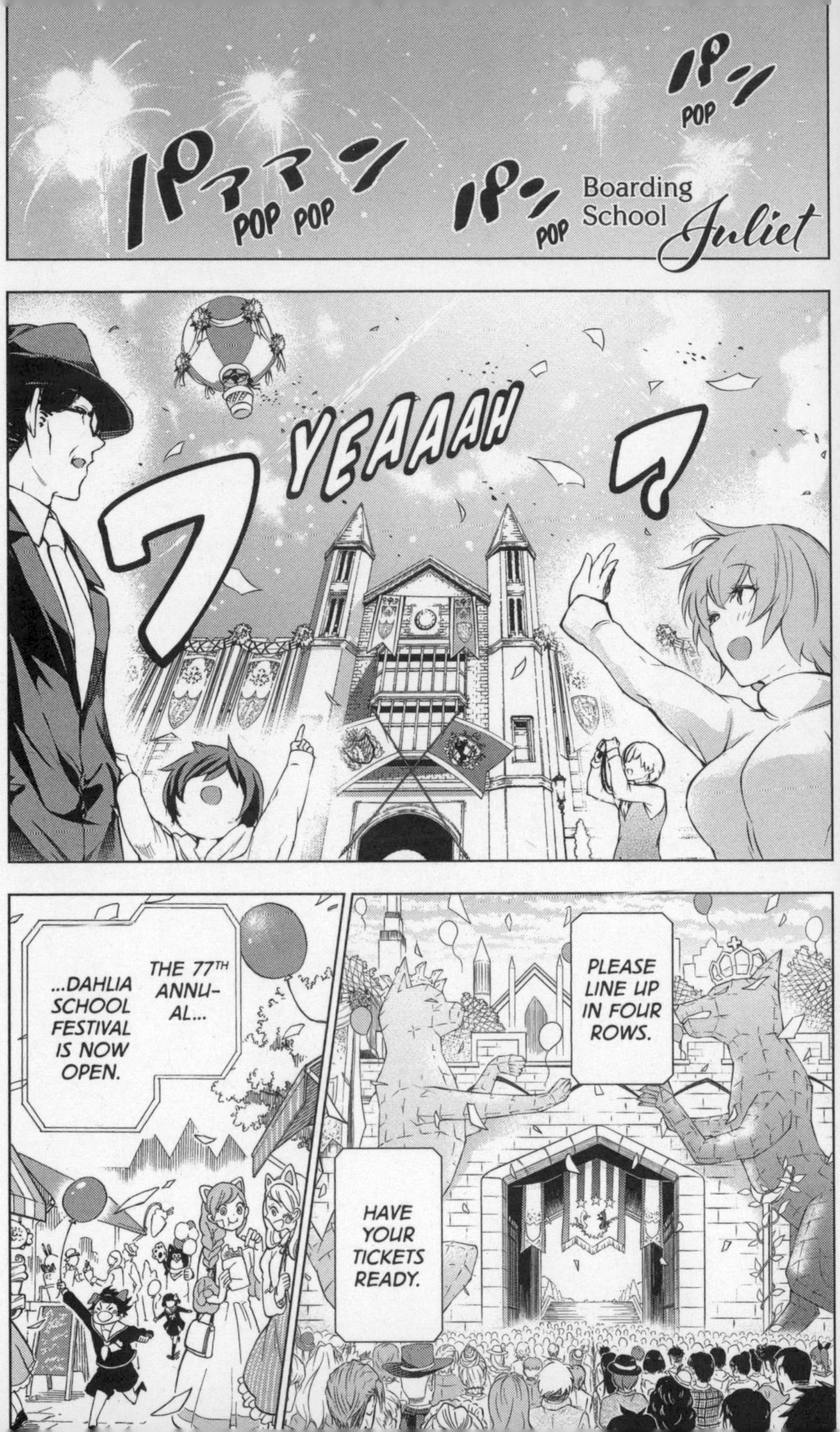
パッ
POP
パッ
POP
パァァンッ
POP POP
Boarding School Juliet
YEAAAH
PLEASE LINE UP IN FOUR ROWS.
HAVE YOUR TICKETS READY.
THE 77TH ANNU-AL...
...DAHLIA SCHOOL FESTIVAL IS NOW OPEN.

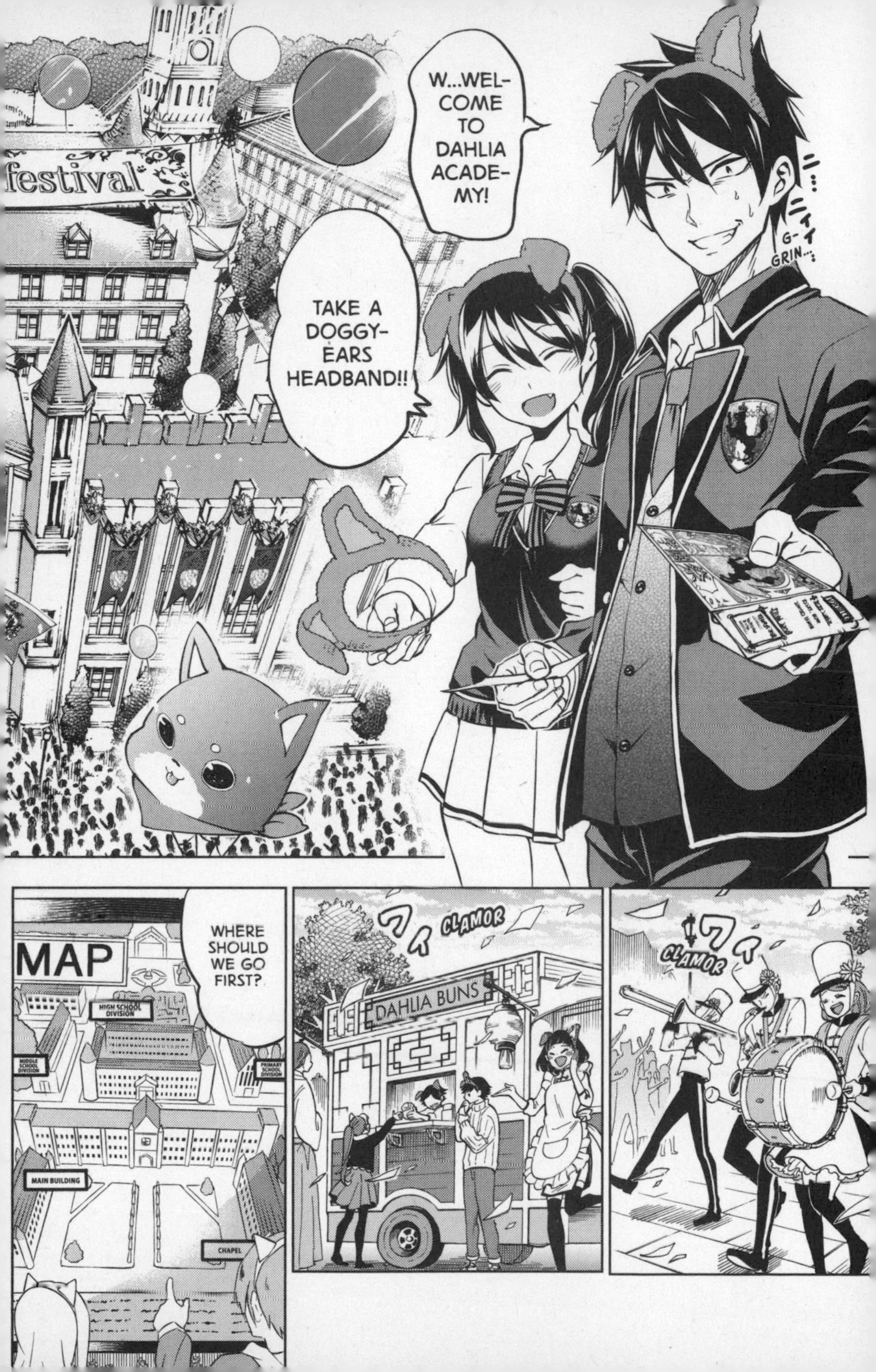
festival
W...WEL-COME TO DAHLIA ACADE-MY!
ニ…ニイイ
G-GRIN…;
TAKE A DOGGY-EARS HEADBAND!!
ワイ
CLAMOR
ワイ
CLAMOR
DAHLIA BUNS
WHERE SHOULD WE GO FIRST?
MAP
HIGH SCHOOL DIVISION
MIDDLE SCHOOL DIVISION
PRIMARY SCHOOL DIVISION
MAIN BUILDING
CHAPEL

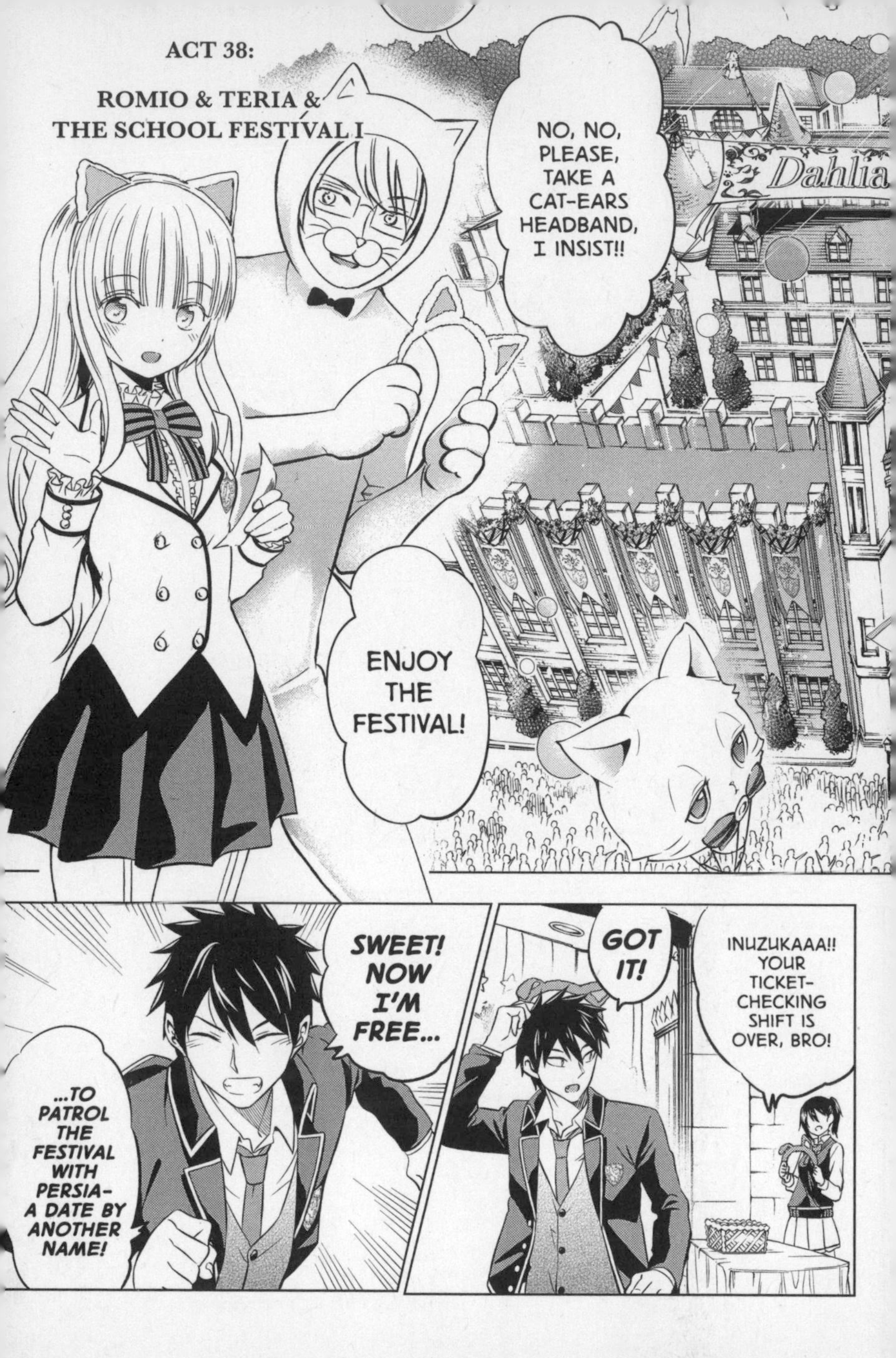
ACT 38:
ROMIO & TERIA & THE SCHOOL FESTIVAL I
NO, NO, PLEASE, TAKE A CAT-EARS HEADBAND, I INSIST!!
Dahlia
ENJOY THE FESTIVAL!
INUZUKAAA!! YOUR TICKET-CHECKING SHIFT IS OVER, BRO!
GOT IT!
SWEET! NOW I'M FREE...
...TO PATROL THE FESTIVAL WITH PERSIA- A DATE BY ANOTHER NAME!

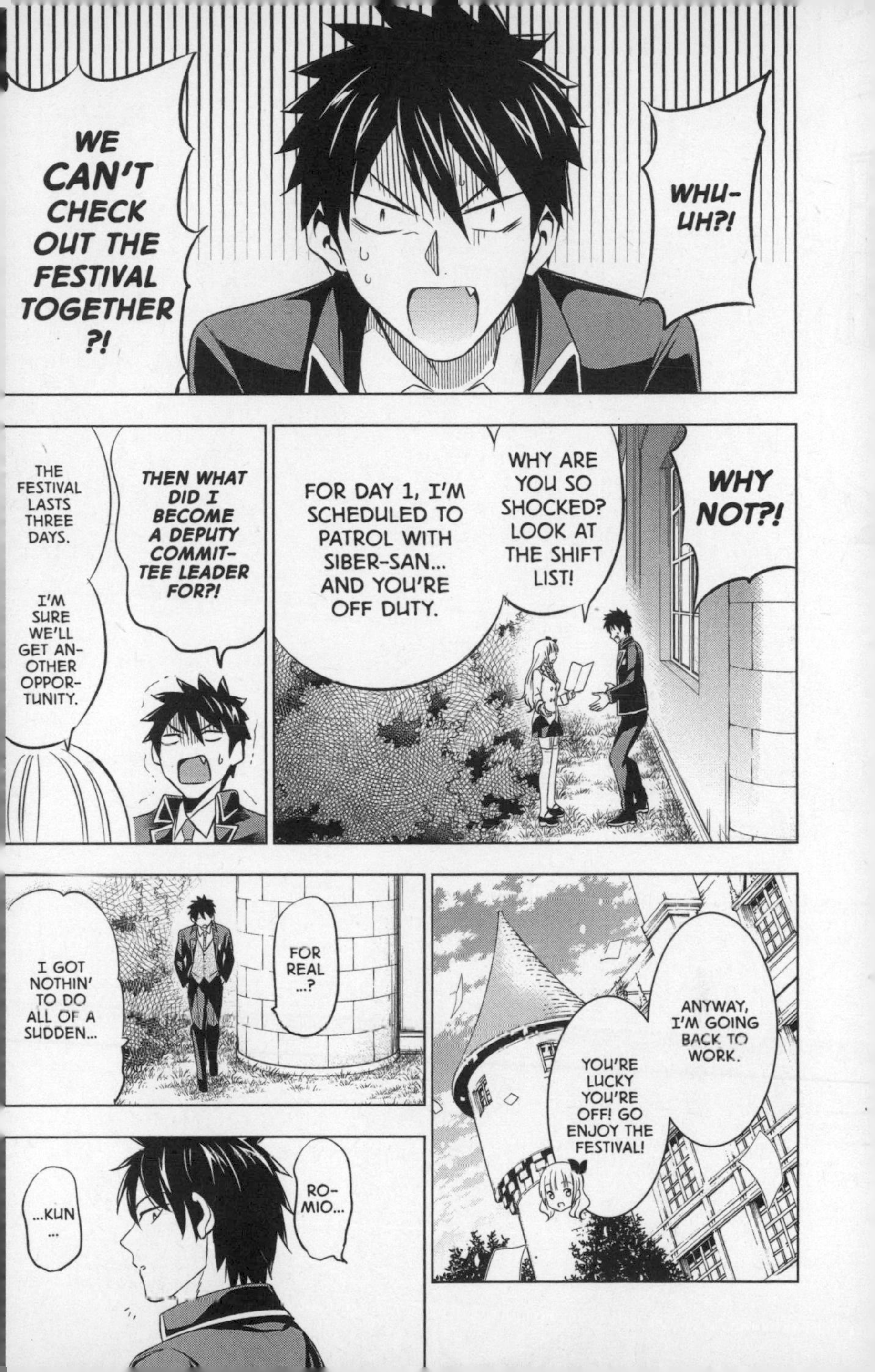
WHU-UH?!
WE CAN'T CHECK OUT THE FESTIVAL TOGETHER?!
WHY NOT?!
WHY ARE YOU SO SHOCKED? LOOK AT THE SHIFT LIST!
FOR DAY 1, I'M SCHEDULED TO PATROL WITH SIBER-SAN... AND YOU'RE OFF DUTY.
THEN WHAT DID I BECOME A DEPUTY COMMIT-TEE LEADER FOR?!
THE FESTIVAL LASTS THREE DAYS.
I'M SURE WE'LL GET AN-OTHER OPPORTUNITY.
ANYWAY, I'M GOING BACK TO WORK.
YOU'RE LUCKY YOU'RE OFF! GO ENJOY THE FESTIVAL!
FOR REAL ...?
I GOT NOTHIN' TO DO ALL OF A SUDDEN...
RO-MIO...
...KUN ...

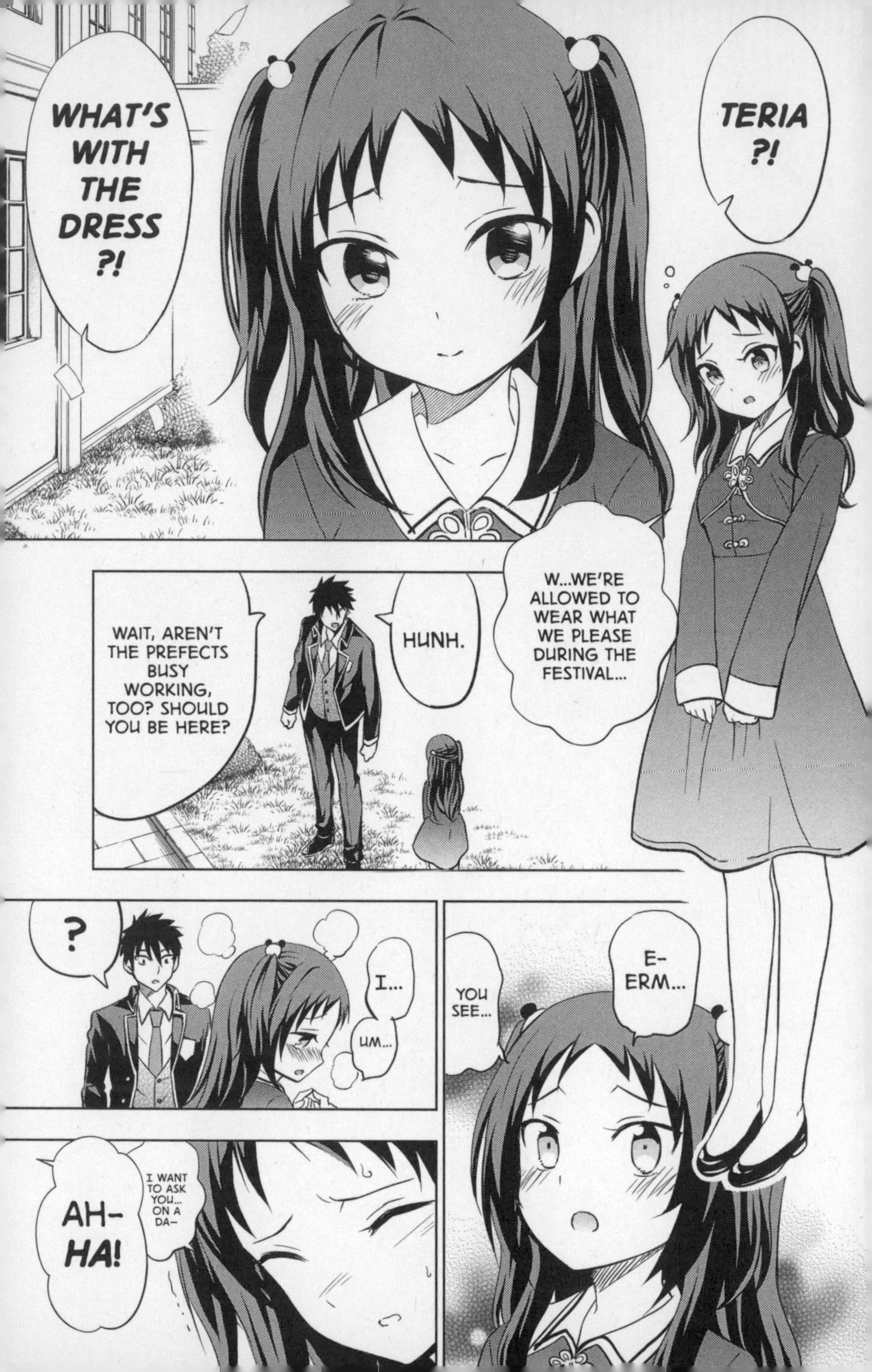
TERIA ?!
WHAT'S WITH THE DRESS ?!
W...WE'RE ALLOWED TO WEAR WHAT WE PLEASE DURING THE FESTIVAL...
HUNH.
WAIT, AREN'T THE PREFECTS BUSY WORKING, TOO? SHOULD YOU BE HERE?
E-ERM...
YOU SEE...
I...
UM...
?
I WANT TO ASK YOU... ON A DA–
AH-HA!

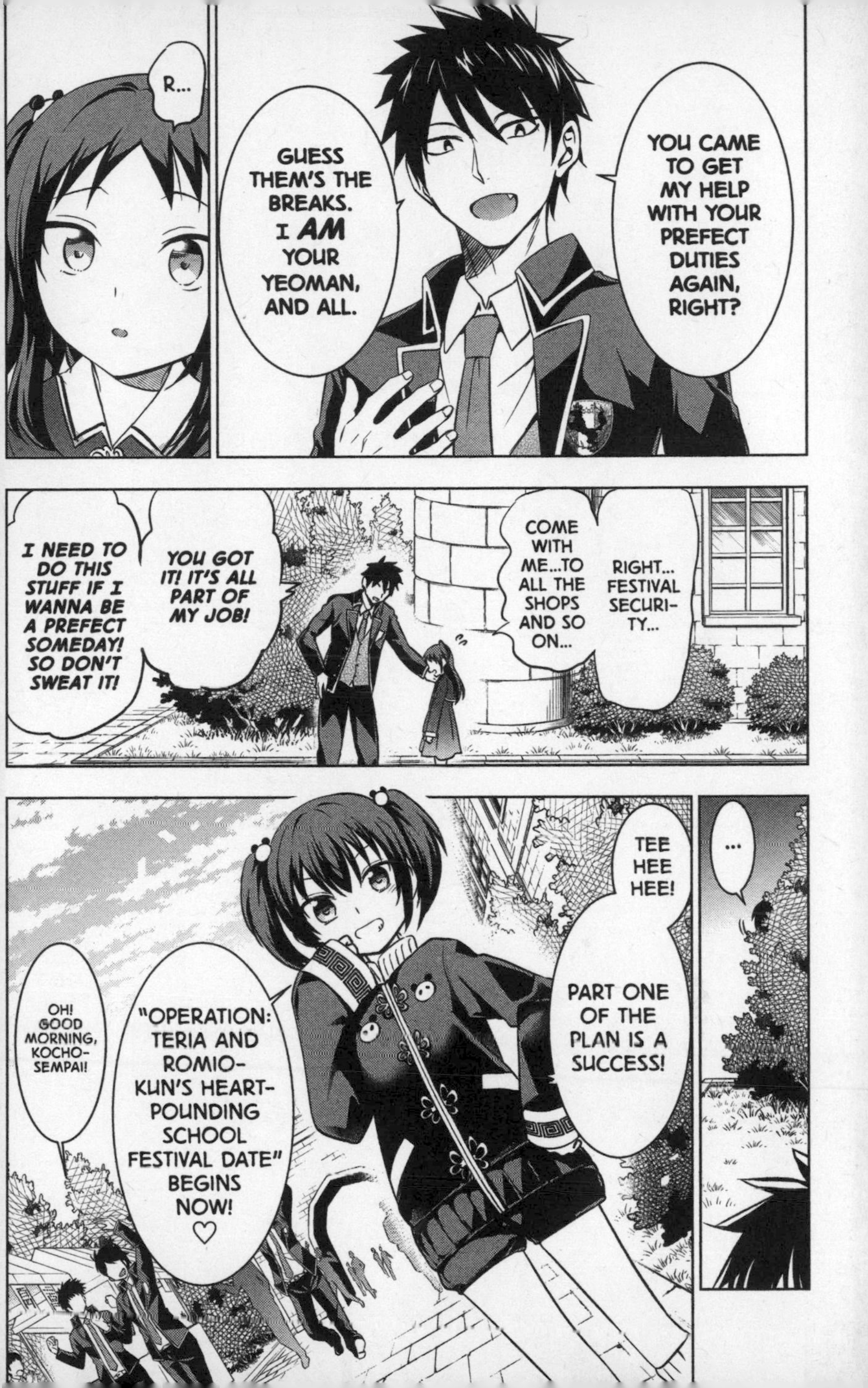
YOU CAME TO GET MY HELP WITH YOUR PREFECT DUTIES AGAIN, RIGHT?
GUESS THEM'S THE BREAKS. I *AM* YOUR YEOMAN, AND ALL.
R...
RIGHT... FESTIVAL SECURI-TY...
COME WITH ME...TO ALL THE SHOPS AND SO ON...
YOU GOT IT! IT'S ALL PART OF MY JOB!
I NEED TO DO THIS STUFF IF I WANNA BE A PREFECT SOMEDAY! SO DON'T SWEAT IT!
...
TEE HEE HEE!
PART ONE OF THE PLAN IS A SUCCESS!
"OPERATION: TERIA AND ROMIO-KUN'S HEART-POUNDING SCHOOL FESTIVAL DATE" BEGINS NOW! ♡
OH! GOOD MORNING, KOCHO-SEMPAI!

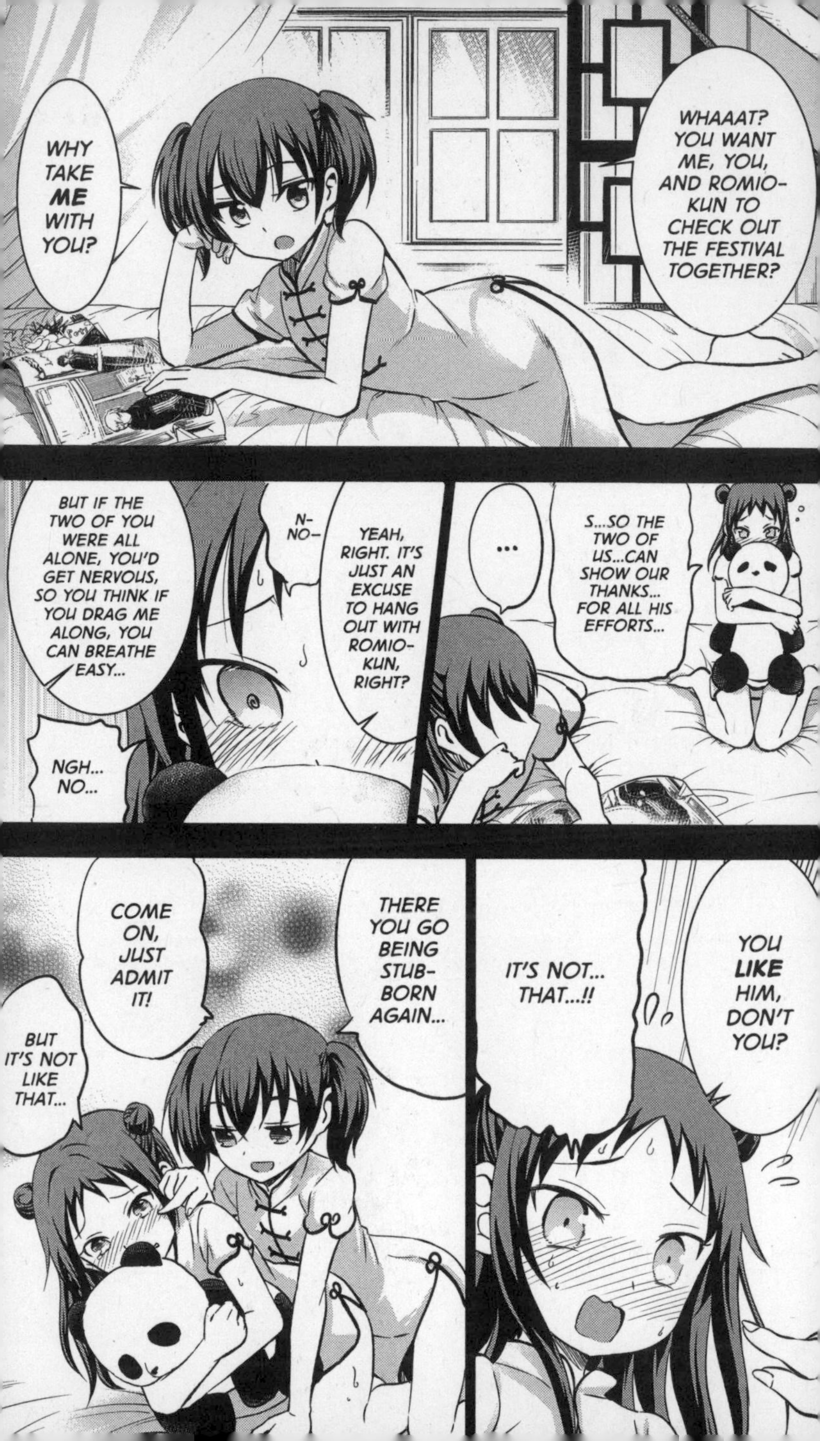
WHAAAT? YOU WANT ME, YOU, AND ROMIO-KUN TO CHECK OUT THE FESTIVAL TOGETHER?
WHY TAKE **ME** WITH YOU?
S...SO THE TWO OF US...CAN SHOW OUR THANKS... FOR ALL HIS EFFORTS...
...
YEAH, RIGHT. IT'S JUST AN EXCUSE TO HANG OUT WITH ROMIO-KUN, RIGHT?
N- NO-
BUT IF THE TWO OF YOU WERE ALL ALONE, YOU'D GET NERVOUS, SO YOU THINK IF YOU DRAG ME ALONG, YOU CAN BREATHE EASY...
NGH... NO...
YOU **LIKE** HIM, DON'T YOU?
IT'S NOT... THAT...!!
THERE YOU GO BEING STUB-BORN AGAIN...
COME ON, JUST ADMIT IT!
BUT IT'S NOT LIKE THAT...

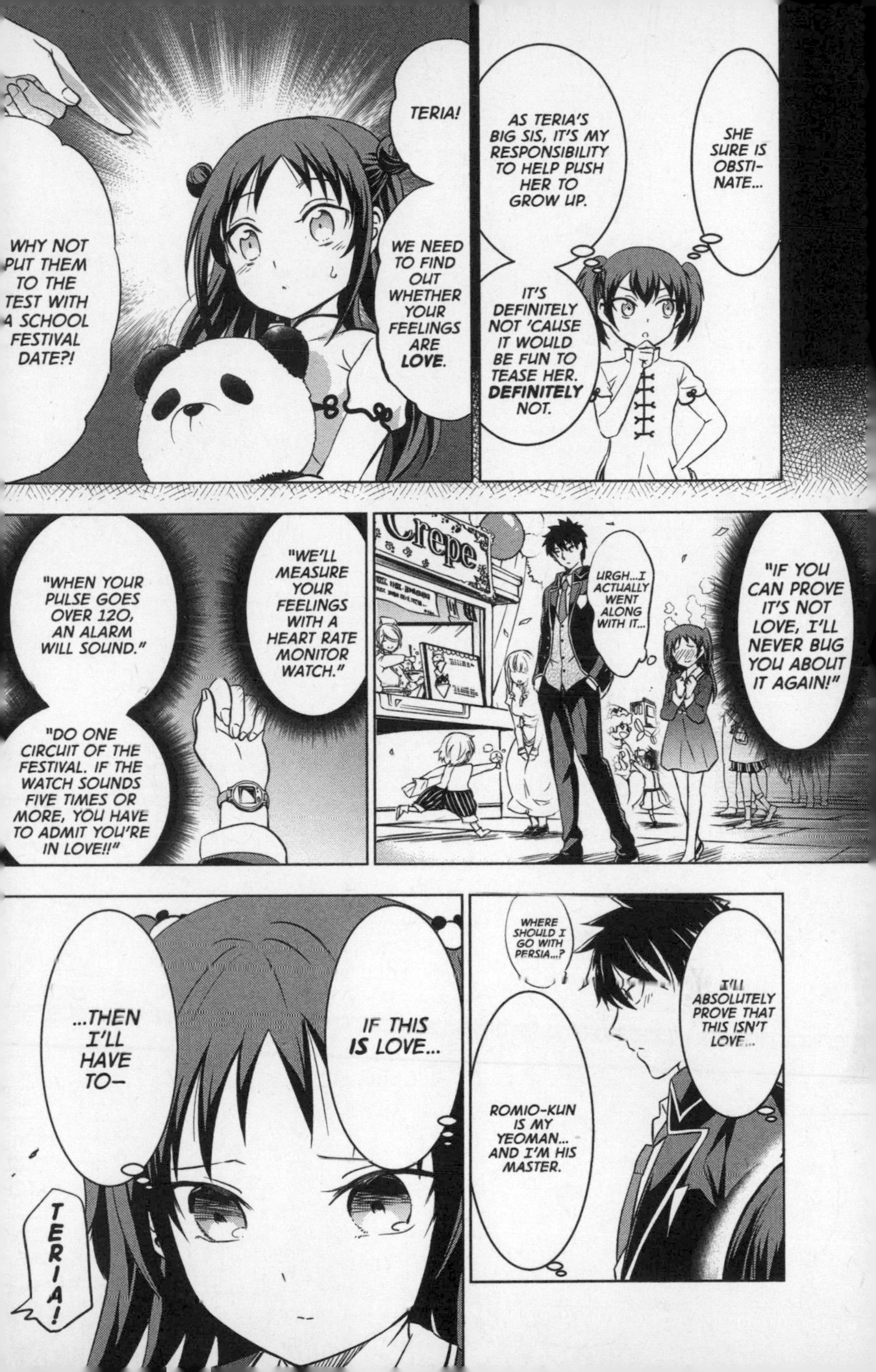
SHE SURE IS OBSTINATE...
AS TERIA'S BIG SIS, IT'S MY RESPONSIBILITY TO HELP PUSH HER TO GROW UP.
IT'S DEFINITELY NOT 'CAUSE IT WOULD BE FUN TO TEASE HER. **DEFINITELY** NOT.
TERIA!
WE NEED TO FIND OUT WHETHER YOUR FEELINGS ARE **LOVE**.
WHY NOT PUT THEM TO THE TEST WITH A SCHOOL FESTIVAL DATE?!
"IF YOU CAN PROVE IT'S NOT LOVE, I'LL NEVER BUG YOU ABOUT IT AGAIN!"
URGH...I ACTUALLY WENT ALONG WITH IT...
Crepe
"WE'LL MEASURE YOUR FEELINGS WITH A HEART RATE MONITOR WATCH."
"WHEN YOUR PULSE GOES OVER 120, AN ALARM WILL SOUND."
"DO ONE CIRCUIT OF THE FESTIVAL. IF THE WATCH SOUNDS FIVE TIMES OR MORE, YOU HAVE TO ADMIT YOU'RE IN LOVE!!"
I'LL ABSOLUTELY PROVE THAT THIS ISN'T LOVE...
WHERE SHOULD I GO WITH PERSIA...?
ROMIO-KUN IS MY YEOMAN... AND I'M HIS MASTER.
IF THIS **IS** LOVE...
...THEN I'LL HAVE TO–
TERIA!

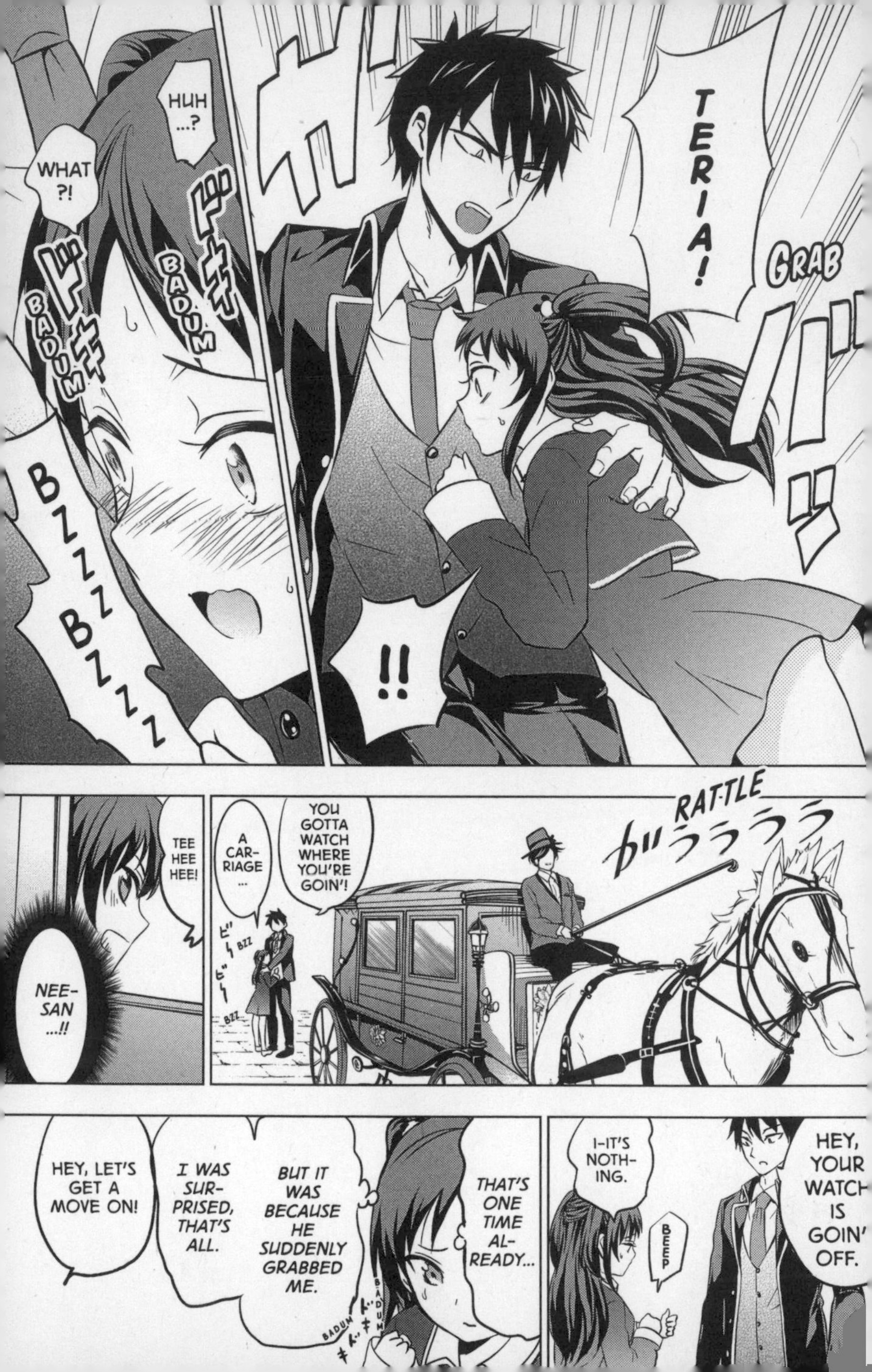
TERIA!
GRAB
!!
HUH ...?
WHAT ?!
BADUM
BADUM
BZZZZ
BZZZZ
RATTLE
YOU GOTTA WATCH WHERE YOU'RE GOIN'!
A CARRIAGE ...
BZZ
BZZ
TEE HEE HEE!
NEE-SAN ...!!
HEY, YOUR WATCH IS GOIN' OFF.
BEEP
I-IT'S NOTHING.
THAT'S ONE TIME ALREADY...
BUT IT WAS BECAUSE HE SUDDENLY GRABBED ME.
BADUM
BADUM
I WAS SURPRISED, THAT'S ALL.
HEY, LET'S GET A MOVE ON!

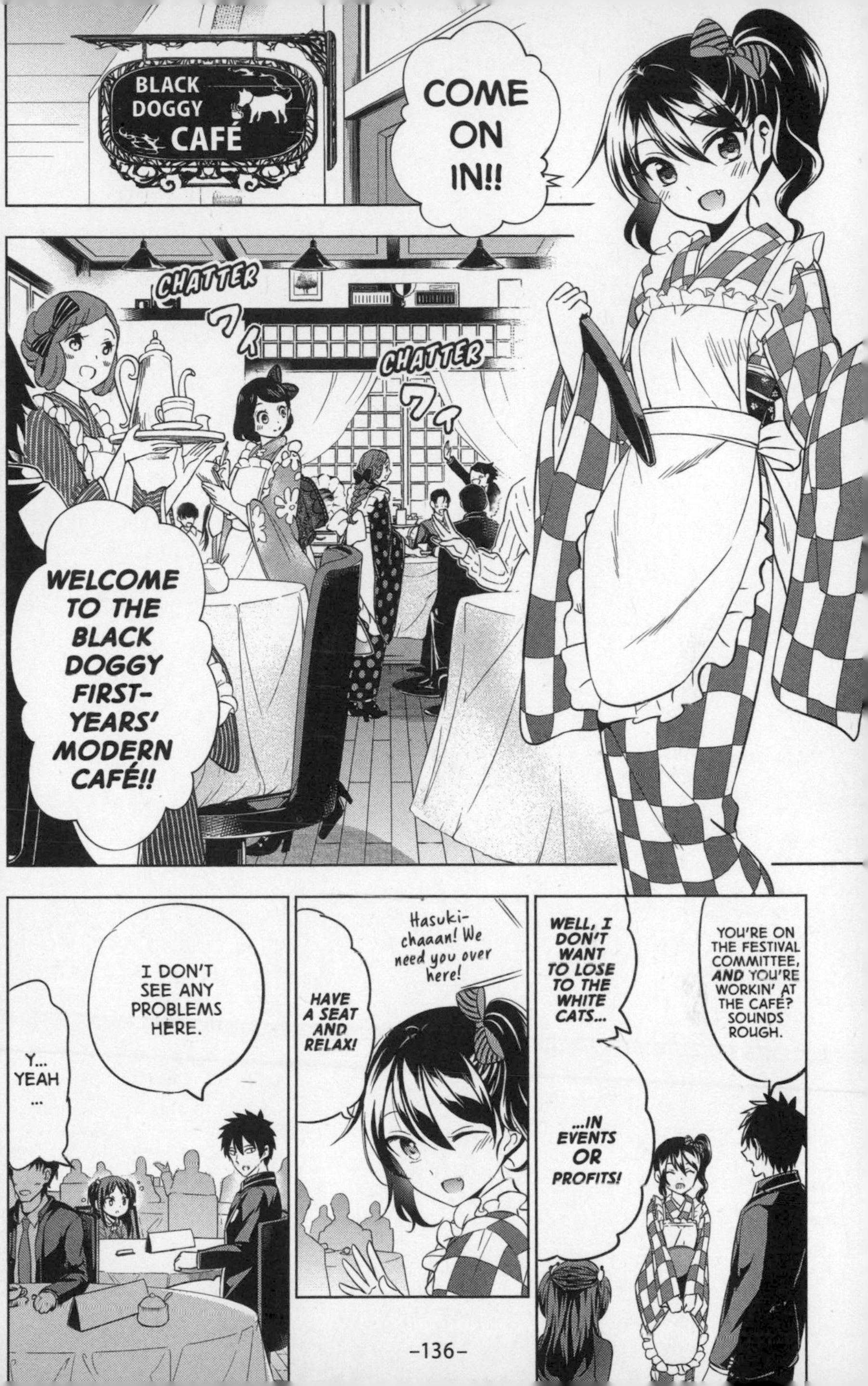
BLACK DOGGY CAFÉ
COME ON IN!!
CHATTER
ワイ
CHATTER
ワイ
WELCOME TO THE BLACK DOGGY FIRST-YEARS' MODERN CAFÉ!!
YOU'RE ON THE FESTIVAL COMMITTEE, AND YOU'RE WORKIN' AT THE CAFÉ? SOUNDS ROUGH.
WELL, I DON'T WANT TO LOSE TO THE WHITE CATS...
...IN EVENTS OR PROFITS!
Hasuki-chaaan! We need you over here!
HAVE A SEAT AND RELAX!
I DON'T SEE ANY PROBLEMS HERE.
Y... YEAH ...

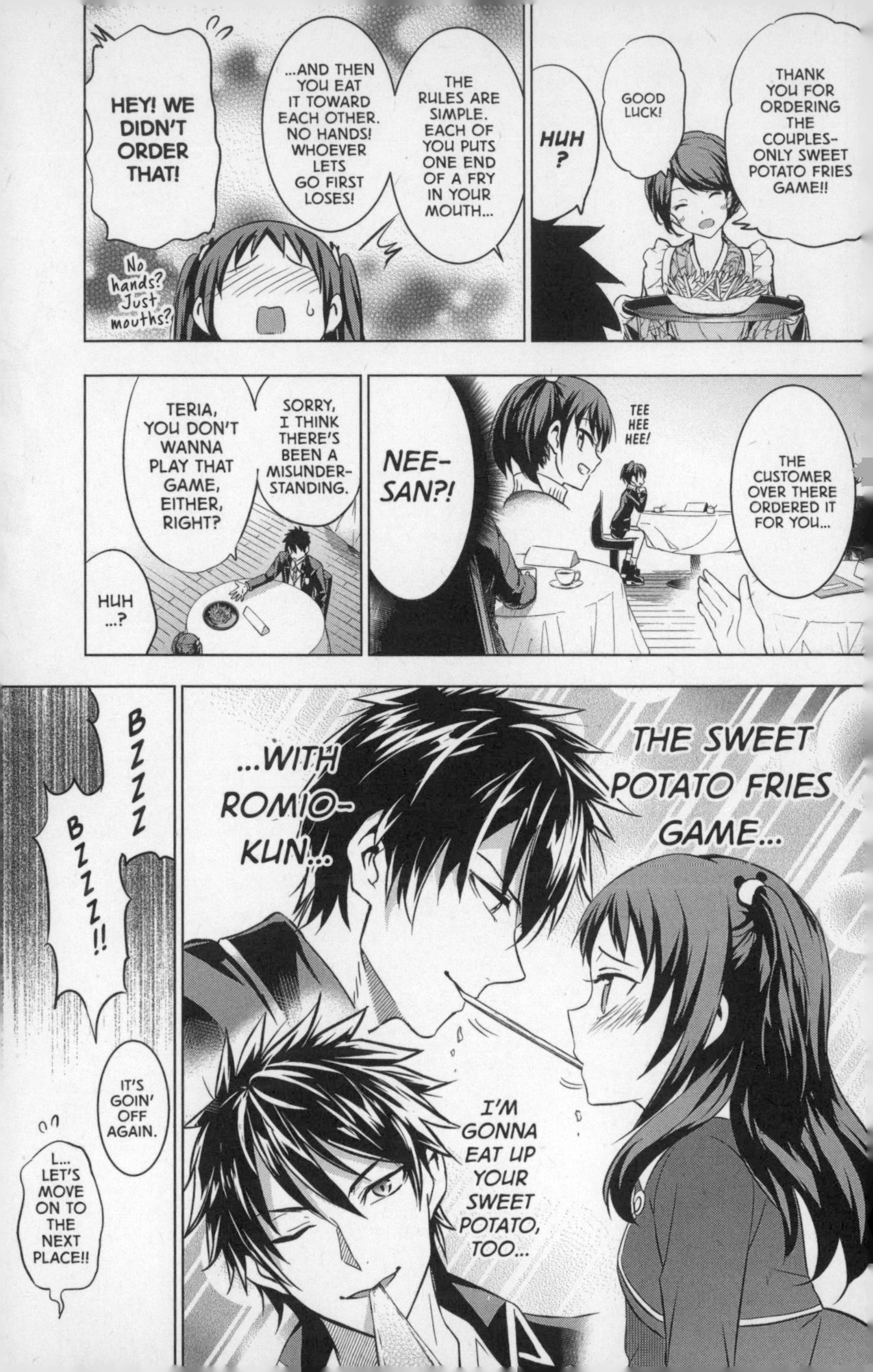
THANK YOU FOR ORDERING THE COUPLES-ONLY SWEET POTATO FRIES GAME!!
GOOD LUCK!
HUH?
THE RULES ARE SIMPLE. EACH OF YOU PUTS ONE END OF A FRY IN YOUR MOUTH...
...AND THEN YOU EAT IT TOWARD EACH OTHER. NO HANDS! WHOEVER LETS GO FIRST LOSES!
HEY! WE DIDN'T ORDER THAT!
No hands? Just mouths?
THE CUSTOMER OVER THERE ORDERED IT FOR YOU...
TEE HEE HEE!
NEE-SAN?!
SORRY, I THINK THERE'S BEEN A MISUNDERSTANDING.
TERIA, YOU DON'T WANNA PLAY THAT GAME, EITHER, RIGHT?
HUH ...?
THE SWEET POTATO FRIES GAME...
...WITH ROMIO-KUN...
I'M GONNA EAT UP YOUR SWEET POTATO, TOO...
BZZZ
BZZZZ!!
IT'S GOIN' OFF AGAIN.
L... LET'S MOVE ON TO THE NEXT PLACE!!

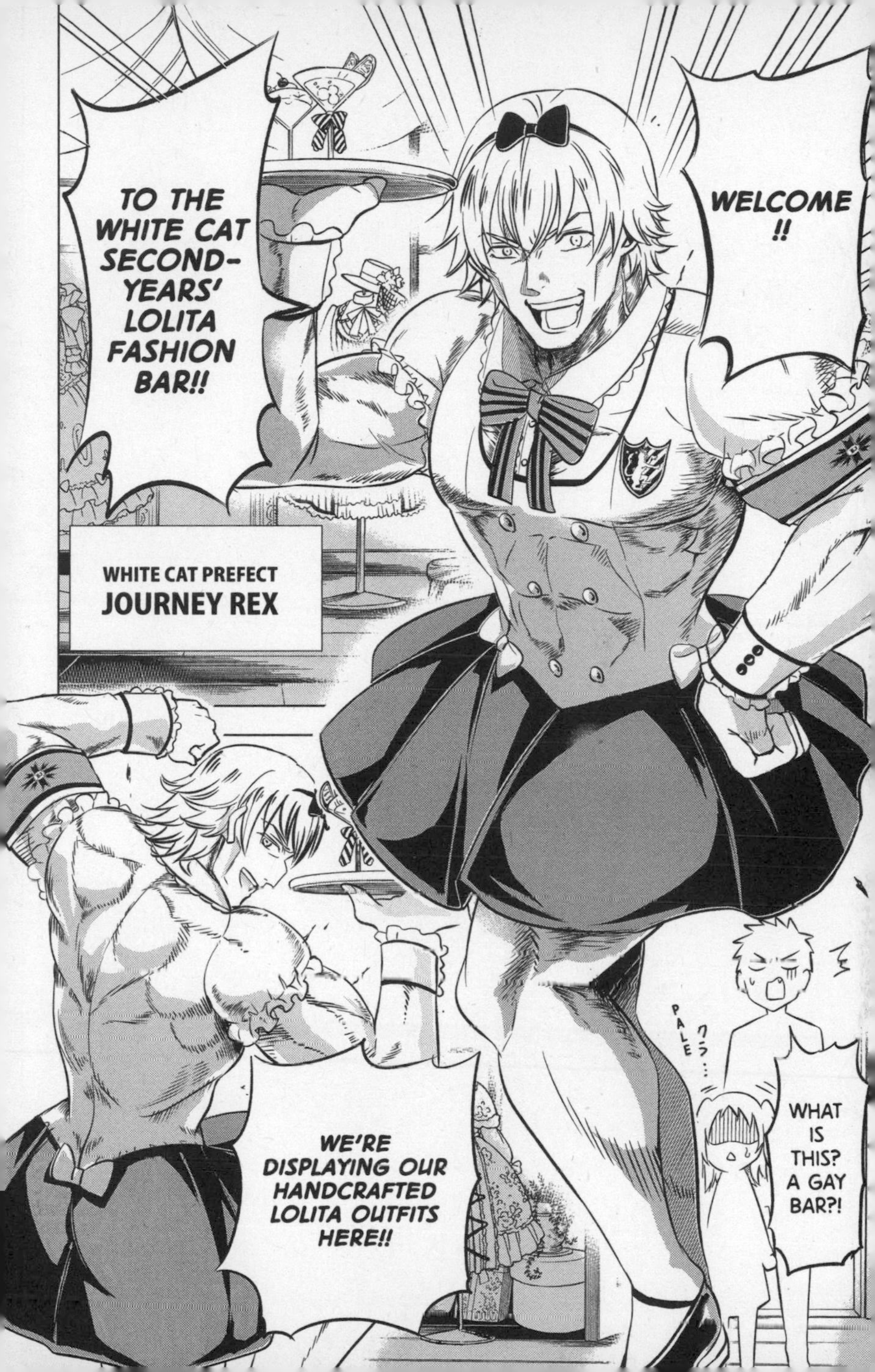
WELCOME!!
TO THE WHITE CAT SECOND-YEARS' LOLITA FASHION BAR!!
WHITE CAT PREFECT
JOURNEY REX
WHAT IS THIS? A GAY BAR?!
PALE
WE'RE DISPLAYING OUR HANDCRAFTED LOLITA OUTFITS HERE!!

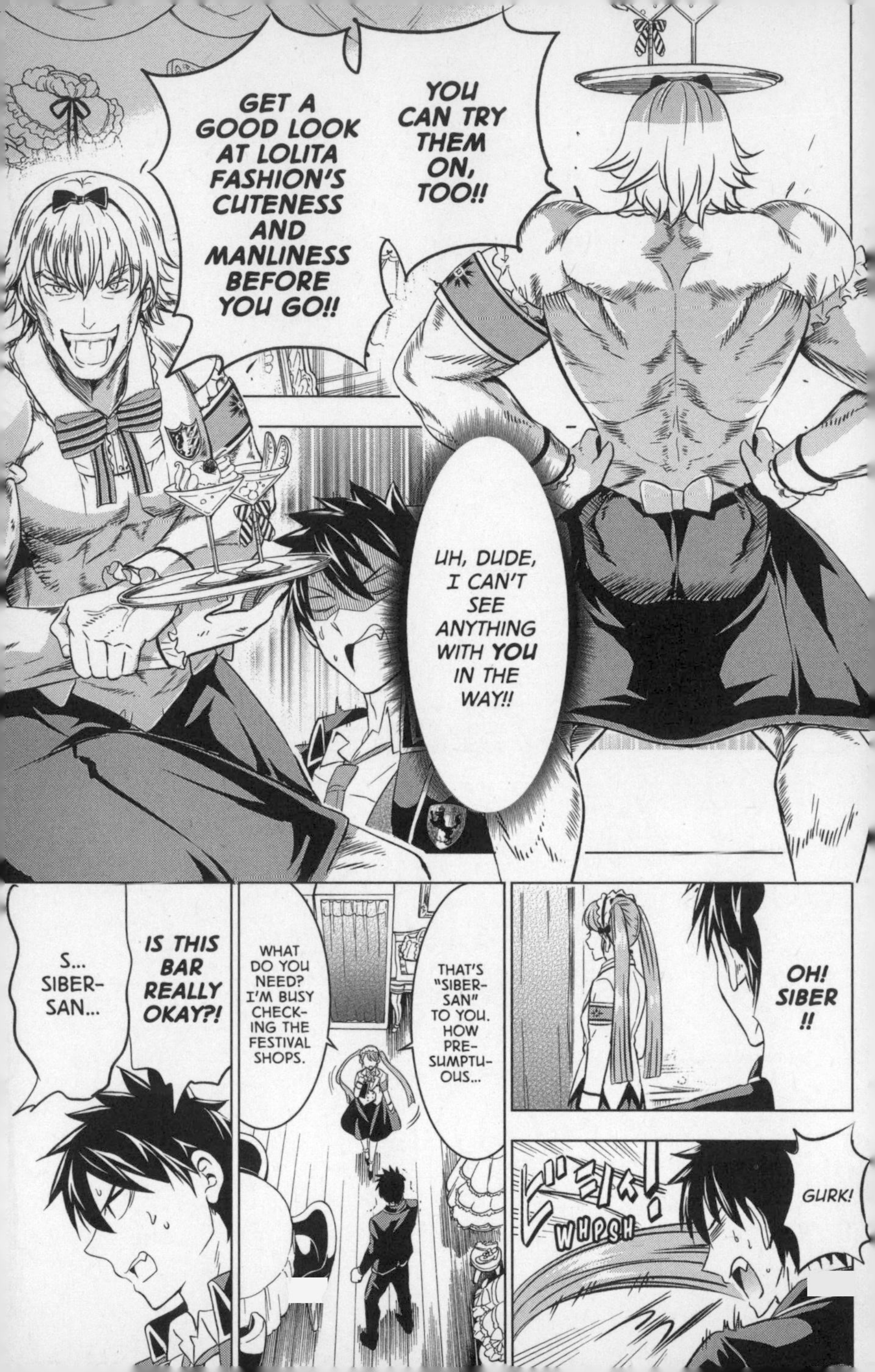

YOU CAN TRY THEM ON, TOO!!
GET A GOOD LOOK AT LOLITA FASHION'S CUTENESS AND MANLINESS BEFORE YOU GO!!
UH, DUDE, I CAN'T SEE ANYTHING WITH YOU IN THE WAY!!
OH! SIBER!!
WHPSH
GURK!
THAT'S "SIBER-SAN" TO YOU. HOW PRE-SUMPTU-OUS...
WHAT DO YOU NEED? I'M BUSY CHECK-ING THE FESTIVAL SHOPS.
IS THIS BAR REALLY OKAY?!
S... SIBER-SAN...

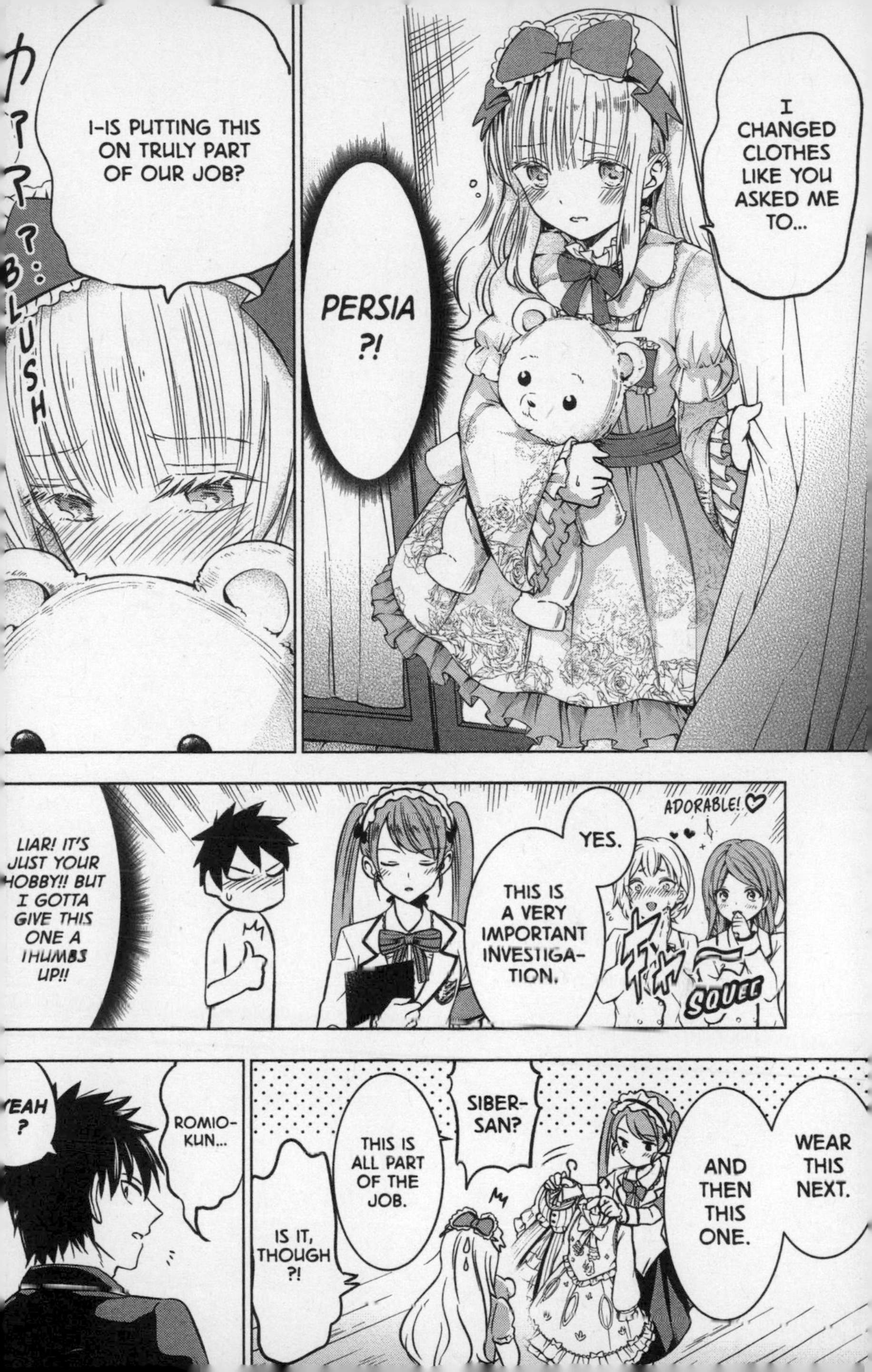
I CHANGED CLOTHES LIKE YOU ASKED ME TO...
PERSIA ?!
I-IS PUTTING THIS ON TRULY PART OF OUR JOB?
BLUSH
ADORABLE! ♡
SQUEE
YES.
THIS IS A VERY IMPORTANT INVESTIGA-TION.
LIAR! IT'S JUST YOUR HOBBY!! BUT I GOTTA GIVE THIS ONE A THUMBS UP!!
WEAR THIS NEXT.
AND THEN THIS ONE.
SIBER-SAN?
THIS IS ALL PART OF THE JOB.
IS IT, THOUGH ?!
ROMIO-KUN...
YEAH ?

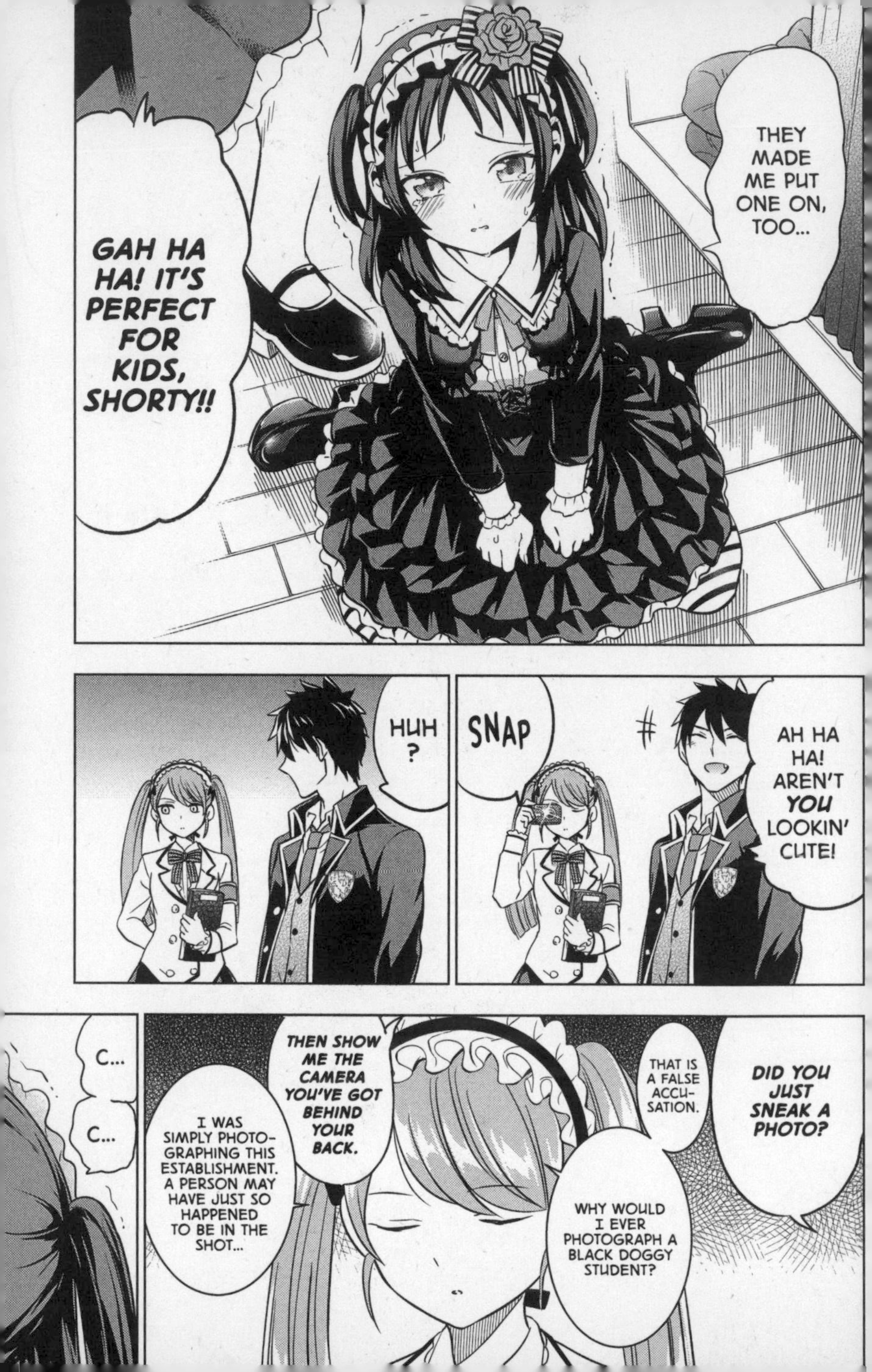
THEY MADE ME PUT ONE ON, TOO...
GAH HA HA! IT'S PERFECT FOR KIDS, SHORTY!!
AH HA HA! AREN'T YOU LOOKIN' CUTE!
SNAP
HUH?
DID YOU JUST SNEAK A PHOTO?
THAT IS A FALSE ACCUSATION.
WHY WOULD I EVER PHOTOGRAPH A BLACK DOGGY STUDENT?
THEN SHOW ME THE CAMERA YOU'VE GOT BEHIND YOUR BACK.
I WAS SIMPLY PHOTOGRAPHING THIS ESTABLISHMENT. A PERSON MAY HAVE JUST SO HAPPENED TO BE IN THE SHOT...
C...
C...

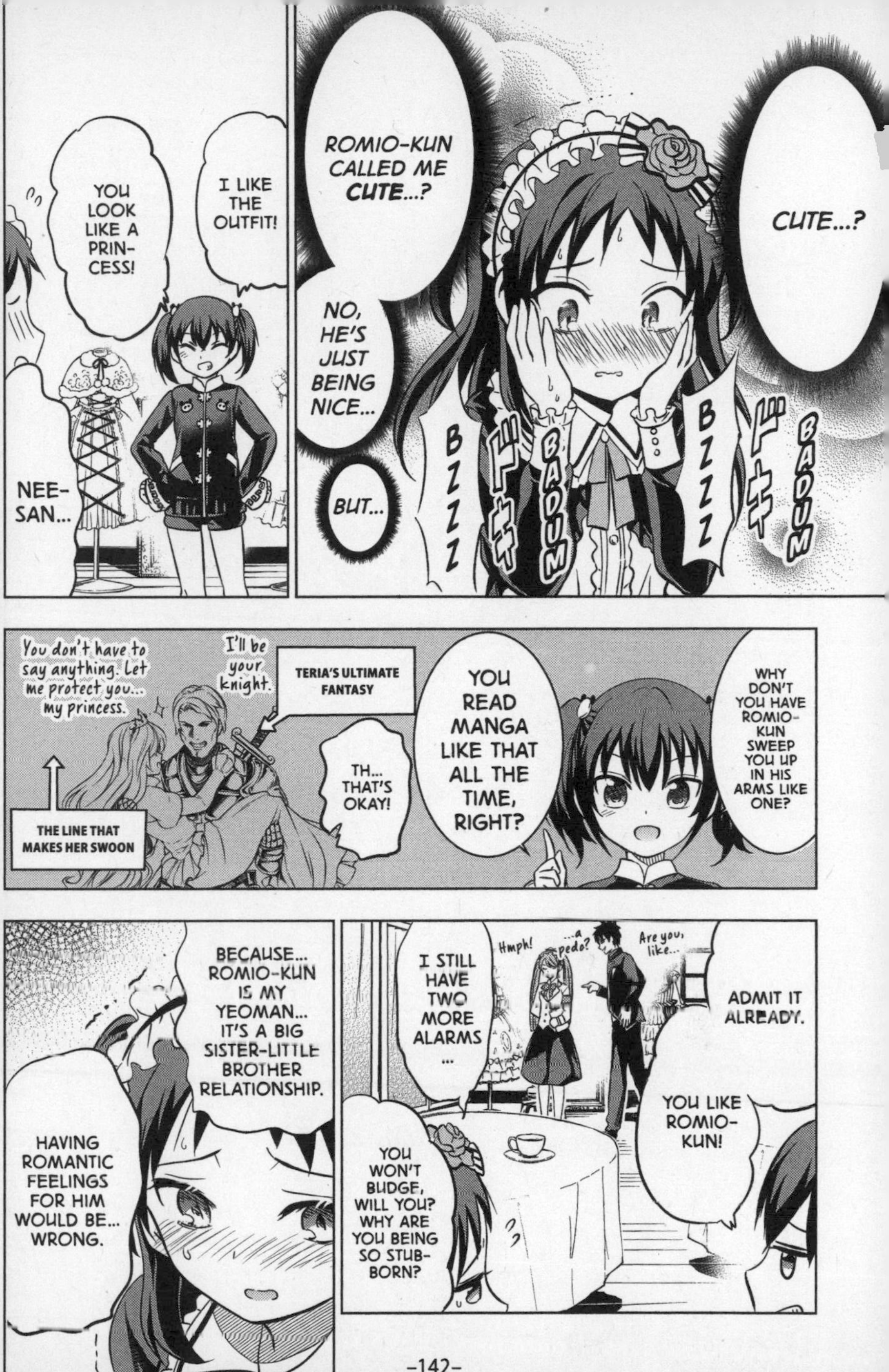
CUTE...?
BADUM
BZZZ
BADUM
BZZZ
ROMIO-KUN CALLED ME CUTE...?
NO, HE'S JUST BEING NICE...
BUT...
I LIKE THE OUTFIT!
YOU LOOK LIKE A PRIN-CESS!
NEE-SAN...
WHY DON'T YOU HAVE ROMIO-KUN SWEEP YOU UP IN HIS ARMS LIKE ONE?
YOU READ MANGA LIKE THAT ALL THE TIME, RIGHT?
TH... THAT'S OKAY!
TERIA'S ULTIMATE FANTASY
I'll be your knight.
You don't have to say anything. Let me protect you... my princess.
THE LINE THAT MAKES HER SWOON
ADMIT IT ALREADY.
Are you, like...
...a pedo?
Hmph!
I STILL HAVE TWO MORE ALARMS...
YOU LIKE ROMIO-KUN!
YOU WON'T BUDGE, WILL YOU? WHY ARE YOU BEING SO STUB-BORN?
BECAUSE... ROMIO-KUN IS MY YEOMAN... IT'S A BIG SISTER-LITTLE BROTHER RELATIONSHIP.
HAVING ROMANTIC FEELINGS FOR HIM WOULD BE... WRONG.

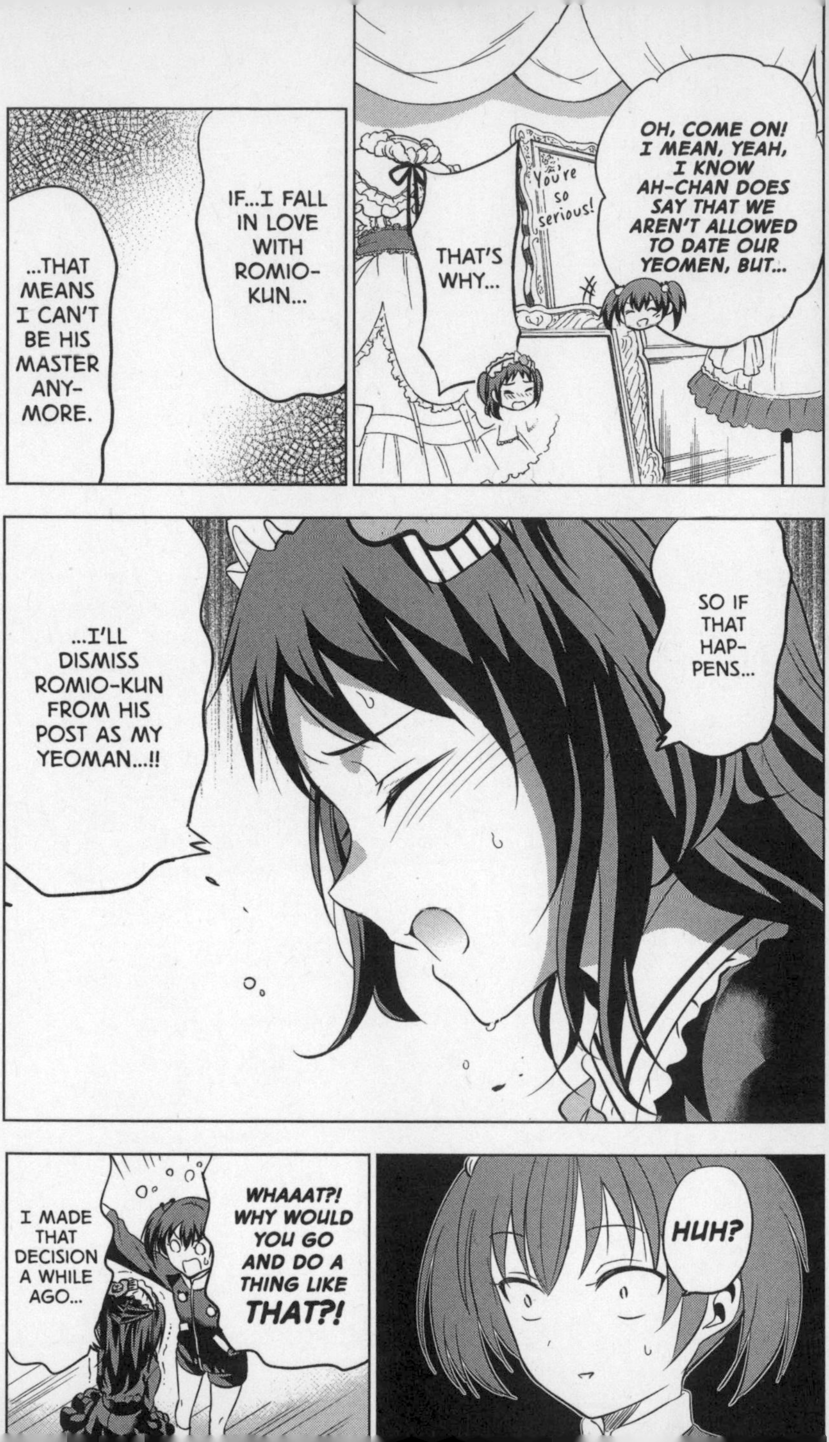
OH, COME ON! I MEAN, YEAH, I KNOW AH-CHAN DOES SAY THAT WE AREN'T ALLOWED TO DATE OUR YEOMEN, BUT...
You're so serious!
THAT'S WHY...
IF...I FALL IN LOVE WITH ROMIO-KUN...
...THAT MEANS I CAN'T BE HIS MASTER ANY-MORE.
SO IF THAT HAP-PENS...
...I'LL DISMISS ROMIO-KUN FROM HIS POST AS MY YEOMAN...!!
HUH?
WHAAAT?! WHY WOULD YOU GO AND DO A THING LIKE THAT?!
I MADE THAT DECISION A WHILE AGO...

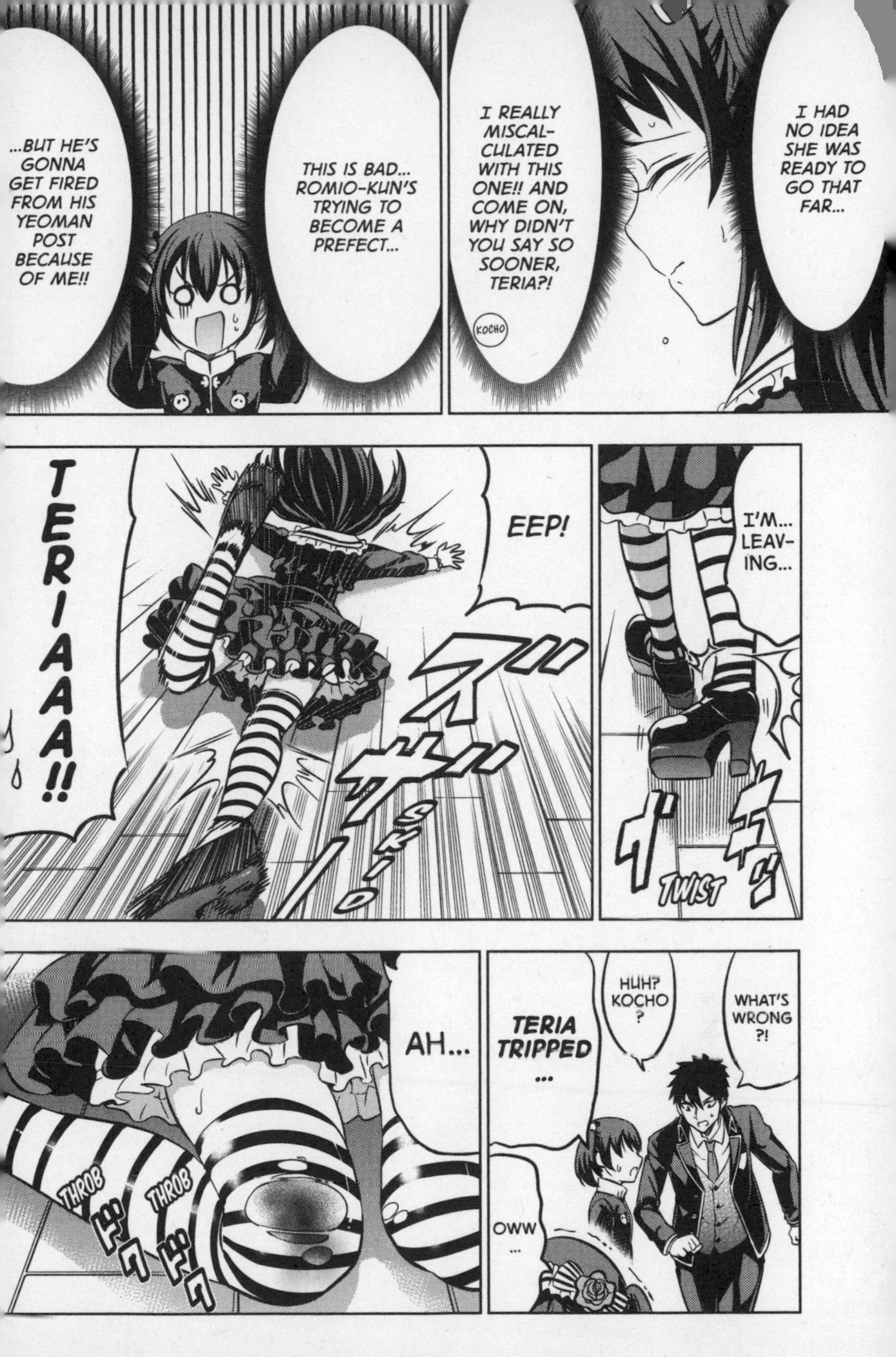
I HAD NO IDEA SHE WAS READY TO GO THAT FAR...
I REALLY MISCAL-CULATED WITH THIS ONE!! AND COME ON, WHY DIDN'T YOU SAY SO SOONER, TERIA?!
KOCHO
THIS IS BAD... ROMIO-KUN'S TRYING TO BECOME A PREFECT...
...BUT HE'S GONNA GET FIRED FROM HIS YEOMAN POST BECAUSE OF ME!!
I'M... LEAV-ING...
TWIST
EEP!
TERIAAAA!!
SKID
WHAT'S WRONG?!
HUH? KOCHO?
TERIA TRIPPED...
OWW...
AH...
THROB
THROB

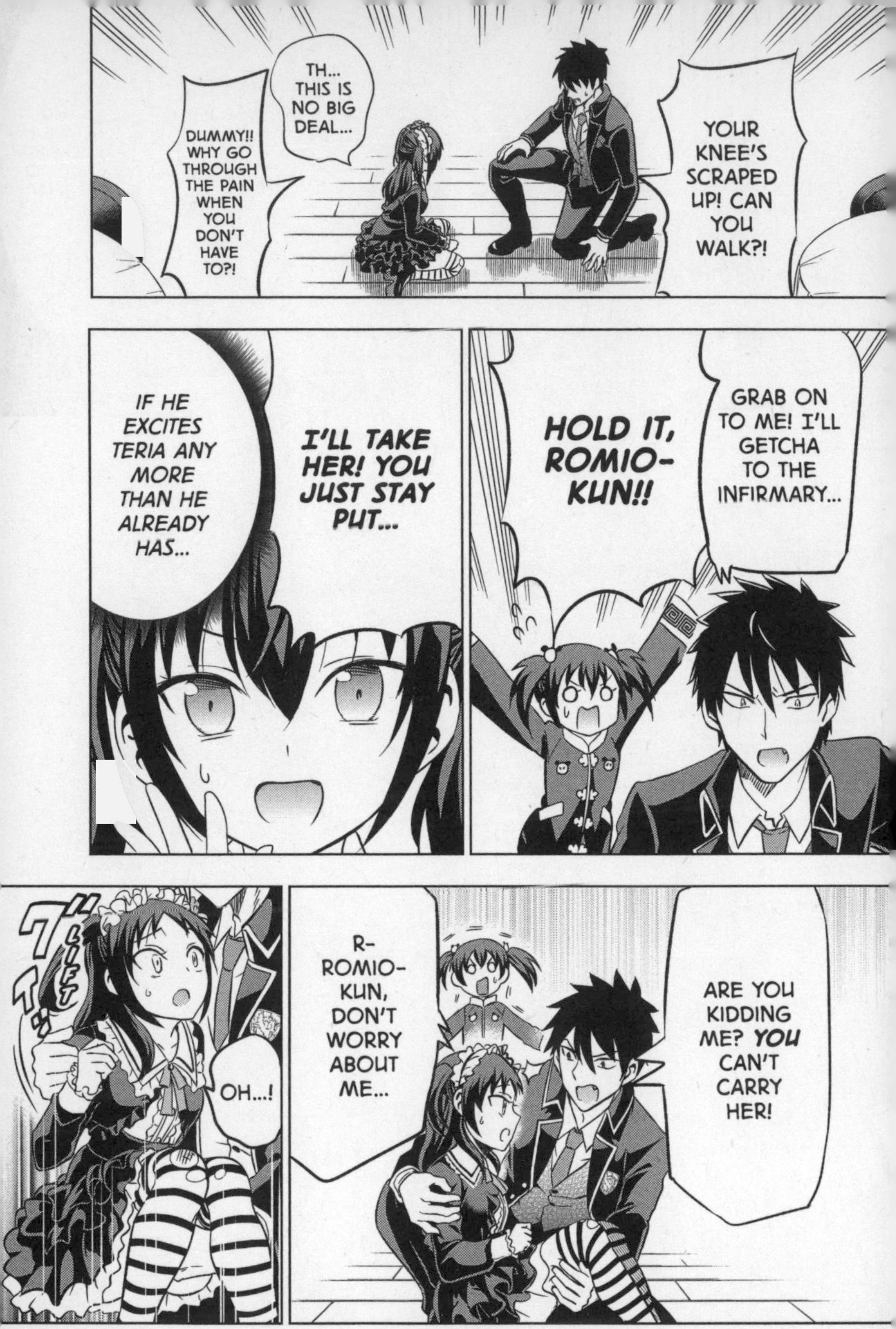
YOUR KNEE'S SCRAPED UP! CAN YOU WALK?!
TH... THIS IS NO BIG DEAL...
DUMMY!! WHY GO THROUGH THE PAIN WHEN YOU DON'T HAVE TO?!
GRAB ON TO ME! I'LL GETCHA TO THE INFIRMARY...
HOLD IT, ROMIO-KUN!!
I'LL TAKE HER! YOU JUST STAY PUT...
IF HE EXCITES TERIA ANY MORE THAN HE ALREADY HAS...
ARE YOU KIDDING ME? YOU CAN'T CARRY HER!
R-ROMIO-KUN, DON'T WORRY ABOUT ME...
OH...!
LIFT

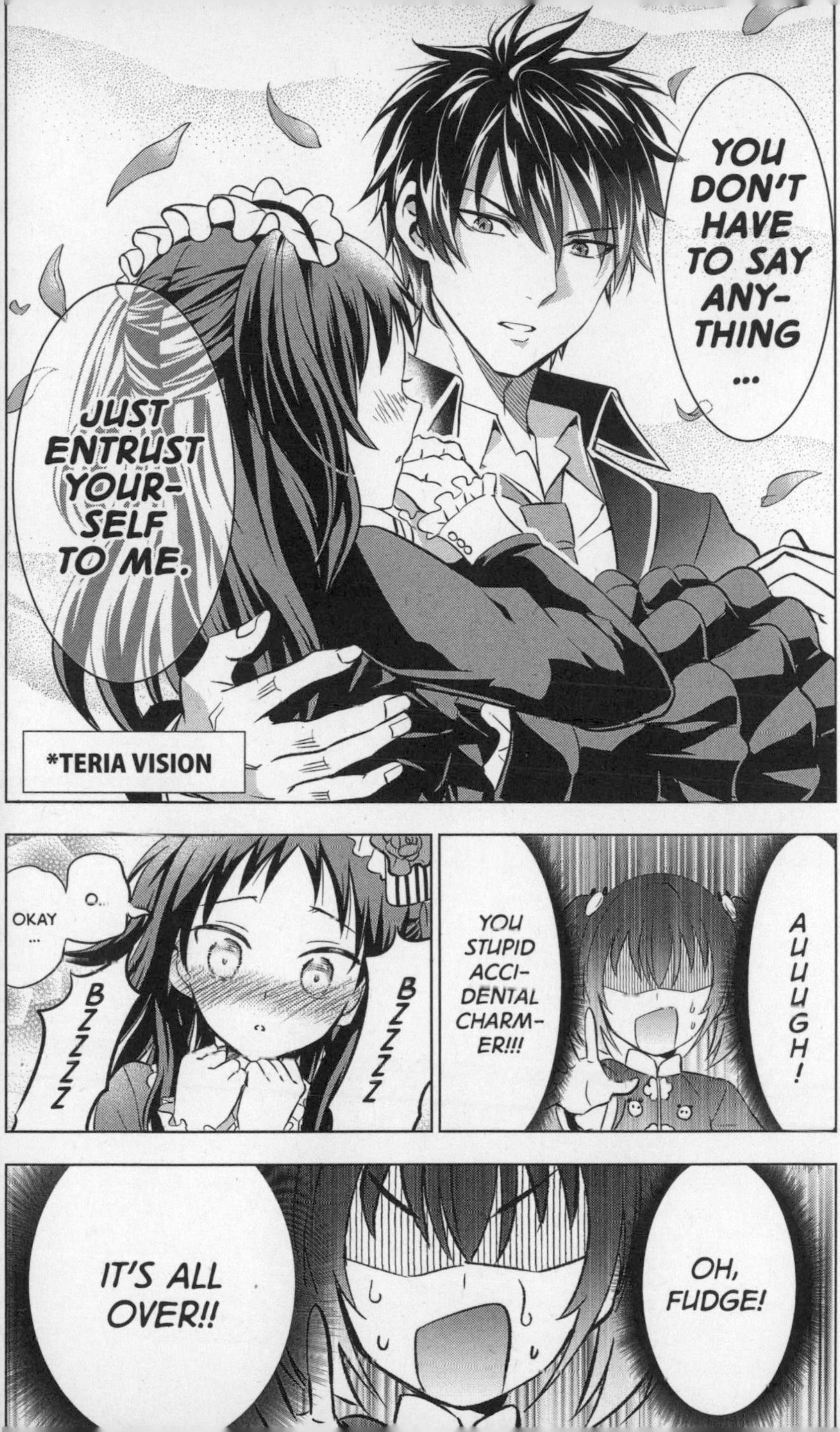
YOU DON'T HAVE TO SAY ANY-THING ...
JUST ENTRUST YOUR-SELF TO ME.
*TERIA VISION
AUUUGH!
YOU STUPID ACCI-DENTAL CHARM-ER!!!
BZZZZZ
O... OKAY ...
BZZZZZ
OH, FUDGE!
IT'S ALL OVER!!

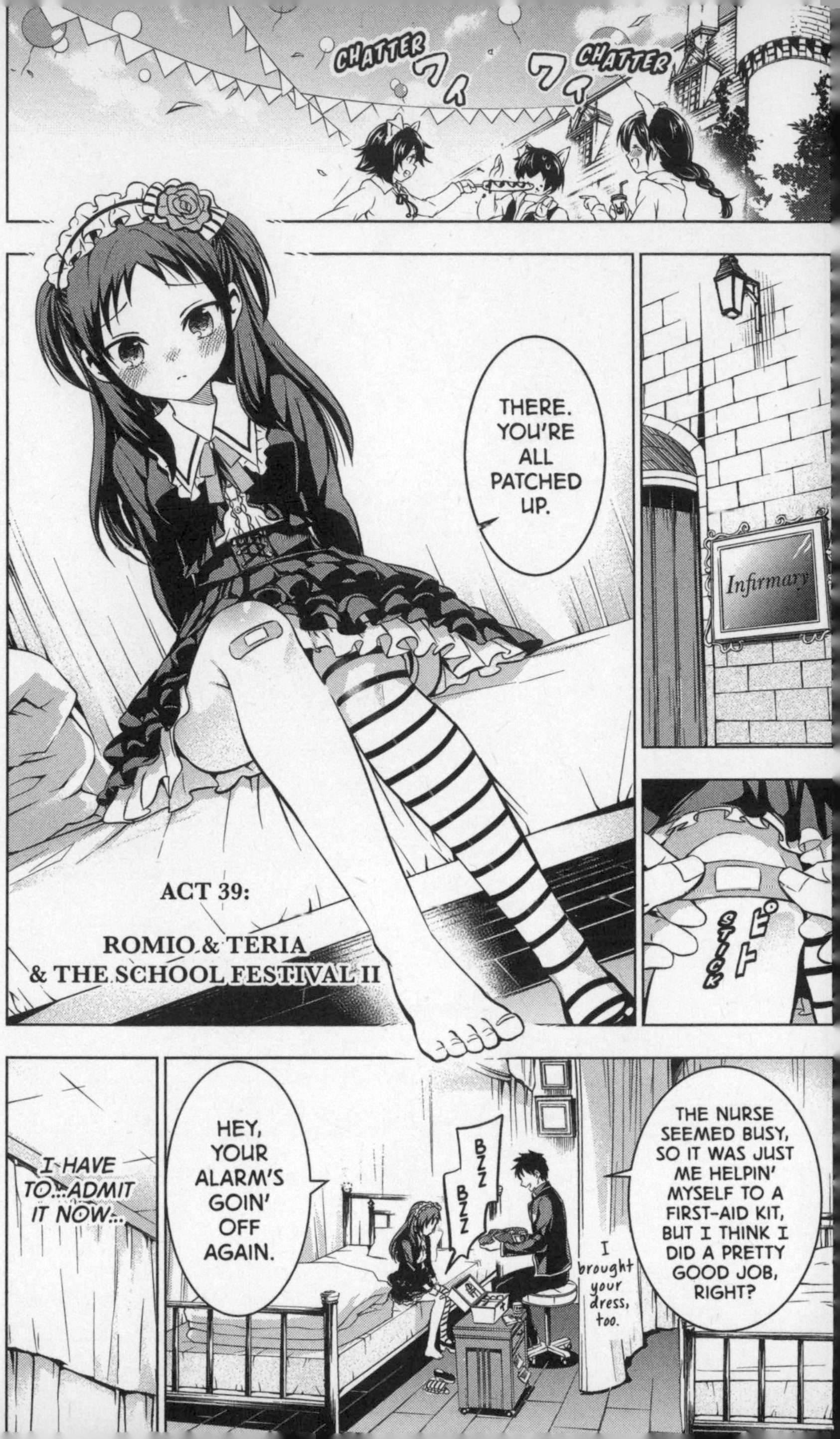
CHATTER
ワイ
ワイ
CHATTER
Infirmary
ピト
STICK
THERE. YOU'RE ALL PATCHED UP.
ACT 39:
ROMIO & TERIA & THE SCHOOL FESTIVAL II
THE NURSE SEEMED BUSY, SO IT WAS JUST ME HELPIN' MYSELF TO A FIRST-AID KIT, BUT I THINK I DID A PRETTY GOOD JOB, RIGHT?
I brought your dress, too.
BZZ BZZ
HEY, YOUR ALARM'S GOIN' OFF AGAIN.
I HAVE TO...ADMIT IT NOW...

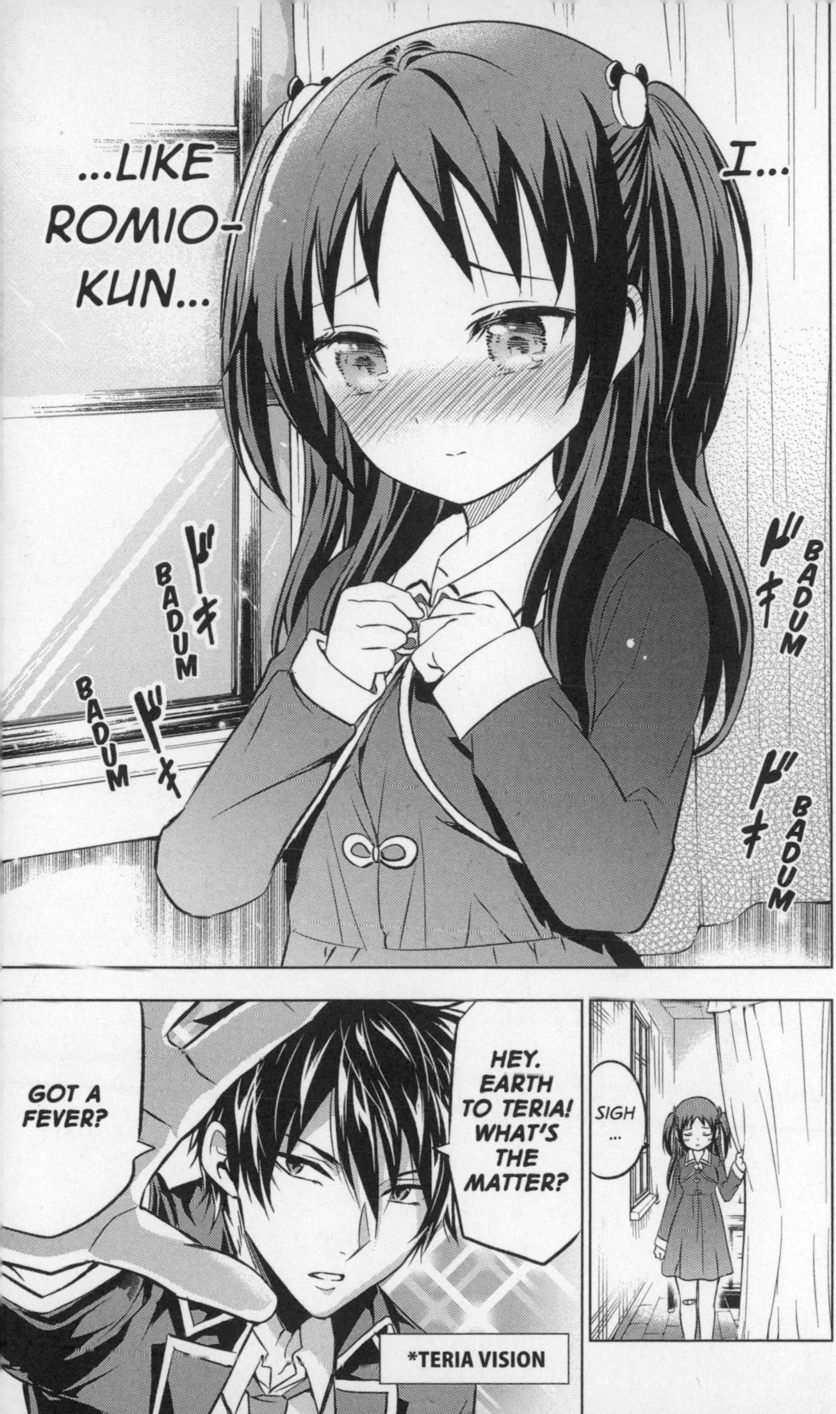
I...
...LIKE ROMIO-KUN...
ドキ BADUM
ドキ BADUM
ドキ BADUM
ドキ BADUM
SIGH ...
HEY. EARTH TO TERIA! WHAT'S THE MATTER?
GOT A FEVER?
*TERIA VISION

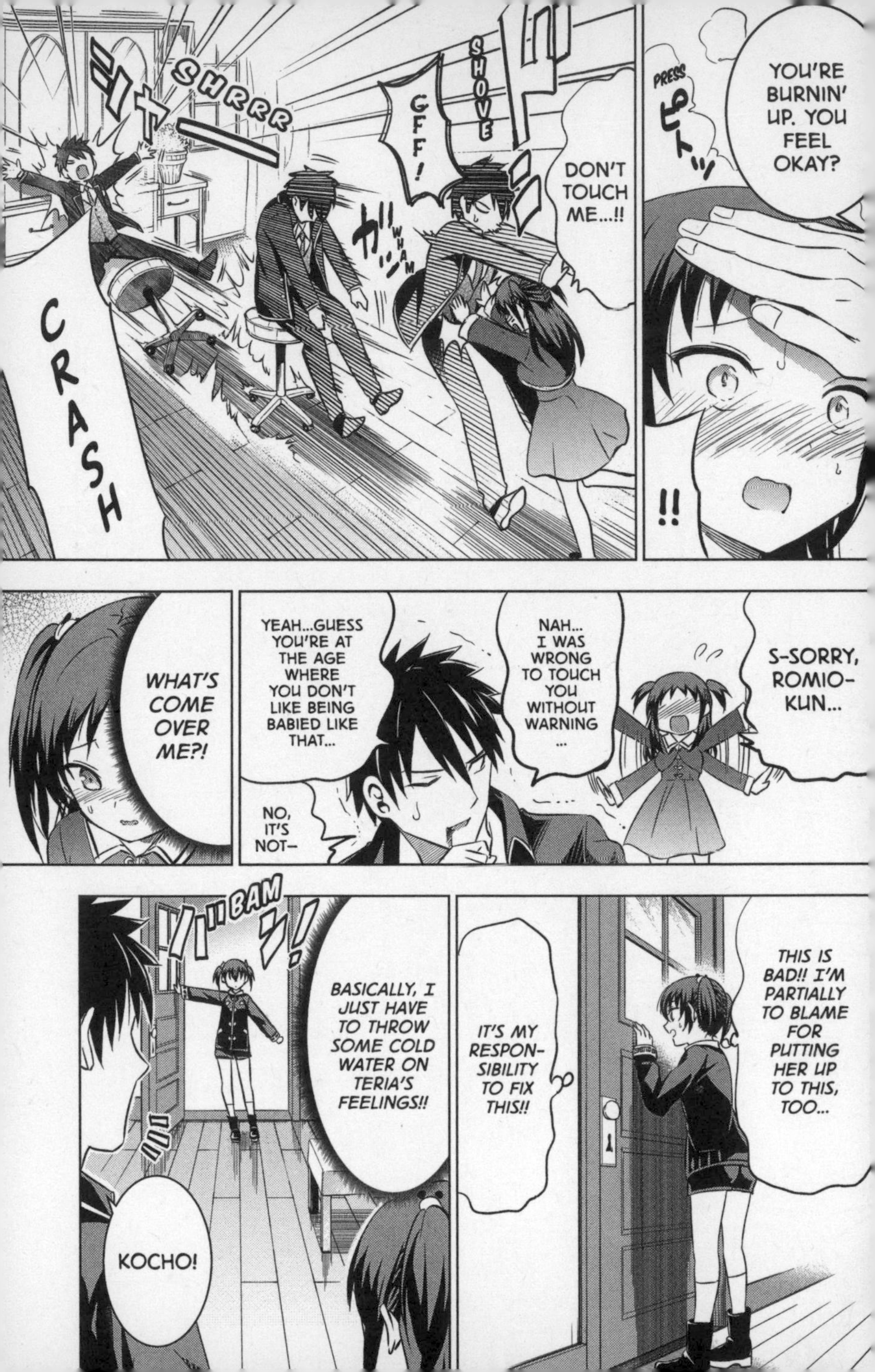
PRESS
YOU'RE BURNIN' UP. YOU FEEL OKAY?
!!
DON'T TOUCH ME...!!
SHOVE
GFF!
WHAM
SHRRRR
CRASH
S-SORRY, ROMIO-KUN...
NAH... I WAS WRONG TO TOUCH YOU WITHOUT WARNING ...
YEAH...GUESS YOU'RE AT THE AGE WHERE YOU DON'T LIKE BEING BABIED LIKE THAT...
NO, IT'S NOT–
WHAT'S COME OVER ME?!
THIS IS BAD!! I'M PARTIALLY TO BLAME FOR PUTTING HER UP TO THIS, TOO...
IT'S MY RESPONSIBILITY TO FIX THIS!!
BAM
BASICALLY, I JUST HAVE TO THROW SOME COLD WATER ON TERIA'S FEELINGS!!
KOCHO!

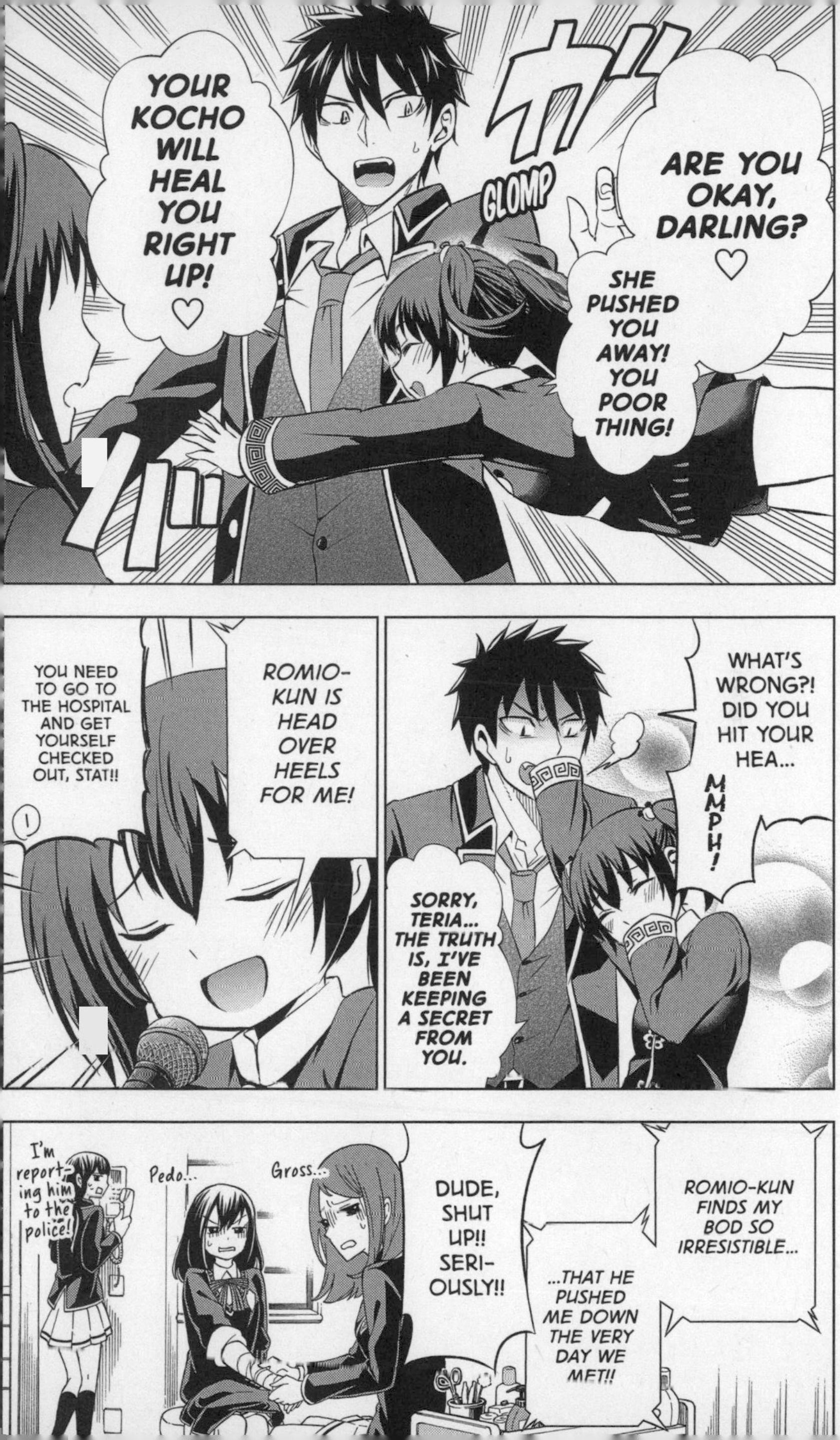
ARE YOU OKAY, DARLING? ♡
SHE PUSHED YOU AWAY! YOU POOR THING!
GLOMP
YOUR KOCHO WILL HEAL YOU RIGHT UP! ♡
WHAT'S WRONG?! DID YOU HIT YOUR HEA...
MMPH!
SORRY, TERIA... THE TRUTH IS, I'VE BEEN KEEPING A SECRET FROM YOU.
ROMIO-KUN IS HEAD OVER HEELS FOR ME!
YOU NEED TO GO TO THE HOSPITAL AND GET YOURSELF CHECKED OUT, STAT!!
!
ROMIO-KUN FINDS MY BOD SO IRRESISTIBLE...
...THAT HE PUSHED ME DOWN THE VERY DAY WE MET!!
DUDE, SHUT UP!! SERI-OUSLY!!
Gross...
Pedo...
I'm reporting him to the police!

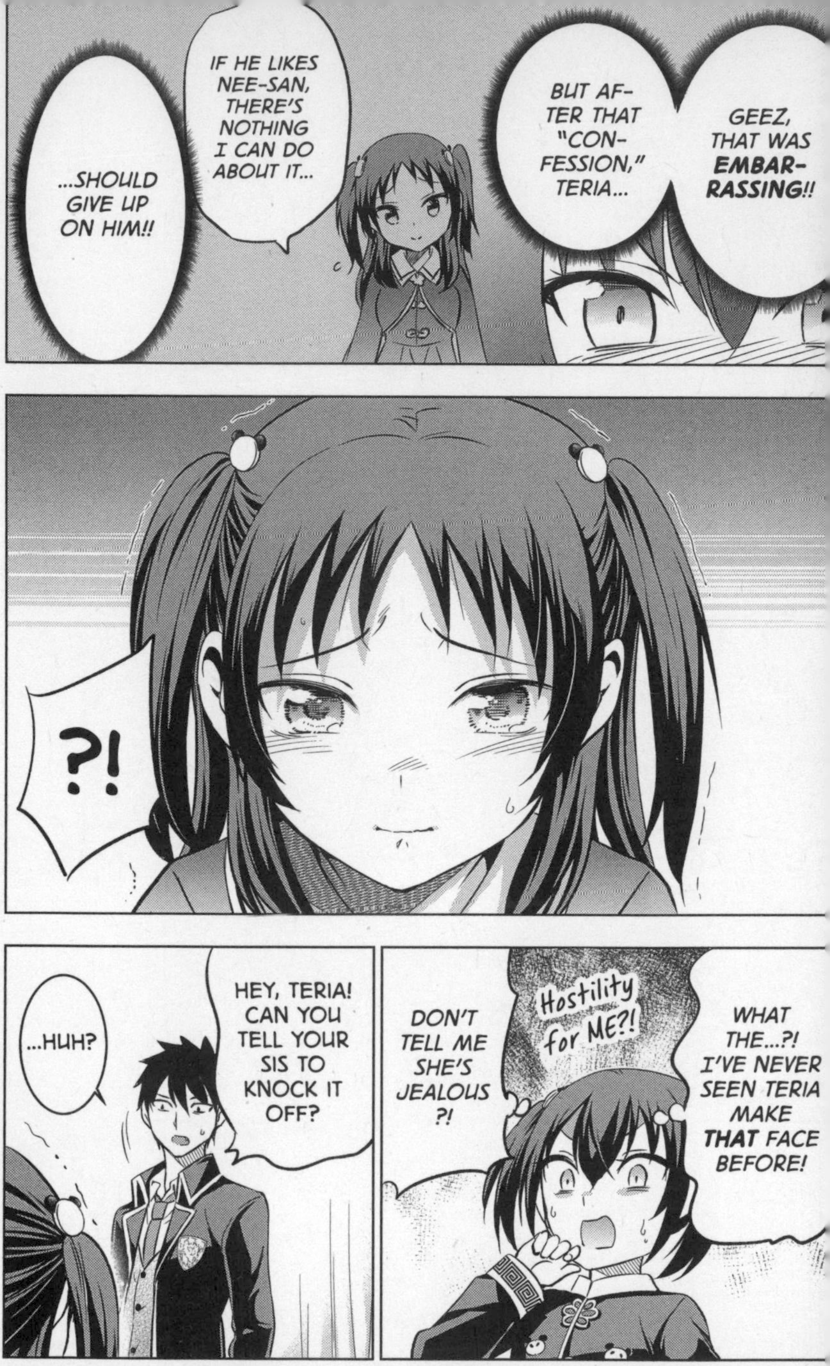
GEEZ, THAT WAS EMBARRASSING!!
BUT AFTER THAT "CONFESSION," TERIA...
IF HE LIKES NEE-SAN, THERE'S NOTHING I CAN DO ABOUT IT...
...SHOULD GIVE UP ON HIM!!
?!
WHAT THE...?! I'VE NEVER SEEN TERIA MAKE THAT FACE BEFORE!
Hostility for ME?!
DON'T TELL ME SHE'S JEALOUS?!
HEY, TERIA! CAN YOU TELL YOUR SIS TO KNOCK IT OFF?
...HUH?

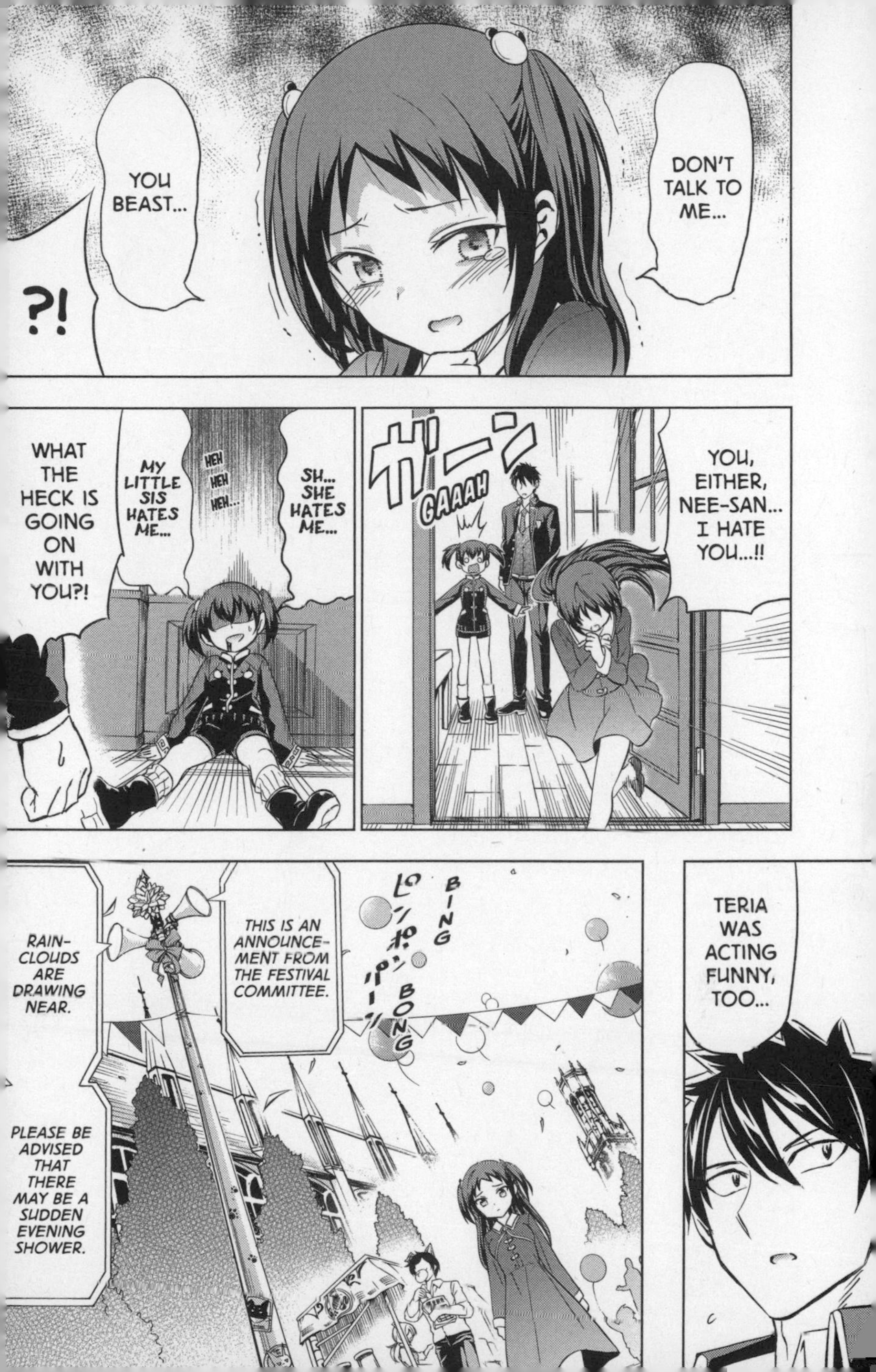
DON'T TALK TO ME...
YOU BEAST...
?!
GAAAH
YOU, EITHER, NEE-SAN... I HATE YOU...!!
SH... SHE HATES ME...
HEH HEH HEH...
MY LITTLE SIS HATES ME...
WHAT THE HECK IS GOING ON WITH YOU?!
TERIA WAS ACTING FUNNY, TOO...
BING
BONG
THIS IS AN ANNOUNCEMENT FROM THE FESTIVAL COMMITTEE.
RAIN-CLOUDS ARE DRAWING NEAR.
PLEASE BE ADVISED THAT THERE MAY BE A SUDDEN EVENING SHOWER.

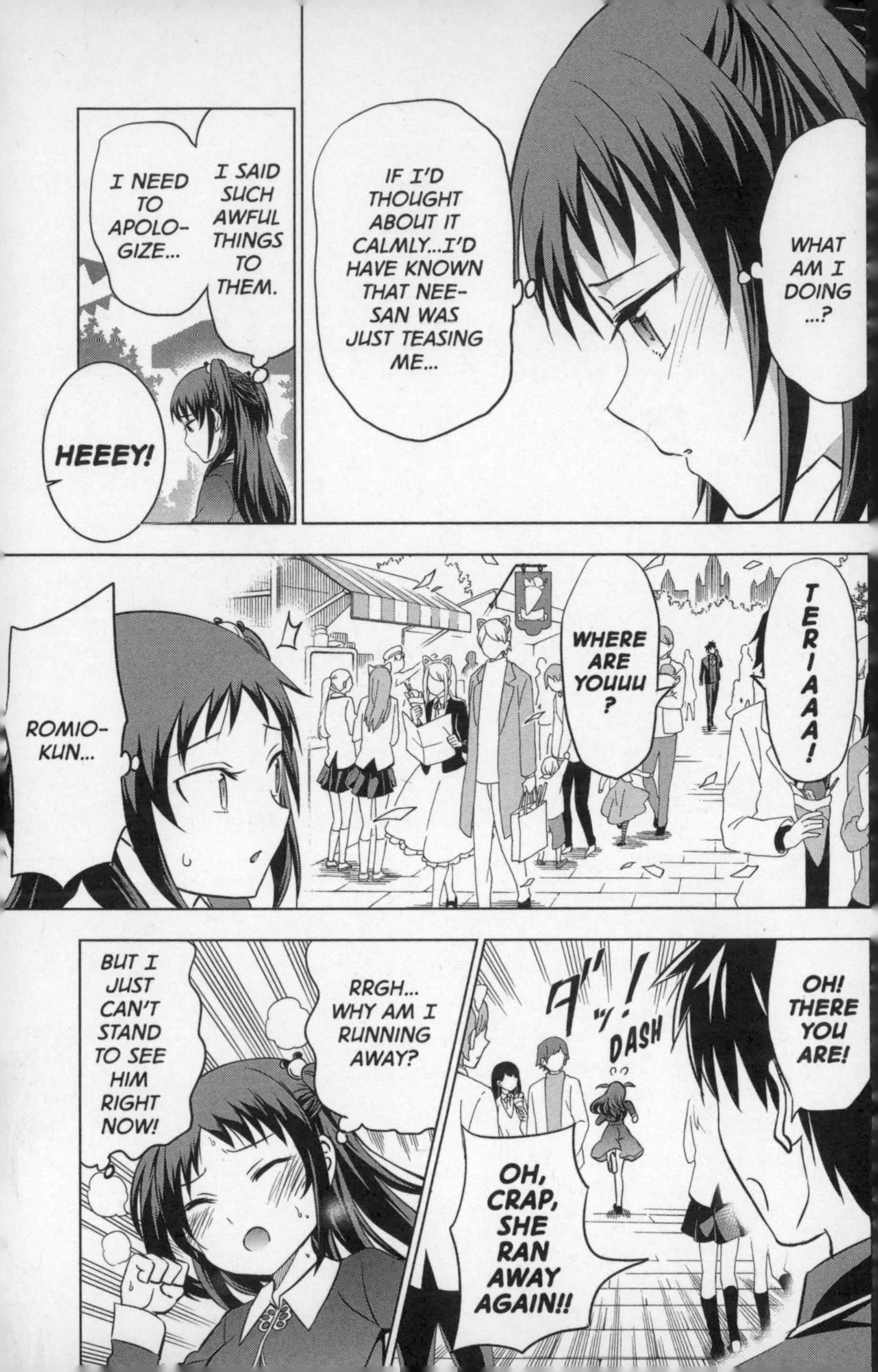
WHAT AM I DOING ...?
IF I'D THOUGHT ABOUT IT CALMLY...I'D HAVE KNOWN THAT NEE-SAN WAS JUST TEASING ME...
I SAID SUCH AWFUL THINGS TO THEM.
I NEED TO APOLOGIZE...
HEEEY!
TERIAAAA!
WHERE ARE YOUUU?
ROMIO-KUN...
OH! THERE YOU ARE!
ダッ!
DASH
OH, CRAP, SHE RAN AWAY AGAIN!!
RRGH... WHY AM I RUNNING AWAY?
BUT I JUST CAN'T STAND TO SEE HIM RIGHT NOW!

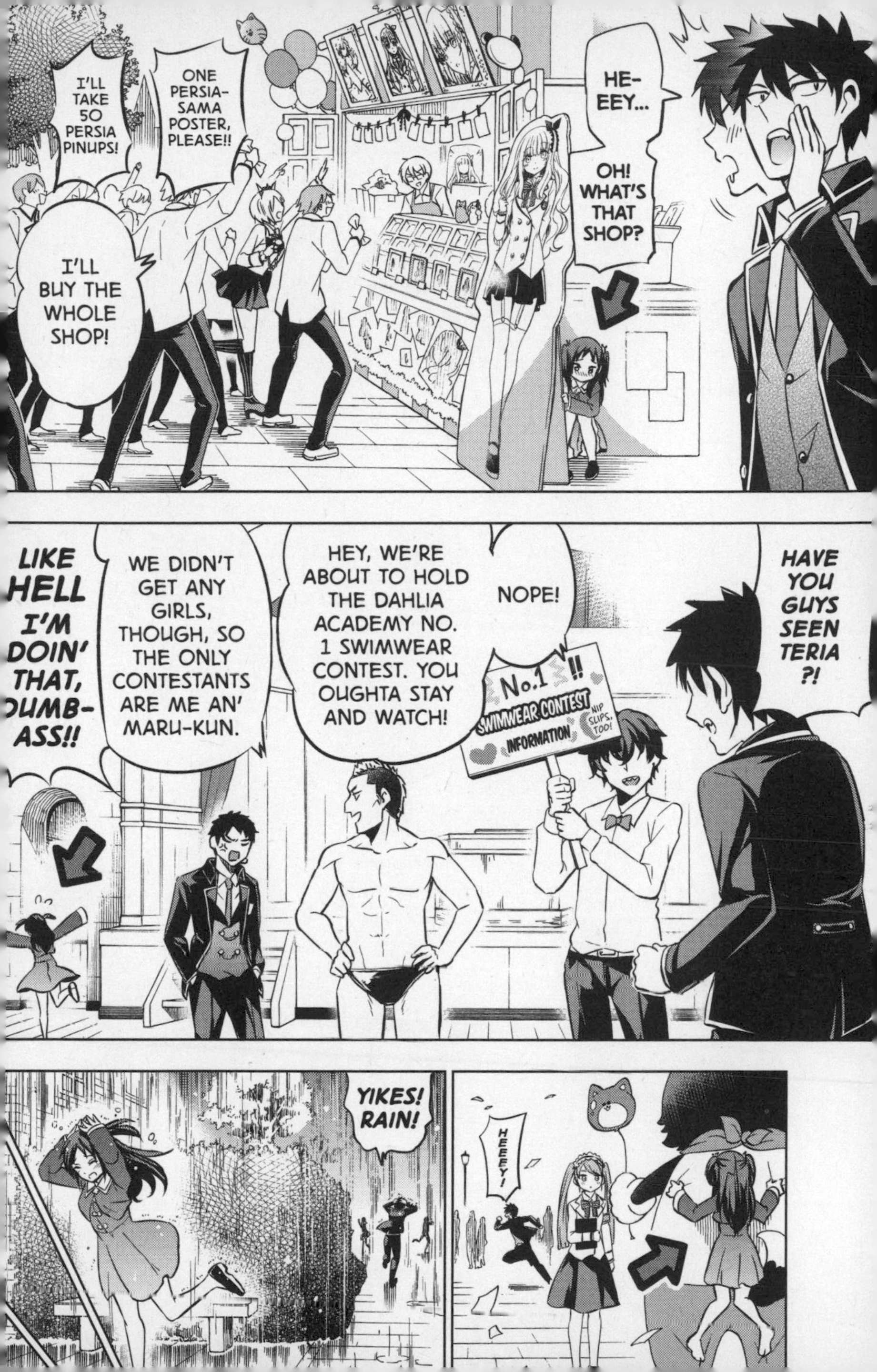
HE-EEY...
OH! WHAT'S THAT SHOP?
ONE PERSIA-SAMA POSTER, PLEASE!!
I'LL TAKE 50 PERSIA PINUPS!
I'LL BUY THE WHOLE SHOP!
HAVE YOU GUYS SEEN TERIA?!
No.1 !! SWIMWEAR CONTEST INFORMATION
NIP SLIPS, TOO!
NOPE!
HEY, WE'RE ABOUT TO HOLD THE DAHLIA ACADEMY NO. 1 SWIMWEAR CONTEST. YOU OUGHTA STAY AND WATCH!
WE DIDN'T GET ANY GIRLS, THOUGH, SO THE ONLY CONTESTANTS ARE ME AN' MARU-KUN.
LIKE HELL I'M DOIN' THAT, DUMB-ASS!!
HEEEEY!
YIKES! RAIN!

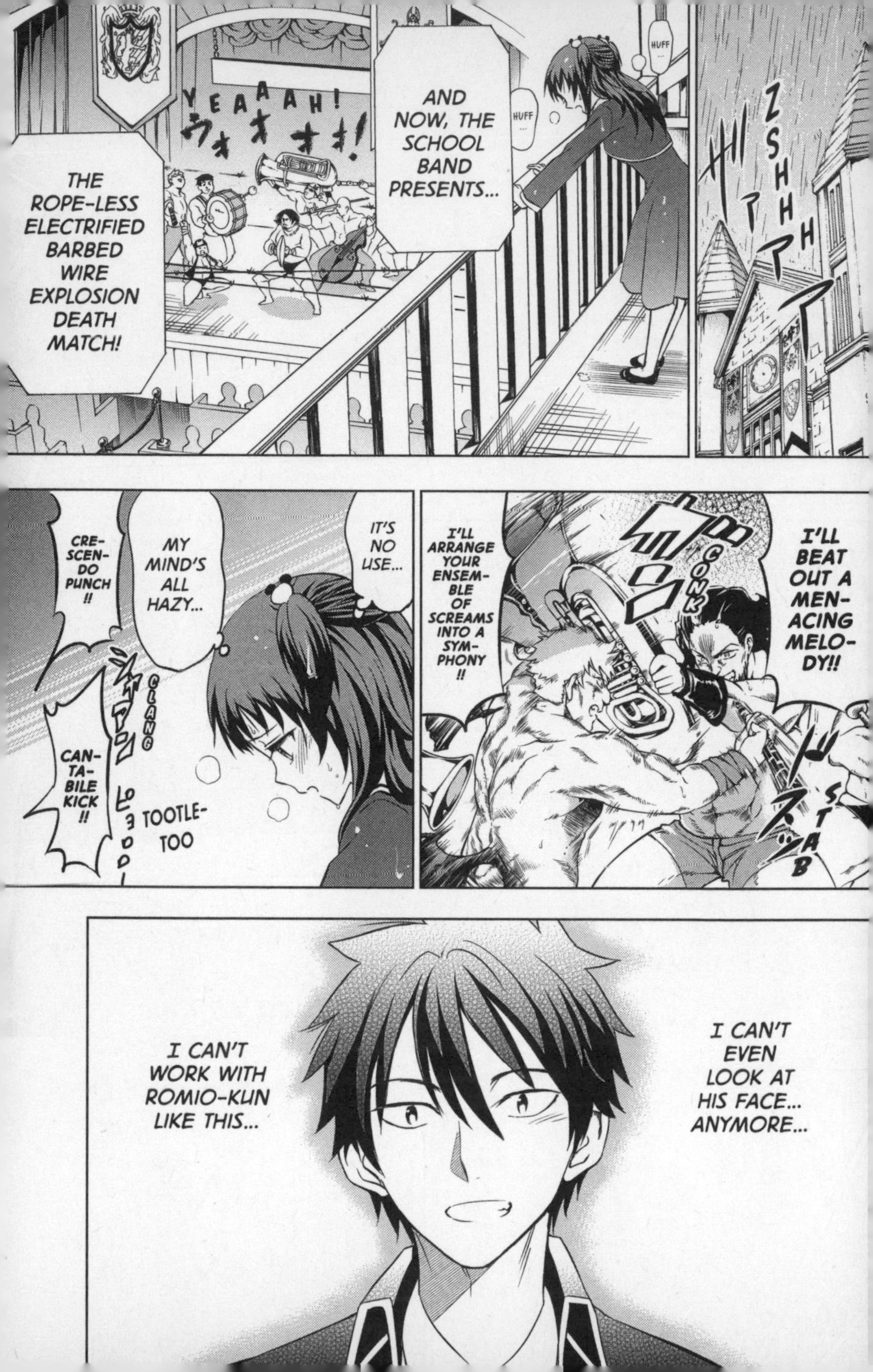
ZSHHH
HUFF...
HUFF...
AND NOW, THE SCHOOL BAND PRESENTS...
YEAAAH!
ウォオオオ!
THE ROPE-LESS ELECTRIFIED BARBED WIRE EXPLOSION DEATH MATCH!
I'LL BEAT OUT A MEN-ACING MELO-DY!!
CONK
I'LL ARRANGE YOUR ENSEM-BLE OF SCREAMS INTO A SYM-PHONY!!
STAB
IT'S NO USE...
MY MIND'S ALL HAZY...
CRE-SCEN-DO PUNCH!!
CLANG
CAN-TA-BILE KICK!!
TOOTLE-TOO
I CAN'T EVEN LOOK AT HIS FACE... ANYMORE...
I CAN'T WORK WITH ROMIO-KUN LIKE THIS...

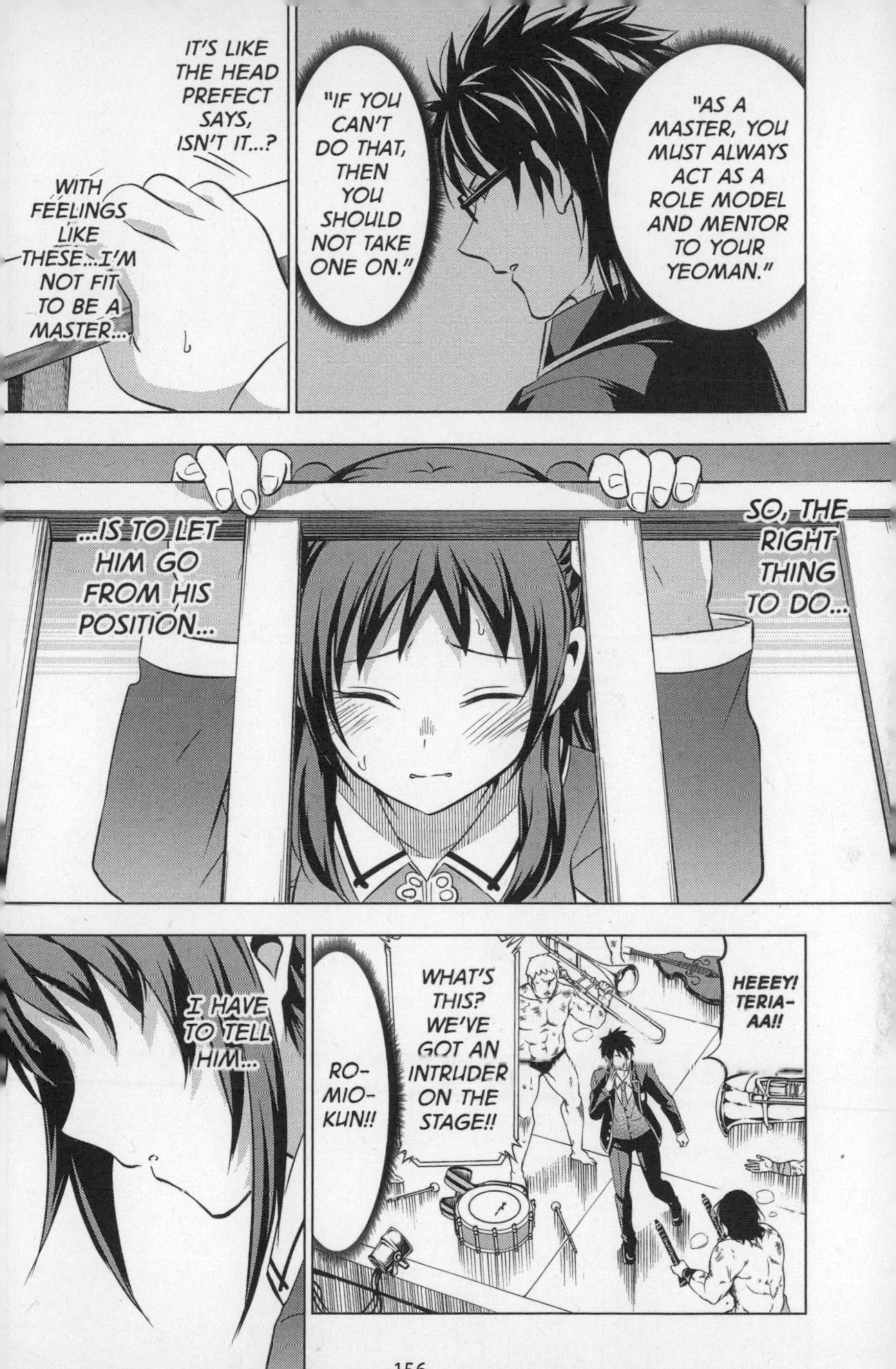
"AS A MASTER, YOU MUST ALWAYS ACT AS A ROLE MODEL AND MENTOR TO YOUR YEOMAN."
"IF YOU CAN'T DO THAT, THEN YOU SHOULD NOT TAKE ONE ON."
IT'S LIKE THE HEAD PREFECT SAYS, ISN'T IT...?
WITH FEELINGS LIKE THESE...I'M NOT FIT TO BE A MASTER...
SO, THE RIGHT THING TO DO...
...IS TO LET HIM GO FROM HIS POSITION...
HEEEY! TERIA-AA!!
WHAT'S THIS? WE'VE GOT AN INTRUDER ON THE STAGE!!
RO-MIO-KUN!!
I HAVE TO TELL HIM...

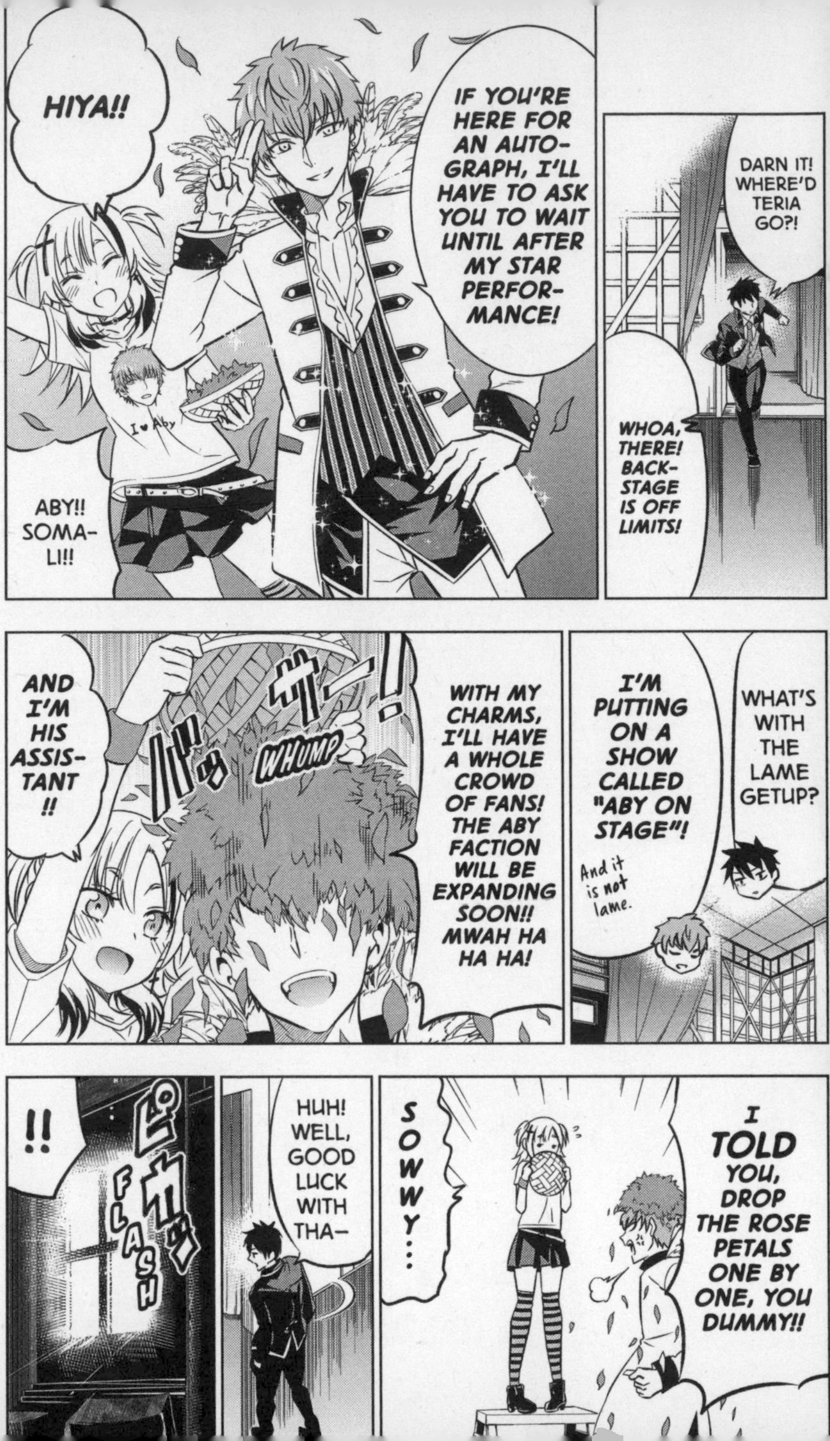
DARN IT! WHERE'D TERIA GO?!
WHOA, THERE! BACK-STAGE IS OFF LIMITS!
IF YOU'RE HERE FOR AN AUTO-GRAPH, I'LL HAVE TO ASK YOU TO WAIT UNTIL AFTER MY STAR PERFOR-MANCE!
HIYA!!
ABY!! SOMA-LI!!
WHAT'S WITH THE LAME GETUP?
I'M PUTTING ON A SHOW CALLED "ABY ON STAGE"!
And it is not lame.
WITH MY CHARMS, I'LL HAVE A WHOLE CROWD OF FANS! THE ABY FACTION WILL BE EXPANDING SOON!! MWAH HA HA HA!
WHUMP
AND I'M HIS ASSIS-TANT!!
I TOLD YOU, DROP THE ROSE PETALS ONE BY ONE, YOU DUMMY!!
SOWWY...
HUH! WELL, GOOD LUCK WITH THA—
!!
FLASH

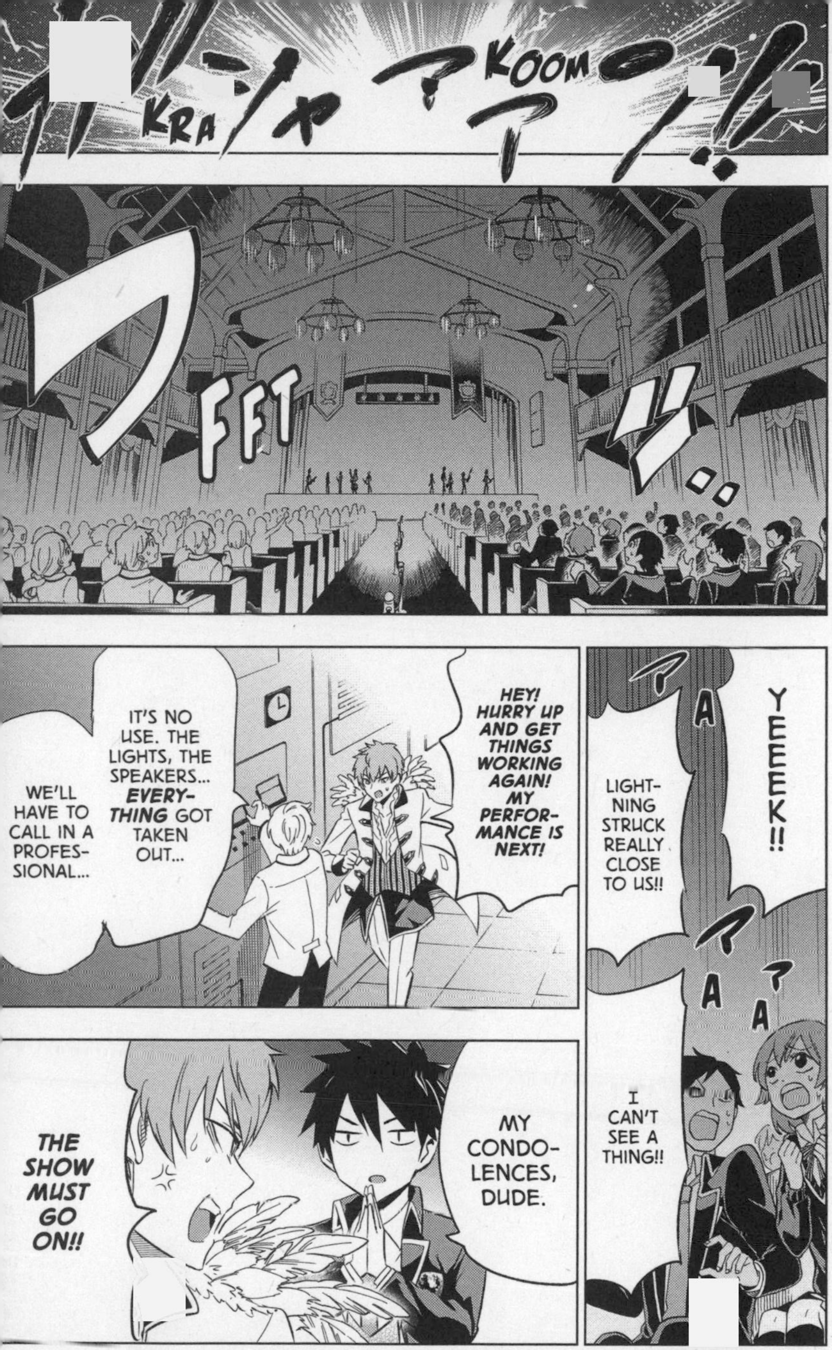
KRA
KOOM
FFT
YEEEK!!
LIGHT-NING STRUCK REALLY CLOSE TO US!!
A
A
A
I CAN'T SEE A THING!!
HEY! HURRY UP AND GET THINGS WORKING AGAIN! MY PERFOR-MANCE IS NEXT!
IT'S NO USE. THE LIGHTS, THE SPEAKERS... EVERY-THING GOT TAKEN OUT...
WE'LL HAVE TO CALL IN A PROFES-SIONAL...
MY CONDO-LENCES, DUDE.
THE SHOW MUST GO ON!!

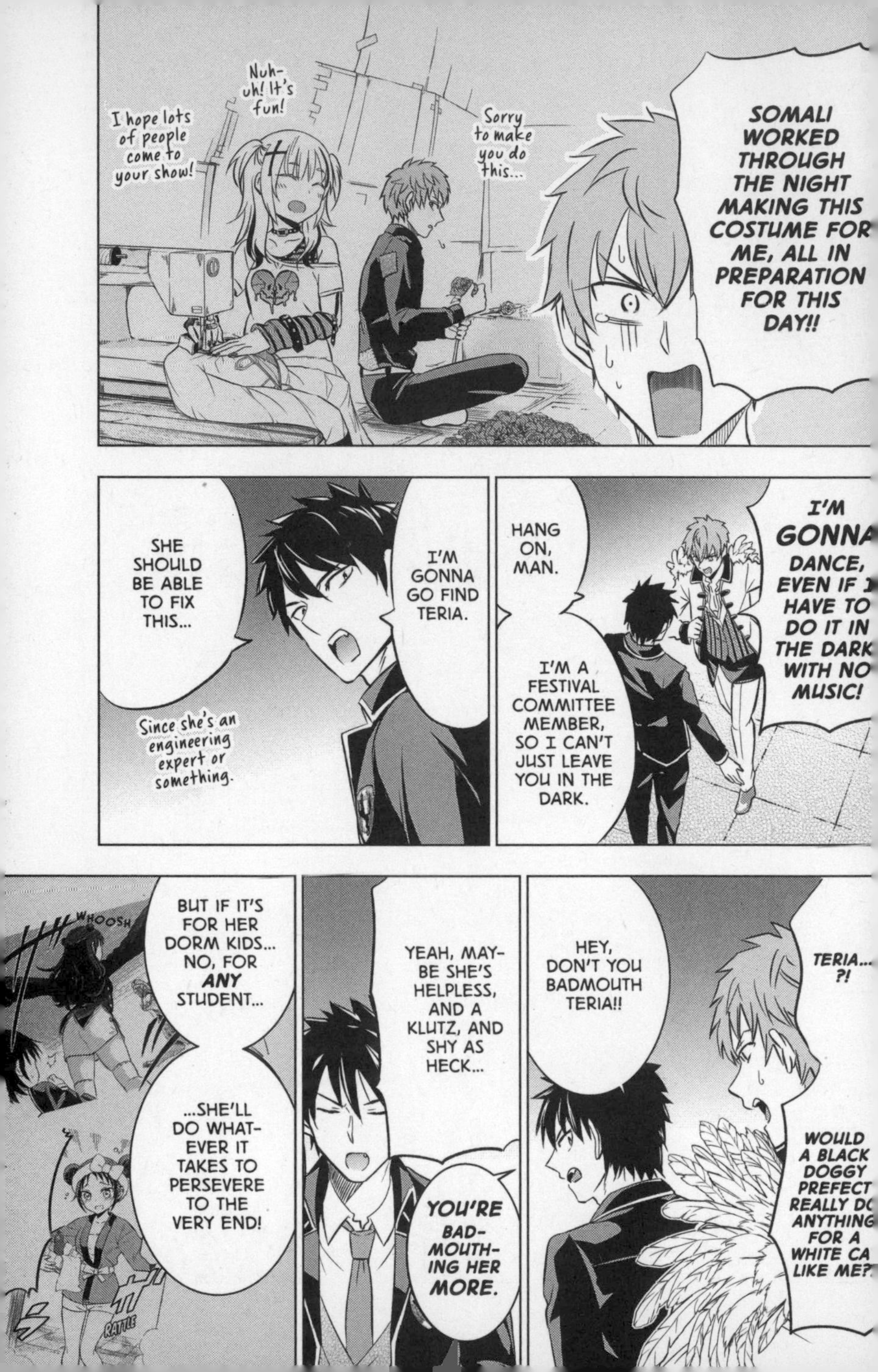
SOMALI WORKED THROUGH THE NIGHT MAKING THIS COSTUME FOR ME, ALL IN PREPARATION FOR THIS DAY!!
Sorry to make you do this...
Nuh-uh! It's fun!
I hope lots of people come to your show!
I'M GONNA DANCE, EVEN IF I HAVE TO DO IT IN THE DARK WITH NO MUSIC!
HANG ON, MAN.
I'M A FESTIVAL COMMITTEE MEMBER, SO I CAN'T JUST LEAVE YOU IN THE DARK.
I'M GONNA GO FIND TERIA.
SHE SHOULD BE ABLE TO FIX THIS...
Since she's an engineering expert or something.
TERIA...?!
WOULD A BLACK DOGGY PREFECT REALLY DO ANYTHING FOR A WHITE CA LIKE ME?
HEY, DON'T YOU BADMOUTH TERIA!!
YEAH, MAY-BE SHE'S HELPLESS, AND A KLUTZ, AND SHY AS HECK...
YOU'RE BAD-MOUTH-ING HER MORE.
BUT IF IT'S FOR HER DORM KIDS... NO, FOR ANY STUDENT...
...SHE'LL DO WHAT-EVER IT TAKES TO PERSEVERE TO THE VERY END!
WHOOSH
RATTLE

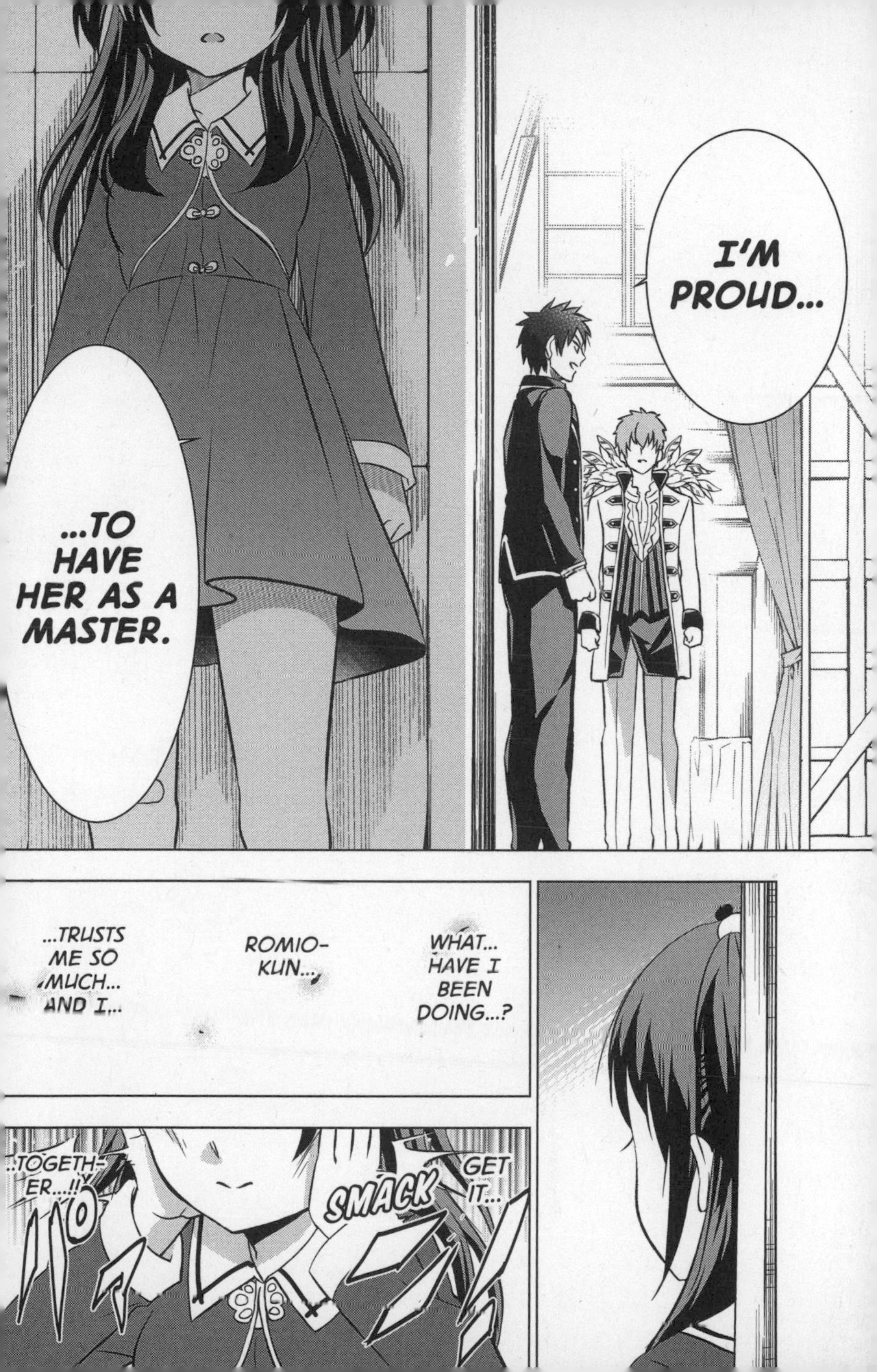
I'M PROUD...
...TO HAVE HER AS A MASTER.
WHAT... HAVE I BEEN DOING...?
ROMIO-KUN...
...TRUSTS ME SO MUCH... AND I...
GET IT...
SMACK
..TOGETH- ER...!!

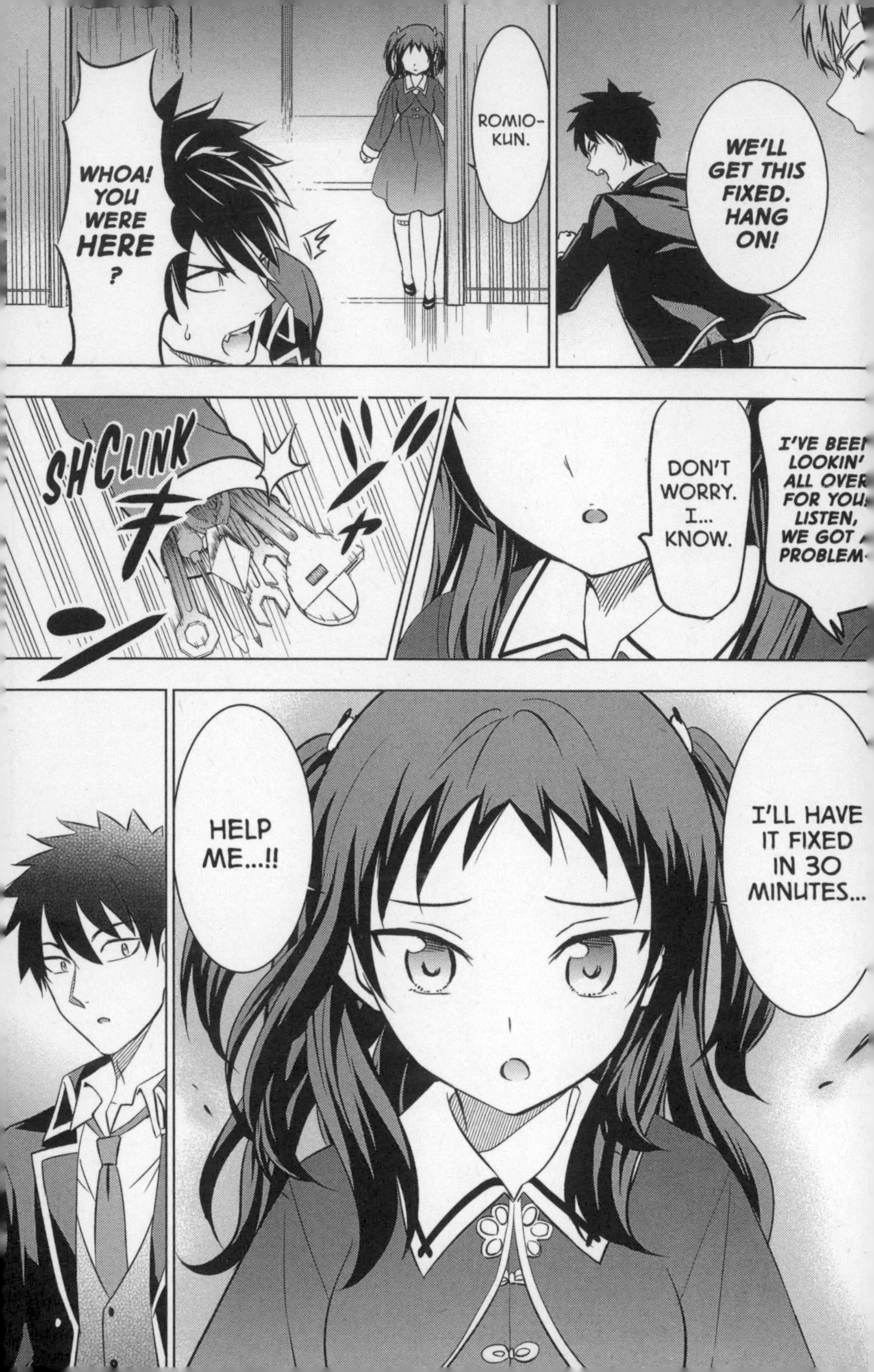
WE'LL GET THIS FIXED. HANG ON!
ROMIO-KUN.
WHOA! YOU WERE HERE ?
I'VE BEE LOOKIN' ALL OVER FOR YOU LISTEN, WE GOT PROBLEM
DON'T WORRY. I... KNOW.
SHCLINK
I'LL HAVE IT FIXED IN 30 MINUTES...
HELP ME...!!

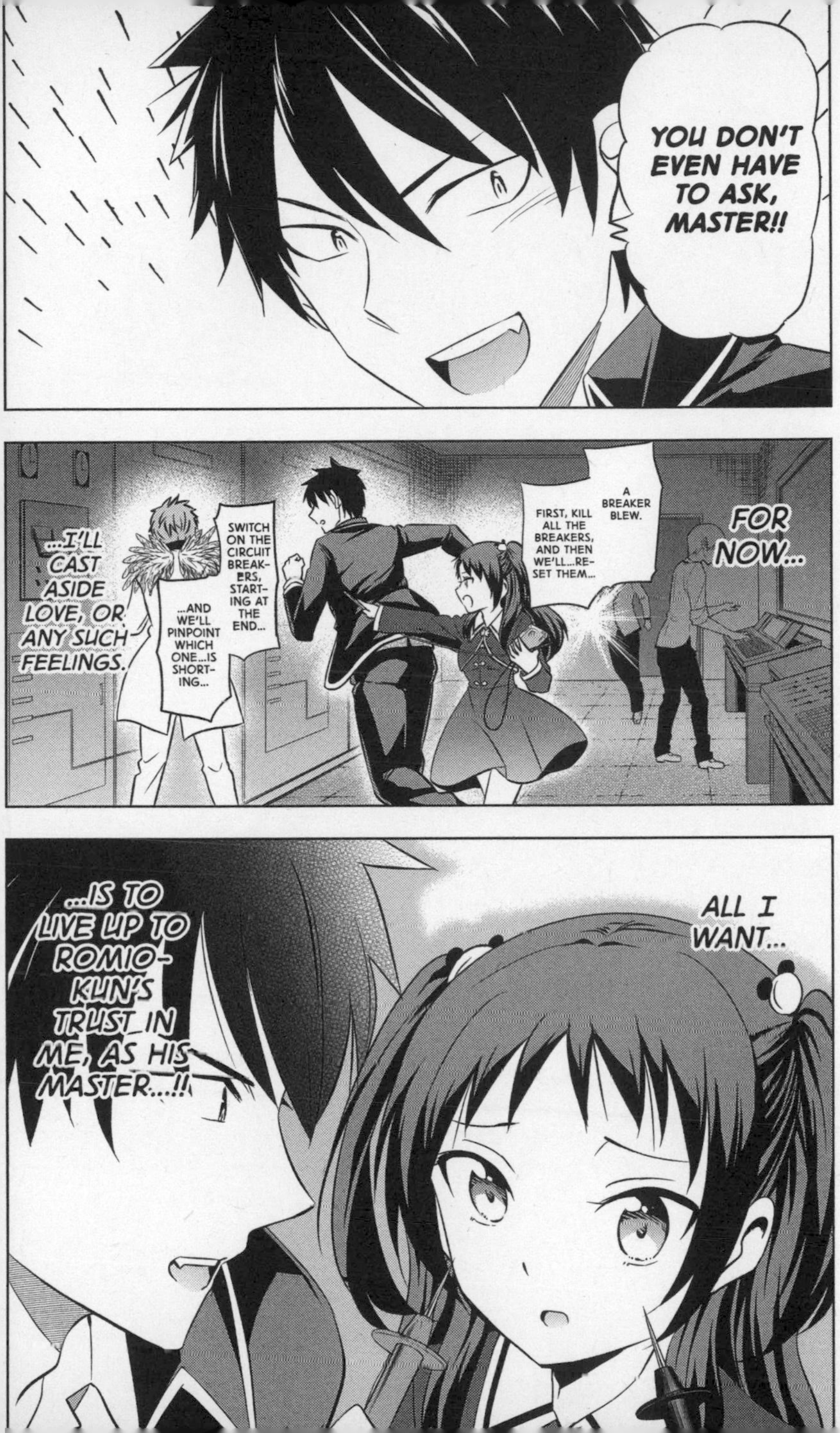
YOU DON'T EVEN HAVE TO ASK, MASTER!!
FOR NOW...
A BREAKER BLEW.
FIRST, KILL ALL THE BREAKERS, AND THEN WE'LL...RE-SET THEM...
SWITCH ON THE CIRCUIT BREAK-ERS, START-ING AT THE END...
...AND WE'LL PINPOINT WHICH ONE...IS SHORT-ING...
...I'LL CAST ASIDE LOVE, OR ANY SUCH FEELINGS.
ALL I WANT...
...IS TO LIVE UP TO ROMIO-KUN'S TRUST IN ME, AS HIS MASTER...!!

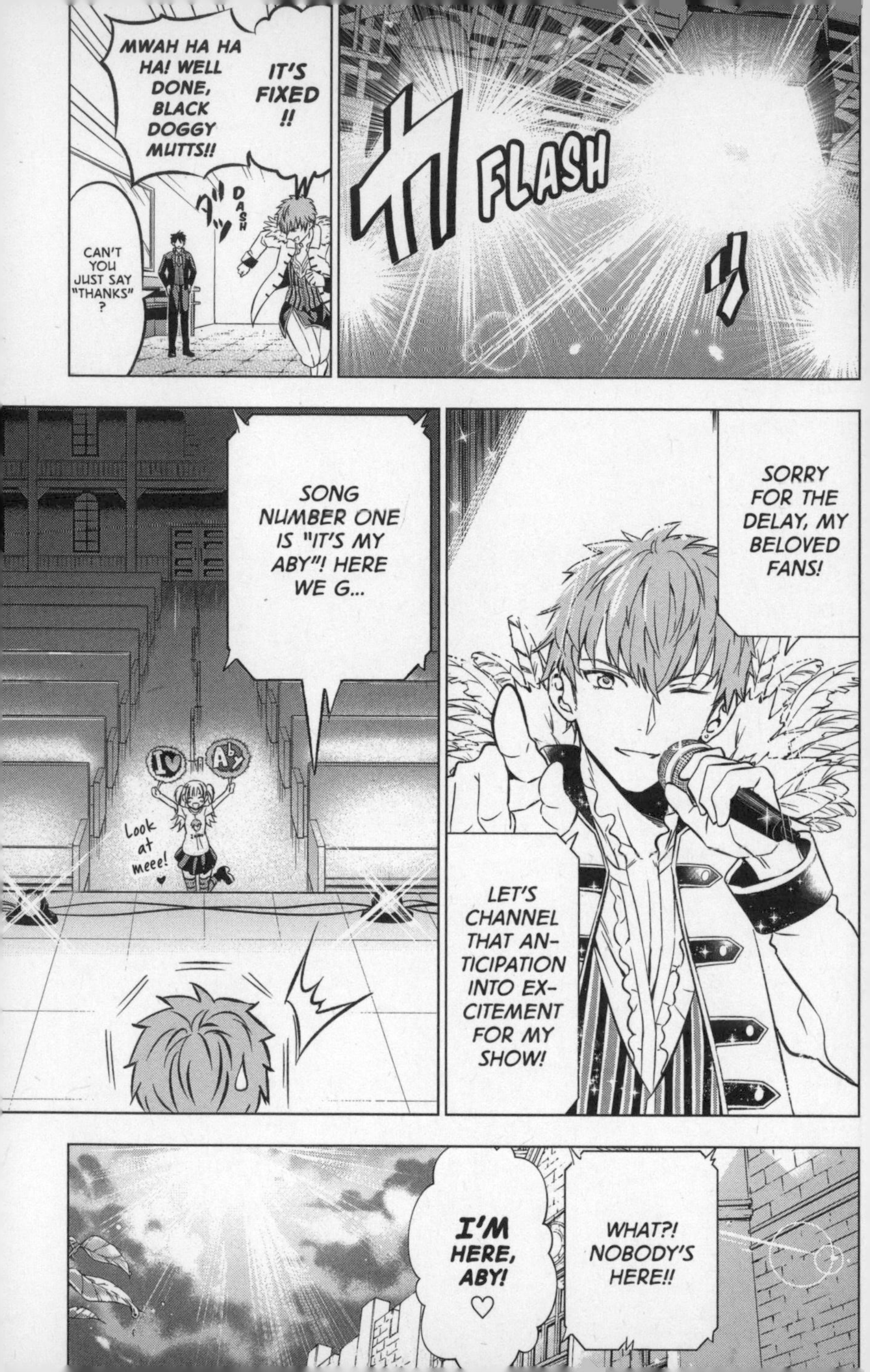
FLASH
IT'S FIXED!!
MWAH HA HA! WELL DONE, BLACK DOGGY MUTTS!!
DASH
CAN'T YOU JUST SAY "THANKS"?
SORRY FOR THE DELAY, MY BELOVED FANS!
LET'S CHANNEL THAT AN-TICIPATION INTO EX-CITEMENT FOR MY SHOW!
SONG NUMBER ONE IS "IT'S MY ABY"! HERE WE G...
Look at meee! ♥
WHAT?! NOBODY'S HERE!!
I'M HERE, ABY! ♡

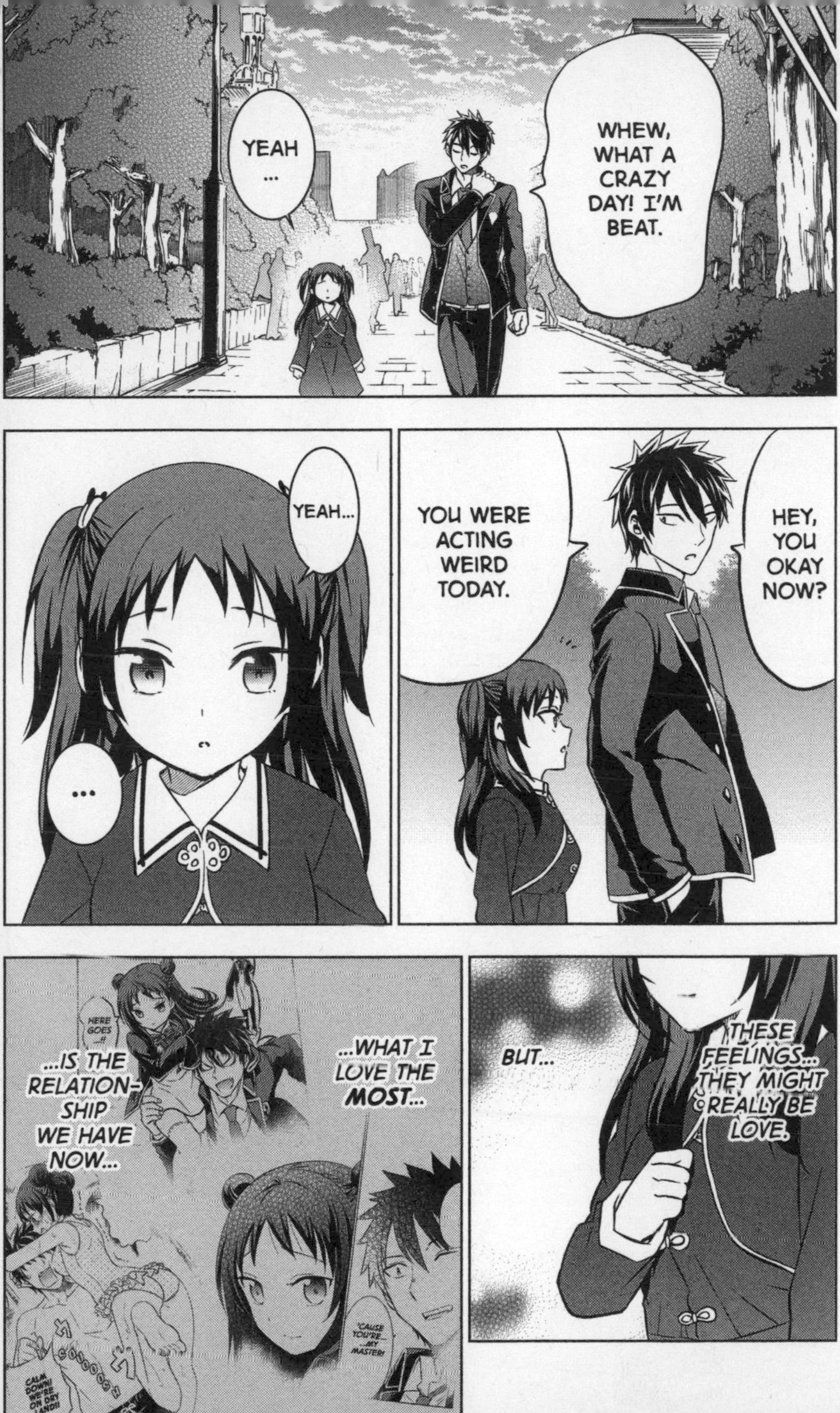
WHEW, WHAT A CRAZY DAY! I'M BEAT.
YEAH ...
HEY, YOU OKAY NOW?
YOU WERE ACTING WEIRD TODAY.
YEAH...
...
THESE FEELINGS... THEY MIGHT REALLY BE LOVE.
BUT...
...WHAT I LOVE THE MOST...
HERE GOES...!!
...IS THE RELATIONSHIP WE HAVE NOW...
'CAUSE YOU'RE... MY MASTER!
CALM DOWN! WE'RE ON DRY LAND!!

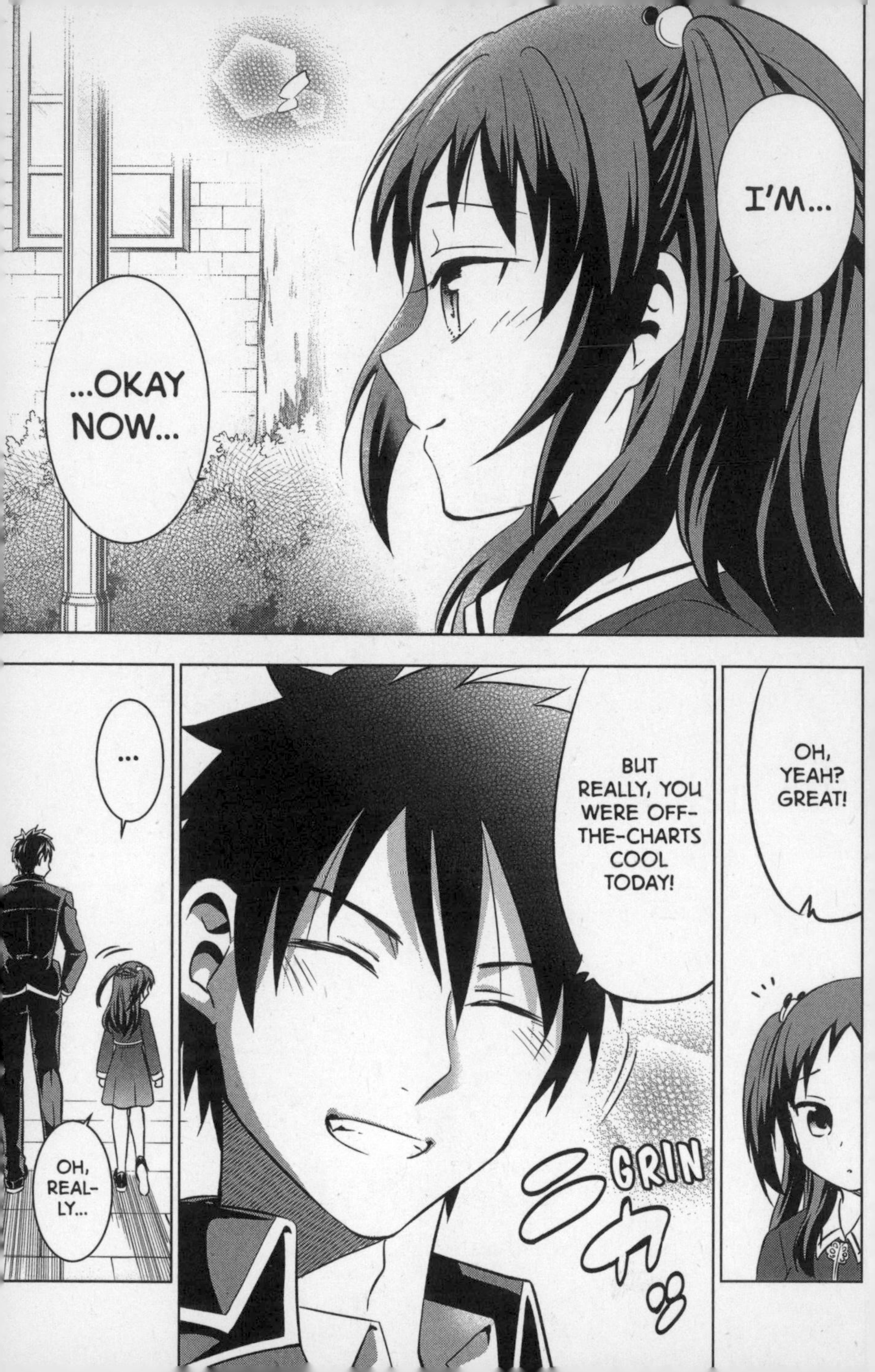
I'M...
...OKAY NOW...
OH, YEAH? GREAT!
BUT REALLY, YOU WERE OFF-THE-CHARTS COOL TODAY!
GRIN
...
OH, REAL-LY...

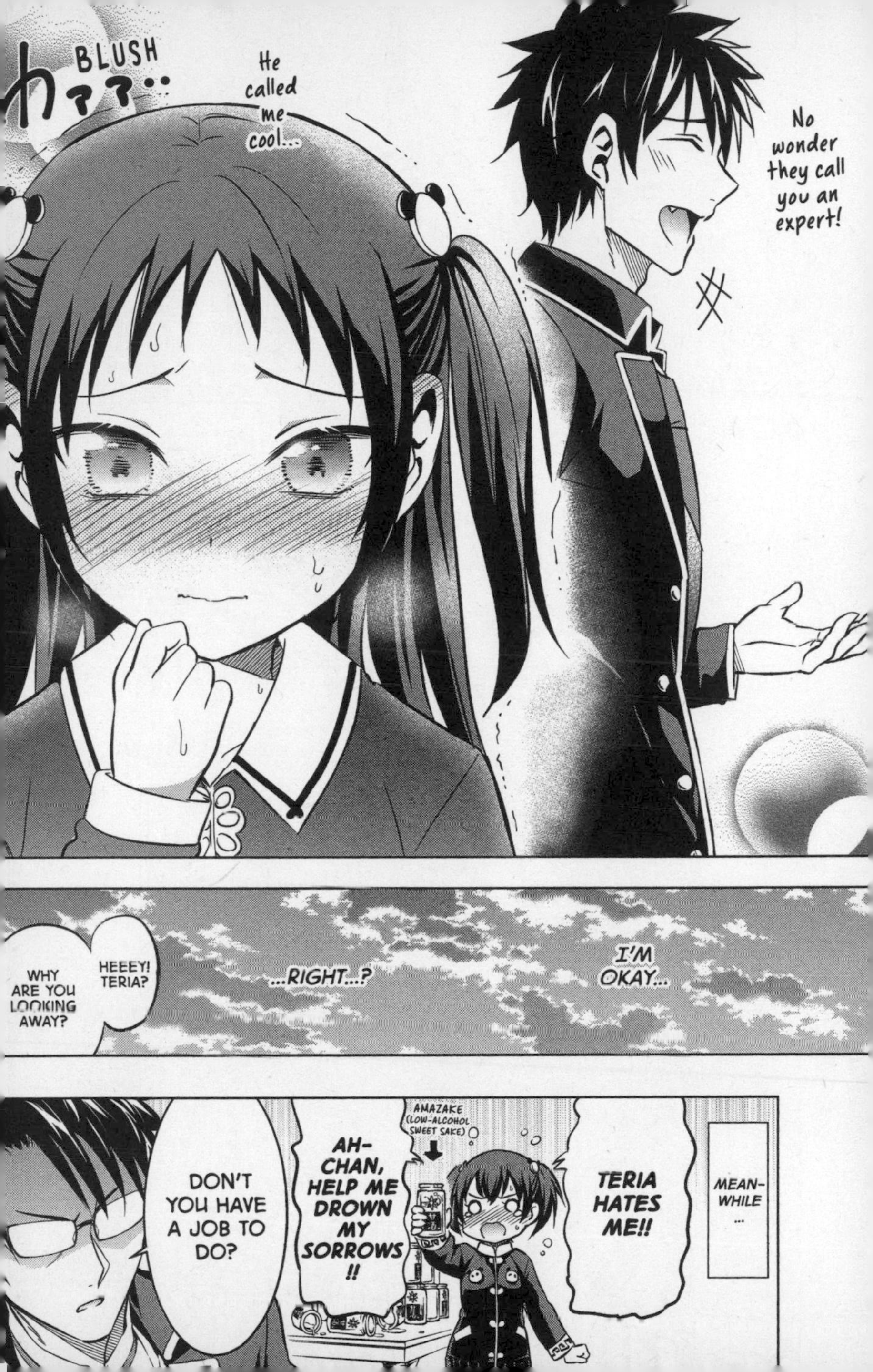
No wonder they call you an expert!
He called me cool...
BLUSH
カァァ‥
I'M OKAY...
...RIGHT...?
HEEEY! TERIA?
WHY ARE YOU LOOKING AWAY?
MEAN-WHILE...
TERIA HATES ME!!
AMAZAKE (LOW-ALCOHOL SWEET SAKE)
AH-CHAN, HELP ME DROWN MY SORROWS!!
DON'T YOU HAVE A JOB TO DO?

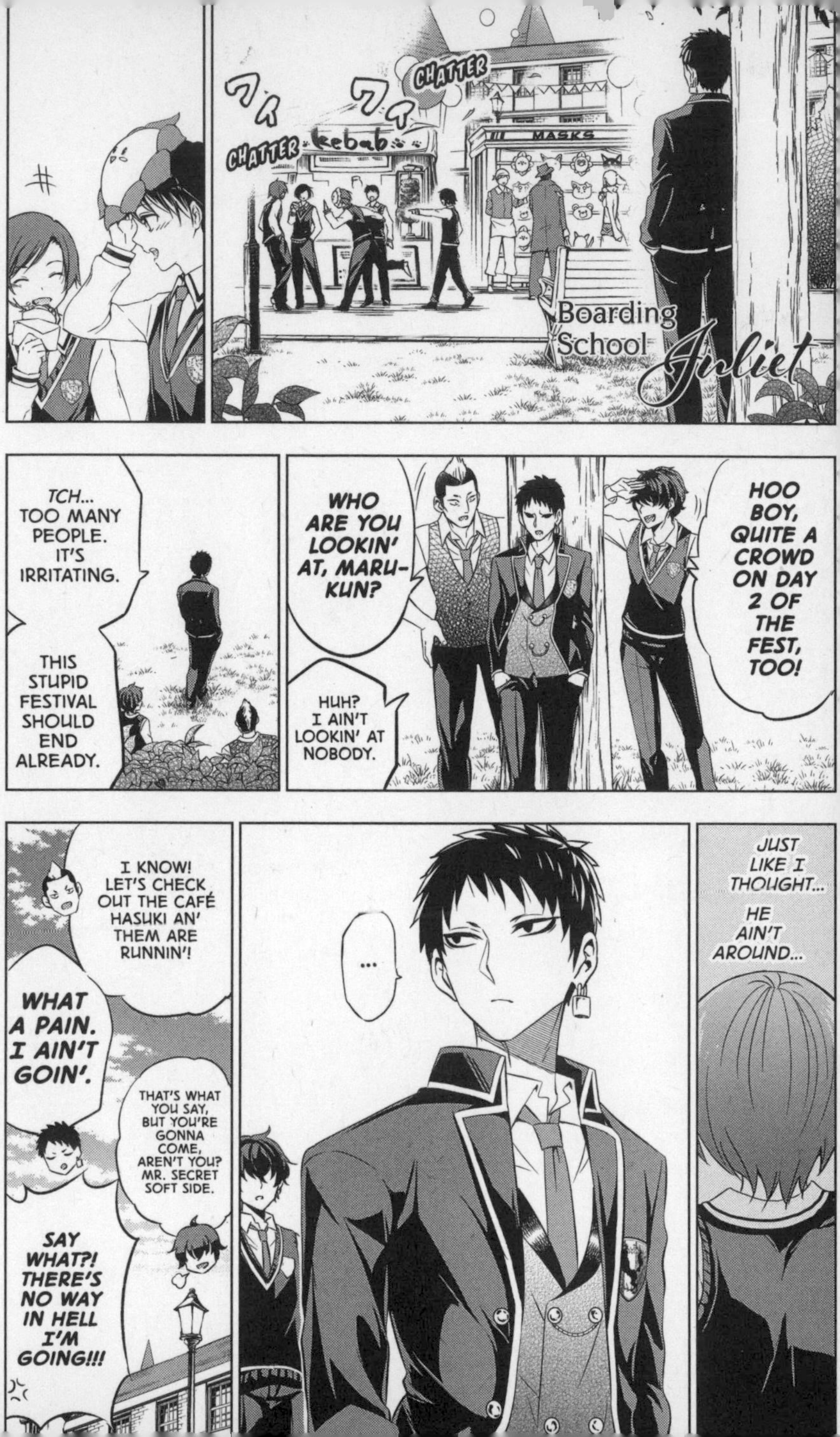
CHATTER
ワイ ワイ
CHATTER
kebab
MASKS
Boarding School Juliet
HOO BOY, QUITE A CROWD ON DAY 2 OF THE FEST, TOO!
WHO ARE YOU LOOKIN' AT, MARU-KUN?
HUH? I AIN'T LOOKIN' AT NOBODY.
TCH... TOO MANY PEOPLE. IT'S IRRITATING.
THIS STUPID FESTIVAL SHOULD END ALREADY.
JUST LIKE I THOUGHT...
HE AIN'T AROUND...
...
I KNOW! LET'S CHECK OUT THE CAFÉ HASUKI AN' THEM ARE RUNNIN'!
WHAT A PAIN. I AIN'T GOIN'.
THAT'S WHAT YOU SAY, BUT YOU'RE GONNA COME, AREN'T YOU? MR. SECRET SOFT SIDE.
SAY WHAT?! THERE'S NO WAY IN HELL I'M GOING!!!

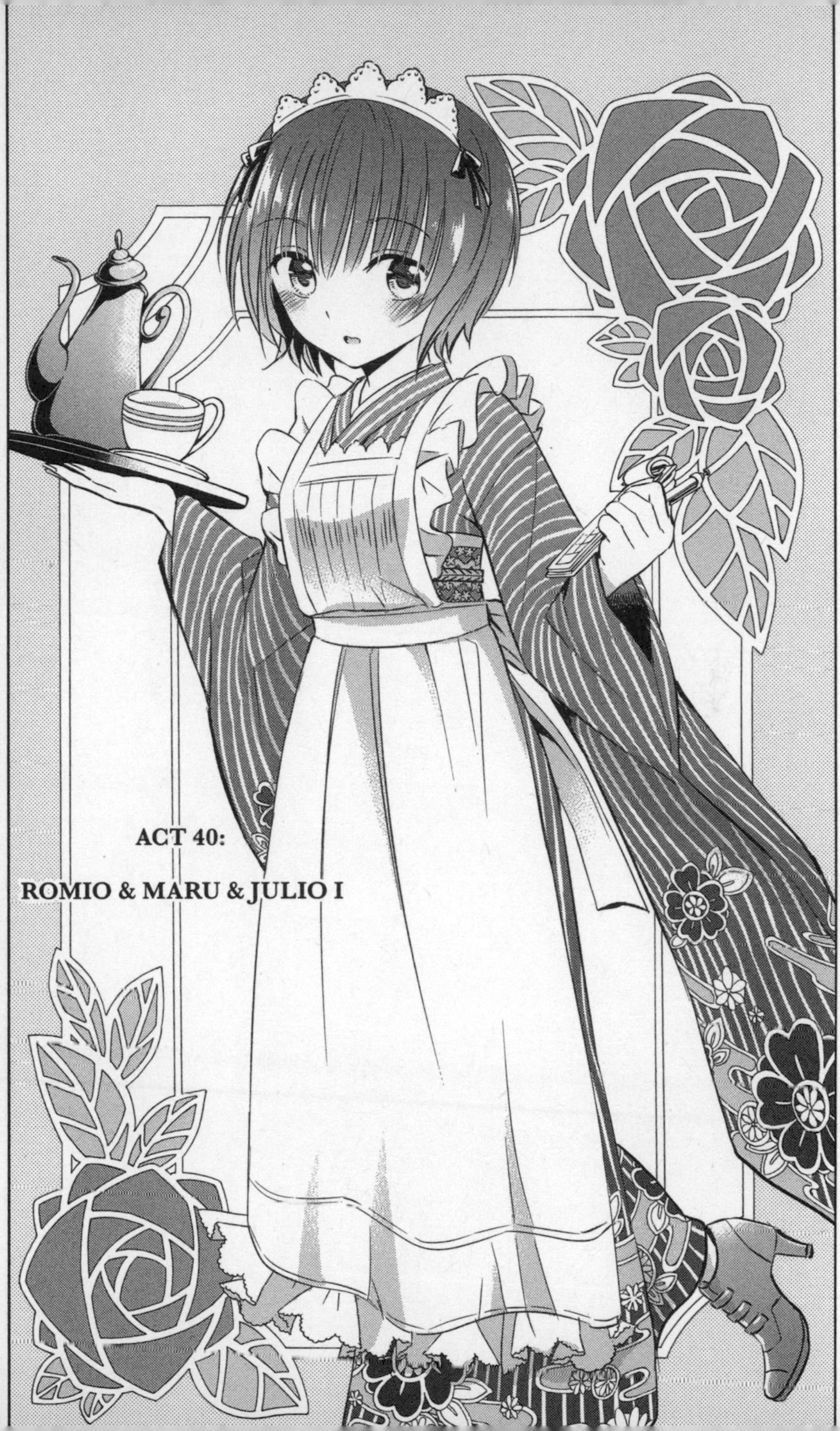
ACT 40:
ROMIO & MARU & JULIO I

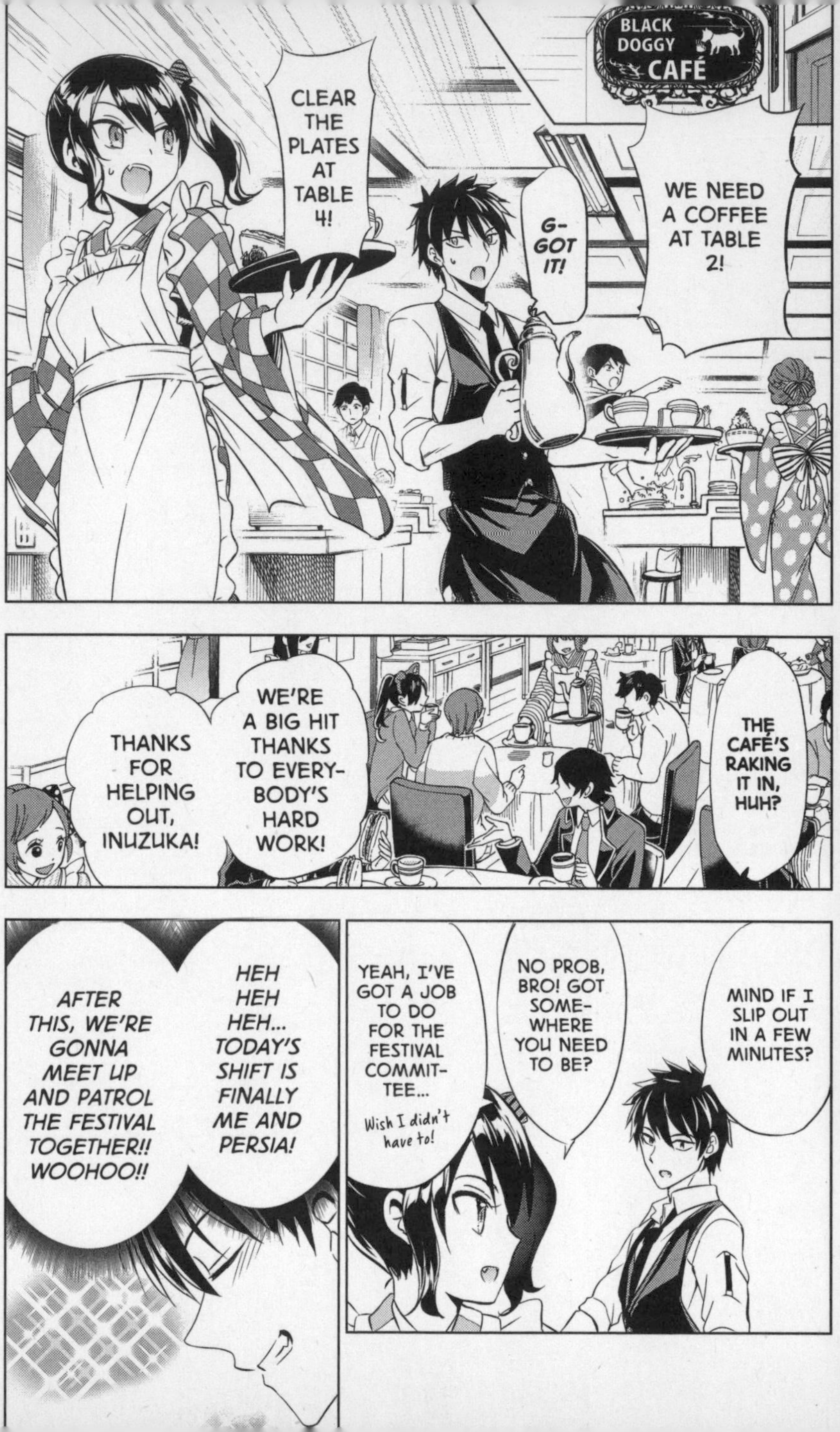
BLACK DOGGY CAFÉ
WE NEED A COFFEE AT TABLE 2!
G-GOT IT!
CLEAR THE PLATES AT TABLE 4!
THE CAFÉ'S RAKING IT IN, HUH?
WE'RE A BIG HIT THANKS TO EVERYBODY'S HARD WORK!
THANKS FOR HELPING OUT, INUZUKA!
MIND IF I SLIP OUT IN A FEW MINUTES?
NO PROB, BRO! GOT SOMEWHERE YOU NEED TO BE?
YEAH, I'VE GOT A JOB TO DO FOR THE FESTIVAL COMMITTEE...
Wish I didn't have to!
HEH HEH HEH... TODAY'S SHIFT IS FINALLY ME AND PERSIA!
AFTER THIS, WE'RE GONNA MEET UP AND PATROL THE FESTIVAL TOGETHER!! WOOHOO!!

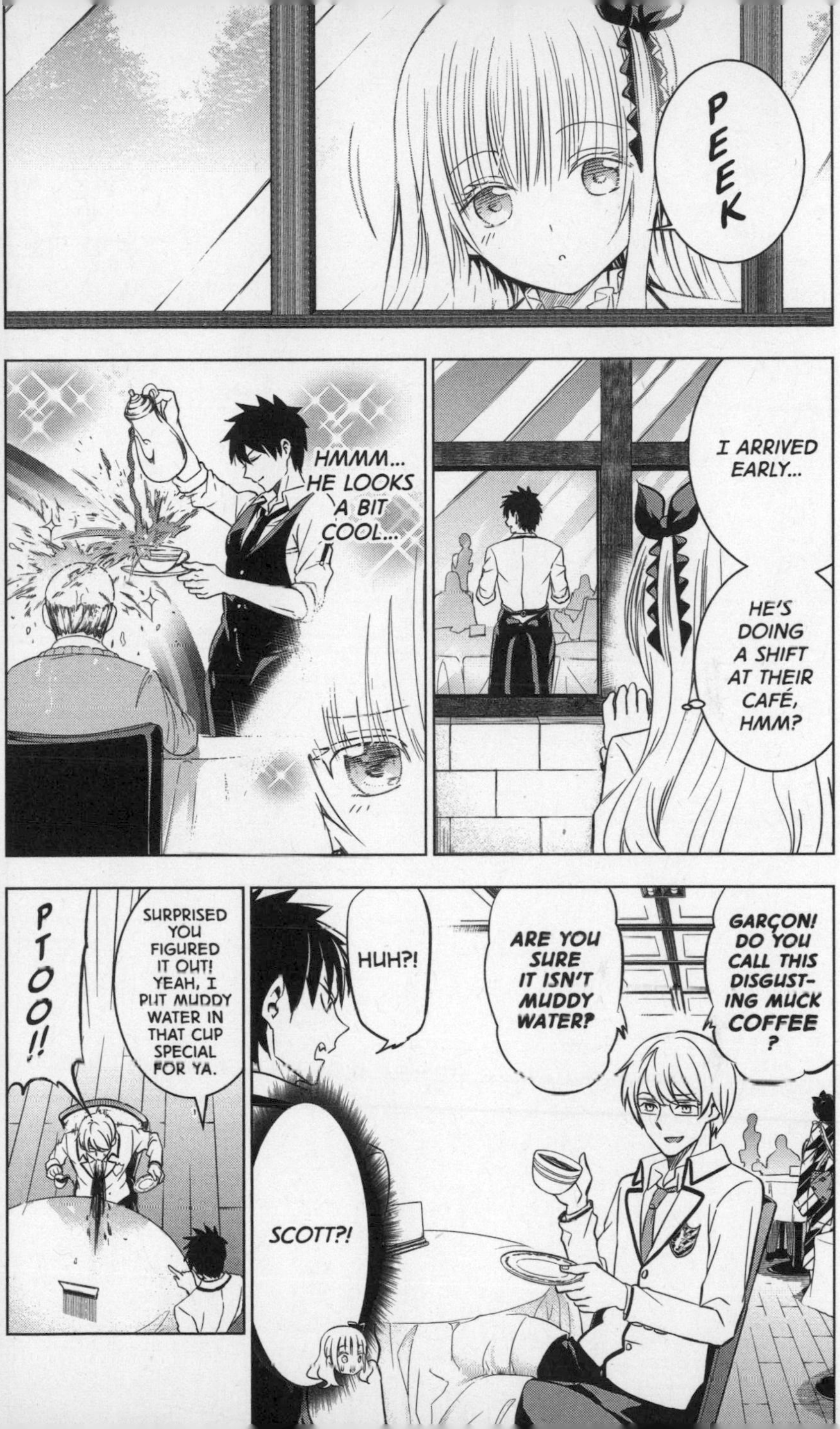
PEEK
I ARRIVED EARLY...
HE'S DOING A SHIFT AT THEIR CAFÉ, HMM?
HMMM... HE LOOKS A BIT COOL...
GARÇON! DO YOU CALL THIS DISGUSTING MUCK COFFEE?
ARE YOU SURE IT ISN'T MUDDY WATER?
HUH?!
SCOTT?!
SURPRISED YOU FIGURED IT OUT! YEAH, I PUT MUDDY WATER IN THAT CUP SPECIAL FOR YA.
PTOOO!!

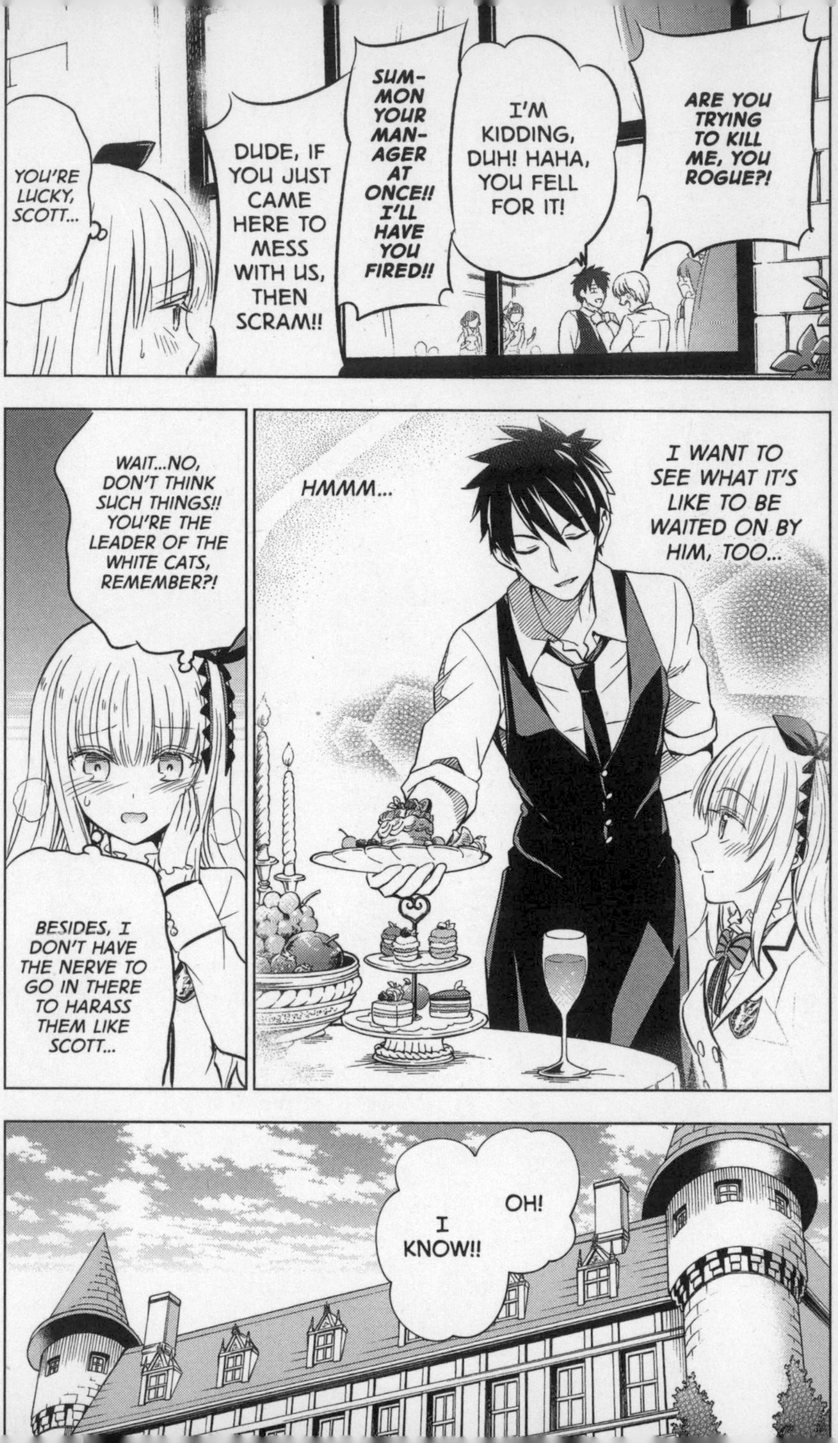
ARE YOU TRYING TO KILL ME, YOU ROGUE?!
I'M KIDDING, DUH! HAHA, YOU FELL FOR IT!
SUMMON YOUR MANAGER AT ONCE!! I'LL HAVE YOU FIRED!!
DUDE, IF YOU JUST CAME HERE TO MESS WITH US, THEN SCRAM!!
YOU'RE LUCKY, SCOTT...
I WANT TO SEE WHAT IT'S LIKE TO BE WAITED ON BY HIM, TOO...
HMMM...
WAIT...NO, DON'T THINK SUCH THINGS!! YOU'RE THE LEADER OF THE WHITE CATS, REMEMBER?!
BESIDES, I DON'T HAVE THE NERVE TO GO IN THERE TO HARASS THEM LIKE SCOTT...
OH!
I KNOW!!

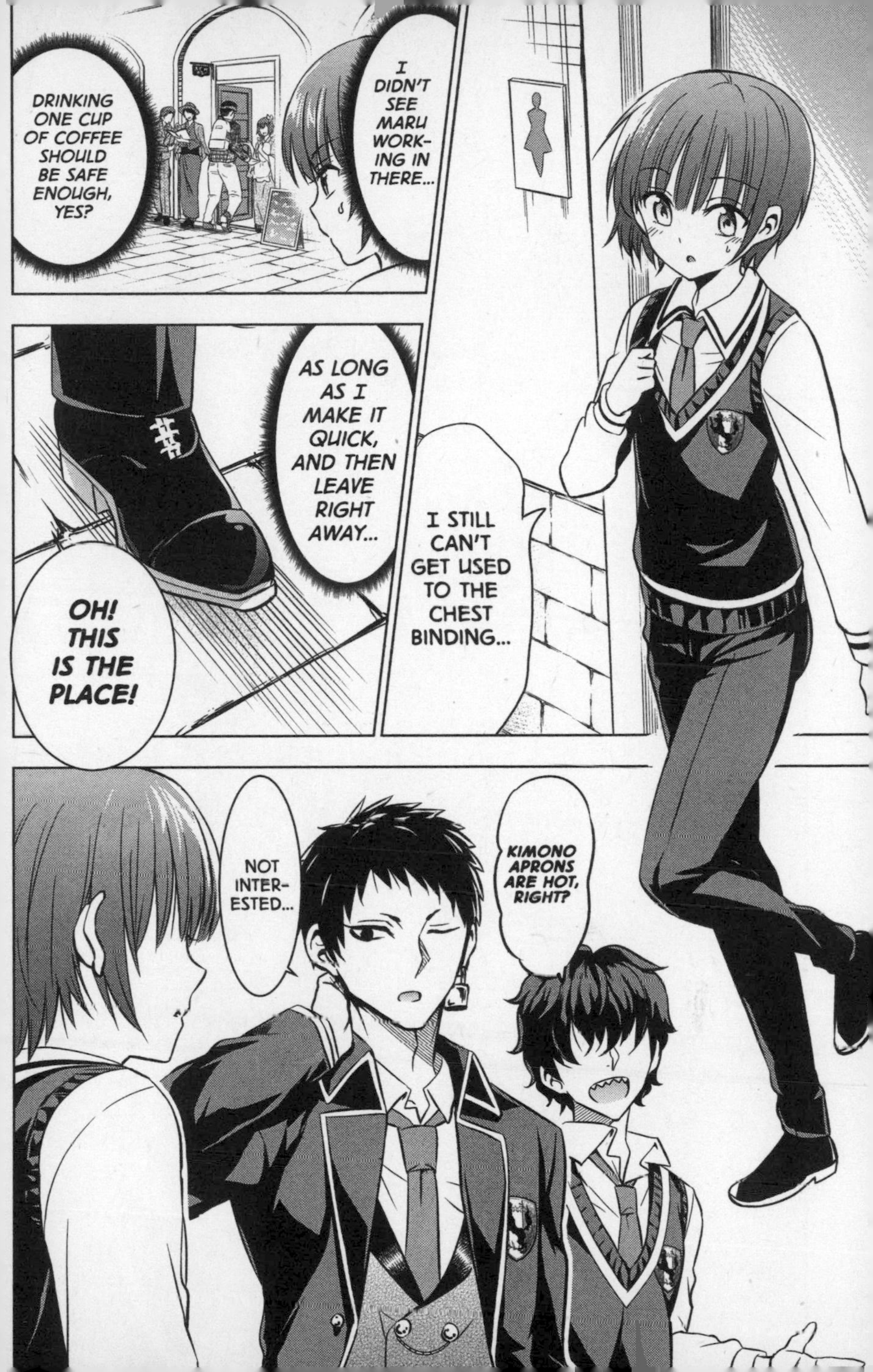
I STILL CAN'T GET USED TO THE CHEST BINDING...
I DIDN'T SEE MARU WORKING IN THERE...
DRINKING ONE CUP OF COFFEE SHOULD BE SAFE ENOUGH, YES?
AS LONG AS I MAKE IT QUICK, AND THEN LEAVE RIGHT AWAY...
OH! THIS IS THE PLACE!
KIMONO APRONS ARE HOT, RIGHT?
NOT INTERESTED...

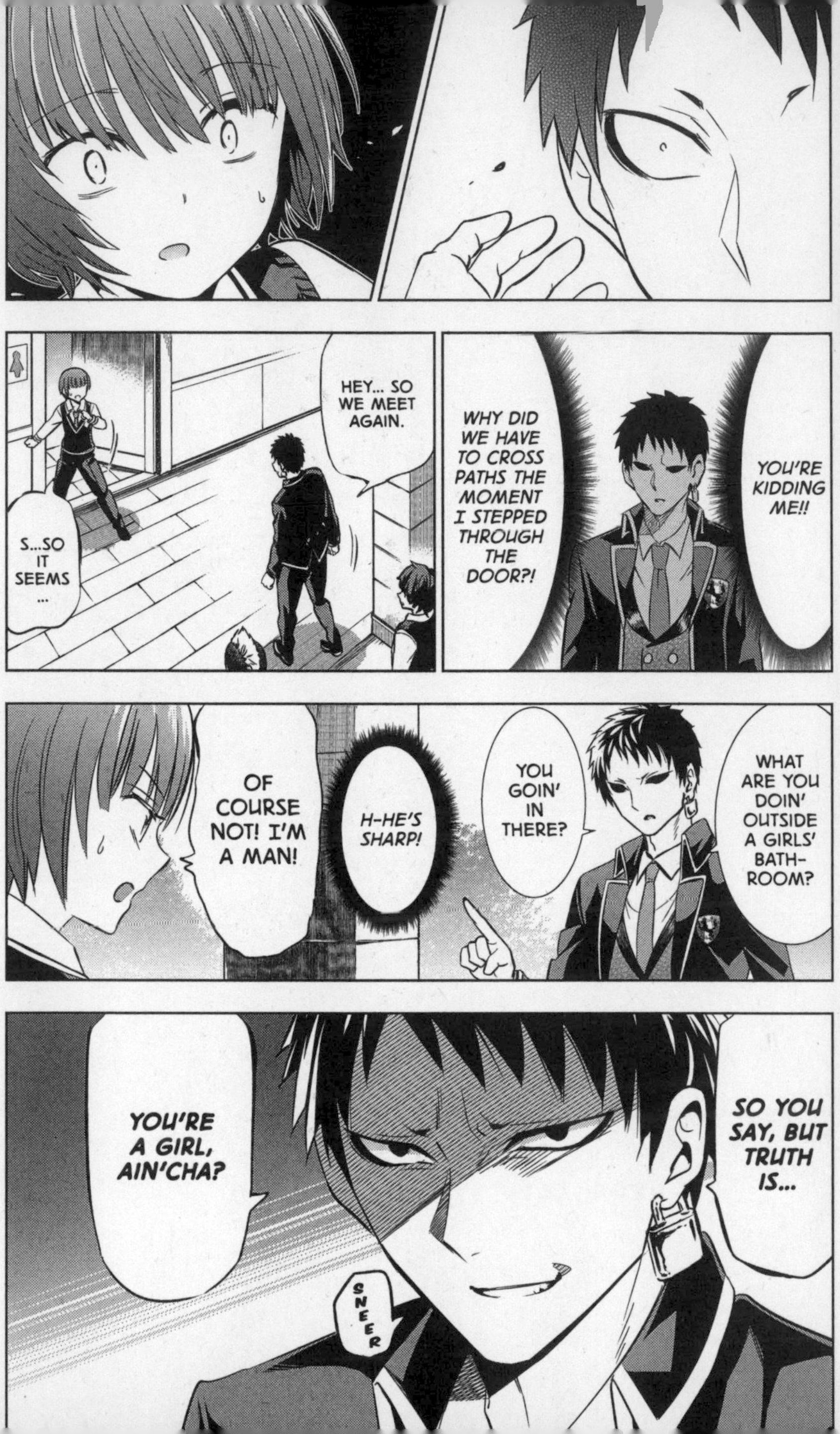
YOU'RE KIDDING ME!!
WHY DID WE HAVE TO CROSS PATHS THE MOMENT I STEPPED THROUGH THE DOOR?!
HEY... SO WE MEET AGAIN.
S...SO IT SEEMS...
WHAT ARE YOU DOIN' OUTSIDE A GIRLS' BATH-ROOM?
YOU GOIN' IN THERE?
H-HE'S SHARP!
OF COURSE NOT! I'M A MAN!
SO YOU SAY, BUT TRUTH IS...
YOU'RE A GIRL, AIN'CHA?
SNEER

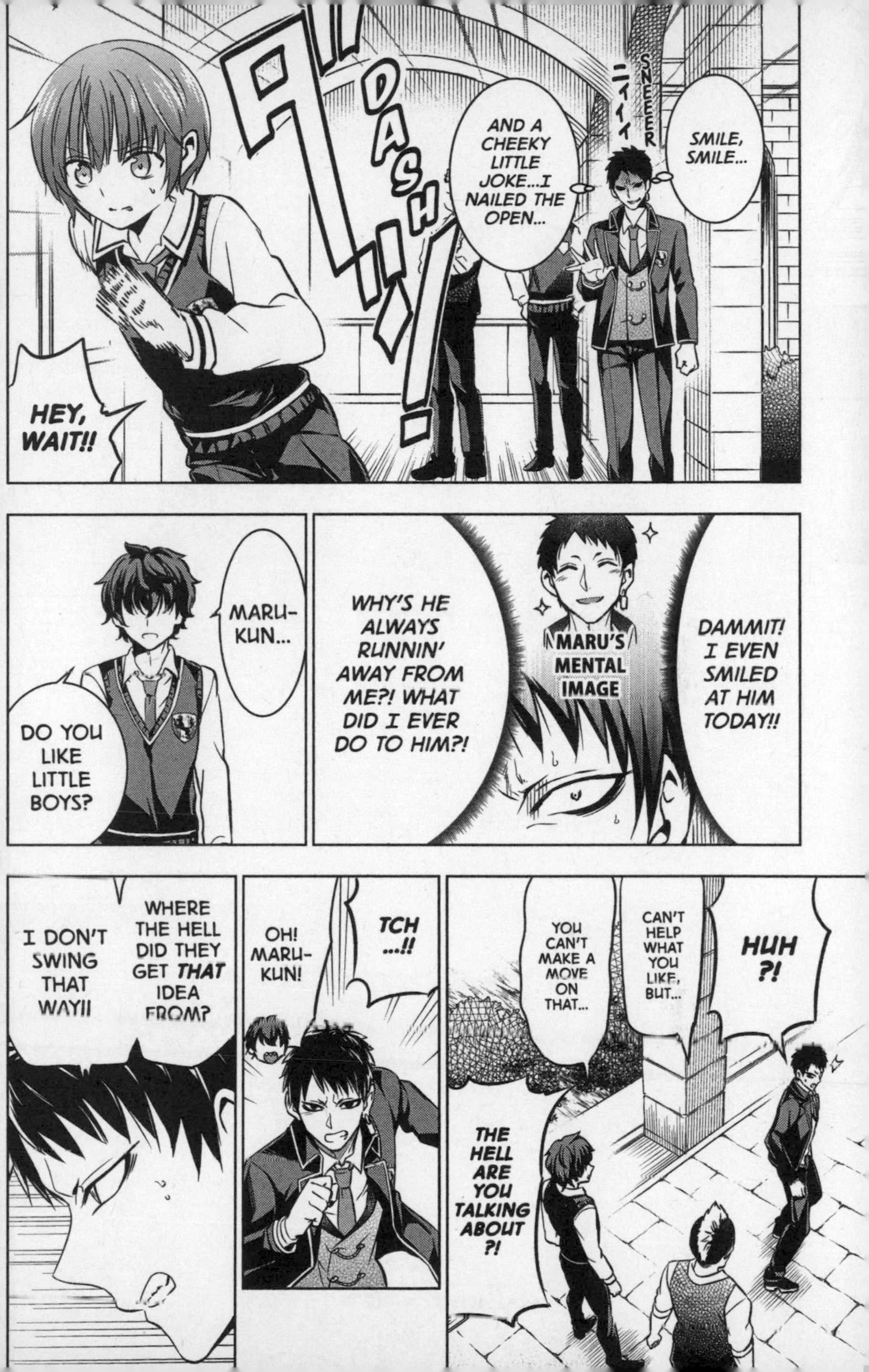
SMILE, SMILE...
SNEEER
AND A CHEEKY LITTLE JOKE...I NAILED THE OPEN...
DASH!!
HEY, WAIT!!
DAMMIT! I EVEN SMILED AT HIM TODAY!!
MARU'S MENTAL IMAGE
WHY'S HE ALWAYS RUNNIN' AWAY FROM ME?! WHAT DID I EVER DO TO HIM?!
MARU-KUN...
DO YOU LIKE LITTLE BOYS?
HUH ?!
CAN'T HELP WHAT YOU LIKE, BUT...
YOU CAN'T MAKE A MOVE ON THAT...
THE HELL ARE YOU TALKING ABOUT ?!
TCH ...!!
OH! MARU-KUN!
WHERE THE HELL DID THEY GET THAT IDEA FROM?
I DON'T SWING THAT WAY!!

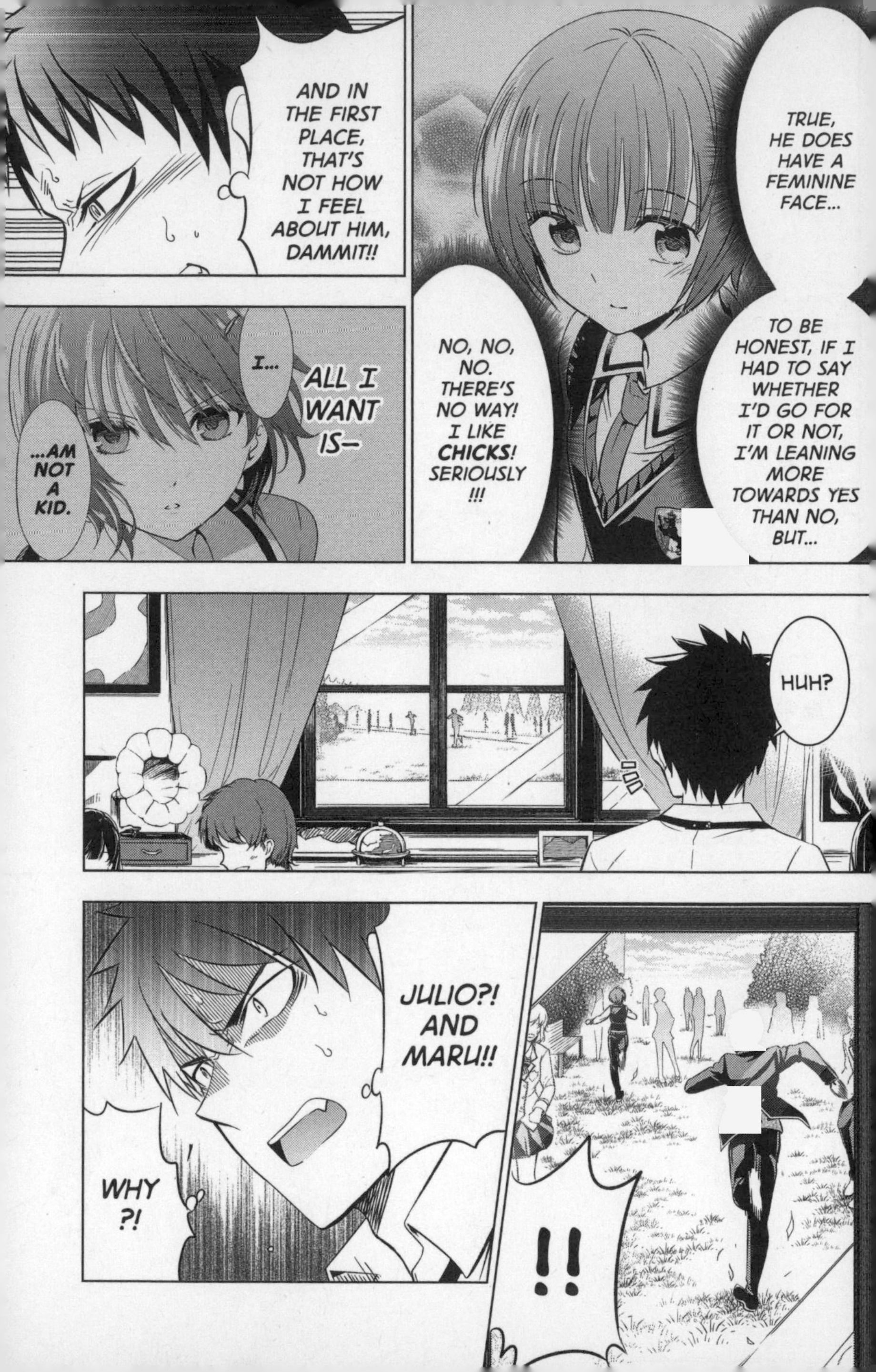
TRUE, HE DOES HAVE A FEMININE FACE...
TO BE HONEST, IF I HAD TO SAY WHETHER I'D GO FOR IT OR NOT, I'M LEANING MORE TOWARDS YES THAN NO, BUT...
NO, NO, NO. THERE'S NO WAY! I LIKE **CHICKS**! SERIOUSLY!!!
AND IN THE FIRST PLACE, THAT'S NOT HOW I FEEL ABOUT HIM, DAMMIT!!
I...
ALL I WANT IS—
...AM NOT A KID.
HUH?
!!
JULIO?! AND MARU!!
WHY?!

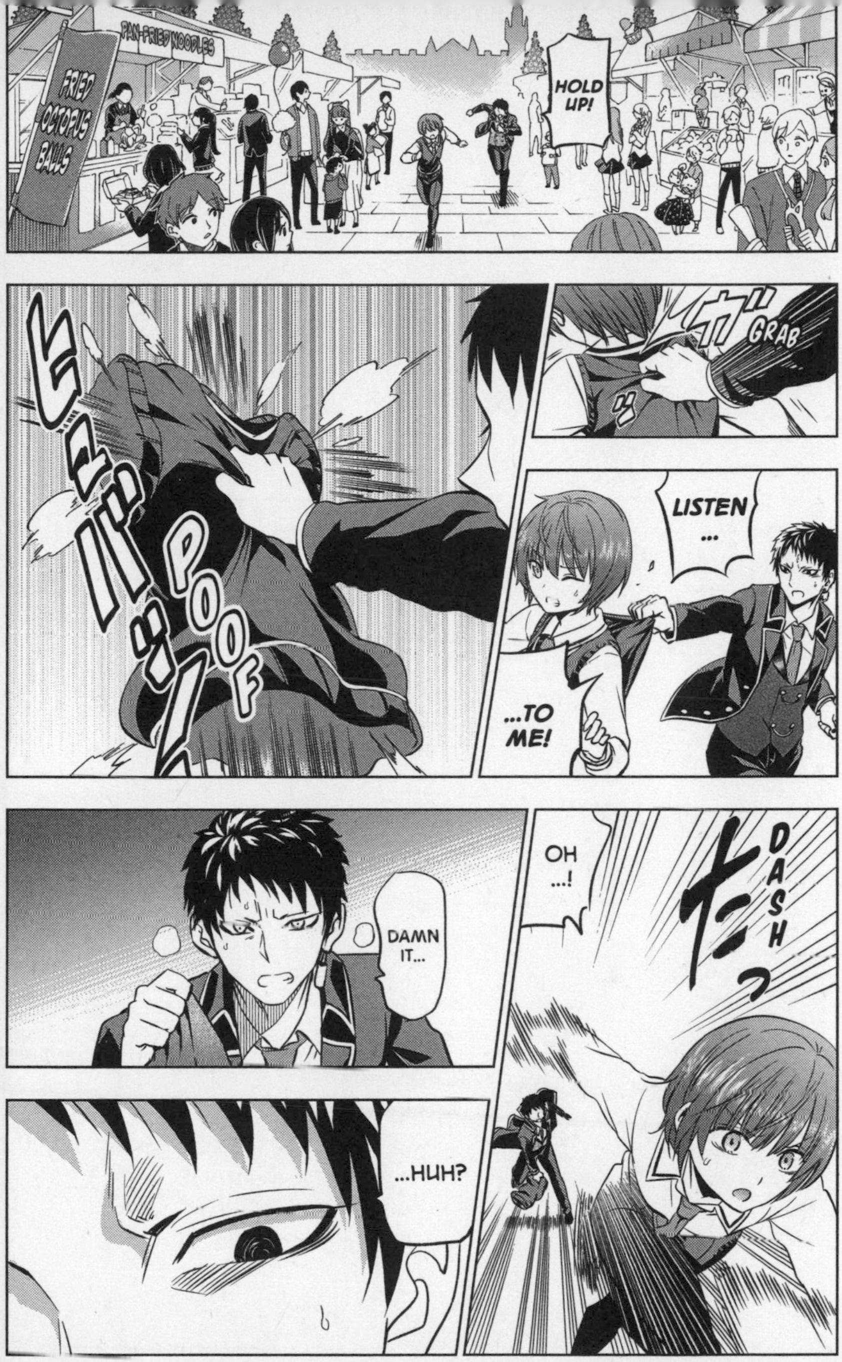
HOLD UP!
PAN-FRIED NOODLES
FRIED OCTOPUS BALLS
GRAB
LISTEN ...
...TO ME!
POOF
OH ...!
DASH
DAMN IT...
...HUH?

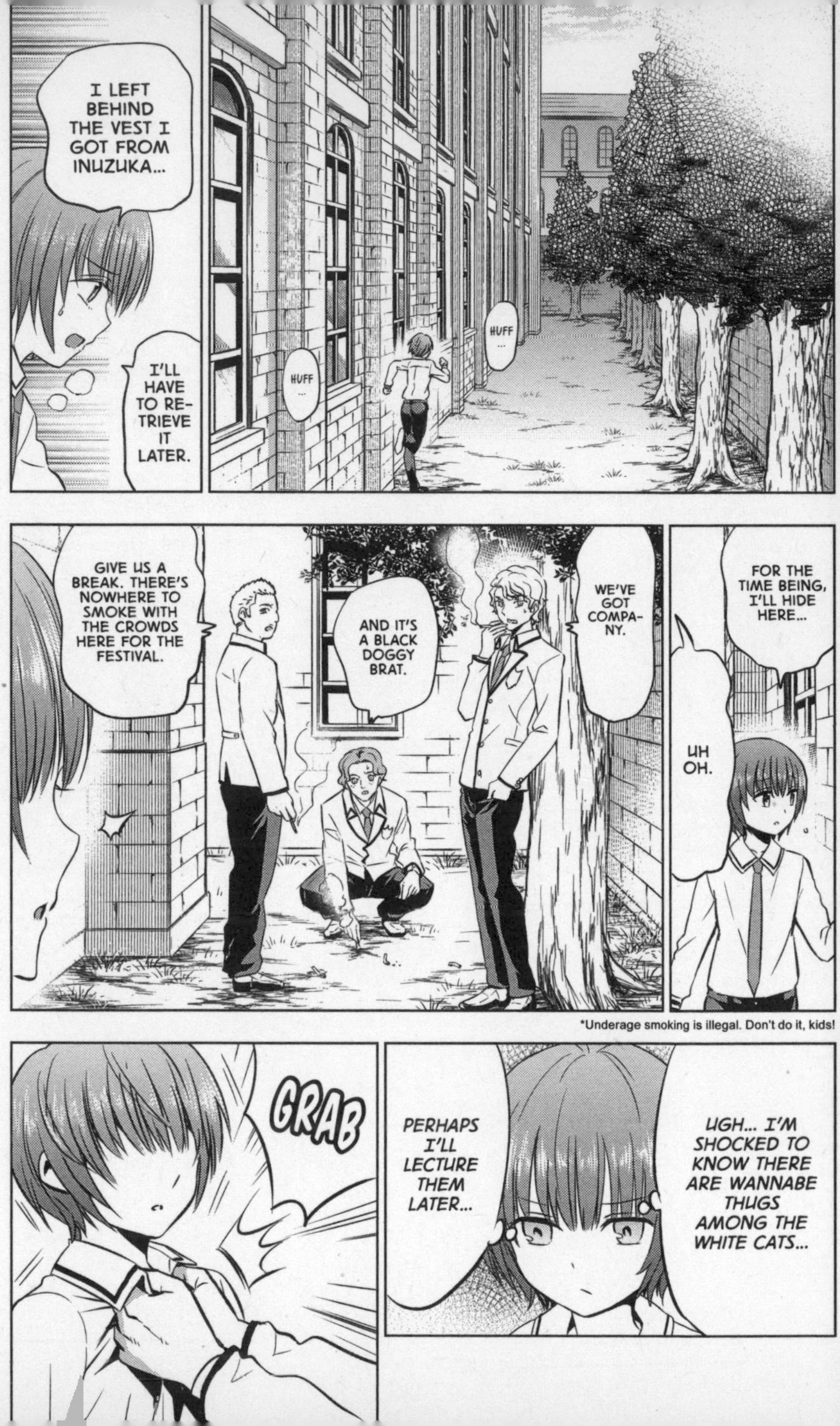
HUFF...
HUFF...
I LEFT BEHIND THE VEST I GOT FROM INUZUKA...
I'LL HAVE TO RE-TRIEVE IT LATER.
FOR THE TIME BEING, I'LL HIDE HERE...
UH OH.
WE'VE GOT COMPA-NY.
AND IT'S A BLACK DOGGY BRAT.
GIVE US A BREAK. THERE'S NOWHERE TO SMOKE WITH THE CROWDS HERE FOR THE FESTIVAL.
UGH... I'M SHOCKED TO KNOW THERE ARE WANNABE THUGS AMONG THE WHITE CATS...
PERHAPS I'LL LECTURE THEM LATER...
GRAB

*Underage smoking is illegal. Don't do it, kids!

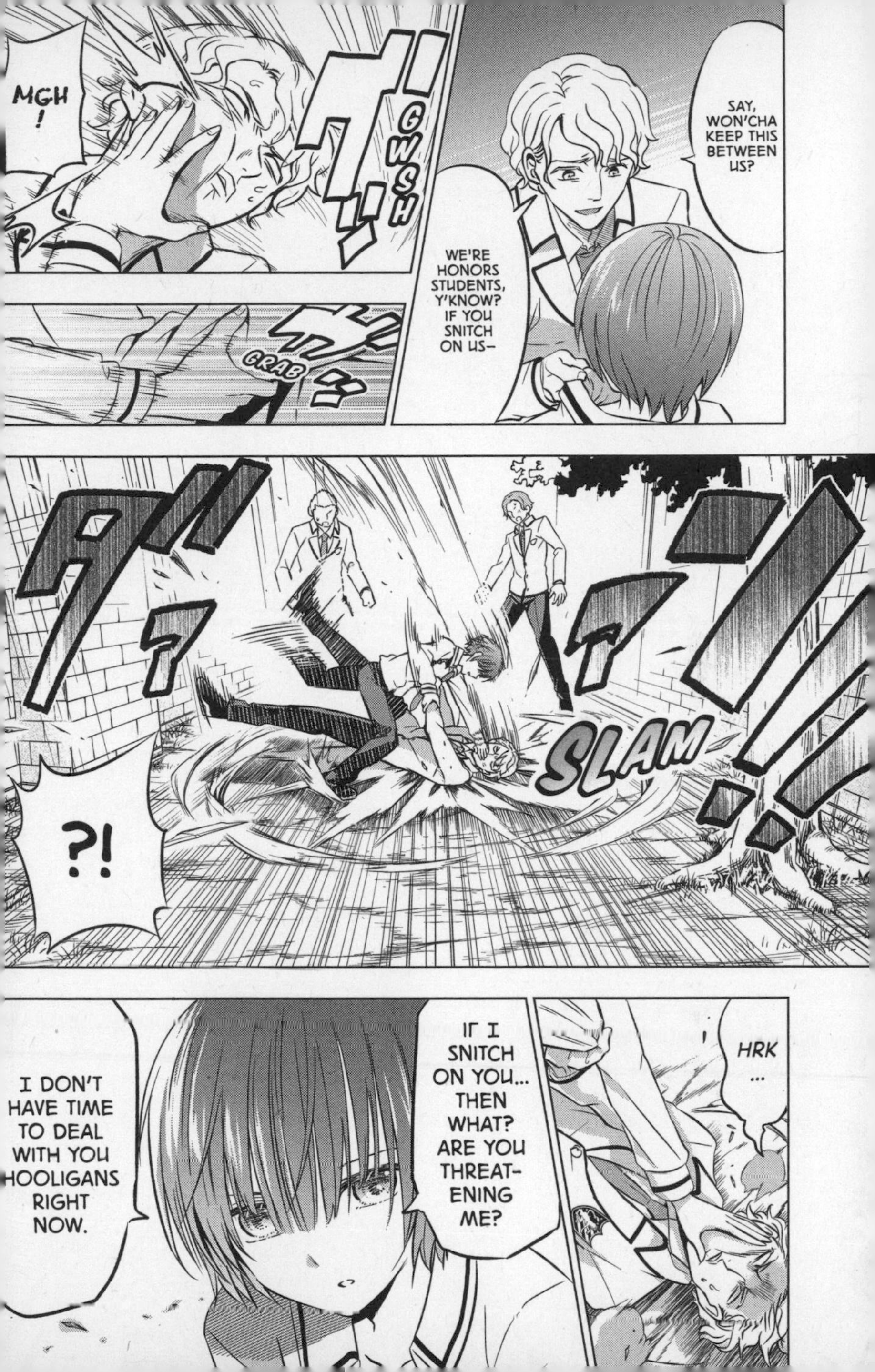
SAY, WON'CHA KEEP THIS BETWEEN US?
WE'RE HONORS STUDENTS, Y'KNOW? IF YOU SNITCH ON US–
MGH!
GWSH
GRAB
SLAM
?!
HRK...
IF I SNITCH ON YOU... THEN WHAT? ARE YOU THREAT-ENING ME?
I DON'T HAVE TIME TO DEAL WITH YOU HOOLIGANS RIGHT NOW.

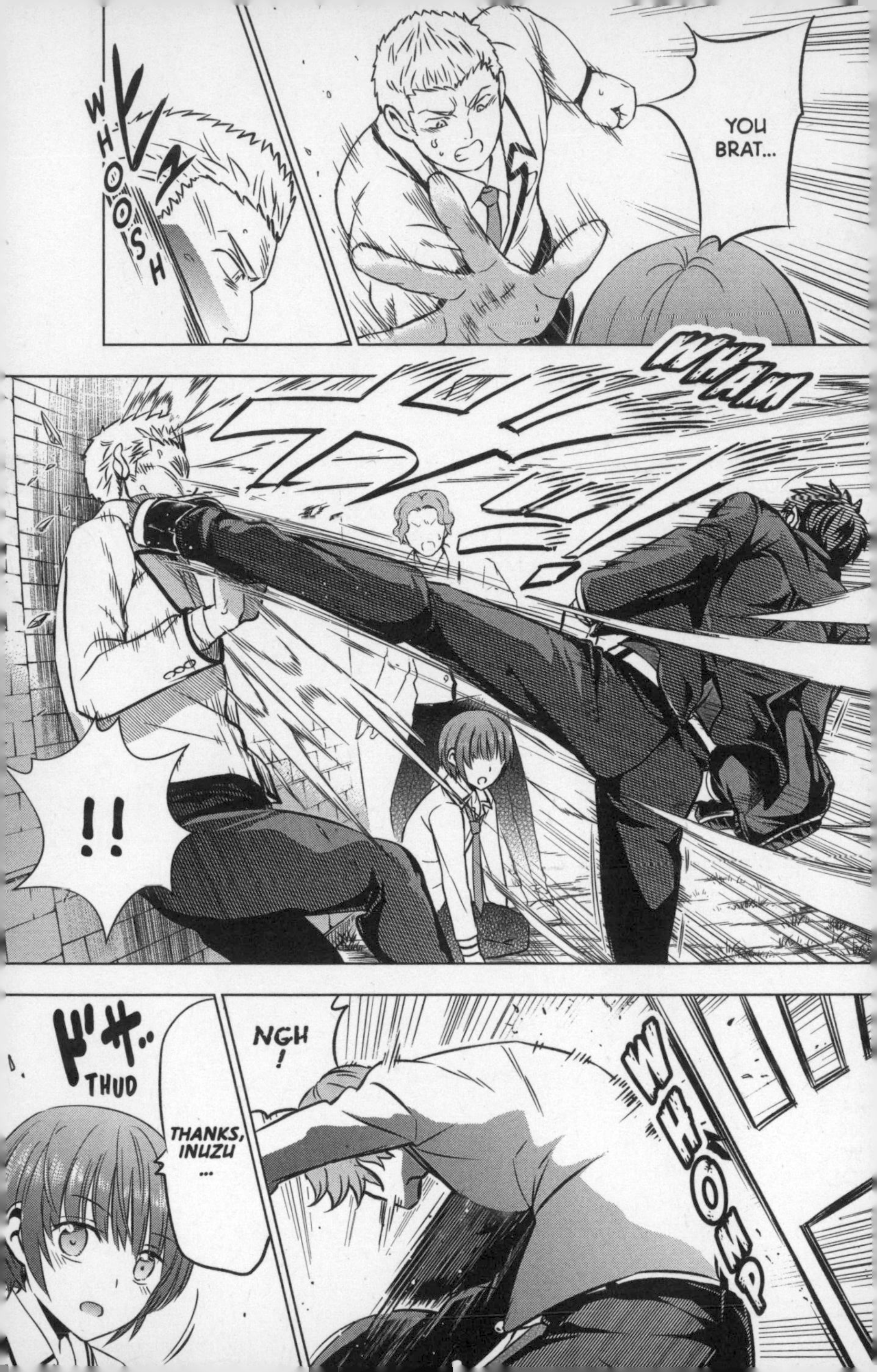
YOU BRAT...
WHOOSH
WHAM
!!
WHOMP
NGH!
ドサッ..
THUD
THANKS, INUZU ...

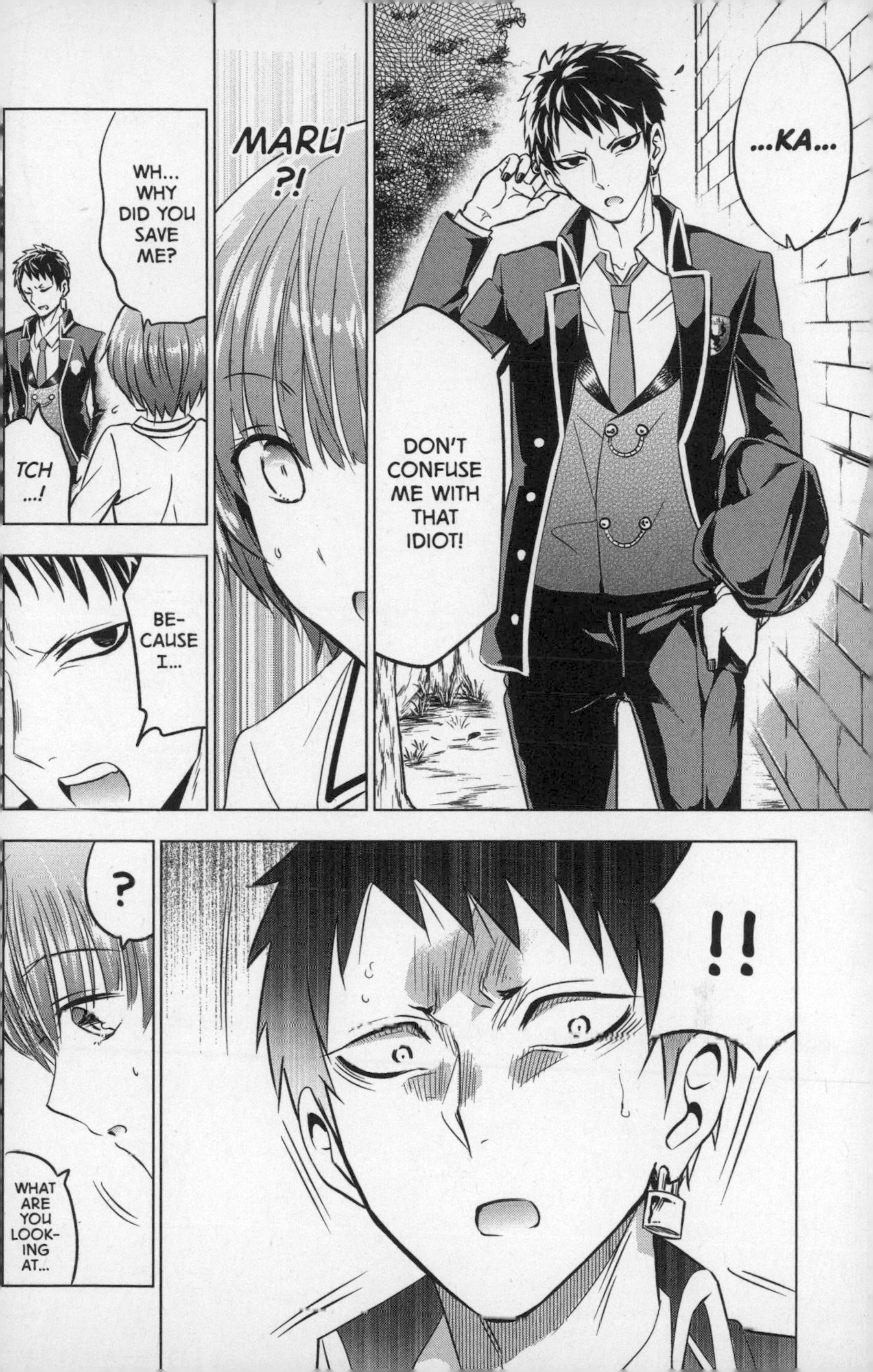
...KA...
DON'T CONFUSE ME WITH THAT IDIOT!
MARU ?!
WH... WHY DID YOU SAVE ME?
TCH ...!
BE-CAUSE I...
!!
?
WHAT ARE YOU LOOK-ING AT...

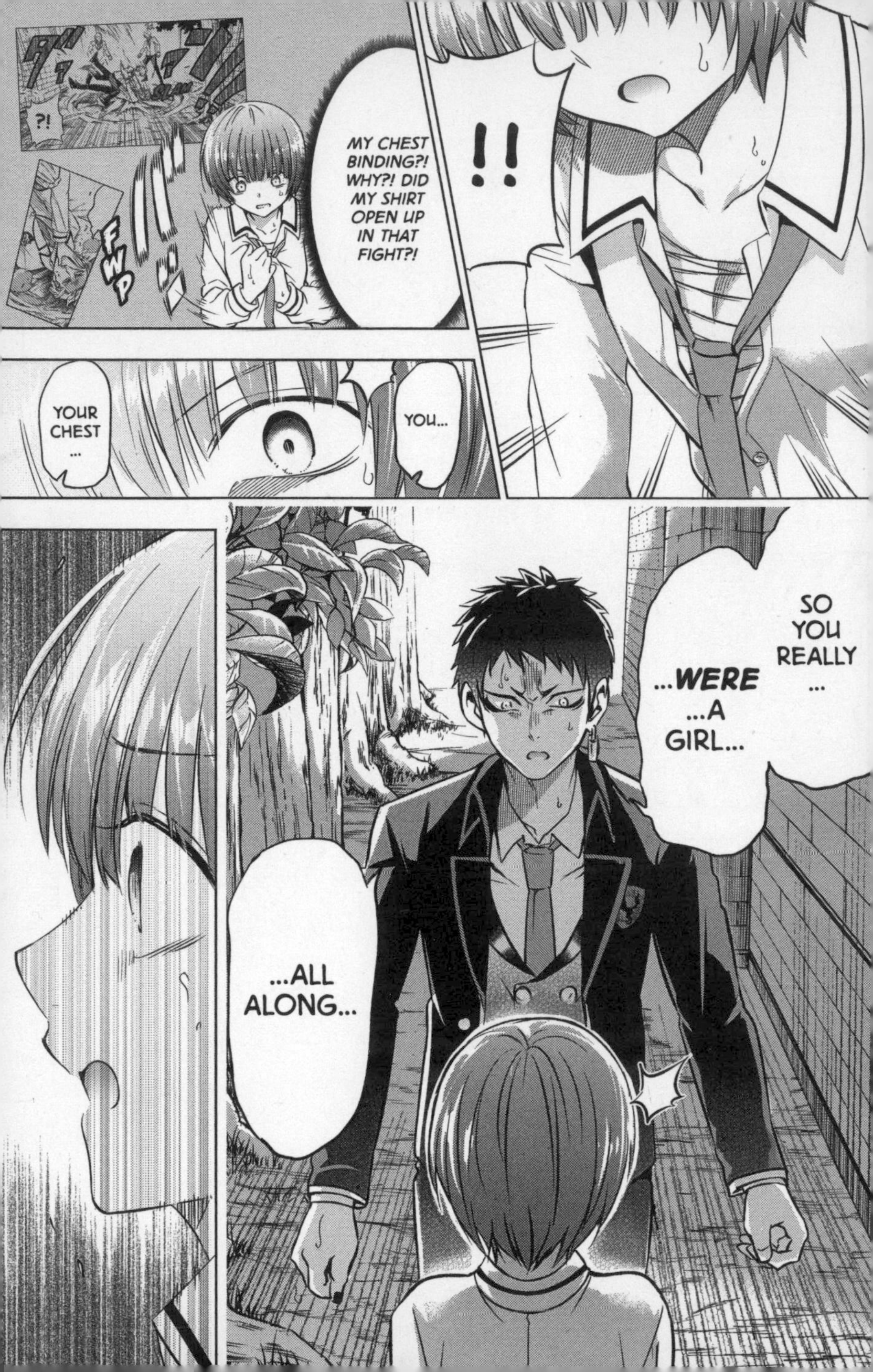
!!
MY CHEST BINDING?! WHY?! DID MY SHIRT OPEN UP IN THAT FIGHT?!
FWP
?!
YOU...
YOUR CHEST ...
SO YOU REALLY ...
...WERE ...A GIRL...
...ALL ALONG...

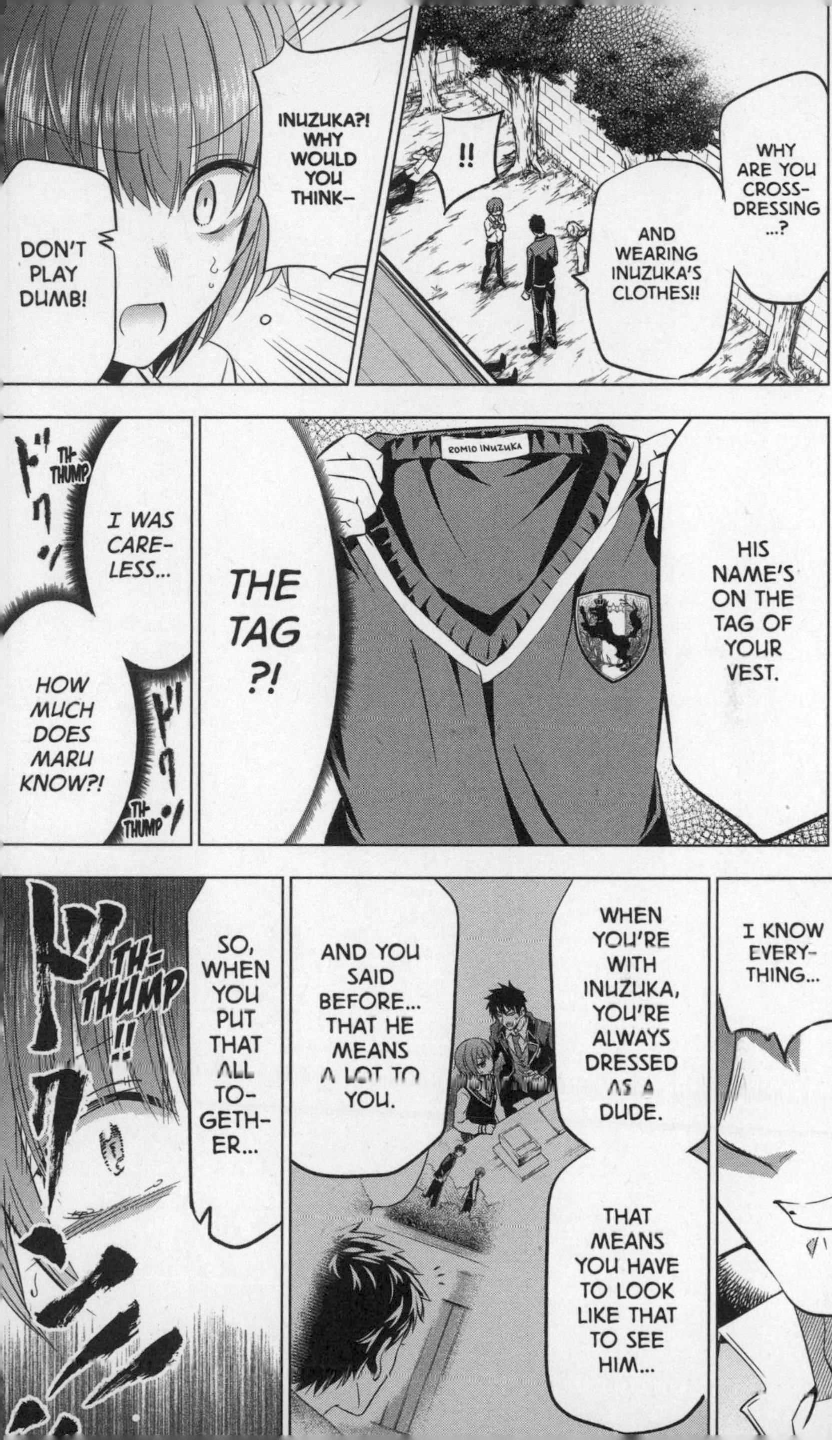
WHY ARE YOU CROSS-DRESSING ...?
AND WEARING INUZUKA'S CLOTHES!!
!!
INUZUKA?! WHY WOULD YOU THINK—
DON'T PLAY DUMB!
HIS NAME'S ON THE TAG OF YOUR VEST.
ROMIO INUZUKA
THE TAG ?!
TH-THUMP
I WAS CARE-LESS...
HOW MUCH DOES MARU KNOW?!
TH-THUMP
I KNOW EVERY-THING...
GRIT
WHEN YOU'RE WITH INUZUKA, YOU'RE ALWAYS DRESSED AS A DUDE.
AND YOU SAID BEFORE... THAT HE MEANS A LOT TO YOU.
THAT MEANS YOU HAVE TO LOOK LIKE THAT TO SEE HIM...
SO, WHEN YOU PUT THAT ALL TO-GETHER...
TH-THUMP!!

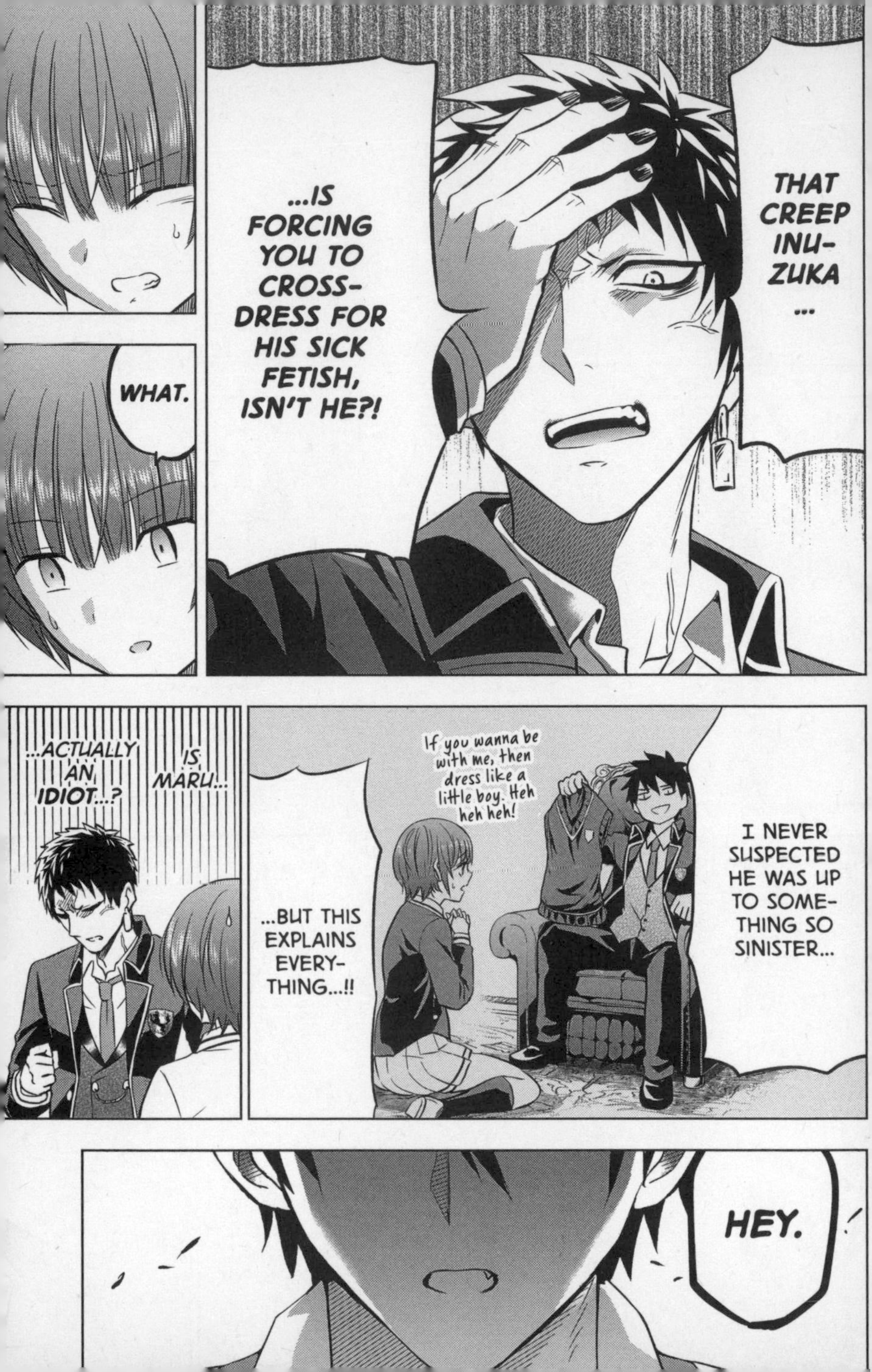
THAT CREEP INU-ZUKA...
...IS FORCING YOU TO CROSS-DRESS FOR HIS SICK FETISH, ISN'T HE?!
WHAT.
I NEVER SUSPECTED HE WAS UP TO SOME-THING SO SINISTER...
If you wanna be with me, then dress like a little boy. Heh heh heh!
...BUT THIS EXPLAINS EVERY-THING...!!
IS MARU...
...ACTUALLY AN IDIOT...?
HEY.

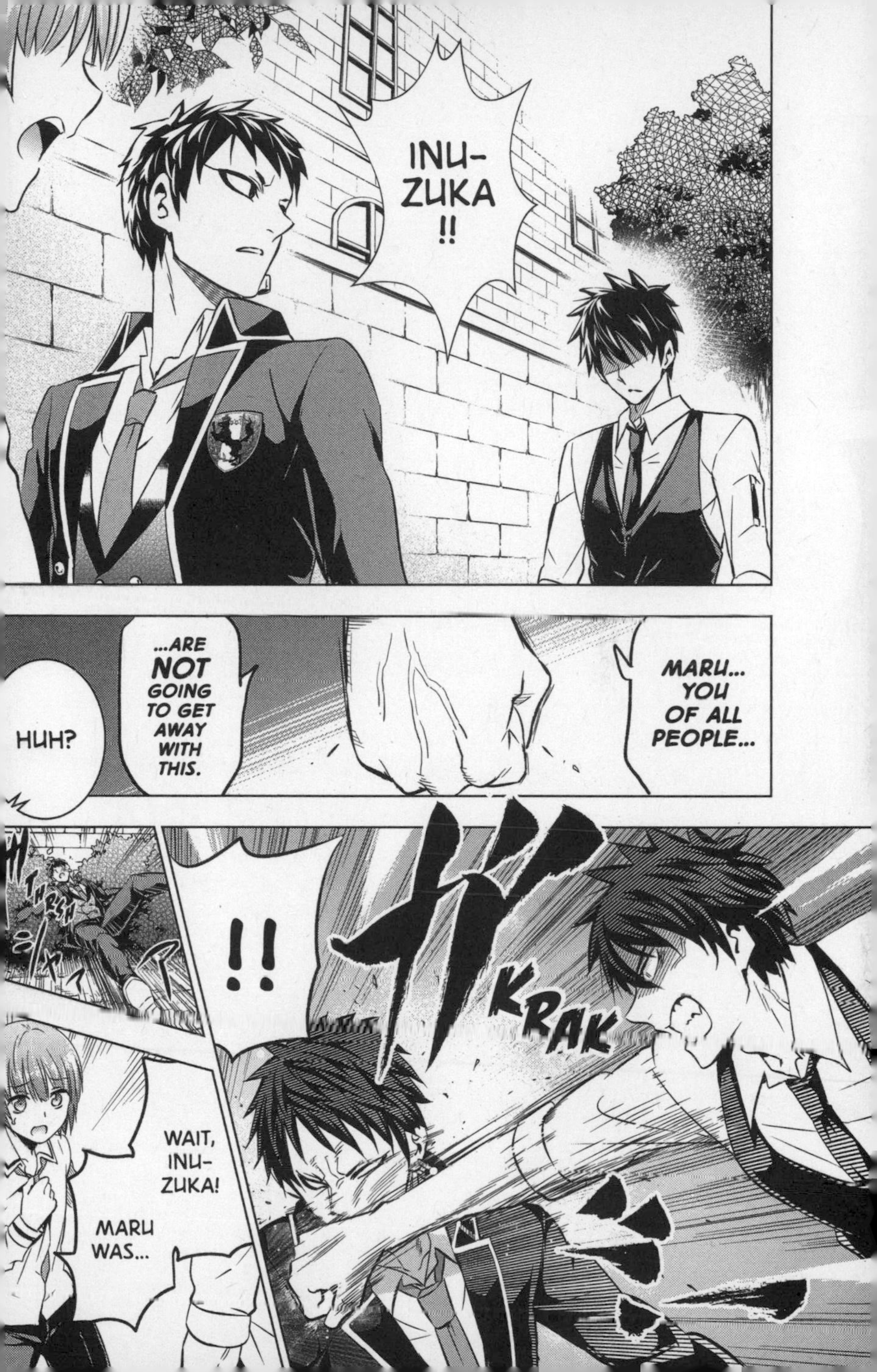
INU-ZUKA !!
MARU... YOU OF ALL PEOPLE...
...ARE NOT GOING TO GET AWAY WITH THIS.
HUH?
!!
KRAK
THRSH
WAIT, INU-ZUKA!
MARU WAS...

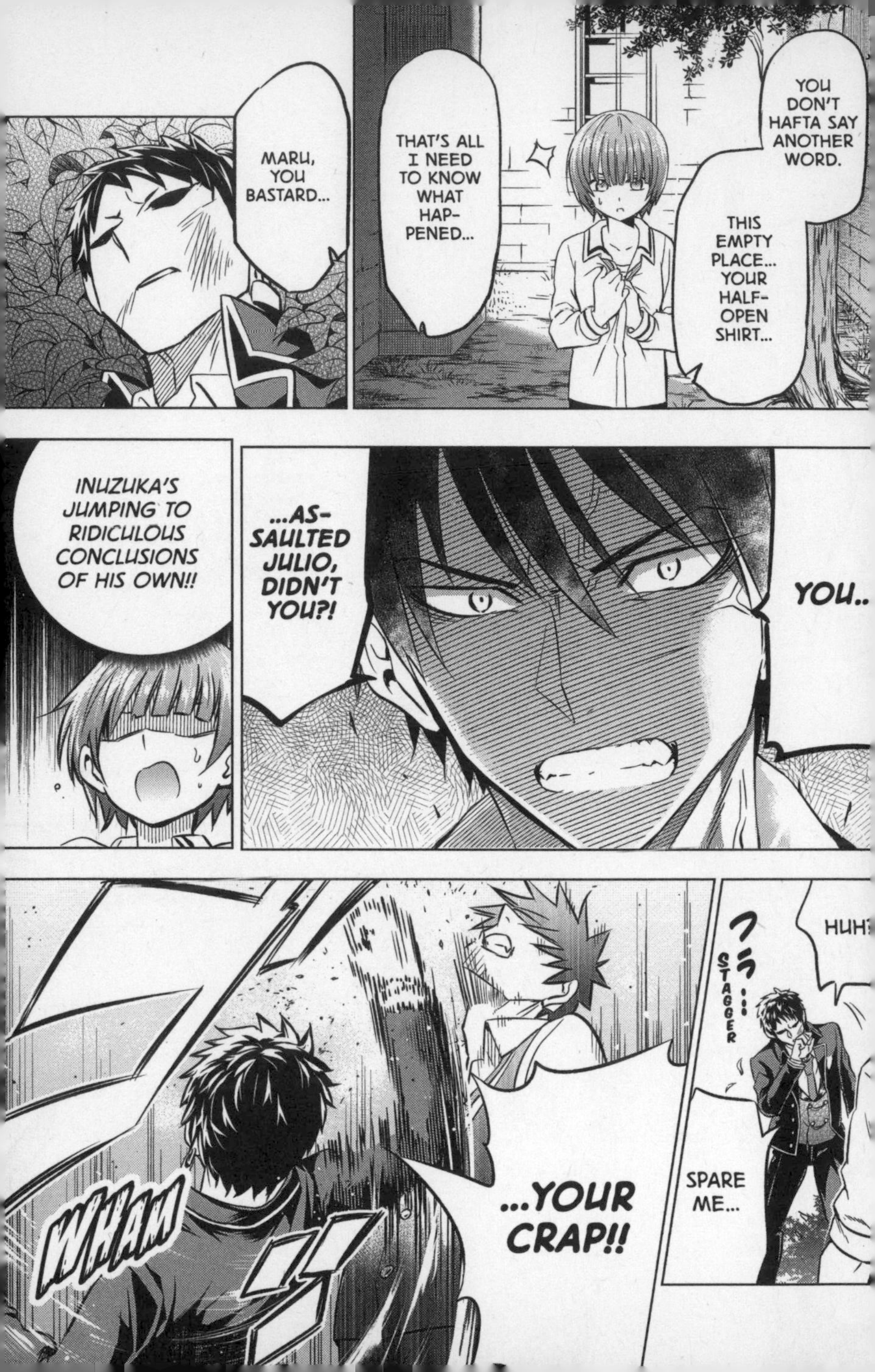
YOU DON'T HAFTA SAY ANOTHER WORD.
THIS EMPTY PLACE... YOUR HALF-OPEN SHIRT...
THAT'S ALL I NEED TO KNOW WHAT HAP-PENED...
MARU, YOU BASTARD...
YOU...
...AS-SAULTED JULIO, DIDN'T YOU?!
INUZUKA'S JUMPING TO RIDICULOUS CONCLUSIONS OF HIS OWN!!
HUH?
フラ...
STAGGER
SPARE ME...
...YOUR CRAP!!
WHAM

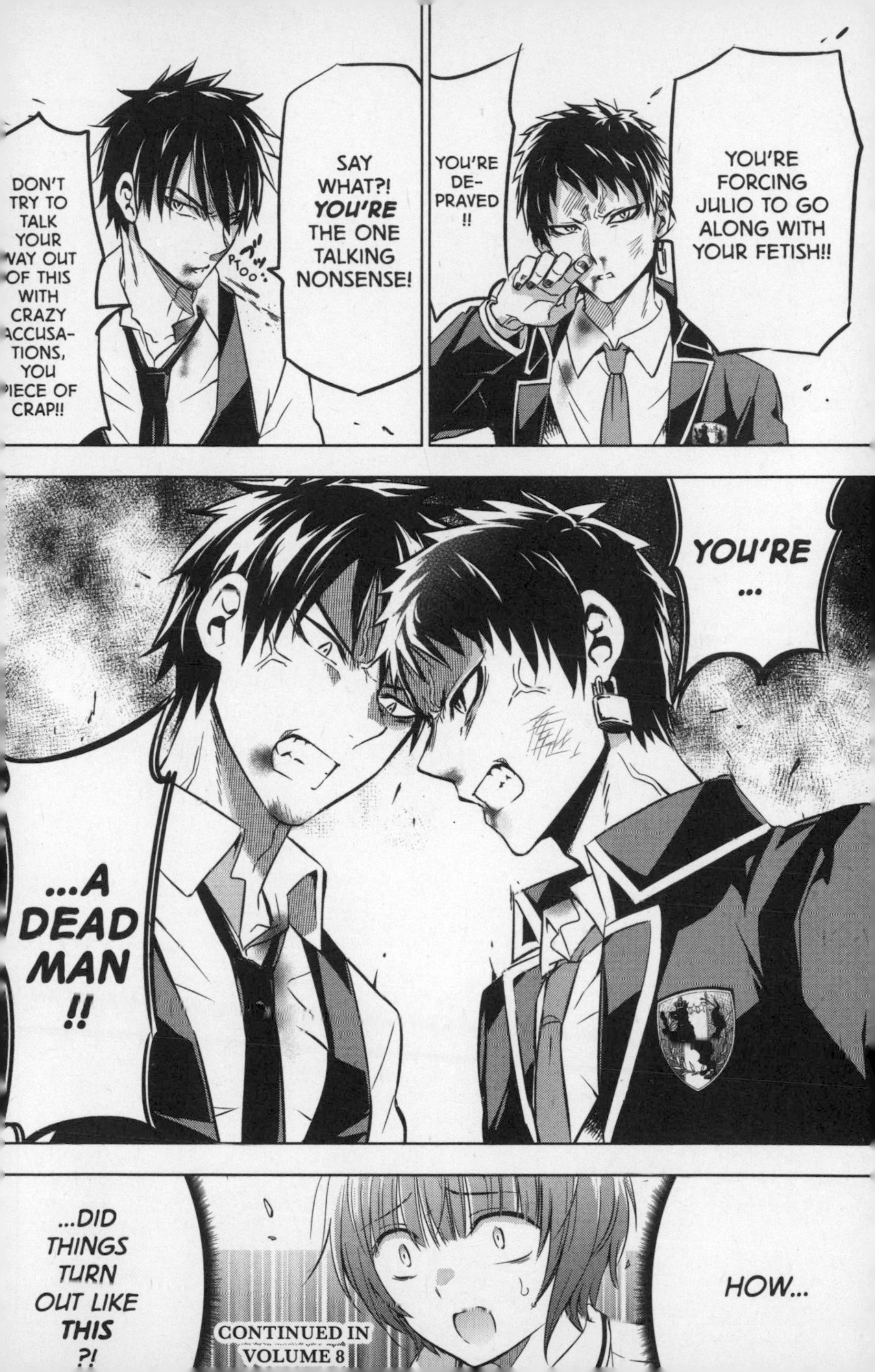
YOU'RE FORCING JULIO TO GO ALONG WITH YOUR FETISH!!
YOU'RE DE-PRAVED!!
SAY WHAT?! *YOU'RE* THE ONE TALKING NONSENSE!
PTOO
DON'T TRY TO TALK YOUR WAY OUT OF THIS WITH CRAZY ACCUSA-TIONS, YOU PIECE OF CRAP!!
YOU'RE...
...A DEAD MAN!!
HOW...
...DID THINGS TURN OUT LIKE THIS?!
CONTINUED IN VOLUME 8

AFTERWORD

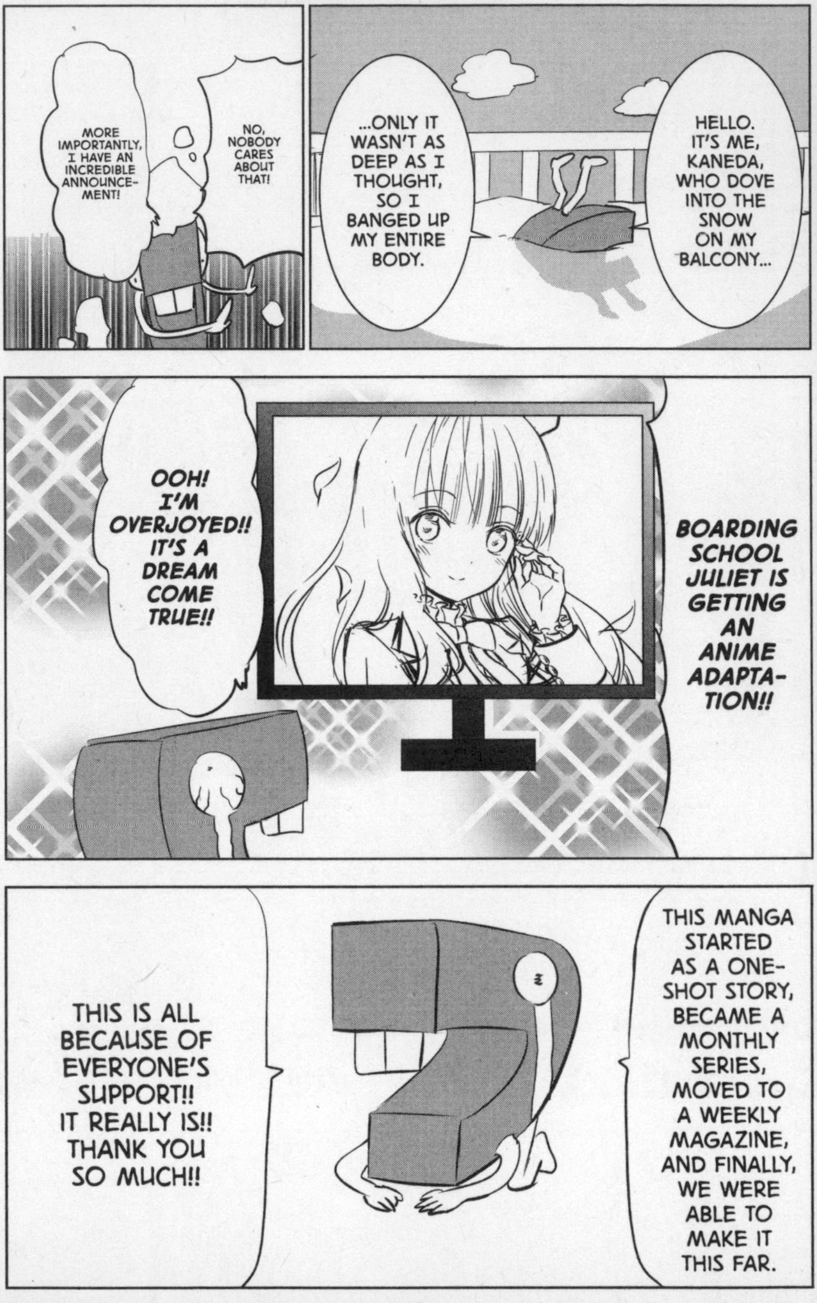
HELLO. IT'S ME, KANEDA, WHO DOVE INTO THE SNOW ON MY BALCONY...
...ONLY IT WASN'T AS DEEP AS I THOUGHT, SO I BANGED UP MY ENTIRE BODY.
NO, NOBODY CARES ABOUT THAT!
MORE IMPORTANTLY, I HAVE AN INCREDIBLE ANNOUNCE-MENT!
BOARDING SCHOOL JULIET IS GETTING AN ANIME ADAPTA-TION!!
OOH! I'M OVERJOYED!! IT'S A DREAM COME TRUE!!
THIS MANGA STARTED AS A ONE-SHOT STORY, BECAME A MONTHLY SERIES, MOVED TO A WEEKLY MAGAZINE, AND FINALLY, WE WERE ABLE TO MAKE IT THIS FAR.
THIS IS ALL BECAUSE OF EVERYONE'S SUPPORT!! IT REALLY IS!! THANK YOU SO MUCH!!

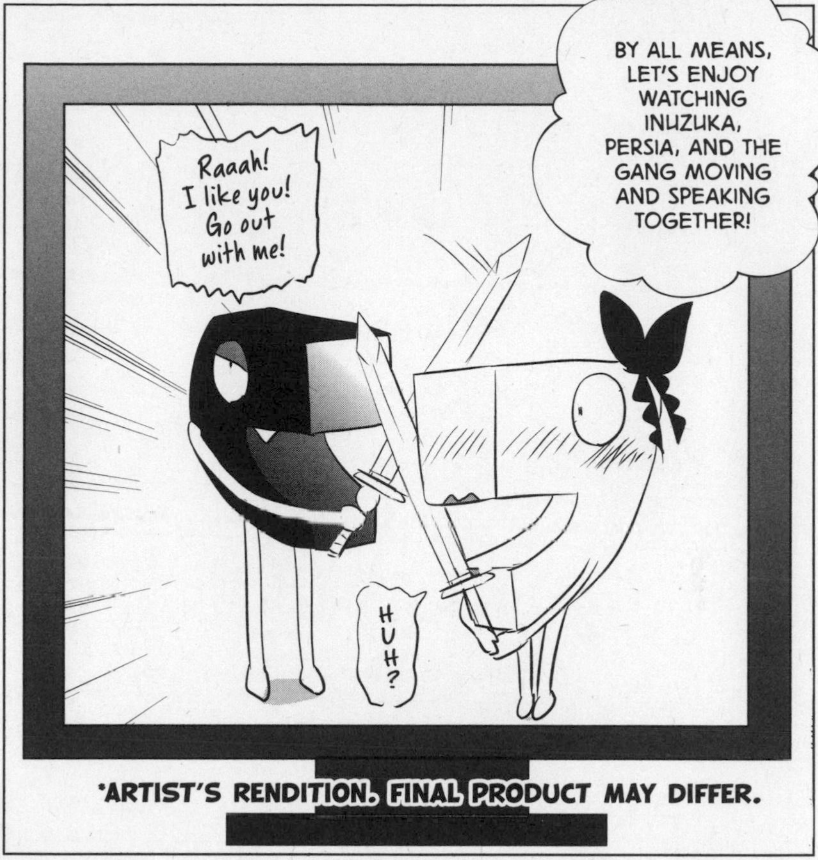
BY ALL MEANS, LET'S ENJOY WATCHING INUZUKA, PERSIA, AND THE GANG MOVING AND SPEAKING TOGETHER!
Raaah! I like you! Go out with me!
HUH?
*ARTIST'S RENDITION. FINAL PRODUCT MAY DIFFER.

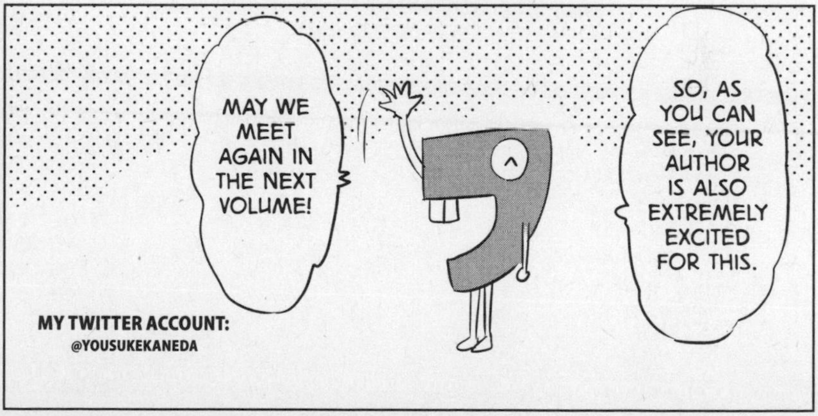
SO, AS YOU CAN SEE, YOUR AUTHOR IS ALSO EXTREMELY EXCITED FOR THIS.
MAY WE MEET AGAIN IN THE NEXT VOLUME!
MY TWITTER ACCOUNT:
@YOUSUKEKANEDA

STAFF LIST

Allow me to introduce the staff members who help create the pages of *Boarding School Juliet*!

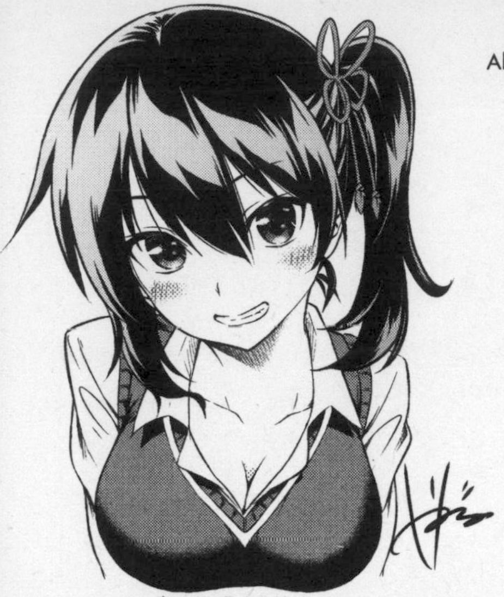

▼ RUREKUCHE
Loves muscles.
Flower master.

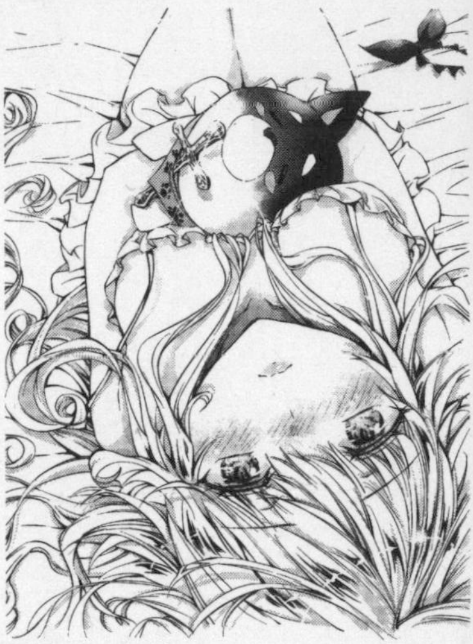

▲ YAGAMI
A DIY genius.
Glossy hair maestro.

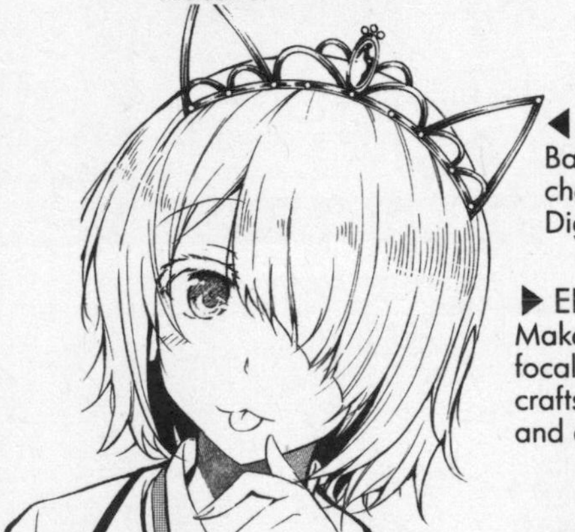

◀ TARO KUROKI
Baseball and 2D idol cheer squad leader.
Digital master.

▶ ERI HARADA
Makes faces into the focal point. Master craftsman of clothes and accessories.

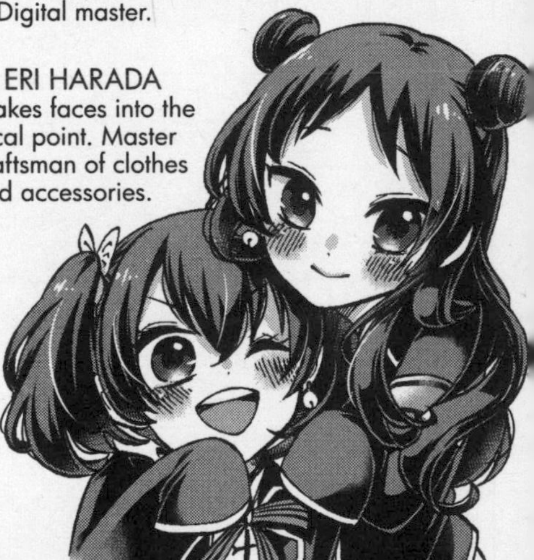

Special ☆ Thanks

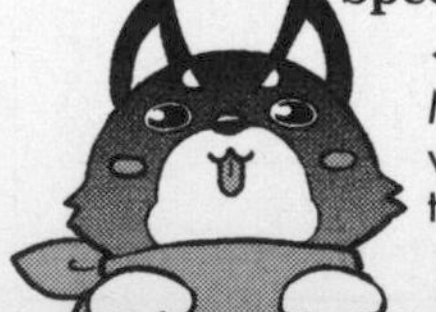

◀ ASUKA
Mayo-loving wizard. Screen tone ascetic.

Thank you!!

WAITING FOR SPRING

A sweet romantic story of a soft-spoken high school freshman and her quest to make friends. For fans of earnest, fun, and dramatic shojo like *Kimi ni Todoke* and *Say I Love You*.

KISS ME AT THE STROKE OF MIDNIGHT

An all-new Cinderella comedy perfect for fans of *My Little Monster* and *Say I Love You*!

LOVE AND LIES

Love is forbidden. When you turn 16, the government will assign you your marriage partner. This dystopian manga about teen love and defiance is a sexy, funny, and dramatic new hit! Anime now streaming on Anime Strike!

Boarding School Juliet volume 7 is a work of fiction. Names, characters, places, and incidents are the products of the author's imagination or are used fictitiously. Any resemblance to actual events, locales, or persons, living or dead, is entirely coincidental.

A Kodansha Comics Trade Paperback Original.

Published in the United States by Kodansha Comics, an imprint of Kodansha USA Publishing, LLC, New York.

Publication rights for this English edition arranged through Kodansha Ltd., Tokyo.

First published in Japan in 2018 by Kodansha Ltd., Tokyo, as *Kishuku Gakkou no Jurietto* volume 7.

ISBN 978-1-63236-786-0

Printed in the United States of America.

www.kodanshacomics.com

9 8 7 6 5 4 3 2 1

Translation: Amanda Haley
Lettering: James Dashiell
Editing: Erin Subramanian and Tiff Ferentini
Kodansha Comics edition cover design: Phil Balsman